ADAM SMITH'S DISCOURSE

Adam Smith's Discourse: Canonicity, Commerce and Conscience challenges the canonic reading of Smith's corpus of writings as constituting a founding statement of modernity and a free market order. Instead of seeing his works as espousing the values of an emerging commercial society, the reading presented here underscores the deep ambivalences and tensions in Smith's texts.

Adam Smith's Discourse examines the textual complexity of all Smith's major works by analysing their stylistic, figurative and rhetorical features and by reading them in the context of Enlightenment discourses on the moral, jurisprudential, political and economic aspects of society. Of central importance for the structure of Smith's discourse is Stoic moral philosophy, which provides a set of values that are fundamentally antithetical to both classical republican virtues and the aspirations of an acquisitive commercial society. Although *The Wealth of Nations* has been celebrated as a clarion call for a modern manufacturing and commercial order, *Adam Smith's Discourse* shows that its attack on mercantilism was based on a critique of what was seen as an overexpansion of trade and manufactures.

Vivienne Brown teaches Economics at the Open University, UK.

ADAM SMITH'S DISCOURSE

Canonicity, commerce and conscience

Vivienne Brown

London and New York

First published 1994
by Routledge
11 New Fetter Lane, London EC4P 4EE

Simultaneously published in the USA and Canada
by Routledge
29 West 35th Street, New York, NY 10001

© 1994 Vivienne Brown

Typeset in Bembo by
Florencetype Limited, Kewstoke, Avon
Printed and bound in Great Britain by
Mackays of Chatham PLC, Chatham, Kent

All rights reserved. No part of this book may be reprinted or reproduced or utilized in any form or by any electronic, mechanical, or other means, now known or hereafter invented, including photocopying and recording, or in any information storage or retrieval system, without permission in writing from the publishers.

British Library Cataloguing in Publication Data
A catalogue record for this book is available from the British Library.

Library of Congress Cataloging in Publication Data
Brown, Vivienne.
Adam Smith's discourse: canonicity, commerce, and conscience/
Vivienne Brown.
p. cm.
Includes bibliographical references and index.
1. Smith, Adam, 1723–1790. I. Title.
B1545.Z7B76   1994
192–dc 20   93–24462
CIP
ISBN 0-415-08160-2 (hbk)
ISBN 0-415-09593-x (pbk)

For Ali and Siby

CONTENTS

	Acknowledgements	ix
	Introduction	1
1	READING ADAM SMITH'S DISCOURSE	9
2	SIGNIFYING VOICES: READING THE ADAM SMITH PROBLEM	23
3	THE DIALOGIC EXPERIENCE OF CONSCIENCE	55
4	TMS AND THE STOIC MORAL HIERARCHY	76
5	JUSTICE AND JURISPRUDENCE	100
6	THE EMERGENCE OF *THE WEALTH OF NATIONS*	142
7	THE SYSTEM OF NATURAL LIBERTY	162
8	CONCLUSION: COMMERCE AND CONSCIENCE	207
	References	221
	Index	234

ACKNOWLEDGEMENTS

I would like to thank Annette Flynn and her colleagues in the library of the Open University for their efficiency and patience in dealing with my numerous Inter-Library Loan requests. I have also appreciated the facilities of the Reading Room of the British Museum and the courtesy of its staff. I would also very much like to thank Alan Jarvis at Routledge for his encouragement.

My greatest debt, of course, is to my family: to my daughters, who have seen so much less of their mother than they have a right to expect, and to Ronnie, who has given me so much support at a time when he was the one who needed it most.

Chapter 2 was first published by Cambridge University Press as 'Signifying voices: reading the "Adam Smith Problem"' in *Economics and Philosophy* 7, 1991, pp. 187–220. Chapter 3 was first published as 'The dialogic experience of conscience: Adam Smith and the voices of Stoicism' in *Eighteenth-Century Studies* 26, 1992–3, pp. 233–60. I would like to thank both journals for permission to use this material here.

INTRODUCTION

Adam Smith's name has become a byword for free market economics. The account of the benefits of free competitive markets found in *An Inquiry into the Nature and Causes of the Wealth of Nations* (WN) is regarded as the classic statement of the virtues of a *laissez-faire* capitalism in which economic agents contribute most effectively to the public good by selfishly pursuing their own interests guided only by the profit motive. Within recent Adam Smith scholarship, however, the political, jurisprudential and moral dimensions of his thought have been explored rather than the economic analysis, and these aspects have been located in terms of the intellectual interests and aspirations of the eighteenth century. Within this larger social matrix, the celebrated view of Smith as primarily an economist – and a dogmatic free market economist at that – appears as a gross caricature; the picture that emerges of Smith is more sceptical, philosophical, and politically focused, and the enthusiasm with which he welcomes the transition to a society based on trade and manufactures is tinged with a more dispassionate recognition of the losses as well as the benefits deriving from commercial society.[1]

These more interdisciplinary advances in recent Adam Smith scholarship have derived in large measure from two discrete but related shifts in interpretative emphasis. First, a major challenge for the modern scholar has become that of understanding Adam Smith's works as the coherent *œuvre* of a lifetime's intellectual activity. Partly this derives from opposition to the earlier view that there is a fundamental inconsistency between *The Wealth of Nations* and Smith's moral philosophy presented in *The Theory of Moral Sentiments* (TMS). The alleged inconsistency – the 'Adam Smith problem' – is now regarded as the product of faulty exegesis based on a misunderstanding of some of the philosophical terms in TMS, but the larger question of the overall relation between the moral philosophy and the economic analysis of commercial society is a recurring interpretative issue. Further discoveries of Smith's lectures have added two extra volumes to the corpus

---

[1] Two outstanding publications are Winch (1978) and Hont and Ignatieff (eds) (1983a).

of Smith's works in addition to TMS (1759) and WN (1776), the only books published during Smith's lifetime. The publication of Smith's *Lectures on Jurisprudence* (LJ) (1896, 1978) and *Lectures on Rhetoric and Belles Lettres* (LRBL) (1963, 1983) have contributed significantly to modern knowledge of the scope of Smith's thinking, but at the same time they have also posed an awesome intellectual challenge for the modern scholar to provide an overarching account of Smith's intellectual project.

Second, the wide scope of Smith's output has resulted in attracting intellectual historians who have sought to understand the historical identity of these works by placing them in their own intellectual context. Providing a historical reconstruction of Smith's output has required situating it within the broad context of Enlightenment social and political thought rather than the history of economics as the prehistory of a narrow set of disciplinary interests. In thus probing the historical identity of Smith's works as part of the expansive canvas of eighteenth-century intellectual history, scholars have also had to respond to current intellectual debates concerning the overall trajectory of eighteenth-century moral and political thought and its antecedents in European Renaissance and post-Renaissance thinking. Crucially important for Smith scholars are the reverberations of debates concerning the ideological origins of liberalism in the two contending vocabularies of natural jurisprudence and civic humanism in eighteenth-century writing in England and Scotland.[2] Within this debate, the jurisprudential language of 'rights' is seen as untranslatable into the civic humanist language of 'virtue', and although this has tended towards a simple dichotomising of the issues, the recognition of the contemporaneous presence of these two paradigmatic vocabularies in eighteenth-century discourse has prompted a more sensitive exploration of the positioning of these alternative vocabularies in Smith's texts.

In repositioning Smith's work within a European context of eighteenth-century thinking, however, recent interdisciplinary scholarship on Adam Smith has been influenced primarily by procedures and debates in the history of political thought rather than in moral philosophy or in economics. Further, in responding to recent developments in political historiography, it has ignored developments in literary theory and textual analysis; in attending to the historical specificity of texts, this scholarly output has neglected the textual specificity of historical thought. Thus, recent research on Adam Smith has failed to address the issue of the textuality of his works and how those works can be read. It attempts to read Smith's texts in the context of their own time, but it is entirely unselfconscious about the act of reading itself. In privileging the notion of historical

---

2 Advocacy of the civic humanist interpretative paradigm is associated with Pocock (1975, 1983).

understanding as the recovery of what the author meant in writing the text, it presupposes that the text itself provides evidence of the author's intentions in writing. There is, however, a massive literature which challenges this as a coherent principle of exegesis.[3] Emphasising the power of language to resist closure of meaning undercuts the author's pre-eminent role as proprietor of the text and problematises the process by which meaning is constructed in the process of reading rather than lying immanent in the text awaiting discovery.

This implies a different conception of the 'meaning' of a text. Traditionally, it has been assumed that the 'meaning' of a text is given by the author's intentions. According to this view, reading a text involves the recovery or reconstruction of authorial intention, and this provides the goal, however elusive, of the interpretative process as well as the overarching criterion of assessment; those interpretations which are thought to provide a greater understanding of the author's intentions are those which are more highly valued. Once it is accepted, however, that language has a kind of fecundity with a potential proliferation of different readings, it is no longer axiomatic that the 'meaning' of a text is given by authorial intent. The notion of historical reconstruction then becomes deeply problematic because, without such an assumption, the author's intention becomes irrecoverable and there are no means of testing an interpretation against it. All that is possible is the attempt to read the various texts with the greatest possible fidelity, but this leaves as an issue of judgment in each particular case just how those texts should be read. For this reason, the 'meaning' of a text is now seen as the product of a process of reading rather than implanted by the author in the act of writing.[4]

This is the point of departure for this book which attempts a reading of Smith's works that engages with the complexity of the texts, and with their stylistic, figurative and rhetorical forms. One result to emerge from this is that the stylistic forms of Smith's texts are not homogeneous, and that this is indicative of their different ethical structures. This allows a recasting of the old 'Adam Smith problem' by showing how the stylistic differences between TMS and WN are also constitutive of their different ethical standing. This, in turn, provides a reading of the moral assessment of commercial society in Smith's texts which highlights the Stoic structure of Adam Smith's discourse. It is argued that TMS is sharply critical of aspects of the new commercial society of the day and that, in some respects, economic activities are morally derogated in spite of the acknowledged

---

3 It is impossible to do justice to the literature which has developed in relation to this argument. Writers whose works have been influential include Jacques Derrida, Michel Foucault and Richard Rorty.
4 This argument is elaborated in the following chapter and in Brown (1993).

material benefits that they bring. This moral assessment of commercial society is also consistent with the economic reading presented of WN, which emphasises not the advantages of competitive markets and an expansion of trade, but rather the overexpansion of trade and manufactures at the expense of agriculture, the more beneficial activity.

As this book is problematising the process of reading Smith's discourse, the first chapter examines the *Lectures on Rhetoric and Belles Lettres* to see if it contains a theory of reading that might aid the modern reader of Smith's texts. LRBL recommends the 'plain style' approach to writing and communication, in which the beauty of style derives from the clear and accessible way in which the author conveys his meaning to readers. Recourse to figurative language and rhetorical forms by itself contributes nothing of beauty and may well be harmful in that it may impede the clear expression of the author's thoughts and sentiments. The chapter argues, however, that this model of communication is unsatisfactory as a self-description of the style and methods of LRBL and as a general model for reading Adam Smith's discourse. Drawing on recent work in literary theory, it argues, for example, against the exegetical assumption of an overarching authorial intentionality as a key to unlock the ultimate meaning of the works. The argument of this book will not rely on such an assumption, although it is widespread in the secondary literature which cross-reads one text of Smith against another in order to fill in supposed gaps and clarify the meaning of what are thought to be obscure passages. As meanings are produced by reading a text in terms of a specific discursive context, one text can be read in terms of another only if both share the same discursive frame. The assumption of a unified authorial intentionality, together with the practice of cross-reading, amounts to the presumption that the same discursive context is appropriate for reading all of Smith's texts. It is argued in the following chapters that this is not the case and that different discursive frames are appropriate at different moments in Smith's texts. This underlines the textual heterogeneity of Smith's works in that a range of different discourses are involved in the construction of their meaning, but this heterogeneity is not to be understood simply in terms of the presence or absence of consistency of authorial purpose.

The 'Adam Smith problem' has been declared by some commentators to be a pseudo problem as the 'same man' wrote both TMS and WN and there are no inconsistencies between the two works. Chapter 2, however, explores the different styles of these two works by drawing on recent literary theory and on Mikhail Bakhtin's work on the development of the novel.[5] Bakhtin argued that what he called novelistic discourse is characterised by a 'dialogic' style incorporating a range of 'voices' representing different cul-

---

5 See, for example, Bakhtin (1981, 1984, 1986).

INTRODUCTION

tural, political and axiological views, and within this category he included ethical discourses such as Stoic and other self-interrogative discourses. By contrast, although such a contrast can only be indicative and comparative rather than absolute, discourses of a scientific and authoritarian nature tend to be more monologic in style with the controlling didactic voice in command of the text denying any space to opposing views. Chapter 2 argues that TMS may be read as a dialogic discourse where the model of conscience represented metaphorically by the impartial spectator is based on an interplay of moral 'voices', whereas WN may be read as a monologic discourse or scientific text where the didactic voice endeavours to assert its controlling jurisdiction over the domain of the text. A result of this reading is that only self-command and beneficence qualify as truly moral virtues encompassed within the dialogic model of conscience represented by the impartial spectator, whereas prudence and justice are denominated as lower-order virtues. The significance of this for interpreting the overall moral assessment of commercial society is that it is the public virtues associated with the market and civic life that are presented as second-order virtues, whereas it is the private virtues that qualify as the truly moral virtues.

Another aspect of dialogism is a generalised intertextuality such that the argument of a text can be seen as a response to, or a refrain from, other discourses outside the text in question. This provides one account of the importance of discursive context in reading a text and generating meaning. Once the assumption of an originating author imbuing the text with meaning has been laid aside, meanings are then seen as the product of the process of reading, in which different outcomes are the product of the application of different discursive frames of reference. Bakhtin's account of dialogism in Stoic discourses thus provides a Stoic ethical context for reading the model of the impartial spectator and the account of the virtues in TMS, and this is further explored in chapters 3 and 4. In chapter 3, Stoic and other discourses of conscience are examined as a route into exploring the limits and textual tensions of the model of the impartial spectator which are products of the simultaneous dependence on, yet ultimate rejection of, the Stoic philosophy in TMS. Chapter 4 examines the ways in which the moral hierarchies of Stoicism structure the discourse of virtue in TMS. Developing the argument introduced in chapter 2 – that only beneficence and self-command constitute truly moral virtues while justice and prudence are denominated lower-order virtues – this chapter argues that the ordering of virtues in TMS reflects the influence of the Stoic categories of 'morally good acts' and merely 'proper functions' or 'indifferent acts'.

Justice is a second-order virtue and so the dialogism of conscience associated with the truly moral first-order virtues is absent from its portrayal in TMS and in LJ. As the text of LJ is structured in terms of justice, it too (along with WN) takes a monologic and not a dialogic form and cannot be regarded as lying on the same moral plane as TMS. Thus, recognising that commercial society must abide by the rules of justice is not sufficient to restore fully its moral credentials. It is therefore a feature of Smith's texts that the higher-order virtues are those associated largely with a person's private life, whereas the public virtues of justice and prudence are accorded a second-order status. This ranking of the virtues is symptomatic of the depoliticisation of virtue in Stoic moral philosophy, which is also reproduced in Smith's texts. Chapter 5 examines justice and jurisprudence in TMS and LJ. It argues that the Stoic foundations of the natural jurisprudence revived by Grotius facilitated a fusion of ethical and jurisprudential language, but that in Smith's texts the ethical basis of natural law founded in the natural reason of the individual moral agent is largely divorced from jurisprudence, which is instead represented as an area of jurisdiction for historically constituted civil governments. This shift away from the traditional categories of natural law is traced across LJ, showing that this process is more developed in LJB than in LJA, thus questioning the practice of reading these two texts as alternative versions of the same authorial statement. In foregrounding the historical processes of legal development and in withdrawing from a political definition of virtue, LJ and TMS are also displacing the notion of a 'legislator', the legendary figure of civic humanism who takes charge not only of the political ordering of society but also, to some degree, its morals and organisation of economic life. Although WN makes reference to the 'science of a statesman or legislator', this is used in an oppositional sense to refer to the economic discourses of state regulation against which WN is arguing.

Chapters 6 and 7 examine the economic arguments to be found in LJ and WN. Chapter 6 argues that there is a significant shift in the basis of the economic argument from LJ to WN. While LJ are still constructed to some degree in terms of the state regulationist discourse of 'police', where the state's object is to secure cheapness and plenty, by the time of WN, 'police' is used to refer to the discourses of the mercantile system and the agricultural system of the Économistes, each of which proposes to favour one economic sector over the others. According to this reading, 'political oeconomy' is the name given to the systems that WN is opposing and is not a self-description. In chapter 7 a rhetorical analysis of WN argues that the forms of argumentation and illustration in WN serve to fortify the monologic trajectory of WN in which the mercantile system is rhetorically displaced as a serious contender to the system of natural liberty. In this sense, the rhetorical devices of WN underpin its monologic ambition of presenting the system of natural liberty as the only coherent and rational economic system. According to this system, agriculture should be developed before manufactures and foreign trade, and it was for this reason that the mercantile system is accused of perverting the natural order of development of Europe. The account of competitive prices and the market mechanism which has been made so much of in interpretations of WN is thus of minor importance in the analytical arguments for the system of natural liberty, and was to some degree recognised by the time WN was published. The ultimate argument against the mercantile system, therefore, is not so much that it interferes with market prices, but that it has resulted in overdeveloping trade and manufactures relative to agriculture, the most beneficial of all activities. Although this interpretation of WN may be unfamiliar to modern readers, it was well recognised by the early readers of WN. Early critics and defenders of WN associated its arguments with the system of the Économistes and there was at the time considerable support for the view that agriculture was the most beneficial form of economic activity.

Finally, Chapter 8 draws together the results of the previous chapters in order to consider the moral assessment of commercial society that is at work in Adam Smith's texts. It argues that the Stoic structure of the argument in TMS not only slights economic and materialistic activities, but even to some degree derogates the virtues associated with the marketplace and political activity. WN's system of natural liberty is not a celebration of trade and manufactures, not even a sceptical celebration of them, but is directed at arguing that trade and manufactures had assumed too prominent a place in contemporary society. Far from being paradoxical, the invective aimed at merchants and manufacturers is congruent with the argument that the sectoral composition of economic activity had become distorted in favour of manufacturing and mercantile interests; it is also consistent with the fierce denunciation in TMS of the vanity and empty materialism of commercial society with its baubles and trinkets, its pride and envy. Far from being an anachronistic apologia for a newly emerging capitalist society, Adam Smith's discourse marks out the moral impatience of Stoic moral philosophy for the material goods and worldly ambitions that are ultimately seen as things indifferent.

Adam Smith's works have come to be seen as the classic statement of liberal capitalism. *The Wealth of Nations* is regarded by economists as a founding document in the canon of the history of economic thought from which modern economic analysis may trace its own descent. In providing a genealogy for modern economics, WN functions as a canonic text which supplies a history and a justification for present intellectual and political practices. By questioning the received interpretation of Adam Smith's works in the canon, the reading offered in this book is also engaging with the construction of that canon. The meanings of texts are not simply given to later generations but are produced through certain practices of reading; as part of this process, authority is vested in canonic texts whose meanings are then subject to a continuous process of reappropriation. For this reason, recovering the meaning of historical texts is always situated within the context of modern disciplinary interests and cannot amount to a pure retrieval of the past. By making explicit the textual and discursive nature of the construction of such meanings, this book is offered as a contribution towards an understanding of the formation of the canon itself.[6]

---

6 Brown (1993) examines canonicity and the history of economic thought.

1
READING ADAM SMITH'S DISCOURSE

1

Adam Smith was a product of that period when expansive and curious minds were unrestrained by the disciplinary boundaries that have since come to separate the various products of professional academic endeavour, and a glance at the titles associated with his name will be sufficient to alert the modern reader to the range of topics covered in his lectures and writings on the commercial society of his own day. But how are Smith's texts to be read? How can a modern reader come to understand Adam Smith's analysis of commercial society? Within economics, a new awareness of the significance of rhetoric for reading and understanding texts has become evident,[1] and so it might be thought that Smith's *Lectures on Rhetoric and Belles Lettres* (LRBL) could be used as a guide for reading his own works; Smith as author might guide his modern reader through his own texts.[2] Such an approach, however, requires that Smith is the best guide to his own works, and that LRBL does provide a rhetorical account that can be applied to Smith's other texts. In examining LRBL, this chapter will argue that this is not the case, and that the theory of language presented there is not a helpful one for reading Smith's texts.

2

Smith's *Lectures on Rhetoric and Belles Lettres* has been hailed by modern commentators as a significant recasting of the ancient notions of rhetoric into a form more suitable for a modern era as a 'general theory of all branches of literature' (Howell 1975, p. 20).[3] Emphasising communication

---

[1] On rhetoric and economics, see McCloskey (1986, 1990), Klamer *et al.* (1988).
[2] For example, Endres (1991).
[3] Also see Lothian (1963), Bevilacqua (1965, 1968), Spence (1974), A. Skinner (1983) and Hogan (1984).

as a general aim of all speech and writing as opposed to the classical emphasis on persuasion as the goal of a specific form of communication, Smith's lectures encompass the four fields of history, poetry (and fiction), didactic writing, and rhetorical discourse/oratory. Communication is perceived as the conveyance of the author's thoughts to the audience/reader:

> the perfection of stile consists in Expressing in the most concise, proper and precise manner the thought of the author, and that in the manner which best conveys the sentiment, passion or affection with which it affects or he pretends it does affect him and which he designs to communicate to his reader.
>
> (LRBL i.133)

Thus, to read a text is to share the author's thoughts and sentiments. A well-written text must have a determinate and univocal meaning concomitant with the author's intended meaning; to read Adam Smith's texts is to explore Adam Smith's intended meaning. Further, LRBL argues that both the language and style of a piece of discourse 'not only expresses the thought but also the spirit and mind of the author' (LRBL i.v.47). To read Adam Smith's texts is therefore to explore the spirit and mind of Adam Smith himself.

If an author is to achieve this communicative aim, it is necessary to adopt a clear, plain and perspicuous style. Such easy writing 'makes the sense of the author flow naturally upon our mind without our being obliged to hunt backwards and forwards in order to find it' (LRBL i.10), and it is this clear representation of the author's thoughts which constitutes the true beauty of style. Arguing against the view that beauty of language derives from figures of speech, LRBL puts the view that figurative language and other embellishments are not only unnecessary for good style but may well prove to be counterproductive in obscuring the author's sense. Whilst not proscribing the use of such figures altogther, it is argued that they should be used sparingly and only when they 'suit the sentiment of the speaker' (LRBL i.73): 'Upon the whole then, Figures of speech give no beauty to stile: it is when the expression is agreeable to the sense of the speaker and his affection that we admire it' (LRBL i.76).

In spite of the transcribed form of these lectures, Smith's own elegant eighteenth-century prose carries his reader along. As he himself says, his approach is 'no more than common sense' (LRBL i.133), and the sympathetic reader might well be inclined to agree. But, appeals to common sense understandings often function as a means of discouraging further scrutiny of the theoretical presuppositions involved, or as evidence of certain taken-for-granted assumptions that represent the implicit theorising of an age. Smith's own endorsement of plain language here is characteristic of some eighteenth-century views of language which rejected what had come to be seen as an over-elaborate and ornate dependence on the prescriptions of ancient rhetoric. Although this traditional rhetoric had included the five parts of invention, disposition, style, memory and delivery, the Renaissance emphasis on the third part – style or elocutio – had by the seventeenth and eighteenth centuries provoked a reaction against what was seen as 'flowery' eloquence. Historians of rhetoric are not agreed on the extent or on the causes of this movement towards a plain style, nor on the relative influence of different emphases within ancient rhetoric in changing conceptions of the role of rhetoric, but the growing authority of the natural sciences and the Royal Society together with the influence of John Locke's *Essay Concerning Human Understanding* (first published 1690) have been identified as significant factors in this change.[4] The proponents of plain style argued that such a style alone without figures and tropes (or at least without excessive ornamentation) is sufficient in order to transmit an author's thoughts to others' minds; according to this view, the communicative power of language is largely independent of its figurative uses which may, if not unchecked, lead to misrepresentation or even deceit.[5] Thus, plain language is held to be both norm and exemplar, and the rhetorical figures are held to be potentially deceptive as they may subvert the meaning intended by the author, or may secure persuasion by moving the passions even where the argument itself is not compelling. LRBL cautions against such ornaments and argues that they are suitable only when they truly 'suit the sentiment of the speaker'. Locke's *Essay* too considers the 'abuse of words' where the wilful misuse of words impairs the communicative process. One of these abuses is that of figurative language which can distort clear communication: 'all the artificial and figurative application of words eloquence hath invented, are for nothing else but to insinuate wrong ideas, move the passions, and thereby mislead the judgment; and so indeed are perfect cheats' (Locke 1959, III.x.34, vol. 2, p. 146).[6]

Beside these wilful faults, Locke's *Essay* also considered the imperfections that naturally inhere in language. It is argued there that words have no natural connection with the ideas they stand for, but take on an arbitrary signification. Because of this, an agreed and unambiguous signification for words is not always possible, especially in the case of more complex and

---

4 See Lothian (1963, pp. xxxi–xxxiii), Howell (1971), Kennedy (1980), Vickers (1985, 1988).
5 It was a widespread eighteenth-century assumption that 'figures are a mere embellishment or added beauty and that the plain meaning, the tenor [i.e. with respect to metaphor], is what alone really matters, and is something that, "regardless of the figures", might be gathered by the patient reader' (Richards 1971, p. 100). This contrasts with the traditional view that rhetorical figures perform an important expressive function: 'the ultimate power of rhetoric in written communication was thought to reside in the figures and tropes, the last stage in the elaboration of persuasive composition' (Vickers 1988, p. 294).
6 The importance of Locke for the new rhetoric is discussed in Howell (1967, 1971, pp. 489–502).

abstract words such as are found in philosophical discourse. This problem of the inherent uncertainty of language is not mentioned in LRBL, but it does occur in the *Lectures on Jurisprudence* (LJ). In the discussion of contracts and contractual obligation, it is argued that the validity of contracts was retarded by the inherent uncertainty and ambiguity of language which was exacerbated by the primitive state of society in early times (LJA ii.46, 48–9). Early contracts were made by the utterance of verbal signs and oaths and only much later did the use of obligatory written contracts become widespread (LJA ii.53–4). Here, the distinction is drawn between written and oral language where it is oaths (oral language) that take priority over written language as better able to signify the will of the contracting parties:

> At this time no contract could be made but amongst those who actually uttered the words by which the contract was comprehended. An oath can only be taken from one who actually delivers it from his own mouth. A written and signed oath is of no effect. Writing is no naturall expression of our thoughts (which language is,) and therefore is more dubious and not so setled in the meaning. Oaths we may observe are most in use amongst barbarous and uncivilized nations; as they are there thought necessary to signify plainly the will of the person; as the language is not fixt in its meaning; and in the state of the greatest barbarity, an oath is thought necessary to confirm every thing that is delivered.
>
> (LJA ii.53–4)

According to this account, it is not only that written language follows speech historically, but that writing is a less natural expression of thought than speech is. In the case of speech, the physical presence of the speaker facilitates a direct expression of the speaker's thought to the listener without the intermediation of writing or the physical distanciation implied by the absence of the writer at the moment of reading. Thus, not only is all language uncertain and ambiguous to some degree, but written language is more uncertain than speech in signifying the will of the person.[7] This argument is not made in LRBL, which treats written and spoken discourse as equivalent forms of utterance. But the underlying model of communication that both LRBL and LJA accounts presuppose is that the veracity and reliability of language is measured in terms of its ability to signify the will, sentiments and thoughts of the author.

Thus, the author is the originating will that defines the meaning of a text. Here 'meaning' is construed as a pre-linguistic or non-linguistic entity which is somehow immanent in the text, bestowed there by the author, and thereafter waiting for a sympathetic reader to find it and restore the work's

---

[7] The classic statement of this argument is to be found in Plato's *Phaedrus*.

originary meaning. As meaning is present in the work, it is to some degree indicative of the historical identity of the author whose intentions are made manifest by the discovery of the meaning of the work. Appealing though this approach may be in terms of commonsense notions of language, it has been massively questioned in the twentieth century, since the power of language to resist closure of meaning has provided compelling evidence that meanings are not so much present in the text but are constructed by the process of reading. Rather than being a 'nugget of sense' deposited by the author for the sympathetic reader to find,[8] the meaning of a text is to some degree the product of the interpretative apparatus that is brought to bear upon it.

It is in this sense that the expression 'death of the author' has become influential.[9] This does not imply that the name denoting authorship is of no interest, nor that the historical circumstances attaching to the period in which the author lived are irrelevant. Indeed, the connection linking *The Theory of Moral Sentiments* and *The Wealth of Nations* is that they are both authored by Adam Smith, and so for the purposes of this book there is an irreducible interest in the works attached to a single name. But it is part of the argument of what is to follow that the facts of authorship cannot be used to provide a principle of interpretation. The personality and predelictions of Adam Smith (to the extent that such knowledge is available) will not be used as a way of discovering the intended meaning of his works. Crucially, this implies that the principle of authorial intention will not be used here to read the texts associated with Adam Smith's name. One implication of this approach is that the richness of a text may be explored independently of the question as to whether the author was aware of these textual devices. It thus facilitates a more rigorous attention to the literariness of the texts, which includes issues such as style and figurative language.

Thus, in spite of the seductive elegance of Smith's perspicuous prose, the theory of communication and plain language in LRBL is not adopted in this book as a guide to reading Smith's discourse. Although LRBL recommends a clear, plain style as the one that will convey the author's sense to the reader, there are a number of difficulties associated with this account. First, although LRBL eschews figurative language, it is unable to avoid it even at those moments when it is extolling plain style and cautioning its hearers to be wary of figurative discourse. If the style is perspicuous, LRBL argues, the reader is able to follow the sense of the author as plain writings are those where 'one half asleep may carry the sense along with him' (LRBL i.10); plain language is here commended using figurative language, and this

---

8 Cf. Rorty (1984, p. 55).
9 Short statements may be found in Wimsatt and Beardsley (1954), Barthes (1977) and Foucault (1986).

continues into the account of obscure writers whose 'meaning is not to be discovered without great attention and being altogether awake' (LRBL i.v.10). Similarly, the use of metaphor is criticised using metaphor; ornaments or flowers in language such as allegory and metaphor are condemned on the grounds that they 'are very apt to make ones stile dark and perplex'd. Studying much to vary the expression leads one also frequently into a dungeon of metaphorical obscurity' (LRBL i.13). Here the power of the 'darkness' of figurative language takes the text deep into the metaphor of the 'dungeon of metaphorical obscurity'. These metaphorical expressions induce the text to make exaggerated claims both for the preferred style (that the reader may carry the sense even though half asleep) and against the criticised style (that it leads into a dungeon of obscurity).

Second, given that throughout LRBL it is taken as axiomatic that a clear, plain and easy style will lead to successful communication, it is not explained what role sympathy plays in this process. The author's sentiment is conveyed by means of sympathy, a crucial concept underlying the model of successful communication in LRBL:

> When the sentiment of the speaker is expressed in a neat, clear, plain and clever manner, and the passion or affection he is possessed of and intends, *by sympathy*, to communicate to his hearer, is plainly and cleverly hit off, then and then only the expression has all the force and beauty that language can give it.
> (LRBL i.v.56 original emphasis; also i.96)

In spite of its importance, LRBL does not provide an account of how the sympathetic process works or even whether it refers to the author or the reader. That is, it is not explained whether it is the author's sympathy with the communicative needs of the audience which determines how the communication is to be effected, or whether it is the audience's sympathy with the situation of the author that allows them to understand the text, or both together fused in a moment of hermeneutic truth.[10] At a number of points in LRBL, literary communication and morality are held to embody analogous principles; just as the wise man in his conversation and behaviour will assume a character that is natural to him, so too will a good author speak naturally in a way that suits his own sentiments and character (LRBL

---

10 Commentators have argued that LRBL is dependent at this point on Smith's lectures on moral philosophy delivered contemporaneously with the rhetoric lectures at Glasgow and later published as *The Theory of Moral Sentiments* in 1759. In TMS, sympathy refers to an imaginative faculty by means of which a moral agent imagines himself in the situation of another and experiences in his imagination what he would feel if he were in the other's place. This process is at the heart of the making of moral judgments as without this imaginative reconstruction of the moral event, the moral agent would be unable to form a judgment about it, but this does not answer the question as to how sympathy is part of the process of communication.

i.133–5).[11] This apparently analogous role of sympathy in the process of communication, however, is not explained in LRBL. Most commentators seem to assume that it is the reader's sympathy that is operative here,[12] but if plain writing is itself sufficient to convey the author's thoughts to his readers, it is not clear what additional role sympathy is supposed to play. LRBL says that a person even half asleep may carry the sense along with him, and so no imaginative effort seems to be required. This suggests that the reader's sympathy may better be described as the result of the reading process; plain writing has enabled the reader to share the author's thoughts and this end-state may be described as sympathy with the author.[13]

These difficulties with the communicative model based on plain style are illustrated by LRBL's endorsement of Jonathan Swift's writing. LRBL assesses a number of writers and writing styles, but it is Jonathan Swift who receives the most fulsome acclamation as a writer of the most perspicuous English, whose plain prose most surely and properly reflects the author's own mind and spirit. And yet Swift is one of the great ironists of the English language, whose clarity cannot be taken at face value as providing the author's intended meaning. In its account of Swift's ridicule, LRBL argues that 'The most common manner in which he [i.e. Swift] throws ridicule on any subjects when he speaks in an other character is to make them express their admiration and esteem for those things he would expose' (LRBL i.120). Thus, to understand the point of the irony is to construe the meaning of the text as other than what it is actually stating, as Swift makes his characters express views that are not consonant with the author's intended meaning. LRBL here takes this process of ironic reading as entirely straightforward, but the history of Swiftian scholarship shows that the identification and interpretation of Swift's irony has proved to be troublesome.[14] Further, the account in LRBL is based on the reader's understanding of the artistic tension between the unstated ironic meaning and a given literal meaning. But identification of the ironic meaning depends on the interpretation of the so-called literal meaning, since different interpretations of the 'literal' meaning will produce different interpretations of the ironic meaning. If neither the ironic nor the 'literal' meaning can be regarded as given or unproblematic to the reader in that they are both produced as a result of specific reading strategies, the obviousness of Swift's

---

11 Bevilacqua (1965, 1968) argues that the concept of propriety in LRBL is based on a moral–aesthetic concept of propriety and not on the classical concept of rhetorical propriety.
12 For example, Bevilacqua (1965, p. 54), (1968, pp. 562–3, 567); Spence (1974, pp. 95–7).
13 Aristotle's notion of propriety of expression in relation to feeling relates to the way in which spectators or listeners can share and sympathise with the speaker's feelings if he expresses himself in a way that rings true for them (Vickers 1988, p. 296).
14 For example, Fish (1989) discusses irony together with some difficulties in identifying and interpreting it in Swift's writing.

irony is undermined and this complicates the notion of an author's intended meaning based on clear style.

Another problem relates to the categorisation of 'rhetoric' in LRBL. While recasting the subject matter of the field of rhetoric and *belles lettres* as a general study of the requirements of communication broadly conceived, LRBL also refers to rhetorical discourse in a much narrower sense, as a specific form of discourse. In this narrower sense, rhetorical discourse as 'persuasion' is contrasted with didactic discourse with seeks sober conviction,[15] and here the distinction between the deceits of a persuasive rhetoric and the clarity of a plain style is central to the theory of language and communication put forward in LRBL. The main division presented in LRBL is a threefold distinction between historical/narrative, didactic, and rhetorical/oratorical discourse. The historical/narrative discourse states the facts without being predisposed to any party to the transactions, whereas the other two forms of discourse are designed to prove some proposition. Didactic discourse employs a strict proof applied to 'our reason and sound judgement' whereas rhetorical/oratorical discourse is 'adapted to affect our passions and by that means persuade us at any rate' (LRBL ii.14). Elsewhere this distinction is described in the following terms:

> [Didactick discourse] . . . proposes to put before us the arguments on both sides of the question in their true light, giving each its proper degree of influence, and has it in view to perswade no farther than the arguments themselves appear convincing. The Rhetoricall again endeavours by all means to perswade us; and for this purpose it magnifies all the arguments on the one side and diminishes or conceals those that might be brought on the side conterary to that which it is designed that we should favour. Persuasion which is the primary design in the Rhetoricall is but the secondary design in the Didactick. It endeavours to persuade us only so far as the strength of the arguments is convincing, instruction is the main End. In the other Persuasion is the main design and Instruction is considered only so far as it is subservient to perswasion, and no farther.
>
> (LRBL i.149–50)

Here LRBL reproduces the classic account of rhetorical discourse as that designed to persuade at all costs whereas didactic discourse is that which attempts to secure conviction on the basis of reasoned argument. This distinction between reason and passion, conviction and persuasion, has been central to the history of rhetoric since Plato's dialogues and was evident too in Locke's *Essay*, a history in which reason and truth are counterposed to

---

15 It has been argued that Smith's 'view is pejorative with regard to the rhetorical and propitious with regard to the historical' (Bevilacqua 1965, p. 56).

rhetoric, which is portrayed as as a fallen, deceitful and potentially dangerous form of discourse.[16] Recent histories of rhetoric have engaged critically with this version of the distinction between didactic and rhetorical discourse, where it is argued that as all discourse is constructed linguistically, it is impossible rigorously to separate the linguistic forms of an argument from the substantive content of that argument; in this sense the search for 'truth' is always located within forms of discourse and their interpretative and rhetorical strategies.[17] According to this account, even in texts which ostensibly are directed to maintaining the distance between didactic and rhetorical discourse, the two domains keep impinging on one another.

It was argued above that, even in its moments of greatest disdain for figurative language, LRBL cannot avoid expressing itself figuratively. Similarly, in spite of its fundamental distinction between didactic and rhetorical discourse, the text of LRBL acknowledges that these two forms of discourse cannot be kept separate. Thus the 'didactick writer sometimes assumes an oratorial stile tho it may be questioned whether this be altogether so proper' (LRBL i.84). Cicero is given as a prime example of such a mixed style, but most other writers should also be included, and it seems that Aristotle and Machiavelli are perhaps the only two didactic writers who have assiduously maintained the didactic style: 'They trust solely to the strength of their arguments and the ingenuity and newness of their thoughts and discoveries to gain the assent of their readers' (LRBL i.85; cf. i.12–13). Thus it turns out that the distinction between didactic and oratorical/rhetorical discourse is not sustainable in practice in view of the complex interweaving of styles in a particular text. Although the distinction is elsewhere maintained as an unproblematic division of discourses, if two writers only can be adduced as examples of a pure didactic style, this suggests that the distinction itself is less helpful as a demarcation across discourses than as a means of examining discursive complexity within a text. But in this case the distinction between didactic and oratorical/rhetorical styles points to the interdependence of different styles and modes of argument within a text, rather than the separation of different modes of enquiry across different types of discourse. But this, in turn, serves to pose the question of the textual interdependence of classically demarcated genres of discourse together with the interplay of conviction and persuasion within any text.

Further, given this classification of discourse, what kind of discourse is Adam Smith's course of university lectures on rhetoric and *belles lettres*?

---

16 See, for example, Plato's *Georgias* for the classic confrontation of philosophy and rhetoric, and Locke's *Essay Concerning Human Understanding* (III.x.34) for a statement of the harmful effects of rhetoric, 'that powerful instrument of error and deceit'.
17 For example, Vickers (1988, chapters 2 and 3).

LRBL is a serious piece of work that does not rouse the passions but appeals rather to sober judgment and reason. It therefore seems to be aimed at conviction as far as the case admits rather than persuasion at all costs, and so would seem to be a clear example of didactic discourse. On the other hand, it cannot be said that it puts the arguments fairly on both sides of the question. In brushing aside ancient rhetoric, for example, as 'generally a very silly set of Books' (LRBL i.v.59), it is hardly presenting a fair-handed account that puts the arguments on both sides in their true light. Furthermore, LRBL is not above resorting to metaphorical exaggeration in order to emphasise a point, as its criticism of figurative language shows. LRBL selects evidence to demonstrate its own points but it does not consider the counter evidence. Thus, in arguing a specific case, one that is redefining the general field of rhetoric and *belles lettres*, it could be said that LRBL remains closer to the narrow sense of rhetorical discourse than to didactic discourse.[18]

The 'commonsense' view of language put forward in LRBL is thus one that grounds the meaning of a text in the intended meaning of the author, and a clear and plain style is thought best to communicate this meaning and hence constitute the beauty of style. But this section has argued that such a theory of language is not satisfactory for exploring the complexity of Smith's own texts and further that Smith's LRBL fails at crucial moments to exemplify its own theoretical position with respect to communication. LRBL lacks self-consciousness about its own resort to figurative language at just that moment when it is criticising figurative language, and it fails to provide an account of the working of sympathy in a process of perspicuous linguistic communication. Although the distinction between didactic and rhetorical genres is presented as a fundamental distinction of discourse, the admission that only two writers can be adduced as good examples of didactic discourse, together with the hybrid nature of the discourse of LRBL, results in an undermining of the validity of this central distinction. As an account of writing and communication, then, LRBL at crucial moments fails to persuade; it does not exemplify its own stated position and the power of language is shown not to be entirely under the author's control even as he speaks/writes.

---

18 Lothian's Introduction to LRBL argues just this. Commenting on Dugald Stewart's account of Smith's lectures: 'It is clear from this that Smith deliberately proposed to make an emotional rather than an intellectual appeal to the interest of the students, to stimulate their feelings and their aesthetic sense, rather than their powers of reasoning' (Lothian 1963, p. xvi).

The reading of Adam Smith's discourse to be presented in this book therefore does not attempt to apply the model of communication described in LRBL. In particular, it does not lay claim to uncovering or recovering Smith's own intentions in his lectures and writing. Such a claim could only be strictly justified if there existed independent evidence, over and above the texts themselves, to which an appeal might be made concerning Smith's intentions. This would constitute objective external evidence against which the textual exegesis could be tested, but no such evidence or higher court of appeal exists. The only evidence of Smith's thinking and intentions is provided textually, by his books, lecture courses and assorted manuscript fragments. All that can ever be offered, then, is a reading of these texts. In the secondary literature on Smith, however, it has become an exegetical convention to ascribe specific intentions to Smith, but such inferences are the result of a specific reading and are not independent of it. Such inferences are commonplace in the secondary literature in intellectual history as a result of the widespread assumption that the meaning of a text is governed by authorial intentionality, the assumption that underlies LRBL, and such claims function powerfully in commanding support for particular recoveries and discoveries of their author's intentions.

A reading of any text can take place only within an interpretative frame of some sort. Readings that privilege the notion of authorial intentionality assume to themselves a prior knowledge of which discursive frame out of all possible ones constitutes the relevant intellectual parameters for the author at the moment of writing. Once it is accepted that this is something which is unknowable independently of the act of reading, then the choice of interpretative frame becomes a recognised part of the act of reading itself. Rational reconstructions assume that the appropriate frame is provided exclusively by modern discourses, and these discourses are usually discipline based. Historical reconstructions assume that it is found in discourses that were contemporary (or antecedent) to the author's act of writing.[19] This latter approach might give the impression that historical reconstructions are able to place a writer's thoughts in historical context without the modern contaminations that infect rational reconstructions, but this assumes that the choice of frame and its interpretation can be indepen-

---

19 It has been argued that what is central is what the author meant in writing the text (the illocutionary act) rather than the meaning of the text itself (the illocutionary force), but the acceptance that the illocutionary force of an utterance may be unintended 'due to the richness of our language' (Q. Skinner 1988, p. 266) renders problematic the reading of texts as a guide to intended illocutionary acts. The result is that, in spite of adherence to the importance of authorial intentions in recovering the historical identity of texts, the 'traditional figure of the author' is none the less left in 'extremely poor health' (Q. Skinner 1988, p. 276).

dent of modern trends in historical research. In both rational and historical reconstructions, it is the selected frame that gives the interpretation its distinctive features; in each case, the choice is a decision taken within the context of modern disciplinary interests and modern intellectual priorities.[20] Such choices are not independent of the discipline's sense of its own canon, whether the effect is to strengthen the existing canon or to give support to dissenting or rival canons. Seen in this sense, the different interpretations of past authors' intentions often amount to rival reappropriations of these past authors in the service of modern struggles over the construction of the discipline's perceived canon, and in this contest the shared assumption of authorial intentionality is used to buttress the shared commitment to the notion of the canon itself.

This book will attempt to read Adam Smith's discourse as part of the contending discourses of the Enlightenment, but it does not privilege the notion of an originating author whose sentiments and intentions can be called upon to buttress the textual analysis presented. The only evidence that can be adduced to support this reading is the evidence of the texts themselves, with the result that the author of this book does not claim independently to know Smith's mind as corroborating evidence for the interpretation offered here. One implication of this approach is that the issue of the coherence and consistency of Adam Smith's *œuvre* is something that has to wait upon the interpretation of the texts, and cannot be used as a prior assumption in reading the texts. This implies that one text cannot be used to explicate obscure or contentious passages in another text, since this presupposes a unitary intentionality, which is precisely one of the questions at issue. Further, this also implies that details of Smith's biography cannot be appealed to in order to settle disputed issues of textual interpretation. The editors of TMS, for example, argue in their Introduction that TMS and WN must be consistent because the 'same man' wrote both works and because, in the Advertisement to the sixth edition of TMS, Smith's words may be understood to mean that he, Smith, conceived of his work as one single, albeit unfinished project (TMS 1976, Introduction, pp. 20, 24). But this kind of argument assumes that Smith's personality and his own understanding of his writings are definitive in interpreting the meanings of the texts and in assessing the overall structural thematicity of his works. These kinds of authorial allusions are rampant in Adam Smith exegesis, and need not be detailed here, but the argument of this book will not rely on them. It was argued in section 2 above that Smith's lectures on rhetoric are not adequate as a guide for reading either LRBL or any other text. In order to establish the argument of each of the three main texts associated with Adam Smith's name, viz., *The Theory of Moral Sentiments, Lectures on Jurisprudence* and *The*

---

20 See Fish (1980, 1989).

Wealth of Nations, each will be read in its own terms and not cross-read through the others. This involves specifying the discursive frames that are appropriate for each text as part of the process of reading each text separately, and this will then enable the issue of consistency or otherwise across texts to be treated more discriminately. In the final chapter, these separate readings will then be put together in order to comment on Adam Smith's discourse overall.

In reading Adam Smith's discourse through the frame of the discourses of the Enlightenment, this book will be exploring the intertextuality of Smith's texts in the broadest sense. Smith's texts may be understood as forming part of a kaleidoscopic interaction of many different texts, arguments and debates conducted in different languages and in response to different conditions and different arguments. Intertextuality is thus a characteristic of discourse and may be viewed as a form of dialogism in which any utterance or text may by understood in terms of the range of other discourses inflected within it.[21] But further, in the work of Mikhail Bakhtin, dialogism has been explored as a characteristic which is internal to certain discourses.[22] A dialogic text in this sense is one that is structured by an interplay of voices which represent different social, political or axiological positions, whereas a monologic text is one characterised by a single voice. In Bakhtin's writings, the novel is the archetypal form of dialogic discourse and so dialogism is seen as a defining feature of novelistic discourse, but ethical discourses such as Stoic moral philosophy, which comprise self-interrogation or soliloquy, are also considered as dialogic discourses in which the moral agent engages in internal dialogue. By contrast, monologic works are those such as scientific works where this dialogic interplay is absent or peripheral. Attention to the 'voices' at work in a text thus contributes a further understanding of the dialogic nature of discourse. In reading Adam Smith's discourse, this also facilitates an exploration of the stylistic differences between the moral philosophy and the economic and jurisprudential works, and this too will be developed in the following chapters.

4

Rorty (1984) has argued that intellectual history needs canons because our imaginary conversations with the dead are an essential part of that sense of community that cannot easily be relinquished. Within economics, this hermeneutic notion of an ongoing conversation has been popularised by McCloskey (1986), in particular, as an overarching metaphor for economic

---

21 Kristeva (1986), Todorov (1984, chapter 5).
22 Bakhtin (1981, 1984, 1986).

discourse both past and present. What emerges from reading Adam Smith's discourse, however, is just how problematic this conversation is. By presenting a series of close readings that are attentive to the figurative, stylistic and intertextual dimensions of Smith's texts, the picture that emerges in the following chapters is one that is harder to include as a straightforward antecedent of modern thinking or as a constitutive element in the canonic 'great works' that provide the ideological foundations of modern commercial societies. Taking a Bakhtinian notion of canonisation as the process that reduces the dialogic complexity of the past to a single voice for consumption in the present, Adam Smith's discourse shows itself to be more dialogic and less univocal than canonic elevation admits.[23]

---

23 The relation between the assumption of authorial intentionality and canonicity is developed further in Brown (1993).

2

SIGNIFYING VOICES
Reading the Adam Smith problem

1

The 'Adam Smith problem' has traditionally been concerned with the issue of authorial integrity: the issue of how a single author, Adam Smith, could have written two such apparently dissimilar, even contradictory, works as *The Theory of Moral Sentiments* and *The Wealth of Nations*.[1] As the problem to be resolved was the single authorial origin of two such works, the perceived incompatibilities between them were explained in terms of Smith's intellectual biography – for example, Smith's travels to France, Smith's meetings with the physiocrats, or the mental incapacities of an ageing man. The current consensus is that the 'Adam Smith problem' is a 'pseudo problem' and that Smith's works represent a unified project,[2] but the same reference to authorial origins now provides the opposite claim that 'the same man' wrote both books.[3] Here the postulate of authorial integrity, of Smith's 'stable integrated character, not subject to deep intellectual

---

1. Summaries of this debate are to be found in Oncken (1897); Morrow (1973, pp. 1–11); Introduction to TMS, edited by D.D. Raphael and A.L. Macfie (1976, pp. 20–5); and Teichgraeber (1981).
2. Variations on the argument in favour of a 'unitary conception' of Smith's works can be found in the editors' Introduction to TMS, pp. 20–5; in Morrow (1973, 1928); Macfie (1967); Campbell (1971); Anspach (1972); Lamb (1974); Young (1986); and Evensky (1987), and accepted without question in Winch (1978). The original charge of an inconsistent view of human nature (with TMS based on sympathy and WN based on self-interest) has been criticised on a number of grounds, including the following: that Smith's concept of sympathy had been grossly misunderstood as benevolence; that self-interest/prudence was treated as one of the virtues in TMS; that self-interested behaviour itself derives from the need for sympathy and spectatorial approval; that the moral justification for property (and hence acquisitive behaviour when restrained by justice) is based on the approval of the impartial spectator; and that natural price and the outcomes of the competitive market are approved by the impartial spectator. The following authoritative statement summarises a diverse literature: 'far from there being any clash between the two books, the later one gives merely a particular development of the broader doctrine in the first. The economic man is the prudent man in the economic sphere. So the economic man also is under the sway of social sympathy and the impartial rulings of the informed spectator' (Macfie 1967, p. 75). An influential dissenting voice can be found in Viner (1928).
3. TMS Introduction, p. 20.

doubts or fissures' (Macfie 1967, p. 76), provides an assurance that such a man is unlikely to have written two entirely different books, an assurance underwritten by a coherent authorial intentionality which guarantees the consistency of the two works.[4]

As explained in chapter 1, the approach taken here will not privilege authorial unity or authorial intentionality as guarantees of consistency but will explore how the texts of TMS and WN can be read and how each produces its effects. Such an analysis would transform the Adam Smith problem. The question, 'How could Smith have *written* two such works?', would be transformed into the problem, 'How are these works to be *read*?' The starting point of this chapter therefore follows neither from the presumption of a unified authorial origin guaranteeing a single meaning, nor from the postulate of a unified authorial design which guarantees a seamless *œuvre*. Instead, this chapter will offer a reading of the two texts where the figurative and stylistic differences between them are shown to be indicative of their different moral positioning. By concentrating on the literariness of Smith's texts, and by exploring the stylistic and moral divergence between TMS and WN, this chapter will demonstrate the textual identity of each of these two works in a way that is not simply reducible to the issue of authorial coherence or consistency.

2

The previous chapter examined the argument of LRBL in favour of a plain and easy style, and it concluded that such an approach to language was inadequate as a guide to reading Smith's own texts. Smith's writing appears easy and elegant, not obscure, but in spite of its own precept it was at times deeply metaphorical and intricately textured.

The primary and emblematic metaphor of the moral discourse of TMS is that of the 'impartial spectator', the mechanism by which a moral agent makes judgments concerning himself[5] and others. The impartial spectator is an imagined spectator; in the case of first-person judgments, the moral agent imagines himself as a spectator to his own actions, whereas in the case of third-person judgments, the agent imagines himself as a spectator to another's actions.[6] The spectator's impartiality is provided by the distancing involved in these imaginative exercises. It is recognised that the sharing of

---

4 'Smith himself provides the best evidence against any idea that there is a conflict between his two works. In the Advertisement to edition 6 of TMS he refers to the final paragraph of the book, which promises another book on law and government, and says that he has "partly executed this promise" in WN. Clearly therefore he regards WN as continuing the sequence of thought set out in TMS' (TMS Introduction, p. 24). Thus, a partly executed intention is held as evidence of the coherence of the two works.
5 The moral agent and the impartial spectator in TMS are male throughout.
6 Raphael (1975).

viewpoints in this imaginary movement is only momentary, and that the spectator cannot, even from this shared viewpoint, go along with the agent's feeling in all its strength. This chapter will be exploring a number of different aspects of the impartial spectator; the point to be made here is that the impartial spectator stands as a metaphor for the mechanism of moral judgment, and that judgment is thus represented figuratively as observation:

> When I endeavour to examine my own conduct, when I endeavour to pass sentence upon it, and either to approve or condemn it, it is evident that, in all such cases, I divide myself, as it were, into two persons; and that I, the examiner and judge, represent a different character from that other I, the person whose conduct is examined into and judged of. The first is the spectator, whose sentiments with regard to my own conduct I endeavour to enter into, by placing myself in his situation, and by considering how it would appear to me, when seen from that particular point of view. The second is the agent, the person whom I properly call myself, and of whose conduct, under the character of a spectator, I was endeavouring to form some opinion. The first is the judge; the second the person judged of.
>
> (TMS III.1.6)

The moral discourse that is presented in TMS is one in which the moral agent takes an active part; imaginatively changing places, the moral agent is watching, looking, seeing, observing his own and others' behaviour and motives with the eye of the impartial spectator. Thus, the moral agent makes judgments not with his own eyes, nor with another's eyes, but with the eyes of the impartial spectator:

> We must view them, neither from our own place nor yet from his [i.e. the other agent's], neither with our own eyes nor yet with his, but from the place and with the eyes of a third person, who has no particular connexion with either, and who judges with impartiality between us.
>
> (TMS III.3.3).[7]

In TMS, seeing, observing, watching from appropriate viewpoints, all constitute the essence of an active process of moral judgment in which the moral agent is absorbed. The more acutely, sensitively and honestly the

---

[7] 'We suppose ourselves the spectators of our own behaviour, and endeavour to imagine what effect it would, in this light, produce upon us. This is the only looking-glass by which we can, in some measure, with the eyes of other people, scrutinize the propriety of our own conduct' (TMS III.1.5); 'But, in order to attain this satisfaction, we must become the impartial spectators of our own character and conduct. We must endeavour to view them with the eyes of other people, or as other people are likely to view them' (TMS III.2.3);

agent enters into this process, the more securely based are his moral judgments and the more morally virtuous are his own actions.

The primary metaphor of economic discourse, however, and one which has come to have enormously powerful resonances, is that of the invisible hand.[8] This metaphor, too, involves vision, but here it is the absence of vision; the hand that oversees the congruence of interest between the individual and the public is both a sightless organ and invisible. If, following the meaning of vision metaphors in TMS, vision refers to moral judgment, then the metaphor of the invisible hand signals that the invisible hand, being sightless and out of sight, is beyond the realm of moral discourse. Metaphorically, this means that the economic analysis of the system of natural liberty in WN is an *amoral discourse*; indeed, moral agents are not present in WN, neither is the impartial spectator, and neither is a moral discussion of the virtues specific to the marketplace.[9] In spite of the absence of these textual references, a moral dimension has, however, been read back into WN by commentators eager to establish the 'unified' nature of Smith's corpus of writing where 'the economic man also is under the sway of social sympathy and the impartial rulings of the informed spectator' (Macfie 1967, p. 75).[10] Emanating from an untheorised reliance on the assumption of authorial unity,[11] such readings achieve their results by transposing citations across different texts, thereby violating the textual identity of the works in question and glossing over crucial distinctions in the account of the different virtues provided in TMS.

This chapter will provide a detailed textual analysis to support an interpretation of the metaphors of the impartial spectator and the invisible hand which shows how the spectatorial account of moral judgment in TMS strictly pertains only to the higher-order virtues, the truly 'moral virtues' of beneficence and self-command, and that the lower-order virtues of justice and prudence, which concern the economic domain and the marketplace, lie outside the domain of moral discourse proper. Further, by adopting a reading strategy that takes account of the literary character of these texts, the chapter will explore the deeply textured dimensions of TMS that

---

'With the eyes of this great inmate he has always been accustomed to regard whatever relates to himself' (TMS III.3.25), etc.

8 TMS IV.1.10; WN IV.ii.9.

9 The passage in which the invisible hand occurs in TMS is examined below in chapter 4, pp.89–92.

10 Also 'The impartial spectator in fact makes no appearance in the *Wealth of Nations*. He there becomes the impersonal market' (Macfie 1967, p. 104).

11 Cf. Young (1986), which argues that Smith could have explicitly introduced the impartial spectator into WN although, as Smith did not, it has to remain 'somewhat tentative': 'The fact that Smith failed even to mention TMS in WN is even more puzzling, given the argument of my article.' This failure is ascribed to the unfinished nature of Smith's overall work where 'he had not yet explored all these [i.e. Young's] connections himself' (Young 1986, p. 382).

challenge the notion of a unified authorial voice addressing the reader in a straightforward and transparent way.

3

TMS is an account of how moral judgments are made. Crucial to this account is a story about the role of sympathy which follows from an imaginary change of situations between the moral agent and the relevant other. When making third-person moral judgments, the relevant other is the third person concerned. When making first-person moral judgments, the relevant other is the impartial spectator. This story thus involves a range of characters. First, there is the class of moral agents; there are those who are being judged and there are those who are doing the judging, actual spectators and the impartial spectator (as well as the 'all-seeing Judge'). In addition, there is another class of characters who are witnessing these tales of judgment; here there is an author and a reader. But, these two classes of characters are not separate. The reader is frequently aligned with the author as part of a representative humanity with natural and commonsense sentiments which are then deployed by the author in the pursuit of his treatise. In addition, the authorial 'I' periodically enters the action on his own account, sometimes as one of the moral agents and sometimes as the source of authorial interjections interrupting one of the other voices. And, finally, there is the impersonal voice of the author as 'narrator' or 'didactic philosopher', whose text and whose story this is, to weave apparently according to his overall design.

Within any particular section or argument of TMS, then, there may well be a range of 'voices' making up the text and this is a stylistic feature of its presentation. A number of examples may help to make this clear. Part I, section i, chapter 4 considers the propriety or impropriety of the sentiments of others and here two cases are contrasted; in the first case, the judgment is regarding those objects that may be considered not to be in any peculiar relation to the judging or judged parties; in the second case, the judgment does involve objects which are of a peculiar relation to the concerned parties. The first case is presented as follows:

> With regard to those objects which are considered without any peculiar relation either to ourselves or to the person whose sentiments we judge of; wherever his sentiments entirely correspond with our own, we ascribe to him the qualities of taste and good judgment. The beauty of a plain, the greatness of a mountain, the ornaments of a building, the expression of a picture, the composition of a discourse, the conduct of a third person, the proportions of different quantities and numbers, the various appearances which the great machine of the universe is perpetually exhibiting, with the secret wheels and springs

which produce them; all the general subjects of science and taste, are what we and our companion regard as having no peculiar relation to either of us. We both look at them from the same point of view, and we have no occasion for sympathy, or for that imaginary change of situations from which it arises, in order to produce, with regard to these, the most perfect harmony of sentiments and affections. If, notwithstanding, we are often differently affected, it arises either from the different degrees of attention, which our different habits of life allow us to give easily to the several parts of those complex objects, or from the different degrees of natural acuteness in the faculty of the mind to which they are addressed.

When the sentiments of our companion coincide with our own in things of this kind, which are obvious and easy, and in which, perhaps, we never found a single person who differed from us, though we, no doubt, must approve of them, yet he seems to deserve no praise or admiration on account of them. But when they not only coincide with our own, but lead and direct our own; when in forming them he appears to have attended to many things which we had overlooked, and to have adjusted them to all the various circumstances of their objects; we not only approve of them, but wonder and are surprised at their uncommon and unexpected acuteness and comprehensiveness, and he appears to deserve a very high degree of admiration and applause. For approbation heightened by wonder and surprise, constitutes the sentiment which is properly called admiration, and of which applause is the natural expression.

(TMS I.i.4.2–3)

This passage commences with the all-inclusive first person plural; here 'we' refers not only to the author and his readers but to all of humanity. It is the voice of reasonable and humane opinion and it carries along with it a considerable part of the story of TMS. In the opening sentences of this passage, this generalised voice of humanity excludes one other, the person whose sentiments are to be judged. But, once it has been explained that in this situation good judgment is not contentious, and that there is therefore no need for sympathy as a basis for judgment, the voice switches from the 'we' of a generalised humanity to the 'we' that includes only the authorial moral agent and the other person ('We both look at them . . .'). In this case, therefore, the two separate characters are unified by sharing 'the same point of view', which precludes the need for sympathy and its imaginary change of situation. With the start of the next paragraph, the voice returns to the generalised voice of humanity and the companion is once again excluded. In this case, the other person's sentiments excite admiration and applause on the part of humanity. It is at this point that the text then moves into the voice of the detached 'narrator' or 'didactic philosopher' ('For approbation heightened by wonder . . .'), who makes some generalised and elevated statements about the nature of admiration.

Two paragraphs later the opposite case is considered, where the objects are of a peculiar interest to the parties concerned and where a discordance of view is expressed:

> With regard to those objects, which affect in a particular manner either ourselves or the person whose sentiments we judge of, it is at once more difficult to preserve this harmony and correspondence, and at the same time, vastly more important. My companion does not naturally look upon the misfortune that has befallen me, or the injury that has been done me, from the same point of view in which I consider them. They affect me much more nearly. We do not view them from the same station, as we do a picture, or a poem, or a system of philosophy, and are, therefore, apt to be very differently affected by them. But I can much more easily overlook the want of this correspondence of sentiments with regard to such indifferent objects as concern neither me nor my companion, than with regard to what interests me so much as the misfortune that has befallen me, or the injury that has been done me. Though you despise that picture, or that poem, or even that system of philosophy, which I admire, there is little danger of our quarrelling upon that account. Neither of us can reasonably be much interested about them. They ought all of them to be matters of great indifference to us both; so that, though our opinions may be opposite, our affections may still be very nearly the same. But it is quite otherwise with regard to those objects by which either you or I are particularly affected. Though your judgments in matters of speculation, though your sentiments in matters of taste, are quite opposite to mine, I can easily overlook this opposition; and if I have any degree of temper, I may still find some entertainment in your conversation, even upon those very subjects. But if you have either no fellow-feeling for the misfortunes I have met with, or none that bears any proportion to the grief which distracts me; or if you have either no indignation at the injuries I have suffered, or none that bears any proportion to the resentment which transports me, we can no longer converse upon these subjects. We become intolerable to one another. I can neither support your company, nor you mine. You are confounded at my violence and passion, and I am enraged at your cold insensibility and want of feeling.
>
> In all such cases, that there may be some correspondence of sentiments between the spectator and the person principally concerned, the spectator must, first of all, endeavour, as much as he can, to put himself in the situation of the other . . .
>
> (TMS I.i.4.5–6)

Again, this passage starts with the generalised 'we' and the third person other, but it quickly moves into the first person singular and the other ('My companion'). The text then returns momentarily to the 'we' signifying both the 'I' and his companion ('We do not view them . . .'), but as these two agents do not share the same viewpoint, this 'we' is ruptured and the text reverts to the separated first and third person singular ('But I . . .', 'me' and 'my companion') and even uses the adversarial form of 'I' and 'you' when it is the opposition of views that is being stressed. The paragraph finally concludes with an impassioned dialogue between the outraged 'I' and the oppositional 'you'. In a calmer voice, which restores equanimity to the text, the subsequent paragraph returns to the impersonal didactic philosopher's voice with its detached references to the spectator and the other; here it is argued that a correspondence of sentiments between the spectator and his companion can be achieved only on the basis of a sympathetic viewpoint (i.e. an imaginary change of places) on the part of the spectator.

These passages set up a range of 'voices' that are responding to each other and answering each other.[12] Instead of having a constant, unchanging, authorial voice controlling the text, there is a range of different voices at work within the text. In this case, in order to examine the way in which the text works, we need to consider the effects of this interplay of voices. In his theory of the novel, Mikhail Bakhtin identified the interplay of voices in a text as the characteristic feature of what he termed 'novelistic discourse'.[13] Analysing European literary and philosophical materials from classical Greece through to the twentieth century, Bakhtin argued that this play of voices served to displace the authorial voice as the centre of the work,

---

[12] As far as I am aware, only Heilbronner (1982) and Evensky (1987) refer to the different 'voices' of TMS, but those arguments are different from the one presented here. Heilbronner (1982) distinguishes between the positive and the normative voices of TMS: 'TMS is written in two voices, one that is distanced from the spectacle of human conduct and that comments on its frailties and foibles with a philosophical resignation; another that exhorts and extols, scolds and rebukes. The two voices obviously belong to Smith the empirical observer and Smith the moral instructor, and the change in rhetorical stance reflects as well Smith's dual role as instructor of and guide to the sons of the gentry entrusted to his charge . . . The sociology of Smith's rhetoric has never, to my knowledge, been made the subject of a study.' (Heilbronner 1982, p. 429, n. 6). Evensky (1987) argues that this takes into account only Smith the empirical observer, and so attempts a more comprehensive reconstruction of the unitary nature of Smith's writings by taking into account Smith the moral philosopher, 'who sees the world as the Design of the Deity, a perfectly harmonious system', as well as Smith the empirical observer, who 'sees that the real world is not the Design of his ideal vision' (Evensky 1987, pp. 447–8). It is surely right to signal the need to listen to the different voices at work in TMS and WN, but in this chapter it will be argued that this emphasis on a simple bifurcation between positive and normative voices is not adequate for exploring the complexity of TMS.

[13] Bakhtin's first book *Problems of Dostoevsky's Art* received serious literary attention when it was published in Leningrad 1929, but for largely political reasons he and his work fell into obscurity until the late 1950s when the book was rediscovered. A second edition of this book was published in Moscow (1963) as *Problems of Dostoevsky's Poetics*, followed by

producing a *dialogic* form of discourse characterised by multivocity and heterodoxy: 'The novel can be defined as a diversity of social speech types (sometimes even diversity of languages) and a diversity of individual voices, artistically organized' (Bakhtin 1981, p. 262). Bakhtin counterposed the dialogic form of novelistic discourse to its other: the *monologic* form of discourse, where a single unitary voice of authority or tradition is at work controlling the text (texts such as a scientific discourse or what Bakhtin termed the epic form). In particular, Bakhtin notes the significance of multivocity in cases of conscience, confession and repentance, and his references here include Stoic philosophers such as Marcus Aurelius and Epictetus, whose works are cited and discussed at length in TMS.[14] At times, the dialogic and the monologic are counterposed in an absolute way, but Bakhtin's later writings also stressed that no language could be entirely closed in that all language, being socially and historically active, is dialogic and open to new interpretations or re-accentuations in spite of the impression of unity provided by the dominance of the authorial voice.[15]

TMS bears many of the characteristics of Bakhtin's dialogic or novelistic discourse,[16] and this is aligned with a number of distinctive features of the moral discourse presented there. First, the dialogic form of the text produces a particular reading experience for the reader of TMS. Second, the dialogic form of moral discourse comes to epitomise the nature of moral judgment itself. In this way, the stylistic form of TMS reproduces the discursive character of the making of moral judgments, and it is for this reason that an exploration of the literary style of TMS is in some measure constitutive of understanding the moral argument itself. Finally, the author's own voice becomes part of the inherent dialogism of the argument in that the author's voice is decentred: instead of being the one and only voice of the text, the author's voice becomes refracted and loses its certainty. Tracing through these features of the dialogism of TMS therefore provides a route for discussing the account of moral judgment and virtue presented there.

Rabelais and his World in Moscow (1965), and literary essays were later republished in the West under the titles of *The Dialogic Imagination* and *Speech Genres and Other Late Essays*. For a biography, see K. Clark and M. Holquist (1984). See also Todorov (1984), Morson (1986a) and Lodge (1987).

14 Bakhtin (1981, pp. 349–50).
15 This chapter will explore just one aspect of this contrast between dialogism and monologism. Later chapters will examine different aspects of intertextuality in TMS and WN.
16 Marshall (1984, reprinted in Marshall 1986, chapter 7) argues that TMS should be regarded as a 'philosophical novel' characterised by its dominant figure of the theatre where 'Smith is as concerned as a novelist with the fictions that we use to represent others and ourselves' (Marshall 1986, p. 3). Griswold argues that: 'So permeated with examples, stories, literary references and allusions, and images is the *TMS* that at times it presents the character of a novel; narrative and analysis are interwoven throughout' (Griswold 1991, p. 217). This chapter will argue that the text of TMS not only treats of fictions, but also displays a dialogic form that may be denoted as novelistic in Bakhtin's terms.

One consequence of the dialogic form of TMS is that the reader's own sympathies and responses are constructed by the text. Sometimes the reader is enlisted alongside the author as part of the inclusive 'we' signifying commonsense humanity;[17] sometimes the reader identifies with the 'you' who is being posited as a counterpoint, even sometimes an unsympathetic counterpoint, to the authorial 'I'; and sometimes the reader becomes invisible, so to speak, in the presence of the detached and elevated tone of the didactic voice. This 'novelistic' style of TMS means that the reader is drawn into the story by the need to play a number of different parts and express, or concur with, a number of different moral judgments as the treatise progresses. In this way, the reader is required by the text to take up the role of an impartial spectator: not a passive spectator, viewing a spectacle and simply responding to and sharing the given, expressed feelings of the characters, but a moral spectator as constructed by the text itself, who makes impartial observations or moral judgments. These moral judgments are made on the basis of a spectatorial sympathy and so require an active imaginative response, as this sympathy is possible only if the spectator changes places in order to imagine, not the other's feelings, but what his own feelings would be if he were in the other's situation.[18] Thus, here there is a process of doubling, where the treatise offers a discourse on the nature of moral judgment by deploying the character of the impartial spectator, but at the same time, the text of this discourse is casting the reader as spectator; in order to read the text, the reader must re-enact the story being told in the text. As the impartial spectator becomes a moral mirror to individual moral agents, so the discursive form of TMS becomes a textual mirror of the mechanisms of moral judgment and control. The readers of TMS share the sentiments of the inclusive 'we' of generalised and impartial humanity, and so are validating the mechanisms of the device of the impartial spectator. When cast as the unsympathetic 'you' of Smith's impassioned dialogue, the reader feels the burden and the stigma of being the unsympathetic and partial spectator as seen by the enraged (authorial) moral

---

17 On the issue of gender, the author and his readers are designated as male: 'The fair-sex, who have commonly much more tenderness than ours, have seldom so much generosity' (TMS IV.2.10): here the possessive pronoun, encompassing the author and his readership, excludes women.
18 It is therefore misleading simply to rely upon the first account of sympathy provided at TMS I.i.1.5 ('Pity and compassion are words appropriated to signify our fellow-feeling with the sorrow of others. Sympathy, though its meaning was, perhaps, originally the same, may now, however, without much impropriety, be made use of to denote our fellow-feeling with any passion whatever') as this identification of sympathy with a fellow-feeling for any passion, was amended and spectatorial sympathy was identified as the imaginative reconstruction of the other's situation: 'Upon some occasions sympathy may seem to arise merely from the view of a certain emotion in another person . . . This, however, does not hold universally, or with regard to every passion . . . Sympathy, therefore, does not arise so much from the view of the passion, as from that of the situation which excites it' (TMS I.i.1.6,7,10).

agent. Here, the reader is made to experience the impropriety of such partial judgment by the mechanism of withdrawal of authorial approbation at this point in the text ('I am outraged at your cold insensibility and want of feeling'), an approbation that the disinterested reader of a treatise might normally expect from the author. And so here again, the mechanism of control through approbation that takes place within the text mirrors that which is being laid out by the formal treatise itself.

In constituting the reader as moral agent, the dialogic form of the text thus provides a powerful illustration of the moral agent at work and the nature of moral judgments that are at the heart of TMS. But the dialogic form of this moral discourse also epitomises the dialogic nature of moral judgment itself. Moral judgment involves listening to the 'voice' of the impartial spectator:

> It is reason, principle, conscience, the inhabitant of the breast, the man within, the great judge and arbiter of our conduct. It is he who, whenever we are about to act so as to affect the happiness of others, *calls to us, with a voice capable of astonishing the most presumptuous of our passions*, that we are but one of the multitude, in no respect better than any other in it . . .
>
> (TMS III.3.4, emphasis added)[19]

In this way, moral judgment is defined by a dialogic relation between the moral agent and the impartial spectator; the moral agent listens not only to his own voice and the voices around him but, most importantly, he listens to the voice of the impartial spectator. This account of the dialogic nature of moral judgment has important implications for the designation of the virtues. Crucially, it means that only those virtues that are subject to this dialogic process are the truly 'moral virtues', the other virtues being of a lower, amoral order. In the account of the virtues in TMS, it is self-command and beneficence that alone qualify as the truly moral virtues, whereas justice and prudence are designated as lower-order virtues.

The practice of self-command is quintessentially a dialogic one, where the moral agent listens to the voice of the impartial spectator. Here the 'man of real constancy and firmness, the wise and just man who has been thoroughly bred in the great school of self-command . . . has never dared to forget for one moment the judgment which the impartial spectator would pass upon his sentiments and conduct.' It is therefore with the 'eyes of this great inmate' that he views his own outward conduct and inward sentiment (TMS III.3.25). In Part VI, it is argued that 'the real man of virtue, the only

---

19 In each of the following two paragraphs, 'the man within immediately calls' to remind the agent that he values himself too highly (TMS III.3.5,6).

real and proper object of love, respect, and admiration' is he who 'governs his whole behaviour and conduct according to those restrained and corrected emotions which the great inmate, the great demi-god within the breast prescribes and approves of' (TMS VI.iii.18). Here, crucially, the impartial spectator both 'prescribes and approves'. The impartial spectator 'prescribes' corrected emotions because in the absence of any other source of moral guidance, it is the impartial spectator alone who provides the moral agent with the dialogic process that defines the making of moral judgments; this means that the responsibility for the making of a moral judgment lies with the individual as a matter of private conscience. The impartial spectator also 'approves', however, and it is this approval which provides the moral compulsion inherent in conscience. This distinction is an important one for understanding the hierarchy of virtues in TMS for, although all the virtues are underwritten by the moral force of the impartial spectator's approval, they are not all dependent on the dialogic presence of the impartial spectator to prescribe the right course of moral action for the individual agent.

In the case of beneficence, the other truly moral virtue, the impartial spectator again prescribes as well as approves. One aspect of the dialogic nature of the moral discourse in TMS is its 'openness'; if moral judgments are the outcome of a dialogic process, then they can not be predetermined or rule-bound. The essence of moral judgment involves taking account of the fine distinctions pertaining to the circumstances of the case, with its own contingencies and private motivations.[20] The impartial spectator is ideally placed to do just this, as his location with respect to the moral agent provides impartiality, while his knowledge of the circumstances of the case enables him to make an informed judgment. But his judgments are never a foregone conclusion, his 'rules' are not knowable in advance; if that were so then the impartial spectator would no longer need to prescribe for individual cases. Given the nicety of any moral situation, the process of judging involves attention to the delicate details of the case, and it was for this reason that moral judgments are not predetermined or rule-bound in the strict sense, but must by necessity be open:

> The general rules of almost all the virtues, the general rules which determine what are the offices of prudence, of charity, of generosity, of gratitude, of friendship, are in many respects loose and inaccurate,

---

20 'When a philosopher goes to examine why humanity is approved of, or cruelty condemned, he does not always form to himself, in a very clear and distinct manner, the conception of any one particular action either of cruelty or of humanity, but is commonly contented with the vague and indeterminate idea which the general names of those qualities suggest to him. But it is in particular instances only that the propriety or impropriety, the merit or demerit of actions is very obvious and discernible' (TMS IV.2.2).

admit of many exceptions, and require so many modifications, that it is scarce possible to regulate our conduct entirely by a regard to them.

(TMS III.6.9)

Prudence, however, is the one virtue in this list for which common maxims can be used as general rules, although a very strict adherence to them would be absurd and pedantic. This is not the case with gratitude, where no general rules or precise answers can be given:

> Of all the virtues I have just now mentioned, gratitude is that, perhaps, of which the rules are the most precise, and admit of the fewest exceptions . . . Upon the most superficial examination, however, this rule [i.e. the return of at least equal services] will appear to be in the highest degree loose and inaccurate, and to admit of ten thousand exceptions . . . It is evident, that no general rule can be laid down, by which a precise answer can, in all cases, be given to any of these questions.
>
> (TMS III.6.9)

In the section on beneficence in Part VI, this indeterminacy is discussed at length:

> When those different beneficent affections happen to draw different ways, to determine by any precise rules in what cases we ought to comply with the one, and in what with the other, is, perhaps, altogether impossible. In what cases friendship ought to yield to gratitude, or gratitude to friendship; in what cases the strongest of all natural affections ought to yield to a regard for the safety of those superiors upon whose safety often depends that of the whole society; and in what cases natural affection may, without impropriety, prevail over that regard; must be left altogether to the decision of the man within the breast, the supposed impartial spectator, the great judge and arbiter of our conduct. If we place ourselves completely in his situation, if we really view ourselves with his eyes, and as he views us, and listen with diligent and reverential attention to what he suggests to us, his voice will never deceive us. We shall stand in need of no casuistic rules to direct our conduct.
>
> (TMS VI.ii.1.22)[21]

Here the central themes of TMS recur: vision metaphors signal judgment ('if we really view ourselves with his eyes, and as he views us'); the 'voice'

---

21 The passage continues: 'These it is often impossible to accommodate to all the different shades and gradations of circumstance, character, and situation, to differences and distinctions which, though not imperceptible, are, by their nicety and delicacy, often altogether undefinable.'

of the impartial spectator signals the dialogic nature of moral discourse; and moral judgment itself is 'open' and indeterminate, not rule-bound or predetermined ('to determine by any precise rules . . . is . . . impossible', moral judgment 'must be left altogether to the decision of the man within the breast', 'We shall stand in need of no casuistic rules to direct our conduct' as these are 'impossible'). This indeterminacy or openness is an analytical feature of moral judgment and, indeed, underlies the need for the impartial spectator. If precise rules could be laid down, then virtuous behaviour would simply consist of living by those rules, but it is the impossibility of such fixed rules that necessitates adjudication by the impartial spectator as the only way in which moral judgments may be made in the myriad complexity of social life. Thus, the account of the origin and use of general rules of morality shows that these rules are a substitute for, not a form of, moral judgment for those (of 'coarse clay') who are not capable of making such judgments themselves (TMS III.4–6).[22] These general rules are essential for the 'very existence of human society' by providing guidelines for decent behaviour in the case of those incapable of making moral judgments, and by helping to correct the misrepresentations of self-love (the 'mysterious veil of self-delusion'), but they are amoral in the sense that their observance does not require the making of moral judgments. Hence, a regard to these general rules of morality is designated as a sense of duty, not as moral judgment proper: 'The regard to those general rules of conduct, is what is properly called a sense of duty, a principle of the greatest consequence in human life, and the only principle by which the bulk of mankind are capable of directing their actions' (TMS III.5.1).[23] The moral foundation of these rules, however, derives from their concurrence with the natural approval or disapproval elicited by different forms of behaviour; the rules of morality are therefore 'ultimately founded upon the experience of what, in particular instances, our moral faculties, our natural sense of merit and propriety, approve, or disapprove of' (TMS III.4.8). Thus, the rules have a

---

[22] Some commentators have been misled by the passage at TMS VI.iii.1 ('The man who acts according to the rules of perfect prudence, of strict justice, and of proper benevolence, may be said to be perfectly virtuous'), in thinking that moral judgment in TMS is rule-governed. The point of this passage, however, is to introduce the chapter on self-command by making the distinction between the knowledge of what is right and the ability to do what is right, where this ability depends in large measure on self-command. The passage itself continues as follows: 'But the most perfect knowledge of those rules will not alone enable him to act in this manner: his own passions are very apt to mislead him; sometimes to drive him and sometimes to seduce him to violate all the rules which he himself, in all his sober and cool hours, approves of. The most perfect knowledge, if it is not supported by the most perfect self-command, will not always enable him to do his duty' (TMS VI.iii.1).

[23] This passage continues: 'Many men behave very decently, and through the whole of their lives avoid any considerable degree of blame, who yet, perhaps, never felt the sentiment upon the propriety of which we found our approbation of their conduct, but acted merely from a regard to what they saw were the established rules of behaviour' (TMS III.5.1).

certain moral force, not simply because they are the rules, but because they embody approved responses (TMS III.4.7–12).[24]

Following from their dialogic nature, however, moral judgments proper are freely subscribed to and freely acted upon. As participation in a process of open dialogue is freely entered into, and as commitment to agreement or consensus is freely given, so moral discourse and moral commitment is free, not coerced. This point is made forcefully early in TMS where beneficence 'is always free' and 'cannot be extorted by force' (TMS II.ii.1.3). Moral discourse is the discourse of the free; moral virtue is not an obligation which can be forced, but is left to the freedom of agents' wills. This freedom is epitomised by the dialogic nature of moral judgment and moral discourse which are non-deterministic, open, and voluntarily entered into. Their powers and compulsive attractions are those of persuasion, argument, reason, the love of approbation and human sociability. Moral discourse is part of social discourse; it is learnt as part of social life and it partakes of the same motivations and forms of persuasion that constitute the socialised communication of everyday life. The moral imperative, where morally virtuous behaviour is free and cannot be extorted by force, thus derives from the agents' need for social approval via the impartial spectator. It is therefore free and non-obligatory only in a legalistic or formal sense; as the moral agent is a social being whose views of proper conduct are shaped by society, his moral sentiments are shaped and given compulsion by the need for approval. The account both of moral openness and of moral freedom thus underscores the crucial role of the mechanism of the impartial spectator, without whom the character of moral virtue would be undefined and the moral imperatives to virtuous action would be absent.

This account of the ways in which the dialogic form of TMS epitomises the mechanism of moral judgment has not considered the author's place in the interplay of voices.[25] Where is the author's voice, and how does this voice control and guide the story of TMS? An important effect of a dialogic style is that the author's own voice is decentred. Instead of being the one and only voice of the text, the authorial voice becomes one among many; instead of controlling the text, it takes the risk of being upstaged or of finding its own uncertainties inscribed within the dialogic structure. And this too can be seen unfolding in TMS. The 'dark' side of TMS has on occasion been remarked on,[26] but it has been difficult for commentators to know how to read this other side of TMS with its cynicism about vanity and self-deceit, and its pessimism and irony about virtue's place in this

---

24 Laws, as the rules of justice, also come into this category, as discussed below, pp. 47–50. Significantly, the passage at TMS III.4.7–12, which explains the moral foundation of rules, includes references to legal rules and justice.
25 Other than noting that the authorial voice is gendered, male. See notes 5 and 17 above.
26 For example, Brissenden (1969), Ignatieff (1986) and Mitchell (1987).

world. By considering the interplay of voices in the text, the status and authority of this dissenting voice can be located.

Of all the voices in the text, it is the detached, didactic voice of the philosopher that seems to be controlling the text. Its impersonal form seems to speak from a position located outside the interplay of first, second and third person voices. Very often this didactic voice summarises and generalises the discourse of the interplay of voices, and here it speaks with an undisputed textual authority; examples of this can be seen at the end of each of the passages quoted above, the first example commencing: 'For approbation heightened by wonder . . .' (TMS I.i.4.3), and the second commencing: 'In all such cases . . .' (TMS I.i.4.6). On other occasions, the textual authority of the didactic voice summarises or builds upon the inclusive first person plural signifying generalised humanity. Here the voice of humanity is used as an informal way of introducing and illustrating the more elevated or general arguments provided by the didactic voice. An example of this is provided by the passage where the word 'spectator' is first introduced:

> Neither is it those circumstances only, which create pain or sorrow, that call forth our fellow-feeling. *Whatever is the passion which arises from any object in the person principally concerned, an analogous emotion springs up, at the thought of his situation, in the breast of every attentive spectator.* Our joy for the deliverance of those heroes of tragedy or romance who interest us, is as sincere as our grief for their distress, and our fellow-feeling with their misery is not more real than that with their happiness. We enter into their gratitude . . .
> (TMS I.i.1.4, emphasis added to didactic voice)

The first sentence introduces the theme of the paragraph, and this is performed in the inclusive first person plural. The didactic voice of the second sentence generalises this point in an impersonal manner. Then there is a return to the earlier voice of humanity, which illustrates the general philosophical point by reference to the stories of tragedy and romance.[27]

Sometimes, the didactic voice is used to add a refinement or a correction to the general view, or even to provide a common reference point to what

---

27 Another example may be provided by the passage which first introduces the impartial spectator: 'The insolence and brutality of anger, in the same manner, when we indulge its fury without check or restraint, is, of all objects, the most detestable. But we admire that noble and generous resentment which governs its pursuit of the greatest injuries, not by the rage which they are apt to excite in the breast of the sufferer, but by the indignation which they naturally call forth in that of the impartial spectator; which allows no word, no gesture, to escape it beyond what this more equitable sentiment would dictate; which never, even in thought, attempts any greater vengeance, nor desires to inflict any greater punishment, than what every indifferent person would rejoice to see executed' (TMS I.i.5.4). Here the first sentence is an inclusive first person plural sentence, but the following one is a hybrid one; it starts off in the first person plural but then is transformed into an impersonal didactic one by the time that the impartial spectator is introduced.

might otherwise seem to be out of place, or too low and vulgar, to be included within the more elevated tone of the didactic voice. As an example of the former, the first and provisional definition of sympathy is presented as a refinement of the ordinary understanding of the word: 'Pity and compassion are words appropriated to signify our fellow-feeling with the sorrow of others. Sympathy, though its meaning was, perhaps, originally the same, may now, however, without much impropriety, be made use of to denote our fellow-feeling with any passion whatever' (TMS I.i.1.5). The first sentence, with the first person plural voice, carries the ordinary meaning, while the second sentence as the didactic voice introduces an extended and more philosophical meaning. As an example of the latter, the detached didactic voice differentiates between virtue and mere propriety in the first sentence in the following passage, but the 'low' illustration of this is delivered in the more familiar tone of generalised humanity:

> There is, in this respect, a considerable difference between virtue and mere propriety; between those qualities and actions which deserve to be admired and celebrated, and those which simply deserve to be approved of. Upon many occasions, to act with the most perfect propriety, requires no more than that common and ordinary degree of sensibility or self-command which the most worthless of mankind are possest of, and sometimes even that degree is not necessary. Thus, to give a very low instance, to eat when we are hungry, is certainly, upon ordinary occasions, perfectly right and proper, and cannot miss being approved of as such by every body. Nothing, however, could be more absurd than to say it was virtuous.
>
> (TMS I.i.5.7)

Here the use of the familiar voice of humanity is inserted to provide a low illustration of the more general philosophical point.

On other occasions, however, the didactic voice becomes deeply critical, as when it intervenes to mark the moral inadequacy of conventional human judgments, thus transforming the voice of the generalised first person from being representative of a naturally humane, if commonsense, approach, to being indicative of the degeneracy of conventional moral views.[28] In the chapter on the origin of ambition and the distinction of ranks, the description of ambitious emulation is conducted in the first person plural:

---

28 'This "common language" – usually the average norm of spoken and written language for a given social group – is taken by the author precisely as the *common view*, as the verbal approach to people and things normal for a given sphere of society, as the *going point of view* and the going *value*. To one degree or another, the author distances himself from this common language, he steps back and objectifies it, forcing his own intentions to refract and diffuse themselves through the medium of this common view that has become embodied in language (a view that is always superficial and frequently hypocritical)' (Bakhtin 1981, pp. 301–2, original emphasis).

> From whence, then, arises that emulation which runs through all the different ranks of men, and what are the advantages which we propose by that great purpose of human life which we call bettering our condition? To be observed, to be attended to, to be taken notice of with sympathy, complacency, and approbation, are all the advantages which we can propose to derive from it.
>
> (TMS I.iii.2.1)

Taking this passage out of context, some commentators have mistakenly thought that Smith was commending or endorsing the attempt to 'better our condition' but, as the style and tone change markedly in the course of this long paragraph, such a complacent interpretation is open to doubt. Although this paragraph commences in the first person plural voice, it switches midway to the detached didactic voice which introduces a darker and more sceptical tone, thus overturning any impression of an easy acceptance of the prevailing mores of ambition and avarice. Describing how the man of rank and distinction is observed by all the world, the paragraph concludes with this sentence:

> It is this, which, notwithstanding the restraint it imposes, notwithstanding the loss of liberty with which it is attended, renders greatness the object of envy, and compensates, in the opinion of mankind, all that toil, all that anxiety, all those mortifications which must be undergone in the pursuit of it; and what is of yet more consequence, all that leisure, all that ease, all that careless security, which are forfeited for ever by the acquisition.
>
> (TMS I.iii.2.1)

Here the detached voice is emphasising the penalties attached to the pursuit and achievement of ambition, but yet these penalties are seen as adequate compensation 'in the opinion of mankind'. In this way, the text offers 'the opinion of mankind' as the commonplace defence of ambition but, at the same time, by switching the voice and style of presentation, the text refuses to condone it. Throughout this chapter, the didactic voice is both explaining vanity and the distinction of ranks, and also intruding with an opposing view that is deeply critical of 'this disposition of mankind'. Whilst analysing the power of both social prestige and social shame, the didactic voice is quite savage in its denunciation of these 'natural' dispositions.

This denunciation is also apparent in the additional chapter on the corruption of moral sentiments. Here, the ordinary humanity of the inclusive plural voice turns out to have been composed all along of two discrete groups; the one group is composed of 'the wise and the virtuous chiefly, a select, though, I am afraid, but a small party, who are the real and steady admirers of wisdom and virtue'. The other group, the 'great mob of mankind', are 'the admirers and worshippers . . . of wealth and greatness' (TMS I.iii.3.2). Thus, the sentiments of the great mob of mankind have been corrupted by their own natural disposition to admire those of wealth and rank, and indeed, this is seen as a 'natural' disposition: 'That kings are the servants of the people, to be obeyed, resisted, deposed, or punished, as the public conveniency may require, is the doctrine of reason and philosophy; but it is not the doctrine of Nature' (TMS I.iii.2.3). Thus, in these passages, the didactic voice is denying the impartiality of the inclusive 'we', an impartiality that is necessary for the formation of moral judgments. An effect of this for the reader seeking authorial approbation is to identify with the select group of the wise and the virtuous. As the text notes that the order of society is itself based on the widespread admiration of the powerful, this inclusion within the select cannot be possible for everyone in society, although it is feasible for the readers of a book such as TMS.

But in criticising the inclusive voice of humanity, the didactic voice loses some of its autonomy and certainty as it answers and responds to the plural voice of generalised humanity. Its own utterances are sometimes interjected by a pure authorial 'I', as in the passage above (I.iii.3.2) where the interjection 'I am afraid' is placed within the didactic voice. In addition, in answering the plural voice, the didactic voice becomes engaged with this voice more intimately in the form of a 'hybrid' mode of utterance, where the voice changes within a sentence even though there may be no formal markers to signify this shift.[29] This occurs at the moment when the didactic voice switches into the plural inclusive voice, as, for example, in the first sentence of the additional chapter:

> This disposition to admire, and almost to worship, the rich and the powerful, and to despise, or, at least, to neglect persons of poor and mean condition, though necessary both to establish and to maintain the distinction of ranks and the order of society, is, at the same time, the great and most universal cause of the corruption of our moral sentiments.
>
> (TMS I.iii.3.1)

This sentence would be a straightforward utterance of the didactic voice were it not for the move into the plural voice at the end, a move that is symptomatic of and necessitated by the text's both sharing and criticising these sentiments. Thus, the apparent purity of the philosophic voice is

---

29 'What we are calling a hybrid construction is an utterance that belongs, by its grammatical (syntactic) and compositional markers, to a single speaker, but that actually contains mixed within it two utterances, two speech manners, two styles, two "languages", two semantic and axiological belief systems' (Bakhtin 1981, p. 304).

undermined by a dialogic reorientating and fracturing of its own voice as it critically engages with the formal argument of the text.

Although it is chapter 3 of this section of TMS that roundly denounces the corruption of moral sentiments, the mechanism by which this corruption occurs is traced first in the preceding chapter, and this is effected by hybrid utterances where dialogised interventions of the philosophic voice enter the structure of the text. The first intrusion of this voice opens the second paragraph, and here there are no linguistic markers to signify this shift:

> When we consider the condition of the great, *in those delusive colours in which the imagination is apt to paint it*, it seems to be almost the abstract idea of a perfect and happy state. It is the very state which, in all our waking dreams and idle reveries, we had sketched out to ourselves as the final object of all our desires.
>
> (TMS I.iii.2.2 emphasis added)

This passage is written in the voice of plural humanity, but the emphasised clause is an interjection by another voice, apparently the didactic voice, which dislodges the presuppositions of the plural voice. Later in this paragraph, this voice again interjects the plural voice of humanity when the text explains that kings and lovers interest us most in the theatre because their happiness appears to be superior to that of others: 'Those two situations are the chief which interest us upon the theatre; because, *in spite of all that reason and experience can tell us to the contrary, the prejudices* of the imagination attach to these two states a happiness superior to any other' (TMS I.iii.2.2, emphasis added). This oppositional voice also enters into the didactic voice: 'Of such mighty importance does it appear to be, *in the imaginations of men*, to stand in that situation which sets them most in the view of general sympathy and attention' (TMS I.iii.2.8, emphasis added).

What each of these interpellations shows is that the mechanism of corruption is the imagination itself, the basis of all sympathetic and moral observations. This means that the detached didactic voice, the most authoritative voice within the text, is also critical and subject to criticism, not only concerning the moral standing of conventional judgments, but also concerning the reliability of the mechanism by which moral judgments are properly formed. The impartiality of the observations of the spectator, and hence the moral standing of those observations, derive from the activity of the imaginative change of place which engenders sympathy. But if the imagination itself is delusory and subject to prejudice, opposing the lessons of reason, philosophy and experience,[30] then it cannot reliably effect the

---

30 The imagination is opposed to reason, philosophy and experience at TMS I.iii.2.2–3 and III.3.28.

change of place which is necessary for moral judgments to be made in the first place.[31] This uncertainty about the moral mechanisms that are at the heart of the argument of TMS is played out stylistically through the interplay of voices in the text of TMS, where the doubts are expressed by the voice that is the most authoritative. The text of TMS both affirms and denies the effectiveness of the mechanisms of imagination and sympathy that are the central core of its moral discourse.

4

The openness and uncertainty of the text of TMS, an openness portrayed figuratively by the metaphor of the impartial spectator and by the representation of judgment as observation, is rendered stylistically in its multivocal dialogism. By comparison, WN stands as a largely single-voiced monologic text,[32] with its expressed certainties and intellectual order.[33] Most of the text of WN is expressed in a voice corresponding to that of the impersonal and didactic philosopher, and the tone is detached and dispassionate.[34] Occasionally an authorial voice does intervene. Sometimes this is in order to signal the structure of the argument that is about to be presented; for

---

31 In the most wise and virtuous person, the self and the impartial spectator 'almost' merge to be a single unified moral being; if such a merger were a real possibility, the voice of the impartial spectator would truly become the agent's own voice, but a complete merging of the identity of the agent with the impartial spectator is not technically possible and this is part of nature's design, even for the wisest and firmest man (TMS III.3.28). The failings of the imagination cannot therefore be ascribed simply to human frailty. This is examined further in chapter 3.

32 It should be stressed that the style of WN is monologic only with reference to the particular form of dialogism analysed here in TMS; see n. 15 above and chapter 7 below, pp. 162–4, 191–6.

33 The monologic work 'contains only *one cognitive subject*, all else being merely *objects* of its cognition' (Bakhtin 1984, p. 71). Discussing the monologic novel: 'Whatever discourse types are introduced by the author-monologist, whatever their compositional distribution, the author's intentions and evaluations must dominate over all the others and must form a compact and unambiguous whole. Any intensification of others' intonations in a certain discourse or a certain section of the work is only a game, which the author permits so that his own direct or refracted word might ring out all the more energetically' (Bakhtin 1984, pp. 203–4).

34 It might be thought that this stylistic difference may be attributable to the different circumstances surrounding the origins and writing of these two works. TMS had its origins in Smith's lectures on moral philosophy, whereas WN represented largely a new piece of work although derived from sections of LJ. It might be thought therefore that the more dialogic style of TMS is attributable to its early career as student lectures, whereas WN represents the more detached style appropriate to a considered piece of writing. Against this, however, is the evidence that TMS was substantially reworked for publication, and that the new passages included in the sixth edition bear the same dialogic form as the earlier editions. Further, as LJ is the direct transcriptions of student notes, it would be expected to take an even more dialogic form if this style were simply the result of a lecture room presentation, but this is not the case; stylistically LJ is similar to WN not TMS. The

example, it is announced that the three aspects of the regulation of the exchangeable value of commodities are to be covered in the following three chapters: 'I shall endeavour to explain, as fully and distinctly as I can, those three subjects in the three following chapters, for which I must very earnestly entreat both the patience and attention of the reader . . .' (WN I.iv.18), and here a rare appeal is made to the reader. Sometimes the first person singular is used when introducing an example or illustration of a point, as shown by the following case which is inserted within the didactic voice: 'There is no city in Europe, I believe, in which house-rent is dearer than in London, and yet I know no capital in which a furnished apartment can be hired so cheap' (WN I.x.b.52). Sometimes, too, this voice is used for clarifications to the didactic voice: 'By advantage or gain, I understand, not the increase of the quantity of gold and silver, but that of the exchangeable value of the annual produce of the land and labour of the country . . .' (WN IV.iii.c.3). There is also an example of a rare intrusion of the authorial voice in the discussion of the corn trade where the authorial 'I' intervenes to argue against the system of bounties: 'I answer, that . . .' and 'I answer, that this might be . . .' (WN IV.v.a.8,10). On another occasion, this voice is used as a distancing device, for example, following a self-conscious use of metaphorical language: 'It [stock] then spreads itself, if I may say so, over the face of the land . . .' (WN I.x.c.26). Thus, WN is not undifferentiated stylistically, but a crucial contrast with TMS is that these different kinds of authorial interventions do not challenge the formal meaning of the didactic voice. Similarly, there is an occasional use of the first person plural voice denoting commonsense or common opinion, but this is used to illustrate or reinforce the official voice of the text, and there is no evidence that the official voice is critically engaging with the other's argument. For example, the famous passage introducing the self-interested character of economic exchange is expressed in the plural voice:

> It is not from the benevolence of the butcher, the brewer, or the baker, that we expect our dinner, but from their regard to their own interest. We address ourselves, not to their humanity but to their self-love, and never talk to them of our own necessities but of their advantages.
>
> (WN I.ii.2)

The switch into the plural voice to describe the economic significance of self-interested behaviour may well carry with it a set of moral resonances for the reader who is accustomed to the stylistic devices of TMS, but the

---

evidence of the origins of these two works therefore does not challenge the argument of this chapter that the stylistic differences between TMS and WN are symptomatic of their different moral positioning.

contrast with TMS lies in the absence here of any dissenting interplay between this plural voice and the detached, didactic voice.

The monologic style is the style that Bakhtin identified as the one used in scientific treatises or what he termed the 'epic': texts where a single unified voice determined the text and its story. It was especially used, according to Bakhtin, whenever the arguments represented a powerful tradition of ideas that brooked no heterodox challenges to itself, or wherever the pursuit of scientific understanding excluded the presentation of alternative views on a basis that posed a potential challenge to the main argument (Bakhtin 1981, p. 351). This is the style of WN as a scientific treatise explaining the system of natural liberty, and it is also the style of the *Lectures on Jurisprudence*.

In TMS, it is argued that in the case of the subjects of 'science and taste', it is their conformity with what is right, accurate and 'agreeable to truth and reality' that first recommends them (TMS I.i.4.4) and that sympathy is inoperative here as 'We both look at them from the same point of view, and we have no occasion for sympathy, or for that imaginary change of situations from which it arises, in order to produce, with regard to these, the most perfect harmony of sentiments and affections' (TMS I.i.4.2). Thus, the subjects of science and taste are objective; all may look at them from the same point of view and sympathy is redundant. In the course of time, however, their utility 'gives them a new value' (TMS I.i.4.4) and so comes to be emphasised as a rejoinder to those who, lacking a 'taste for such sublime discoveries, endeavoured to depreciate them as useless' (TMS IV.2.7). Although the approval of any theoretical system thus lies in its being right and accurate, it may well be appropriate to emphasise the utility of the subject for those who have no taste for 'sublime discoveries', but by this is meant not David Hume's argument concerning the ultimate end in view, but the aesthetic adaptation of means to ends where appreciation depends on a love of system and of the beauty of order (TMS IV.1). This is discussed for the system of public police, which is provided as an example of the more general case where utility is perceived to lie in the aesthetic appreciation of the artful adaptation of means to ends rather than in an appreciation of those ends themselves (TMS IV.1.11). Here, in order to arouse the interest of those without a taste for 'sublime discoveries', it is necessary to emphasise the utility attendant upon those systems; in this way the arguments for propagating public police are based on counterposing two different accounts of the source of utility and not on opposing a moral against a utilitarian justification of public police.[35]

The monologic style of WN is thus entirely in accord with the scientific

---

35 By construing the argument of TMS concerning the utility of economic ends as a moral argument concerning the ethics of economic policy, some commentators have implicitly endorsed Hume's theory concerning the approbation of virtue on the basis of utility, by arguing that Smith's own political economy should be understood as a branch of ethics but

standing attributed to systems of public police in TMS, without reference to either sympathy or an imaginary change of places. This means that WN has no place for the moral discourse of TMS; in this sense WN is an amoral discourse. For this reason, the multivocity and the spectatorial sympathy of TMS become redundant, to be replaced by the more overly didactic and detached style which characterises the monologism of WN. This is not to say, however, that none of the virtues described in TMS are to be found in WN. It has been established in the literature that economic self-interest is denominated as a virtue in TMS when understood as a form of prudence restrained by justice. The existing literature also unanimously emphasises that although it is TMS which treats of the virtues (whereas WN does not), still WN may take as a presupposition the theory of morality contained in TMS.[36] But the crucial point is that the virtue of economic self-interest is treated differently in TMS from the higher moral virtues of beneficence and self-command, the true objects of moral discourse as defined by the structure of the argument in TMS, and it is this differential treatment in TMS itself that signals a different moral status for WN, a difference epitomised by the absence of the impartial spectator from the pages of WN. The distinction between the character of virtue and the mechanism of the principle of approbation (TMS VII.i) is a crucial one, underlying the central argument of TMS that a moral judgment is made when virtue is identified by way of the impartial spectator mechanism. But this means that only beneficence and self-command unambiguously fall within the ambit of moral judgment according to the spectatorial account of the way that moral judgments are made. The status of the other two virtues in TMS, justice and prudence, is of a lower order;[37] although clearly denominated as virtues, they none the less stand outside the discourse signified as moral discourse by the arguments of TMS.

---

which, in order to be persuasive, was presented in WN on the basis of considerations of utility; see Lindgren (1973) chapters IV–VI.

36 'It would appear that the *Wealth of Nations* is simply a special case – the economic case – of the philosophy implicit in the *Moral Sentiments*. It works out the economic side of that 'self-love' which is given its appropriate place in the developed ethical system of the earlier book. For self-love is there an essential element in virtue, or in the good life of society' (Macfie 1967, pp. 75–6). Summarising the literature, Winch (1978) writes: 'The *Theory of Moral Sentiments* contains Smith's general theory of morality or psychology; it consistently operates on a higher level of theoretical generality and with a lower degree of empirical realism than the *Wealth of Nations*. The latter work can, therefore, be regarded as a specialised application to the detailed field of economic action of the general theories of social (including economic) behaviour contained in the earlier work, which means that it can properly be used to supply background assumptions to the *Wealth of Nations*, particularly on questions involving individual motivation and social conduct', although it is also cautioned that this does not provide a warrant 'for regarding the *Theory of Moral Sentiments* as a court of higher appeal on all disputed matters' (Winch 1978, p. 10).

37 There is also a 'superior prudence' as applied to great generals, statesmen and legislators which is directed to 'greater and nobler purposes than the care of the health, the fortune, the rank and reputation of the individual' and is combined with 'many greater and more

One important distinction between justice and beneficence relies upon the contrast between the freely donated character of the moral virtue of beneficence and the obligation attaching to the virtue of justice:[38]

> There is, however, another virtue, of which the observance is not left to the freedom of our own wills, which may be extorted by force, and of which the violation exposes to resentment, and consequently to punishment. This virtue is justice: the violation of justice is injury . . . And upon this is founded that remarkable distinction between justice and all the other social virtues . . . that we feel ourselves to be under a stricter obligation to act according to justice, than agreeably to friendship, charity, or generosity; that the practice of these last mentioned virtues seems to be left in some measure to our own choice, but that, somehow or other, we feel ourselves to be in a peculiar manner tied, bound, and obliged to the observation of justice.
> (TMS II.ii.1.5)

In this case, virtue is not free but may be extorted by force; for this reason, too, the impartial spectator is redundant in matters of justice in the sense that compulsion is provided by the law itself and there is no need for the moral imperative provided by the impartial spectator. The distinction between the 'rules' of justice and the 'precepts' of the other virtues such as friendship, generosity and charity signifies, too, that the impartial spectator is not required for the agent to come to know what is in accordance with justice; the agent is not required to make any legal judgments but merely to follow the rules of justice that are laid down in the system of positive laws of that country. Thus, justice is also unlike beneficence in that it is rule-determined:

> There is, however, one virtue of which the general rules determine with the greatest exactness every external action which it requires. This virtue is justice. The rules of justice are accurate in the highest degree, and admit of no exceptions or modifications, but such as may be ascertained as accurately as the rules themselves, and which generally, indeed, flow from the very same principles with them.
> (TMS III.6.10)[39]

---

splendid virtues, with valour, with extensive and strong benevolence, with a sacred regard to the rules of justice, and all these supported by a proper degree of self-command' (TMS VI.i.15).

38 See discussion on p. 37 on the freedom of beneficence.

39 'The rules of justice may be compared to the rules of grammar; the rules of the other virtues, to the rules which critics lay down for the attainment of what is sublime and elegant in composition. The one, are precise, accurate, and indispensable. The other, are loose, vague, and indeterminate, and present us rather with a general idea of the perfection we ought to aim at, than afford us any certain and infallible directions for acquiring it' (TMS III.6.11). Also TMS VII.iv.1.

To live justly does not require the making of moral or legal judgments; agents simply have to obey the rules and this can be achieved without reference either to the moral guidance or the approbation of the impartial spectator. This is in contrast with the 'perfectly innocent and just man' (TMS VI.ii.intro.2), whose heightened moral consciousness makes him aware of the impartial spectator's approval of those positive laws of a state which are based on the principles of natural jurisprudence. For such a man alone, the positive laws are morally redundant.

The rules of justice are established by the state or commonwealth, and are given to the agent, but the principles on which they are (or ought to be) based are the subject of a science, that of natural jurisprudence (TMS VI.ii.intro.2). The significance of this reference to science is that the principles of justice are the subject of the science of jurisprudence and not of moral discourse. As noted above, the scientificity of a subject has important implications for it as a mode of discourse because scientific subjects are not amenable to moral judgment or impartial spectator mechanisms. Although Smith's lectures on jurisprudence were not prepared for publication by Smith, they are available now in the form of two sets of student notes,[40] and these notes are similar in style to the monologism of WN rather than the dialogism of TMS. Correspondingly, the appearances of the impartial spectator in LJ have a different function compared with TMS: in TMS the mechanism by which individual moral judgments are made as a basis for individual moral action is provided by the impartial spectator; in LJ the impartial spectator is introduced to vouchsafe the moral standing of codified laws that are in accordance with natural jurisprudence,[41] not to describe how a person comes to decide what is just behaviour.[42] The laws thus constitute a system of general rules that are sufficient for the precise guidance of just behaviour, and a person may act justly without ever consulting the impartial spectator. A person may even act justly by sitting still and doing nothing,[43] a state of moral inactivity that could never describe the morally virtuous person who has a dialogic relation with the impartial spectator and who actively takes responsibility for making moral judgments. According to the argument of TMS, moral judgments are

---

40 A statement of Smith's intention to publish his account of the general principles of law and jurisprudence is provided in the Advertisement to TMS and TMS VII.iv.37.
41 LJA i.35–8, 42–4, 77, ii.43–5, v.18; LJB 150, 154, 181–2.
42 Thus laws embodying the principles of natural jurisprudence are necessarily approved by the impartial spectator; the historical formation of these rules in the past may even be seen as the outcome of a long process of impartial spectator decisions (TMS III.4.8–11), but their existence and codification now mean that agents do not need the impartial spectator to prescribe what it is that constitutes just behaviour. When the impartial spectator is introduced into the text of LJ, however, the style is marked by a momentary extension in the range of voices; for example, an imaginary dialogue between the occupier and the challenger is presented at LJA i.37.
43 TMS II.ii.1.9.

'made' not 'given'; what are 'given' are 'rules' which may have a certain obligatory force, but they are distinguished from moral judgments proper.[44]

Justice is a 'negative virtue'; by itself it has little positive merit although it has some propriety about it:

> Though the breach of justice, on the contrary, exposes to punishment, the observance of the rules of that virtue seems scarce to deserve any reward. There is, no doubt, a propriety in the practice of justice, and it merits, upon that account, all the approbation which is due to propriety. But as it does no real positive good, it is entitled to very little gratitude. Mere justice is, upon most occasions, but a negative virtue, and only hinders us from hurting our neighbour.
>
> (TMS II.ii.1.9)

This means that the impartial spectator's response here is asymmetric; just actions do not require reward (as there is but little merit), whereas unjust actions do require punishment (as there is demerit).[45] This shows that the proper context for understanding the impartial spectator's attitude towards justice is that of the proper redress for injuries received, and it is in this context that the impartial spectator appears in the discussion of occupation as the primary and original form of private property at the opening of LJA where the context is that of injury:

> How is it that a man by pulling an apple should be imagined to have a right to that apple and a power of excluding all others from it – and that an injury should be conceived to be done when such a subject is taken [from] the possessor. From the system I have already explain'd, you will remember that I told you we may conceive an injury was done one when an impartial spectator would be of opinion he was injured, would join with him in his concern and go along with him when he defended the subject in his possession against any violent attack . . .
>
> (LJA i.35–6)[46]

In this passage, the spectator 'goes along with' and 'justifies' the possessor in

---

44 As an example of this, the discussion of punishment shows how laws may be disregarded or circumvented if they do not correspond with moral judgments based on the impartial spectator (LJA ii. 89–91, LJB 181). Here disregarding a law would be the result of a moral judgment in a way that simply abiding by the rules of justice would not, although the latter would still constitute virtuous behaviour.
45 In the discussion of punishment, mankind 'approves' as well as 'goes along with' punishment for the violation of justice (TMS II.ii.1.5,7). In the discussion of the race for honours in the following chapter, the indulgence of the impartial spectator is restricted to being able to 'go along with' the aspirations and behaviour of the agent (TMS II.ii.2.1).
46 The impartial spectator appears in LJ in three distinct contexts, viz.: property rights, contract and punishment. The more detailed notes in LJA show that the common link

defending his property because he 'goes along with' his reasonable expectation that his property implies exclusive use. But his approval of the defence of property is of a different order from the approval of the exclusive property as such; the first is approval of the punishment of demerit, whereas the latter is associated with the absence of merit. For this reason, the impartial spectator's approval of punishment for the violation of property does not imply an equivalent approval for the institution of property as such.

Prudence is the other virtue discussed in TMS that is seen as especially appropriate to the economic domain of WN, and it too has been cited as an example of the virtuous character of economic behaviour upon which WN is premissed.[47] As a broad, inclusive category, prudence combines care of the health, fortune, rank and reputation, with economic self-interest generally regarded as falling within its ambit as long as it is restrained by the rules of justice. In many of the discussions in TMS, prudence is grouped together with beneficence and self-command; this occurs in the distinction between the freely given moral virtues and the obligatory nature of justice, and it also occurs in the distinction between the rule-governed nature of justice on the one hand, and the open-ended character of beneficence, self-command and prudence on the other. It is made clear that the proverbial maxims of prudence may be used to some degree as general rules, especially in the ordinary and everyday cases of private interest, although not in the extraordinary and important cases,[48] but self-interest does not have the same moral standing as beneficence and self-command. In the assessment of the virtue of prudence in Part IV, 'superior reason and understanding' and 'self-command' are the two qualities which comprise prudence (TMS IV.2.6–8). The first quality (reason/understanding) is approved of as right or accurate according to the approval of any subject that comes under science or taste (TMS I.i.4.4) and therefore lies outside moral judgment. The second quality, self-command, is approved of under propriety and utility, but it is the deferment of pleasure and the physical and mental labour that are approved, rather than the seeking after material wealth:

> Hence arises that eminent esteem with which all men naturally regard a steady perseverance in the practice of frugality, industry, and application, though directed to no other purpose than the acquisition of fortune. The resolute firmness of the person who acts in this manner, and in order to obtain a great though remote advantage, not only

---

between these three contexts is injury, and that the impartial spectator's sympathy is directed to the injuries received; LJA i.35–8, 42–4, 77, ii.43–5, 89–91; LJB 150, 154, 181.
47 For example, Macfie (1967, pp. 71–81).
48 TMS III.6.6–7, 9.

gives up all present pleasures, but endures the greatest labour both of mind and body, necessarily commands our approbation.

(TMS IV.2.8)

It is the firmness and perseverance, not the acquisition of fortune, that is approved by the spectator; indeed the text refers rather contemptuously to the ultimate purpose of the self-denial ('though directed to no other purpose than the acquisition of fortune'), underlining the point that it is the perseverance and the self-denial, not the economic orientation of the behaviour or the motivation, that is admired.

This account of the sources of approbation in prudent behaviour is repeated in Part VI, where the parallel treatment of the three virtues allows a direct comparison of the ways in which the virtues are described and commended. In the chapter considering prudence, the approbation of the impartial spectator is called upon only once with respect to industry and frugality, and even here it is not the economic pursuit of wealth as such that is approved of, but the self-command that 'industry and frugality' are thought to imply:

> In the steadiness of his industry and frugality, in his steadily sacrificing the ease and enjoyment of the present moment for the probable expectation of the still greater ease and enjoyment of a more distant but more lasting period of time, the prudent man is always both supported and rewarded by the entire approbation of the impartial spectator, and of the representative of the impartial spectator, the man within the breast . . . He cannot therefore but approve, and even applaud, that proper exertion of self-command, which enables them to act as if their present and their future situation affected them nearly in the same manner in which they affect him.
>
> (TMS VI.i.11)

This passage shows that the object of the impartial spectator's approval, even applause, is the self-command that enables economic agents to act as if their present and their future affected them to the same degree that it affected him.[49] It is thus the powers of self-command that are applauded, not economic activities as such, the same self-command that was earlier identified in Part IV as the one aspect of prudence of which the impartial spectator could approve.[50]

Thus, the impartial spectator's approval of prudence is limited to the present denial of economic pleasures, rather than the pursuit of economic

---

49 'The moral quality of prudence depends on its association with the Stoic virtue of self-command' (Introduction to TMS, p. 9).
50 The prudent man of TMS is thought to be the frugal man of WN (Introduction TMS, p. 18); the frugal man's behaviour, however, may indicate 'not only a trifling, but a base and selfish disposition' (WN II.iii.42).

pleasures, and it is but a 'cold esteem', not a very 'ardent love or admiration' (TMS VI.i.14).[51] This restricted spectatorial endorsement stands in sharp contrast to the abundance of references to sympathy and the impartial spectator in the discussions of the moral virtues of beneficence and self-command in sections ii and iii of Part VI. Prudence is approved of, even in this limited way, only if the 'race for wealth, and honours, and preferments' is restrained by the laws of justice (TMS II.ii.2.1), but the virtue of justice stands outside moral discourse and is only a negative virtue. Thus, economic agents occupy a shadowy, twilight space in the moral universe, somewhat outside the site of moral discourse proper where the resplendent moral virtues shine in the approving light of the impartial spectator's eye. The inclusion of economic behaviour within the domain of the virtues follows not from the particular character of economic activity or material objectives, but almost in spite of them. The prudent man of industry and frugality is virtuous in so far as he works hard, does not break the law, and denies present pleasures; it is his self-denial that earns the approval of the impartial spectator, and little else, but this is not sufficient to earn his keep in the company of truly moral men practising the moral virtues. For this reason, the impartial spectator has no place in the discourse of WN.

It is not only the mechanism of the impartial spectator that is absent from the pages of WN; sympathy and the imaginative change of places are also absent. It has been remarked that the self-interested behaviour of WN may be understood as non-tuism in the sense that an economic agent does not consider the other agent, the 'you', of an economic transaction.[52] The moral behaviour of TMS was always located with reference to others, their views, and the degree to which a moral agent's behaviour could be assured of their sympathy and approbation; and this was signified directly in the text by its multivocity, including its direct references to 'you'. By contrast, the non-tuism of the text of WN excludes both sympathy and the presence of other voices apart from that of the author/philosopher. In view of the fact that commercial exchange involves a reciprocity of relations where there would always be present the other of the exchange, this absence is striking. It is sometimes argued that market relations in WN presuppose anonymity,[53] but one of the few passages where different characters – 'you' and 'I' – enter the text and deal directly with each other is the one introducing market exchange:

---

51 Cf. TMS VI.iii.13; VI.Conclusion.5.
52 Commenting on sympathy and self-interest in Adam Smith's work, Wilson (1976, p. 81) refers to Wicksteed's emphasis on non-tuism rather than egoism in economic transactions: ' "Non-tuism" is necessary if the market is to work satisfactorily just as "non-tuism" is necessary for a decent game of football or of chess. Without "non-tuism" the game will be spoiled.'
53 Viner (1960, p. 60) and Macfie (1967, p. 104).

> Whoever offers to another a bargain of any kind, proposes to do this. Give me that which I want, and you shall have this which you want, is the meaning of every such offer; and it is in this manner that we obtain from one another the far greater part of those good offices which we stand in need of. It is not from the benevolence of the butcher . . .
>
> (WN I.ii.2)

Interpretations of this passage tend to emphasise the demotion of benevolence in WN, but the significant feature of this relationship that is entirely absent from TMS is the *symmetry* of the exchange relation: when an offer of this sort is made, it is matched by a reciprocal offer, where each party to the exchange is saying 'Give me what I want and you shall have what you want'. In this symmetric exchange, there is no need for an imaginary change of places or for sympathy, because everyone knows that the other is in the same position as themselves: being a symmetrical relation, the exchange relation provides its own mirror and has no need of spectator mechanisms to achieve reflection. Here, the rules of the game are provided by the rules of justice relating to property and contract, and these rules are clearly laid out for each of the parties to the transaction. The agents are economic agents, not moral agents, and economic agents are owners of property[54] in the form of land, labour and capital. In the system of natural liberty in WN, economic agents as property owners may use their property as they wish in the sense that they are subject not to moral imperatives, but to the laws relating to property and contract.

5

The history of changing legal and political conceptions of property was a long one without a simple teleology. It forms part of the larger set of discourses within which WN must be located, and where the economic analysis of WN cannot be read as an endorsement of 'liberal capitalism' or as a prescient anticipation of modern principles of competitive markets. But the possibility of reconstructing the broader evaluation of the natural progress of opulence and the growth of commercial societies that is to be found in WN cannot be furthered by attempting to inject the moral discourse of TMS into the text of WN on the grounds that the 'Adam Smith problem' has been resolved and that 'the same man wrote both works'. This chapter has challenged both this mode of reading the Adam Smith problem and the substantive results derived from such readings. It has argued that the form,

---

54 'Dominium, or the full right of property. By this a man has the sole claim to a subject, exclusive of all others, but can use it himself as he thinks fit, and if he pleases abuse or destroy it . . . Property is to be considered as an exclusive right by which we can hinder any other person from using in any shape what we possess in this manner' (LJA i.16–17).

style and moral import of TMS and WN carry the reader along different tracks: the former is a 'dialogic', multivocal exploration of moral judgment; the second is a 'monologic', didactic treatise on the system of natural liberty. These differences have contributed to the divergent reading experience sensed by many scholars in attempting to understand these two books as complementary parts of a larger *œuvre*; they also epitomise the moral disjuncture between these two works.[55] This means that to understand the place of 'virtue' in the larger appraisal of commercial society in TMS or WN requires not only an understanding of the textured resonances of the word 'virtue' in eighteenth-century discourse, but also an examination of the significance of the partial uncoupling of virtue from conscience in TMS, where the moral discourse of conscience operates on a different register from that of the lower-order but public virtues of justice and prudence. Even more crucially, it also requires a re-examination of the eighteenth-century context of the economic arguments underlying the system of natural liberty, together with a reading of WN that does not simply reproduce the conventional wisdoms of twentieth-century economic thinking. Accordingly, later chapters will provide an account of LJ and WN, but first the Stoic reverberations of TMS will be examined in the following two chapters.

---

55 Interpretations that attempt to use LJ as a 'bridge' to link TMS with WN thus overlook the extent of the moral disjuncture between the discourse of TMS and that of LJ and WN.

3

THE DIALOGIC EXPERIENCE OF CONSCIENCE

1

The account of conscience in TMS presented in the previous chapter stressed the dialogism of the mechanism of the impartial spectator. The importance of inner debate or soliloquy for ethical discourse has long been recognised; the Delphic maxim 'Know Yourself' provides evidence from antiquity, and written examples of dialogic discourse are available in the works of the Stoic philosopher Marcus Aurelius and the early Christian convert St Augustine.[1] Bakhtin's argument, however, concerned the ways in which this ethical dialogism predisposes certain ethical discourses towards a dialogic style where 'elements of an artistic representation of another's word are possible . . . for example, a representation of the struggle waged by the voice of conscience with other voices that sound in a man, the internal dialogism leading to repentance and so forth' (Bakhtin 1981, p. 350). This chapter will examine the Stoic model of inner debate and its presence in some early eighteenth-century writings, and it will argue that this Stoic model structures the presentation of TMS and its metaphor of the impartial spectator. Further, this chapter will also argue that the tensions in the account of the impartial spectator mechanism, which were considered in the previous chapter, can also be traced to TMS's dependence on, yet ultimate rejection of, the Stoic philosophy.

2

The impartial spectator metaphor provides a view of conscience as soliloquy,[2]

---

1 See Marcus Aurelius (1964) and Augustine (1990, 1991).
2 'A dialogic relationship to one's own self defines the genre of the soliloquy. It is a discussion with oneself' (Bakhtin 1984, p. 120); 'The third and final modification [i.e. to classical forms of biography/autobiography] we will call the *stoic* type of autobiography, . . . Typical . . . is the advent of a new form for relating to one's self. One might best characterise this new relationship by using Augustine's term "Soliloquia", that is, "solitary conversations with oneself" . . . This is a new relationship to one's own self, to one's own particular "I" – with

a dialogic relation with one's own self,[3] a view of conscience which Bakhtin argues was characteristic of philosophers such as Epictetus, Marcus Aurelius and Augustine:

> At the heart of the genre [i.e. soliloquy] lies the discovery of the *inner man* – 'one's own self', accessible not to passive self-observation but only through an *active dialogic approach to one's own self*, destroying that naive wholeness of one's notions about the self that lies at the heart of the lyric, epic, and tragic image of man.
> (Bakhtin 1984, p. 120, original emphasis)[4]

The Stoic writers such as Epictetus and Marcus Aurelius are referred to copiously in the course of TMS but, although the importance of Stoic philosophy for Adam Smith's moral philosophy is generally recognised in

---

no witnesses, without any concessions to the voice of a "third person", whoever it might be. Here the self-consciousness of a solitary individual seeks support and more authoritative reading of its fate in its own self, without mediation, in the sphere of ideas and philosophy. There is even a place here for struggle with "another's" point of view – for example, in Marcus Aurelius. The point of view that "another" takes toward us – which we take into account, and by which we evaluate ourselves – functions as the source of vanity, vain pride, or as the source of offense . . . Despite these new features, even this third modification remains to a significant extent public and rhetorical. There is, as yet, nothing of that authentically solitary individual who makes his appearance only in the Middle Ages . . . Solitude, here, is still a very relative and naive thing. A sense of self is still rooted firmly in the public sphere . . .' (Bakhtin 1981, pp. 144–5).

3 In a fascinating study, Marshall (1984; reprinted as chapter 7 in 1986) links conscience as soliloquy in Shaftesbury's 'Soliloquy or Advice to an Author' with the impartial spectator in TMS, but he emphasises the *theatrical* status of the soliloquy, and the *theatricality* of the metaphor of spectator and spectacle in TMS. The argument of this paper involves stressing the ethical context for the metaphors of theatre and spectacle, and underlining the ethical and Stoic traditions of this inner dialogism. For example, in the *Encheiridion* of Epictetus (which Shaftesbury carried about him, and which is referred to in TMS) God is the ultimate playwright: 'Remember that you are an actor in a play, the character of which is determined by the Playwright: if He wishes the play to be short, it is short; if long, it is long . . . For this is your business, to play admirably the role assigned to you; but the selection of that role is Another's' (para. 17): all quotations from the works of Epictetus are taken from the Loeb translation (Epictetus 1925/8). In the *Philosophical Regimen*, Shaftesbury writes: ' "Is this all? Must I have nothing better to act?" And thus thou becomest one of those seditious and quarrelsome actors that mutiny against the master of the stage. For it is plain, whilst thou art thus affected, thy aim is towards spectators, not towards Him of whose approbation alone thou hast need, since in this respect every part is equally great and worthy if duly accepted and cheerfully, benignly, gratefully, manfully discharged' (Shaftesbury 1900, p. 119). Also 'For just as an actor or dancer has assigned to him not any but a certain particular part or dance, so life has to be conducted in a certain fixed way, and not in any way we like' (Cicero 1931, III.24). Cf. Marcus Aurelius 1964, XII.36. For a discussion of theatrical imagery, see Vickers (1971, especially pp. 189–226).

4 'The Stoics say that man differs from irrational animals because of internal speech not uttered speech . . .' (Sextus Empiricus *Adversus Mathematicos* viii.275; cited in Long 1986, p. 125). In citing this passage, Long argues that the Stoics held that 'A man is a creature who possesses the capacity to see connexions (and to use language) as a natural endowment. To do this is to think articulately, *to speak within oneself*, to order the impressions of experience and to create new ideas from them' (Long 1986, p. 125, emphasis added).

the literature, it has been little explored.[5] The *Meditations* of Marcus Aurelius,[6] for example, are written as a dialogic discourse; translated literally the Greek title means 'To Himself' and these private meditations (not intended for publication) are written as a man's private deliberations with his own conscience. The style ranges across a number of voices, but time and again the author addresses himself directly and interrogates himself: 'To what use am I now putting the powers of my soul? Examine yourself on this point at every step, and ask, "How stands it with that part of me men call the master-part? Whose soul inhabits me at this moment?" ' (Marcus Aurelius 1964, V.11). The 'master-part' here is the *hegemonikon*, the mind or highest part of the Stoic soul,[7] and variously translated into English as the ruling reason, the governing principle, and the commanding faculty. The *hegemonikon* is the site of reason, *logos*, in the soul of man and comprises a spark of the divine fire, the Right Reason or *logos* that is God, the controlling spirit of the universe.[8] This provides a model of conscience where a person may deliberate with himself, with his inner being, and it is this process of rational self-deliberation that constitutes the divine element in man and shows his affinity with God: 'even as Zeus communes with himself, and is at peace with himself, and contemplates the character of his governance, and occupies himself with ideas appropriate to himself, so ought we also to be able to converse with ourselves, not to be in need of others . . .' (Epictetus 1925/8, III.xiii; vol. II, p. 89).[9]

This dialogic scrutiny of oneself is also evident in the private philosophical exercises of the Third Earl of Shaftesbury,[10] a deeply Stoic attempt to reconcile the political responsibilities and social expectations of an eighteenth-century English lord with the philosophical writings of Stoic philosophers such as Epictetus and Marcus Aurelius.[11] Written as a series of private philosophical deliberations, stylistically Shaftesbury's *Philosophical Regimen* (Shaftesbury 1900) follows the *Meditations* of Marcus Aurelius with their direct interrogations of the self, but the substance of the argument draws upon Epictetus as well as Marcus Aurelius. In this dialogic debate,

---

5 Macfie and Raphael discuss the importance of Stoicism for TMS in their Introduction to TMS (pp. 5–10), but their comments have not been developed in the literature on TMS; see also Macfie (1967, pp. 72–81). An exception is Waszek (1984). See also Ignatieff (1986) and Dwyer (1987, chapter 7).
6 All quotations are from the Penguin edition (1964).
7 Inwood (1985, pp. 27–41).
8 'there is a portion of God which is not external but inherent in every human being, namely his own *logos*' (Long 1971c, p. 179).
9 Epictetus also recommends Socrates' habit 'of testing and examining himself' (*Discourses* II.i; vol. I, p. 223); see also *Discourses* IV.iv,ix; vol.II, pp. 323, 395.
10 Published under the title *Philosophical Regimen* in *The Life, Unpublished Letters and Philosophical Regimen of Anthony, Earl of Shaftesbury*, edited by Benjamin Rand, New York, 1900.
11 On Shaftesbury's Stoicism see Rand's Prefatory Introduction to *The Life, Unpublished Letters . . .* (Shaftesbury 1900, pp. xi–xii), Tiffany (1923); and Voitle (1984, ch.4).

the moral agent is urged to 'Learn to be with self, to talk with self. Commune with thy own heart; be that thy companion' (Shaftesbury 1900, p. 144).[12] The 'moral approving or disapproving faculty' is identified as the *hegemonikon*, the 'ruling, leading, commanding part' and this is called upon in the serious play of life[13] to correct the unruly and unreliable 'fancies or appearances' (Shaftesbury 1900, pp. 174–5). The dialogic scrutiny is also prescribed to authors in 'Soliloquy or Advice to an Author'[14] on the grounds that to speak wisely they must first know themselves,[15] and here an author is advised to 'multiply himself into two persons and be his own subject' (Shaftesbury 1964, vol. I, p. 105). Examples of this dialogic method, or soliloquy, are given from the poets and the dramatic arts,[16] but the context here is a lesson in morals. The presence of the Stoic 'daemon' or 'guardian-spirit' is urged as a means of dialogic self-scrutiny:[17]

> that we had each of us a patient in ourself; that we were properly our own subjects of practice; and that we then became due practitioners, when by virtue of an intimate recess we could discover a certain duplicity of soul, and divide ourselves into two parties.
> (Shaftesbury 1964, vol. I, p. 112)

By recognising this division in the soul, the agent could then converse with himself:

---

12 'inquire, listen, and hear what is said *within*. Be it in conversation, amongst friends, or with books, or in ever so seemingly good situation or plausible a circumstance. Is there not a voice that speaks within . . . ?' (Shaftesbury 1900, p. 158, original emphasis).
13 'When the tragedy chances to be over-moving, and the action strikes us, do not we say to ourselves instantly, "This is but a play?" Is not this the correcting, redressing, rectifying part? And how does this part carry itself in that other play – the serious one of life? How does it manage in this scene? Is it here still the same ruling, leading, commanding part? the *hegemonikon*?' (Shaftesbury 1900, p. 175).
14 In *Characteristics of Men, Manners, Opinions, Times* (1964), edited by John M. Robertson, vol. I, pp. 101–234.
15 'He who deals in characters must of necessity know his own, or he will know nothing. And he who would give the world a profitable entertainment of this sort, should be sure to profit, first, by himself. For in this sense, Wisdom as well as Charity may be honestly said to begin at home. There is no way of estimating manners, or apprising the different humours, fancies, passions, and apprehensions of others, without first taking an inventory of the same kind of goods within ourselves, and surveying our domestic fund' (Shaftesbury 1964, vol. I, p. 124). Cf.: 'the ancients gave us the injunction, "Know thyself"' (Epictetus 1925/8, I.xviii; vol. I, p. 127. Cf. III.i; vol. II, p. 11. Also the *Fragments* 1).
16 'By virtue of this soliloquy he [i.e. the actor on the stage] becomes two distinct persons. He is pupil and preceptor. He teaches, and he learns' (Shaftesbury 1964, pp. 105–6). It has been argued that the influence of the *Characteristics* was to reorientate literary criticism away from its traditional concern with plot towards 'vicarious introspection': 'Thus Shaftesbury cast his *Advice to an Author* as a "soliloquy", a form to which he gives the highest praise. He expands the Socratic tradition of "Know thyself". Not meditations or essays written with one eye on the audience, he says – but true soliloquy, self-examination to the very depths of the soul, is what is needed' (Tuvesen 1953, p. 290).
17 'Yet none the less He has stationed by each man's side as guardian his particular genius, – and has committed the man to his care, – and that too a guardian who never sleeps and is not to be beguiled. For to what other guardian, better and more careful, could He have

This was, among the ancients, that celebrated Delphic inscription, Recognise yourself; which was as much as to say, divide yourself, or be two. For if the division were rightly made, all within would of course, they thought, be rightly understood and prudently managed. Such confidence they had in this home-dialect of soliloquy. For it was accounted the peculiar of philosophers and wise men, to be able to hold themselves in talk. And it was their boast on this account, 'that they were never less alone than when by themselves'.

(Shaftesbury 1964, vol. I, p. 113)

Recognising how formidable is this degree of self-scrutiny for ordinary folk, however, it falls to moralists and philosophers to undertake a dialogic scrutiny on behalf of others, and it is at this point in the argument that these dialogic encounters are described in terms of a looking-glass: 'And this, in our default, is what the moralists or philosophers endeavour to do to our hand, when, as is usual, they hold us out a kind of vocal looking-glass, draw sound out of our breast, and instruct us to personate ourselves in the plainest manner' (Shaftesbury 1964, vol. I, pp. 113-14).[18] Here the role of the moralists and philosophers is to instruct their readers in the dialogic interrogation of themselves that their readers fear or are unable to perform themselves. In a mixed metaphor, the looking-glass that provides the objective reflection of the self is a 'vocal looking-glass', and the debate with the self is both auditory and spectatorial.[19]

The spectatorial metaphor for self-knowledge and moral judgment was well established by the time TMS was written,[20] but its account of the

---

committed each one of us? Wherefore, when you close your doors and make darkness within, remember never to say that you are alone, for you are not alone; nay, God is within, and your own genius is within' (Epictetus 1925/8, I.xiv; vol. I, p. 105).

18 Epictetus uses a mirror metaphor twice in the *Discourses*: 'if I say that you do not understand your own self, how can you possibly bear with me, and endure and abide my questioning? You cannot do so at all, but immediately you go away offended. And yet what harm have I done you? None at all, unless the mirror also does harm to the ugly man by showing him what he looks like . . .' (Epictetus 1925/8, II.xiv; vol. I, p. 313). To someone who might criticise the Cynics, Epictetus responds: 'Do you see the spirit in which you are intending to set your hand to so great an enterprise? First take a mirror, look at your shoulders, find out what kind of loins and thighs you have. Man, it's an Olympic contest in which you are intending to enter your name, not some cheap and miserable contest or other' (Epictetus 1925/8, III.xxii; vol. II, p. 149).

19 The soliloquy recommended is a solitary form of encounter as was that of the ancient moralists, where the agent's only companion was to be himself and where he would be far from the eyes of the world: ' 'Tis the hardest thing in the world to be a good thinker without being a strong self-examiner and thorough-paced dialogist in this solitary way' (Shaftesbury 1964, vol. I, p. 112).

20 Although the spectatorial metaphor was also used in a reverse frame where ordinary mortals were the spectators of God's work: 'But God has brought man into the world to be a spectator of Himself and of His works, and not merely a spectator, but also an interpreter' (Epictetus 1925/8, I.vi; vol. I, p. 45). Elsewhere in the *Discourses*, men are the spectators to the pageant and festival organised by God (IV.i; vol. II, pp. 279-81): 'since the divine

impartial spectator was the most well developed, providing an account of conscience that combines the impartiality deriving from distance together with the necessary knowledge of the agent that derives from intimacy. Within this model of conscience as dialogic relation with oneself, the metaphor of vision refers to moral judgment. In TMS the activities of watching, seeing and observing all constitute forms of moral judgment, and the impartial spectator is simply the proper and most objective moral judge: 'We suppose ourselves the spectators of our own behaviour, and endeavour to imagine what effect it would, in this light, produce upon us. This is the only looking-glass by which we can, in some measure, with the eyes of other people, scrutinize the propriety of our own conduct' (TMS III.1.5). Here again, the links with the Stoic tradition are maintained where a proper perspective on an agent's actions is provided by seeing him through the eyes of others.[21] In the description of Stoicism in Part VII of TMS, the account of the relation between the wise Stoic and the divine Being provides a model of Smith's own account of the relation between a moral agent and the impartial spectator:

> He [i.e. the wise Stoic] regards himself in the light in which he imagines the great genius of human nature, and of the world, regards him. He enters, if I may say so, into the sentiments of that divine Being, and considers himself as an atom, a particle, of an immense and infinite system, which must and ought to be disposed of, according to the conveniency of the whole.
>
> (TMS VII.ii.1.20)

The wise Stoic imagines how the divine Being regards a man such as himself, and then he endeavours to enter into that imagined feeling and make it his own.[22] Seen from this lofty perspective, he is but an atom, a

---

Goodness, for the reasons above mentioned, has constituted our sense of beauty as it is at present, the same Goodness might determine the Great Architect to adorn this vast theatre in that manner which should be agreeable to the spectators, and that part which is exposed to the observation of men, so as to be pleasant to them . . .' (Hutcheson 1971a, I.8, p. 96).

21 'Man, according to the Stoics, ought to regard himself, not as something separated and detached, but as a citizen of the world . . . We should view ourselves, not in the light in which our own selfish passions are apt to place us, but in the light in which any other citizen of the world would view us' (TMS III.3.11). 'But we ought to remember how we feel when we hear of the same misfortune befalling others' (Epictetus *Encheiridion* 26), referred to at this point in TMS.

22 'For where the theistical belief is entire and perfect, there must be a steady opinion of the superintendency of a supreme Being, a witness and spectator of human life, and conscious of whatsoever is felt or acted in the universe; so that in the perfectest recess or deepest solitude there must be One still presumed remaining with us, whose presence singly must be of more moment than that of the most august assembly on earth' (Shaftesbury *An Inquiry concerning Virtue or Merit*, p. 268; published in *Characteristics*, vol. I, pp. 235–338); 'remember that Another looks from above on what is taking place, and that you must please Him . . .' (Epictetus 1925/8, I.xxx; vol. I, p. 205).

mere particle, and so he begins to see himself in that light, without undue care for his own destiny except to greet it serenely with inner composure.[23] Analogously, the moral agent of TMS enters into the imagined feelings of the impartial spectator and views himself in that more detached light:

> We can never survey our own sentiments and motives, we can never form any judgment concerning them; unless we remove ourselves, as it were, from our natural station, and endeavour to view them as at a certain distance from us. But we can do this in no other way than by endeavouring to view them with the eyes of other people, or as other people are likely to view them . . . We endeavour to examine our own conduct as we imagine any other fair and impartial spectator would examine it.
>
> (TMS III.1.2)

These different uses of the looking-glass metaphor, however, reveal different approaches to conscience. The story of an amour in Shaftesbury's 'Soliloquy' shows that the soliloquy of conscience involves a debate between two distinct souls representing the good and the ill side of a man's character:

> 'O Sir!' replied the youth, 'well am I now satisfied that I have in reality within me two distinct separate souls. This lesson of philosophy I have learnt from that villainous sophister Love. For 'tis impossible to believe that, having one and the same soul, it should be actually both good and bad, passionate for virtue and vice, desirous of contraries. No. There must of necessity be two: and when the good prevails, 'tis then we act handsomely; when the ill, then basely and villainously.'
>
> (Shaftesbury 1964, vol. I, p. 121)[24]

In the account of the classical poems which presented a range of characters to the audience as a looking-glass in which they might see their own features reflected, there is a division of character into two sorts, the philosophical hero as the perfect character, and the range of second characters who showed the appetites which needed to be overcome.[25] The specular

---

[23] 'Many of the anxieties that harass you are superfluous: being but creatures of your own fancy, you can rid yourself of them and expand into an ampler region, letting your thought sweep over the entire universe, contemplating the illimitable tracts of eternity, marking the swiftness of change in each created thing, and contrasting the brief span between birth and dissolution with the endless aeons that precede the one and the infinity that follows the other' (Marcus Aurelius 1964, IX.32).

[24] In the *Inquiry*, the 'economy' of the passions is discussed at pp. 288–93 in *Characteristics*, vol. I.

[25] 'So that in this genius of writing there appeared both the heroic and the simple, the tragic and the comic vein . . . We might here, therefore, as in a looking-glass discover ourselves, and see our minutest features nicely delineated, and suited to our own apprehension and cognizance' (Shaftesbury 1964, vol. I, pp. 128).

habit of self-inspection thus learnt from these poems would then manifest itself in the use of a private looking-glass, which similarly enabled a person to see the two sides of his character.[26] This view of two persons in one individual self, however, implies a psychological dualism where conscience is the site of a struggle between two independent forces, between the appetites and desires on the one side and reason on the other,[27] but this dualism is Aristotelian not Stoic.

The Stoics argued that the sole centre of consciousness and control was the *hegemonikon*.[28] According to this Stoic view, wayward passions were mistaken judgments rather than the result of a lower or irrational element in the soul,[29] and it was on this basis that the Stoics emphasised that virtue required educating a person's reason rather than eliciting the obedience of the non-rational parts of the soul.[30] In TMS, however, instead of dichotomising the self into reason and the passions, conscience is presented as the attempt to achieve impartiality and moral distance in making judgments, where a moral agent must step outside himself in order to see himself within an appropriate moral perspective. This model of conscience deploys the agent's imagination as the basis for sympathy and the impartial spectator mechanism, and it is this that provides the dialogic element. But in substituting the imagination for reason as the prime moral mover, TMS privileged nature over reason and, ultimately, rejected Stoicism itself.

By presenting conscience as a struggle between the good and the ill sides

---

26 'And, what was of singular note in these magical glasses, it would happen that, by constant and long inspection, the parties accustomed to the practice would acquire a peculiar speculative habit, so as virtually to carry about with them a sort of pocket-mirror, always ready and in use. In this, there were two faces which would naturally present themselves to our view: one of them, like the commanding genius, the leader and chief above-mentioned; the other like that rude, undisciplined and headstrong creature whom we ourselves in our natural capacity most exactly resembled. Whatever we were employed in, whatever we set about, if once we had acquired the habit of this mirror we should, by virtue of the double reflection, distinguish ourselves into two different parties. And in this dramatic method, the work of self-inspection would proceed with admirable success' (Shaftesbury 1964, vol. I, pp. 128–9).

27 'For Appetite, which is elder brother to Reason, being the lad of stronger growth, is sure, on every contest, to take the advantage of drawing all to his own side. And Will, so highly boasted, is at best merely a top or football between these youngsters, who prove very unfortunately matched; till the youngest, instead of now and then a kick or lash bestowed to little purpose, forsakes the ball or top itself, and begins to lay about his elder brother. 'Tis then that the scene changes. For the elder, like an arrant coward, upon this treatment, presently grows civil, and affords the younger as fair play afterwards as he can desire' (Shaftesbury 1964, vol. I, p. 123).

28 'The Stoic psychology of action was monistic in that it placed the power of reason in charge of the process of generating actions, and did not leave room for a power in the soul which might oppose reason and interfere with its control over the actions of the agent' (Inwood 1985, p. 33); also Campbell (1985).

29 In discussion of Seneca's tragedies: 'for the Stoic the passions are sequels of faulty judgment, for the dramatist they are independent forces that fight with reason and pervert it for their own ends' (Sandbach 1975, p. 161).

30 Inwood (1985, p. 139).

of human nature, the 'Soliloquy' emphasises the adversarial nature of these dialogic deliberations. The sermons of Joseph Butler[31] also present an adversarial account of conscience, but here the contest has become more pointed with conscience claiming absolute authority and direction over all the other principles of action:[32] 'conscience or reflection . . . plainly bears upon it marks of authority over all the rest, and claims the absolute direction of them all, to allow or forbid their gratification' (Butler 1970, Preface, p. 8, para. 24).[33] Indeed, Butler's *Sermons* challenge Shaftesbury's *Inquiry* on just this point that conscience should have authority and mastery over a man's nature: 'The not taking into consideration this authority, which is implied in the idea of reflex approbation or disapprobation, seems a material deficiency or omission in Lord Shaftesbury's *Inquiry concerning Virtue*' (Butler 1970, Preface, p. 9, para. 26).[34] In Butler's *Sermons*, a more distinctly Christian virtue becomes obligatory and the task of conscience is to ensure that the moral law, that is, God's law, is enforced.[35] As the law of God is already written in people's hearts, revelation is not essential for right action according to God's law, but by now the fundamental dialogism of the Stoics has been turned into its opposite, a monologic discourse of obligations and duties underwritten by God's will, which instructs and commands obedience.[36]

---

31 *Butler's Fifteen Sermons Preached at the Rolls Chapel*, edited by T. A. Roberts 1970; first published 1726; Preface added to second edition, 1729.
32 Butler 'tried to introduce a principle of authority and obligation into the sense of right and wrong, which was utterly incompatible with Shaftesbury's moral outlook . . .' (Voitle 1984, p. 126).
33 Butler continues in categorical terms; 'Whereas in reality the very constitution of our nature requires, that we bring our whole conduct before this superior faculty; wait its determination; enforce upon ourselves its authority, and make it the business of our lives, as it is absolutely the whole business of a moral agent, to conform ourselves to it. This is the true meaning of that ancient precept, *Reverence thyself*' (Butler 1970, Preface, p. 9, para. 25, original emphasis).
34 The language of mastery and command is also used in the *Philosophical Regimen*, but the source of this mastery and command is the self, the *hegemonikon*, and is connected to the moral agent's freedom and happiness in the knowledge and pursuit of virtue. In this sense, Stoicism was not deontological but eudaimonistic; cf. Long (1971b, p. 103) and Long and Sedley (1987, pp. 398–400).
35 'The apostle asserts, that the Gentiles *do by NATURE the things contained in the law*. Nature is indeed here put by way of distinction from revelation, but yet it is not a mere negative. He intends to express more than that by which they *did not*, that by which they *did* the works of the law; namely, by *nature* . . . What that is in man by which he is *naturally a law to himself*, is explained in the following words: "which shew the work of the law written in their hearts, their conscience also bearing witness . . ."' (Butler 1970, 2.8, p. 30, original emphasis).
36 'Your obligation to obey this law, is its being the law of your nature. That your conscience approves of and attests to such a course of action, is itself alone an obligation. Conscience does not only offer itself to shew us the way we should walk in, but it likewise carries its own authority with it, that it is our natural guide; the guide assigned us by the Author of our nature: it therefore belongs to our condition of being, it is our duty to walk in that path,

This difference between Shaftesbury's *Inquiry into Virtue* and Butler's *Sermons* is also discernible in the marked change in the tone and language of Francis Hutcheson's early writings on moral virtue in *An Inquiry into the Original of our Ideas of Beauty and Virtue* (first published 1725) and *An Essay on the Nature and Conduct of the Passions and Affections* (first published 1728) compared with *A Short Introduction to Moral Philosophy*, which was published in 1747.[37] The earlier works of Hutcheson emphasise the moral sense as an entirely disinterested concern with the well-being and happiness of others: 'so he has given us a Moral Sense, to direct our actions, and to give us still nobler pleasures; so that while we are only intending the good of others, we undesignedly promote our own greatest private good' (Hutcheson 1971a, I.I.1.VIII, p. 124). Although this moral sense is there to 'direct' actions, the paramount concern is the benevolent intention to secure the good of others, and it is this disinterested goodness rather than a regime of authority and compulsion which is the hallmark of this account of the moral sense theory taken from Shaftesbury's *Inquiry*.[38] This disinterested benevolence brings happiness to the perfectly virtuous person, but it is not the expectation of this happiness which prompts benevolent actions, nor is it the obligation to obey God's laws: goodness is truly its own reward and any obligation to moral good can be understood to derive from this commitment to virtuous action – the moral sense itself – independently of any laws as such,[39] although the laws may provide a prop for those whose moral

---

and follow this guide, without looking about to see whether we may not possibly forsake them with impunity' (Butler 1970, 3.5, p. 37).

[37] *Collected Works of Francis Hutcheson*, vols I–VII, facsimile edition, Hildesheim; punctuation modernised in all citations here.

[38] 'Having removed these falsely supposed springs of those actions which are counted virtuous, let us next establish the true one, viz. some determination of our nature to study the good of others; or some instinct, antecedent to all reason from interest, which influences us to the love of others, even as the moral sense, above supposed, determines us to approve the actions which flow from this love in our selves or others' (Hutcheson 1971a, II.2.9, p. 143).

[39] 'To conclude this subject, we may, from what has been said, see the true original of moral ideas, viz. "This moral sense of excellence in every appearance, or evidence of benevolence"; and that we have ideas of virtue and vice, abstractly from any law, human or divine. If any one ask, can we have any sense of obligation abstractly from the laws of a superior? we must answer according to the various sense of the word obligation. If by obligation we understand a determination, without regard to our own interest, to approve actions, and to perform them; which determination shall also make us displeased with our selves, and uneasy upon having acted contrary to this [moral] sense; in this meaning of the word obligation, there is naturally an obligation upon all men to benevolence . . . this internal sense, and instinct toward benevolence, will either influence our actions, or else make us very uneasy and dissatisfied; and we shall be conscious that we are in a base unhappy state, even without considering any law whatsoever, or any external advantages lost, or disadvantages impending from its sanctions . . . But if by obligation we understand a motive from self-interest sufficient to determine all those who duly consider it, and pursue their own advantage wisely, to a certain course of actions; we may have a sense of such obligation by reflecting on this determination of our nature to approve virtue, to be pleased and happy when we reflect upon our having done virtuous actions . . . And all this without relation to a law' (Hutcheson 1971a, II.7.1, pp. 249–51).

sense is defective. By the time of the *Essay*, the criticism of the argument that moral judgment is founded on obligation or duty, includes a reformulation that defines the moral sense or internal obligation towards moral goodness in terms of the response of the spectator: 'That every spectator, or he himself upon reflection, must approve his action, and disapprove his omitting it . . .' (Hutcheson 1971b, II.1, p. 229), but again Hutcheson's account is presented without recourse to the language of authority and compulsion. The *Essay* also examines the conduct of the passions and affections in terms that evoke the discussion of the economy and management of the passions in Shaftesbury's *Inquiry*. But by the time of the *Short Introduction to Moral Philosophy*, moral sense is frequently used synonymously with conscience, and this gives rise to a set of inflections that are more juridical and regulatory than the benign moral sense had been in the earlier writings. The first mention of conscience still carries with it that easy association of the most divine of all senses with what is recommended to us by nature,[40] but the conscience is soon portrayed as certain judge and regulator of life: as the 'judge of the whole of life' which 'assumes a jurisdiction', as 'the governing power in man', 'a right of judging, approving or condemning all the various motions of the soul', and 'destined to command' (Hutcheson 1969, I.1.12, pp. 23–6). These more authoritative and authoritarian inflections on the moral sense as a regulating conscience echo Butler's own treatment of conscience, and may well have been prompted by the influence of the *Sermons* during the 1730s and 1740s.

Vestiges of some of Butler's terminology on the authority of conscience have been discerned in TMS (III.5.5),[41] but this apparent similarity is belied by the essentially deliberative nature of the process of conscience in TMS, where truly moral virtue is not obligatory but is freely given:

> Beneficence is always free, it cannot be extorted by force . . . To oblige him by force to perform what in gratitude he ought to perform, and what every impartial spectator would approve of him for performing, would, if possible, be still more improper than his neglecting to perform it.
>
> (TMS II.ii.1.3)

The reference here is to legal obligation rather than moral obligation, but even so virtue is not represented as a duty. In TMS a sense of duty is defined by a regard to general rules of conduct, but these rules denote a second-order level of virtue for those who are unable to measure up to the full requirements of truly moral behaviour which requires an independent

---

40 Hutcheson 1969, I.1.10, p. 16.
41 See editors' Introduction TMS p. 11; p. 164, n. 1.

moral judgment denoted by an engagement with the impartial spectator (TMS III.5.1; 6.1).[42] In TMS, truly moral outcomes are open; they are not rule-bound or obligatory but are the result of an open process of debate between the moral agent and the impartial spectator, in which the final outcome is neither predetermined nor legislated upon by a theological determinism.[43] But as many people ('the coarse clay' of mankind) are unable to make the fine judgments necessary for independent moral judgment, they have available to them the general rules of conduct which will guide them on decent and honest behaviour.[44] In addition, some of the lower-order virtues may appropriately be determined with respect to the general rules of conduct, for example, the pursuit of private interest in common and mean cases (TMS III.6.5–6), and those which can be determined with any precision or exactness may also be determined by general rules, for example, largely the rules of justice (TMS III.6.8–11). But the truly moral exemplar in TMS remains a person's private deliberations with respect to the views of the impartial spectator.

3

The analogy between the wise Stoic and Smith's moral agent noted above depends on the role of the imagination in providing the mechanism by which the moral gaze of the divine Being (for the Stoic) or the impartial spectator (for TMS) is made accessible to ordinary mortals. In the Stoic system, as recounted in TMS, the imagination provides the wise Stoic with a straightforward access to the divine viewpoint, but TMS's own deeply problematic account of the imagination in the process of moral judgment is revealed by the interplay of different voices at work in the text.

In the first chapter of TMS, having made the clarification in paragraph 10 that sympathy arises not from the view of the passion but from that of the situation, the final paragraphs present a number of illustrations of the imaginative change of places that underlies all moral judgments. In the

---

[42] 'The truly good man [i.e. the Stoic good man] acts on the basis of knowledge, which is not reducible to a set of specifiable moral rules' (Long 1986, p. 215).

[43] 'What matters to the Stoic sage is his disposition, how he is inside. He is free because he feels free, because he makes up his own mind about moral action in accordance with the values prescribed by *orthos logos*' (Long 1971c, p. 175).

[44] 'None but those of the happiest mould are capable of suiting, with exact justness, their sentiments and behaviour to the smallest difference of situation, and acting upon all occasions with the most delicate and accurate propriety. The coarse clay of which the bulk of mankind are formed, cannot be wrought up to such perfection. There is scarce any man, however, who by discipline, education, and example, may not be so impressed with a regard to general rules, as to act upon almost every occasion with tolerable decency, and through the whole of his life to avoid any considerable degree of blame' (TMS III.5.1).

second of these, the didactic voice[45] considers the plight of those who have lost their reason and then it concludes:

> The compassion of the spectator must arise altogether from the consideration of what he himself would feel if he was reduced to the same unhappy situation, and, *what perhaps is impossible*, was at the same time able to regard it with his present reason and judgment.
> (TMS I.i.1.11, emphasis added)

Here, a sceptical interjection in the form of a hybrid utterance within the didactic voice itself challenges the very possibility of the imaginative mechanism on which TMS is built. As it occurs within the didactic voice, its authenticity and authority can hardly be denied, yet it challenges the authoritative account of the possibility of moral judgment that the didactic voice represents.

The final example presented in this chapter concerns sympathy with the dead, and here the text displays a number of voices:

> We sympathize even with the dead, and *overlooking what is of real importance in their situation, that awful futurity which awaits them*, we are chiefly affected by those circumstances which strike our senses, *but can have no influence upon their happiness*. 'It is miserable', we think, 'to be deprived of the light of the sun; to be shut out from life and conversation; to be laid out in the cold grave, a prey to corruption and the reptiles of the earth; to be no more thought of in this world, but to be obliterated, in a little time, from the affections, and almost from the memory, of their dearest friends and relations. Surely, we imagine, 'we can never feel too much for those who have suffered so dreadful a calamity'. The tribute of our fellow-feeling seems doubly due to them now, when they are in danger of being forgot by every body; and, by the vain honours which we pay to their memory, we endeavour, for our own misery, artificially to keep alive our melancholy remembrance of their misfortune . . . *The happiness of the dead, however, most assuredly, is affected by none of these circumstances; nor is it the thought of these things which can ever disturb the profound security of their repose.* The idea of that dreary and endless melancholy, which the fancy naturally ascribes to their condition, arises altogether from our joining to the change which has been produced upon them, our own consciousness of that change, from our putting ourselves in their situation, and from our lodging, *if I may be allowed to say so*, our own living souls in their inanimated bodies, and thence conceiving what would be our emotions in this case. *It is from this very illusion of the imagination*, that the

---

45 This is the detached impersonal voice of the text which speaks with the greatest authority.

foresight of our own dissolution is so terrible to us, and that the idea of those circumstances, *which undoubtedly can give us no pain when we are dead*, makes us miserable while we are alive.

(TMS I.i.1.13, emphasis and quotation marks added)

In this passage there is a complex interplay of voices. The passage seems to commence with the generalised first person plural voice expressing sympathy for the dead, but this becomes a hybrid utterance as it is interjected by a voice which comments upon it by observing that this sympathy is misdirected in so far as it is founded on 'overlooking what is of real importance in their situation'. The sorrowing bereaved bemoan the dead's exclusion from earthly pleasures rather than what is actually awaiting them in their own futurity. After virtually quoting the bereaved sentiments as direct speech (these are signified above by the addition of quotation marks to the original passage), and then following this with first person plural tributes to the dead ('The tribute of our fellow-feeling . . .'), the text offers a rejoinder in the critical didactic voice which replies: 'The happiness of the dead, however, most assuredly, is affected by none of these circumstances . . . security of their repose.' The text then returns to the hybrid mode, where the didactic voice is directly engaging with and criticising the plural voice of humanity; again, interjections mark the presence of the more critical voice: 'if I may be allowed to say so'; 'It is from this very illusion of the imagination'; and 'which undoubtedly can give us no pain when we are dead'. This dialogic succession of voices plays out the undecidability of the text here. The didactic voice has to comment philosophically on the sympathy arising from viewing the situation of the dead, but it does this in such a way as to deny that this sympathy is either appropriate or even possible. If the living were really to sympathise with the dead by changing places in the imagination, it could only be by imagining what is of real importance in the situation of the dead, which is 'that awful futurity which awaits them'. In this case then, changing places in the imagination means to imagine the state of being dead, rather than imagining being alive within someone else's inanimated body. For this reason, the requirement to change places in the imagination must necessarily be problematic, and it is this 'illusion' of an imagination which is unable properly to change situation with another, that signals the difficulties with the sympathetic mechanism. Thus, the problems with the imagination are shown here to follow from the posited difficulties of the model of imagination itself, rather than from any personal moral inadequacies of the agent concerned.[46] Indeed, the causation is the other

---

46 Evensky (1976) argues that the failure of Smith's ideal vision as a moral philosopher derives from man's frailty and imperfectibility which obstructs the divine plan.

THE DIALOGIC EXPERIENCE OF CONSCIENCE

way round; it is because the mechanism of the imagination is a problematic one that it is so hard for the imagination to provide a reliable basis for moral judgments.

The fundamental problem with the mechanism of the imagination is that for it to work properly, the spectators must assume a double identity. In order to appreciate the situation of the other, the spectator must imagine what it is like to be in that situation, but at the same time to observe it as an outsider. Spectators must imagine what it is like to be without reason by using their own mental faculties to perform this imaginative feat; spectators must imagine being dead using their own living and lively imagination. In effect, the spectator is required to perform simultaneously two opposing parts, that of the observer/judge and that of the observed/judged. This imaginary identity of the two characters is achieved when they share the same view, and see with the same eyes.[47] But the interjections in the text declare that this shared vision is inherently problematic.

This is analogous to the problem that is encountered later on in Part III, where conscience requires that a person should be both judge and judged. The difference is that in the former case, the agents have to assume the situation of the other as the one to be judged, as well as retaining their own faculties as judge; in the case of conscience, the moral agents have to assume the situation of the other as judge, as well as retaining themselves as the one judged. In this case concerning conscience, the text reverts to the use of the first person singular, but again it is the authoritative didactic voice that pronounces such a model of conscience to be an impossible one:

> When I endeavour to examine my own conduct, when I endeavour to pass sentence upon it, and either to approve or condemn it, it is evident that, in all such cases, I divide myself, *as it were*, into two persons; and that I, the examiner and judge, represent a different character from that other I, the person whose conduct is examined into and judged of. The first is the spectator . . . The second is the agent . . . The first is the judge; the second the person judged of. *But that the judge should, in every respect, be the same with the person judged of, is as impossible, as that the cause should, in every respect, be the same with the effect.*
>
> (TMS III.1.6, emphasis added)

The passage commences by describing the requirements of conscience in the authorial, first person singular. It concludes in the didactic voice by 'But . . .' and declaring such a model of conscience to be as impossible as

---

47 If it is not possible to share viewpoints in the imagination, then sympathy is not possible. Elsewhere in the text where sympathy is being treated unproblematically, it is recognised that the sharing of viewpoints is only momentary and that the spectator cannot, even from

identifying cause with effect. In spite of this pronouncement by the didactic voice, however, the text continues in the following paragraph as if this doubt had not been expressed and as if the model of conscience had been demonstrated unproblematically.

It is sometimes argued that a heightened form of Stoic self-command provides a coherent basis for the model of the impartial spectator, but here, too, the text is marked by doubts. In the section on the Stoic philosophy in Part III, it is argued that the realisation of Stoic self-command comes close to being a complete internalisation of the impartial spectator and the dictates of conscience as the higher tribunal. This might seem to suggest that if only people were sufficiently virtuous in exercising self-command, the mechanisms of sympathy and conscience would work perfectly. But here, too, in the chapter headed 'Of the influence and authority of conscience', the text distances itself from this conclusion. The man of real constancy and firmness 'does not merely affect the sentiments of the impartial spectator. He really adopts them.' This might appear to represent the one case where the agent and the impartial spectator truly identify with each other, but the text continues: 'He almost identifies himself with, he almost becomes himself that impartial spectator, and scarce even feels but as that great arbiter of his conduct directs him to feel' (III.3.25). Here, the didactic voice is plagued with indecision; the virtuous man 'really' adopts the sentiments of the impartial spectator, but yet only 'almost' identifies with him. On the following page, the wisest and firmest man, he who more than any other has completely internalised the sentiments of the impartial spectator, is made, under the paroxysms of distress, to learn the limits of his only 'almost' having achieved this complete identification. And here, where even the wisest of all cannot completely identify with the impartial spectator of their own conduct, the didactic voice insists that this is so:

> He does not, in this case, perfectly identify himself with the ideal man within the breast, he does not become himself the impartial spectator of his own conduct. The different views of both characters exist in his own mind separate and distinct from one another, and each directing him to a behaviour different from that to which the other directs him.
> (TMS III.3.28)

---

this shared viewpoint, go along with all the agent's feelings in all their strength. This is the 'correct' operation of the spectator mechanism. Sympathy is redundant, however, when the agents already share the same view, as is the case in matters of science and taste where the disinterested attitudes of the agents mean that they share the same view: 'all the general subjects of science and taste, are what we and our companion regard as having no peculiar relation to either of us. We both look at them from the same point of view, and we have no occasion for sympathy, or for that imaginary change of situations from which it arises, in order to produce, with regard to these, the most perfect harmony of sentiments and affections' (TMS I.i.4.2).

The virtuous man exists in a triangle of torment as two opposing views are presented to him and he is pulled in opposite directions, but the text goes on to say that this separation of views has been willed by nature to ensure that he takes proper care of himself:

> When he follows that view which honour and dignity point out to him, Nature does not, indeed, leave him without a recompense. He enjoys his own complete self-approbation, and the applause of every candid and impartial spectator. By her unalterable laws, however, he still suffers; and the recompense which she bestows, though very considerable, is not sufficient completely to compensate the sufferings which those laws inflict. Neither is it fit that it should. If it did completely compensate them, he could, from self-interest, have no motive for avoiding an accident which must necessarily diminish his utility both to himself and society; and Nature, from her parental care of both, meant that he should anxiously avoid all such accidents.
> (TMS III.3.28)

Thus, the opposition in his mind between the two views presented to him is not the result of any frailty or personal inadequacy, but is inevitable and necessary, deriving from the opposition between nature and reason. The text, continuing in the solemn didactic voice, assures the reader that this opposition of views has been decreed by nature. In order that he should take proper care of himself, even the most virtuous man must maintain his own identity distinct and separate from that of the impartial spectator. To identify completely with the ideal man within the breast and become something more than the average man, means that he would become something less than a man; by not taking proper care of himself, he would be endangering himself and rendering himself vulnerable to accident.

Thus, the text of TMS itself displays a radical doubt concerning the viability of the spectator mechanism that forms the basis of the theory of moral sentiments. These doubts are, moreover, expressed by that voice of the text that is the most authoritative and the most philosophical, but as these doubts are interjected into a text that is characterised by a number of distinct voices, they take on the form of a series of responses or observations on the main theses advanced in the text. A crucial feature of the didactic voice in its sceptical utterances is that it is answering and responding to the other voices in the text, using words such as 'but' and 'however' to denote its critical engagement with the other voices. In this way, it could be thought of as a dialogic element within the text that presents the text not only as responding to or making observations on itself, but also as introducing an element of heterodoxy and openness as the text offers sceptical judgments about itself. Indeed, in some respects, this sceptical voice could be seen as the presence of an impartial spectator within the text, making observations on the text from the vantage point of a well-informed (indeed the best-informed) and impartial (indeed the most philosophical) observer and judge.

According to this spectator model, a person's moral integrity, embodying a wholeness and oneness with the impartial spectator and therefore with oneself, is dependent on the sharing of vision with the great inmate of the soul: 'With the eyes of this great inmate he [i.e. the person of 'real constancy and firmness'] has always been accustomed to regard whatever relates to himself' (TMS III.3.25). As a moral sentiment is a moral observation, so to view one's own conduct morally, one must share the vision of the impartial spectator whose own vision, whose own observations, are beyond reproach. But what the text of TMS signifies is that this metaphor of vision and observation as the essence of moral judgment carries with it its own limits and its own impossibilities. Without the certainty of the possibility of single true vision, the moral agent cannot become a unified moral being but must remain fractured and morally ambivalent, subject to bifocal vision and competing voices.

The unity of the moral being, and the authorial voice as the epitome of the moral being, remains an open issue for TMS in a way that does not accord with the Stoic vision of the literal integrity of the virtuous being. The monistic psychology of the Stoics held that the *hegemonikon* is thoroughly rational; what were thought of as 'irrational' passions or vices in Aristotelian philosophy are held by the Stoics to be mistaken and hence inconsistent judgments within the *hegemonikon*. In this case, the conflicts of conscience are debates conducted within reason itself, or more properly, between a defective reason and Right Reason,[48] while the virtuous life was defined by rational consistency, or living in accordance with reason: 'And the particular mind, what? – Part of this general mind, of a piece with it, of like substance (as much as we understand of substance); alike active upon body, original to motion and order; alike simple, uncompounded, ONE, *individual* . . .' (Shaftesbury 1900, p. 139, original emphasis).[49] The foundation of moral integrity for the Stoic is thus provided by Right Reason, the will of Zeus; when the moral agent's reason is in full accord with Right Reason, then inner conflict is impossible. Although it is only the Stoic sage who has reached this ultimate moral goodness by internalising the controlling reason of the universe, and although it is recognised that few men will ever achieve this ideal, yet the idea of the Stoic sage remained a powerful exemplar of moral integrity. In spite of or perhaps in response to this ideal

---

48 'When we respond hastily or foolishly to the presentations we receive, we fall into conflict with our own reason in so far as it has achieved its goal of becoming assimilated to Right Reason which, ultimately, is the will of Zeus' (Inwood 1985, p. 139).

49 Cf. 'According therefore as this recess was deep and intimate, and the dual number practically formed in us, we were supposed to advance in morals and true wisdom. This, they thought, was the only way of composing matters in our breast, and establishing that

of moral wholeness, the private meditations of the Stoic philosophers themselves, however, reveal a more fractured and ambivalent inner soul; Marcus Aurelius in his *Meditations* wrote: 'O soul of mine, will you never be good and sincere, all one, all open, visible to the beholder more clearly than even your encompassing body of flesh?' (Marcus Aurelius 1964, X.1), and Shaftesbury's *Regimen* too reveals the intensity of the dialogic struggle in pursuit of inner wholeness:

> How long is it that thou wilt continue thus to act two different parts and be two different persons? Call to mind what thou art; what thou hast resolved and entered upon; recollect thyself wholly within thyself. Be one entire and self-same man . . .
>
> (Shaftesbury 1900, p. 112; cf. p. 267)[50]

The philosophical unity supporting the integrity of the Stoic man lies in the coincidence of a man's reason with Right Reason, the controlling force in the universe; but this is another way of saying that it is also based on the coincidence of reason and nature, *logos* and *physis*, eliminating any opposition between them.[51] Nature here refers to the nature of the universe, nature in general, but it also refers to individual natures, to man's own nature. Thus, to live in accordance with one's own true nature is to live in accordance with 'Nature' itself, and this is also to live in accordance with Right Reason and the will of God.[52] The ultimate break with Stoicism in

---

subordinacy which alone could make us agree with ourselves and be of a piece within' (Shaftesbury 1964, vol. I, pp. 112–13).

50 Butler too underscored the unitary direction of conscience where, characteristically, emphasis was placed on the subordination and control of the several passions by the legislative authority of reason: 'As the idea of a civil constitution implies in it united strength, various subordinations, under one direction, that of the supreme authority; the different strength of each particular member of the society not coming into the idea; whereas, if you leave out the subordination, the union, and the one direction, you destroy and lose it: so reason, several appetites, passions, and affections, prevailing in different degrees of strength, is not *that* idea or notion of *human nature*; but *that nature* consists in these several principles considered as having a natural respect to each other, in the several passions being naturally subordinate to the one superior principle of reflection or conscience' (Butler 1970, 3.2, p. 35, original emphasis). The *Philosophical Regimen* too had employed the metaphor of legislative power: 'Begin, therefore, and, as a legislator to thyself, establish that economy or commonwealth within, according to those laws which thou knowest to be just; and swear never to transgress what thou hast thus solemly decreed and appointed to thyself' (Shaftesbury 1900, p. 116), but here the framework is a dialogic one as the moral agent is legislating upon his own decrees.

51 'In Stoicism *physis* and *logos* are the key concepts of moral discourse, and for man they are interchangeable' (Long 1971b, p. 104); 'Moreover I take it as common ground that the ultimate ideal, and consequently the essence of the Wise Man, is life in accordance with Nature, which Nature is identifiable with the rational principle found both in the Universe and in the individual man' (Kerferd 1978, p. 127).

52 'What is involved is the achievement of life in accordance with nature at a deeper level at each of the stages [of a Stoic life], until finally life in accordance with nature and life in accordance with reason are identical' (Kerferd 1972, p. 192).

TMS, however, is based on a denial of the coincidence of reason and nature; TMS counterposes nature to reason and it is this oppposition that lies at the basis of the rejection of the Stoic philosophy in Part VII, despite the deeply Stoic tone of much of the book. At the end of the largely sympathetic account of Stoicism, the text concludes: 'The plan and system which Nature has sketched out for our conduct, seems to be altogether different from that of the Stoical philosophy' (TMS VII.ii.1.43), and it is argued against Stoicism that it is nature's will that the events which touch a person most nearly and immediately will be felt most keenly:

> By Nature the events which immediately affect that little department in which we ourselves have some little management and direction, which immediately affect ourselves, our friends, our country, are the events which interest us the most, and which chiefly excite our desires and aversions, our hopes and fears, our joys and sorrows.
> (TMS VII.ii.1.44)[53]

The text, therefore, refers the reader to its own system of moral philosophy by arguing that should those feelings be too vehement, nature has provided a remedy in the form of the real or imagined impartial spectator who 'is always at hand to overawe them into the proper tone and temper of moderation' (TMS VII.ii.1.44). But the earlier account of conscience in Part III has already shown how nature upsets the operation of the impartial spectator even in the ideal case of the man of real constancy and firmness (TMS III.3.28), and so the impartial spectator cannot be proposed here as a solution to the problem of the antithesis of nature and reason.[54]

This leaves TMS without a resolution of the problem posed by the reluctance to accept the Stoic model; indeed it cannot resolve this because the impartial spectator has been set up as an analogue of the wise Stoic's

---

[53] Nature is again set against the reasoning of Stoicism a few paragraphs later: 'The reasonings of philosophy, it may be said, though they may confound and perplex the understanding, can never break down the necessary connection which Nature has established between causes and their effects. The causes which naturally excite our desires and aversions, our hopes and fears, our joys and sorrows, would no doubt, notwithstanding all the reasonings of Stoicism, produce upon each individual, according to the degree of his actual sensibility, their proper and necessary effects' (TMS VII.ii.1.47). Hutcheson had written: 'This may shew the vanity of some of the lower rate of philosophers of the Stoic sect, in boasting of an undisturbed happiness and serenity, independently even of the Deity, as well as of their fellow-creatures, wholly inconsistent with the order of nature, as well as with the principles of some of their great leaders . . . That must be a very fantastic scheme of virtue, which represents it as a private sublimely selfish discipline, to preserve ourselves wholly unconcerned, not only in the changes of fortune as to our wealth or poverty, liberty or slavery, ease or pain, but even in all external events whatsoever, in the fortunes of our dearest friends or country, solacing ourselves that we are easy and undisturbed' (Hutcheson 1971b, I.4.5, pp. 117–18).

[54] At TMS I.iii.2.3 nature is opposed to reason and philosophy in the context of the adulation of the great by the mob of mankind.

divine Being. The wise Stoic regards himself as he imagines the divine Being regards him, but TMS argues that nature disallows this as a feasible view of human nature. TMS then sets up its own analogous model of the impartial spectator, but the problems endemic to the Stoic version cannot be entirely suppressed as nature prevents the complete identification of the moral agent with the impartial spectator, even in the case of the most constant man. Thus, ultimately, imagination and sympathy fail in achieving complete moral wholeness for the moral agent, even for the wisest and firmest of all. Conscience is rendered as an irreducibly dialogic experience, which leaves its mark in certain stylistic features of the text as the dialogic interplay of voices mirrors and reproduces the ethical dialogism of the moral argument itself. In this complex interplay of voices, even the didactic voice of the text, the most authoritative and the most philosophical voice, is unable to achieve a complete resolution in which the sympathetic construction of the impartial spectator achieves a state of moral wholeness for the moral agent.

4

TMS is a systematic treatise on moral philosophy but it also displays many of the features of the dialogic discourse which Bakhtin attributed to ethical texts as well as what he termed novelistic discourse. The style of TMS is marked by a range of different voices which respond to and answer each other in such a way that the main argument advanced by the text is to some degree undermined by the interpellations of the text. Further, the model of conscience and moral judgment that is presented in the text is a dialogic one; moral judgments are the outcome of a dialogic process between the moral agent and the impartial spectator whereby the truly moral outcome cannot be predetermined and, further, the moral agent himself is unable fully to achieve a complete moral integrity. This is not the case for the ideal and perfect Stoic sage, who ultimately identifies himself with the controlling reason in the universe, and where his own reason is in full accordance with nature. This means that even the ideal moral agent of TMS is not the unified, integral moral agent such as we see in the case of the ideal Stoic man, the 'fully finished and completed being' of the monologic hero, but in some respects is a more fractured and struggling moral being.[55]

---

[55] Some dialogic affinities between TMS and Dostoevsky's *Crime and Punishment* are traced in Brown (forthcoming).

4
TMS AND THE STOIC MORAL HIERARCHY

1

In chapter 2, it was argued that the model of moral judgment at work in the metaphor of the impartial spectator results in a hierarchy of virtues; those that derive from the dialogic operation of the impartial spectator are the truly moral virtues, whereas those that derive from the observance of rules or the basic requirements of socially decent behaviour are second-rate or lower-order virtues. Chapter 3 presented a reading of the model of the impartial spectator in the context of Stoic conceptions of inner debate and a literature on soliloquy as the private meditations of the moral agent. This chapter will focus on the lower-order virtues by way of an account of the ways in which the discursive dependence on the Stoic moral hierarchy also structures the discourse of TMS by privileging the private domain of moral debate at the expense of the more public virtues of prudence and justice. Exploring the ways in which the Stoic moral hierarchy leaves its traces on the style and argument of TMS also provides a means of examining the moral status of self-love and prudence and of differentiating them from later, more economistic, conceptions. Once again, in spite of the formal rejection of the Stoic philosophy, it is argued that TMS is operating within a discursive space that is marked by the presence of Stoic categories of thought. The remaining lower-order virtue, justice, is the subject of chapter 5.

2

The Stoics defined moral goodness or virtue as the only good, and moral evil as the only evil, with all else remaining indifferent from a moral point of view.[1] Within this indifferent zone of the 'intermediates' were included not only the objects of worldly ambition such as wealth and greatness, but even

---

1 General accounts of Stoicism can be found in Long (1971a, 1986), Sandbach (1975), Rist (1978a), Long and Sedley (1987).

such constituents of the Aristotelian good life as bodily health, an adequate standard of material comfort, and the pleasures of family and friendship. It was this distinction that underlay the Stoic celebration of 'apathy', where a person accepted with perfect equanimity whatever life had to bring and where everything that lay outside a person's own moral faculty was regarded as indifferent, and it was this identification of the happiness attendant upon virtue as ultimately independent of the pleasures of sociability and civilised life that led to the rejection of Stoicism in TMS. The root distinction itself, however, could not so easily be thrown off but forms a crucial part of the moral foundation of the argument of TMS.

The highest good (*agathon*) for the Stoics related strictly to the inner state of mind, the sphere of moral purpose. The truly virtuous moral agent aspires to a life that is in conformity with nature because he knows and appreciates that this is the highest form of rational life available. For such a person, reason (*logos*) and nature (*physis*) are as one, and all the virtues are present as a unity. This person is the truly wise man, the Stoic sage. The actions of the truly wise person are perfectly moral right acts (*katorthomata*); it is because they are both appropriate acts in themselves and chosen for the right reason, that the moral agent aspires to the highest good. Choosing between alternative actions is something the wise man attends to as part of daily life, but the material outcomes of these choices are indifferent in a moral sense. The wise person, for example, will choose to take care of his health not because a healthy life is an end in itself, but because it is reasonable for a person to do this; such a person, however, will be indifferent to the outcome in a moral sense, in that he will accept ill health or good health with equal composure and happiness. For most people, this ultimate state of wisdom is either not possible at all, or else something that is still being worked towards; for these people 'appropriate acts' are feasible and are to be preferred but, as these actions are not accompanied by the right moral attitude of mind, they are designated simply as appropriate acts or proper functions (*kathekonta*). Thus, an act chosen by a wise man for morally good reasons is designated as a *katorthoma*, whereas the same act chosen for reasons that lie outside the moral purpose is designated as a *kathekon*.[2] In choosing appropriate acts (*kathekonta*), people are guided by what is reasonable as well as by basic precepts or rules of behaviour which provide guidance for those who do not or cannot aspire to the highest good, thus helping them to live decent lives without having to make choices in a moral sense: 'In *kathekonta* these rules are laid down for the use of the agent for the attainment of a certain object, but do not apply to his attitude of mind in the performance of the act. The agent accepts the rules, like the

---

[2] Thus a wise man and an unwise man may sometimes choose the same act though for different reasons. In other cases the wise man's superior reasoning and knowledge of the

opinions of a legal expert, but does not form them or think out the situation for himself' (Kidd 1971, p. 156). In the case of the *kathekonta*, therefore, the relation between the inner state of mind and the material outcome is reversed compared with the situation of the *katorthomata*, as it is the material outcome that is the object of choice whilst the inner state of mind is not. Thus, the distinction between *katorthomata* for the few and *kathekonta* for the many derives from a moral hierarchy where the life of the Stoic sage is achieved only by a few, but it also provides a practical reconciliation of the unworldy aspirations of Stoicism as a moral philosophy, with the demands for a viable code of behaviour for men active in public life in a civilised society.

The distinction between that which is morally good and that which is appropriate underlies Cicero's division of moral philosophy between *De Finibus* and *De Officiis*,[3] a distinction reworked in the Preface to Francis Hutcheson's *Short Introduction to Moral Philosophy*,[4] and accepted in TMS.[5] *De Finibus* presents an account of the three major ethical systems of Hellenistic Greece, providing the Roman audience with a Latin vocabulary for crucial Greek philosophical terms used by the Epicureans, Stoics and Old Academics. In the discussion of Stoicism in Books III and IV, the *summum bonum* is the highest good, while the term for appropriate acts (*kathekonta*) is translated into Latin as *officia*, and perfectly moral right acts (*katorthomata*) are translated as *recte facta* (Cicero 1931, III.20–5). Moral

---

summum bonum may well lead him to choose a different act in otherwise identical circumstances.

3 All citations here are from the Loeb translations.

4 'The design of Cicero's books *de officiis*, which are so very justly admired by all, has been mistaken inconsiderately by some very ingenious men, who speak of these books as intended for a complete system of morals or ethics. Whereas Cicero expressly declares, that the doctrine concerning *virtue*, and the *supreme good*, which is the principal part of ethics, is to be found elsewhere. Nay, in his own books *de finibus*, and *Tusculan questions*, he had previously treated these subjects more copiously. And he tells us expressly, that in his book *de officiis* he follows the *Stoicks*, and uses their way of treating this subject. Now 'tis well known that the *Stoicks* made such difference between *virtue*, which they counted the sole good, and the *officia*, or external duties of life, that they counted these duties among the *things indifferent*, neither morally good nor evil. The design then of these books *de officiis* is this; to shew how persons in higher stations, already well instructed in the fundamentals of moral philosophy, should so conduct themselves in life, that in perfect consistence with virtue they may obtain great interest, power, popularity, high offices and glory' (Hutcheson, Preface to *A Short Introduction to Moral Philosophy*, 1969, pp. ii–iii). In a footnote (p. ii), Hutcheson suggests that Cicero named *De Finibus* as he did in order to avoid using the title *De Virtute* which Brutus had used for a book addressed to Cicero.

5 'The Stoics in general seem to have admitted that there might be a degree of proficiency in those who had not advanced to perfect virtue and happiness. They distributed those proficients into different classes, according to the degree of their achievement; and they called the imperfect virtues which they supposed them capable of exercising, not rectitudes, but proprieties, fitnesses, decent and becoming actions, for which a plausible or probable reason could be assigned, what Cicero expresses by the Latin word *officia*, and Seneca, I think more exactly, by that of *convenientia*. The doctrine of those imperfect, but attainable

worth is designated as the supreme good or telos of a man's life whereas intermediates are indifferent from a moral point of view even though some are to be preferred: 'Accordingly after conclusively proving that morality alone is good and baseness alone evil, the Stoics went on to affirm that among those things which were of no importance for happiness or misery, there was nevertheless an element of difference, making some of them of positive and others of negative value, and others neutral' (Cicero 1931, III.50). Thus, even amongst things indifferent, items such as health, security, safety, friendship and public office would be preferred as possessing a 'moderate value', even though they possessed no moral worth. *De Officiis* is concerned not with an overall presentation of the Stoic ethical system or with the *summum bonum*, but with practical ethics in the form of practical rules for daily living. These are similar to the Stoic '*officia*', that is, the *kathekonta* or appropriate acts,[6] and it is here that the four cardinal virtues of wisdom, justice, fortitude and self-control/temperance are discussed.[7] Here, it is clear that the *officia* constitute a separate and lower order of human endeavour from that which aspires to virtue or the supreme good: 'The performance of the duties (*officia*), then, which I am discussing in these books, is called by the Stoics a sort of second-grade moral goodness, not the peculiar property of their wise men, but shared by them with all mankind' (Cicero 1913, III.15). This implies that much of the discussion of *De Officiis* is concerned with precepts or rules[8] concerning the *officia* in order to guide those who are unable to make proper moral judgments themselves.[9]

This fundamental Stoic distinction between moral worth and appropriate action forms the Stoic moral hierarchy[10] which also structures the discourse

---

virtues, seems to have constituted what we may call the practical morality of the Stoics. It is the subject of Cicero's Offices . . . ' (TMS VII.ii.1.42).

6 Although here the Greek distinction is rendered as that between absolute duty and ordinary duty. Cf. Cicero 1913, I.7–8, III.13–15.
7 Cicero 1913, I.15.
8 There are two different types of rules in *De Officiis*: there are the *praecepta* (passim) which constitute the general advice about the *officia*, and there is also the *formula/regula* in Book III which is directed at those cases where it might be thought (wrongly) that there is a conflict between that which is morally right and that which is expedient; cf. Griffin and Atkins Introduction to *On Duties* (Cicero 1991, p. xxii).
9 'The wise man does not need *praecepta*, since he does not act by external rules, but by his internal *logos*, therefore it is superfluous to give rules to one who knows' (Kidd 1971, p. 164).
10 This distinction might suggest that the Stoic moral hierarchy amounts to a simple binary distinction between the unattainable life of the sage and the morally imperfect life of all other agents, but a more complex system with finer gradations was proposed by the Stoics and is to be found in Cicero's *De Finibus* Book III. Following classic Stoic sources, Cicero presents a sequential development from the earliest stage of the infant through to the ultimate stage of the adult sage such that a person's moral development may be seen as a life-long journey; although it is the sage alone who arrives at the ultimate moral destination, this does not devalue the significance of the moral progress achieved by others. Cicero's presentation here of the Stoic doctrine of *oikeiosis* and the moral development of the individual forms a central part of Stoic ethics and is referred to again at notes 31 and 32

of TMS and underlies the stylistic character of its dialogic movement between voices. Of all the different voices in the text, it is typically the detached didactic voice which speaks for and on behalf of the highest moral virtue. This voice is the most elevated moral voice, the voice representing the point of view of true virtue, and is in contrast with the voice of plural humanity, the voice of the first person plural, which represents at best a second-order of moral worth and at worst the complete absence of moral standing. This switch in voices can be seen, for example, in the discussion of the importance of sensibility for the making of moral judgments:

> A stupid insensibility to the events of human life necessarily extinguishes all that keen and earnest attention to the propriety of our own conduct, which constitutes the real essence of virtue. We can feel little anxiety about the propriety of our own actions, when we are indifferent about the events which may result from them. The man who feels the full distress of the calamity which has befallen him, who feels the whole baseness of the injustice which has been done to him, but who feels still more strongly what the dignity of his own character requires; who does not abandon himself to the guidance of the undisciplined passions which his situation might naturally inspire; but who governs his whole behaviour and conduct according to those restrained and corrected emotions which the great inmate, the great demi-god within the breast prescribes and approves of; is alone the real man of virtue, the only real and proper object of love, respect and admiration.
>
> (TMS VI.iii.18)

The first two sentences are in the first person plural voice of general humanity, and this voice refers to the case where a 'stupid insensibility' prevents the full propriety of conduct which is essential for virtue. Characteristically, the text then switches to the detached didactic voice to denote by contrast the case of a man of perfect sensibility combined with full self-command, who is able fully to adjust his behaviour and his emotions to that which is approved by the impartial spectator. This is the man denoted as the real man of virtue and the only proper object of love, respect and admiration. The switching of voices in this passage from the general voice of humanity to the detached didactic voice is symptomatic of the moral switch from the imperfections of generalised humanity to the rarefied perfection of the real man of virtue who is ostensibly at one with the impartial spectator.

Another switch is made later in this chapter where the text refers to the

---

below, and also in chapter 5 in relation to the Stoic theory of justice. The Stoic doctrine of *oikeiosis* has been the subject of an extensive critical literature; for example, Pembroke

two different standards of judgment that a moral agent may refer to; the one corresponding to 'the idea of exact propriety and perfection', and the other being 'that degree of approximation to this idea which is commonly attained in this world' (TMS VI.iii.23).[11] This and the following paragraph are written mainly in the first person plural from the point of view of commonplace humanity:

> So far as our attention is directed towards the first standard, the wisest and best of us all can, in his own character and conduct, see nothing but weakness and imperfection; can discover no ground for arrogance and presumption, but a great deal for humility, regret and repentance. So far as our attention is directed towards the second, we may be affected either the one way or in the other, and feel ourselves, either really above, or really below, the standard to which we compare ourselves.
>
> (TMS VI.iii.24)

As soon as the text moves to describe the virtuous man, the voice shifts from that of common humanity to that of the detached didactic voice:

> The wise and virtuous man directs his principal attention to the first standard; the idea of exact propriety and perfection. There exists in the mind of every man, an idea of this kind, gradually formed from his observations upon the character and conduct both of himself and of other people. It is the slow, gradual, and progressive work of the great demigod within the breast, the great judge and arbiter of conduct. This idea is in every man more or less accurately drawn, its colouring is more or less just, its outlines are more or less accurately designed, according to the delicacy and acuteness of that sensibility, with which those observations were made, and according to the care and attention employed in making them.
>
> (TMS VI.iii.25)

This long paragraph continues in the same style with the didactic voice describing the wise and virtuous man's continuous exertions after excellence, and the text goes on to compare him with the great artist who can never be truly satisfied with his work, whereas the lesser artist frequently is (TMS VI.iii.26).

This account of two different standards of moral judgment is symptomatic of the moral hierarchies of TMS; as has been noted before, the perfectly wise and virtuous man's pursuit of moral excellence is based on

---

(1971), Kerferd (1972), Striker (1983), Brunschwig (1986), Engberg Pedersen (1986, 1990). See also Long and Sedley (1987) pp. 346–54.

11 These two different standards were first introduced at TMS I.i.5.6–10.

the ideal of the Stoic *sapiens*, whose moral purpose is exclusively committed to the *summum bonum* and in which the ideal unity of *logos* and *physis* is clearly exemplified. For this person alone, all the virtues are united in their most perfect form, and this includes not only self-command and beneficence, the truly moral virtues adjudicated by the impartial spectator, but also the superior versions of justice and prudence which then also become fully moral virtues.[12] As chapter 3 argued above, however, it is only in the rarefied case of the Stoic sage that *logos* and *physis* are united in the complete integrity of the moral agent. In TMS, even the wisest and firmest man is unable fully and completely to identify with the man within the breast, but yet the impartial spectator remains available as the mechanism of moral judgment for all those moral agents who are able to muster the requisite degree of sensibility and self-command, and here inevitably moral judgments are made with reference to both standards (TMS VI.iii.23). Thus, both these two standards of moral judgment fall within the purview of the mechanism of the impartial spectator; although it is the wise and virtuous man who always 'directs his attention to the first standard', this does not devalue the frequent use made by other moral agents of a less elevated standard of moral judgment. In TMS, therefore, moral judgment itself is not exercised exclusively by the small group of truly wise and virtuous men, although they exercise it more consistently with regard to the more elevated standard. The mechanism of the impartial spectator is relevant for all men who attempt to formulate their own moral judgments and, in the exercise of this independent moral judgment, such men are acting as moral agents.[13]

But, it is argued in TMS that not all men are able to exercise an independent moral judgment. The prevalence of self-deceit and the delusions of self-love prevent many from even attempting to make moral judgments. In view of this, TMS outlines an alternative but inferior mode

---

12 'A sacred and religious regard not to hurt or disturb in any respect the happiness of our neighbour, even in those cases where no law can properly protect him, constitutes the character of the perfectly innocent and just man; a character which, when carried to a certain delicacy of attention, is always highly respectable and even venerable for its own sake, and can scarcely ever fail to be accompanied with many other virtues, with great feeling for other people, with great humanity and great benevolence' (TMS VI.ii.Intro.2); 'This superior prudence, when carried to the highest degree of perfection, necessarily supposes the art, the talent, and the habit or disposition of acting with the most perfect propriety in every possible circumstance and situation. It necessarily supposes the utmost perfection of all the intellectual and of all the moral virtues. It is the best head joined to the best heart. It is the most perfect wisdom combined with the most perfect virtue. It constitutes very nearly the character of the Academical or Peripatetic sage, as the inferior prudence does that of the Epicurean' (TMS VI.i.15).
13 'That degree of self-estimation, therefore, which contributes most to the happiness and contentment of the person himself, seems likewise most agreeable to the impartial spectator. The man who esteems himself as he ought, and no more than he ought, seldom fails to obtain from other people all the esteem that he himself thinks due' (TMS VI.iii.50).

of ascertaining proper behaviour for a culpable and self-deceiving humanity, and this is presented as adherence to the 'general rules' of morality (TMS III.4.6–12). The violence and injustice of the selfish passions prevent most people from viewing themselves with the detached eyes of the impartial spectator but, yet, by having regard to these general rules, they may live a life of 'tolerable decency' and 'avoid any considerable degree of blame': 'Those general rules of conduct, when they have been fixed in our mind by habitual reflection, are of great use in correcting the misrepresentations of self-love concerning what is fit and proper to be done in our particular situation' (TMS III.4.12). Characteristically, the chapter on the origin and use of the general rules of morality is carried almost exclusively by the plural voice of fallen humanity, whereas in the following chapter discussing the place and significance of these rules, it is the detached voice which is used. Here, it is argued that only a refined few are able to act with appropriate propriety but that the bulk of mankind, those of 'coarse clay', may yet with the guidance of these rules live a decent life:

> The coarse clay of which the bulk of mankind are formed, cannot be wrought up to such perfection. There is scarce any man, however, who by discipline, education, and example, may not be so impressed with a regard to general rules, as to act upon almost every occasion with tolerable decency, and through the whole of his life to avoid any considerable degree of blame.
>
> (TMS III.5.1)

Regard to these general rules is designated as 'a sense of duty' and the significance of this sense of duty may be enhanced by the view that the important rules of morality are 'the commands and laws of the deity, who will finally reward the obedient, and punish the transgressors of their duty' (TMS III.5.3). Thus, the 'terrors of religion' are seen as enforcing the natural sense of duty and provide increased authority for their observance (TMS III.5.6). But adherence to these general rules strictly falls outside the ambit of moral judgment proper, and so provides only a second-order level of moral activity. If a wife or friend is motivated only by a sense of duty, then, 'Such a friend, and such a wife, are neither of them, undoubtedly, the very best of their kinds . . . Though not the very first of their kinds, however, they are perhaps the second . . .' (TMS III.5.1).

This then raises the question: 'in what cases our actions ought to arise chiefly or entirely from a sense of duty, or from a regard to general rules; and in what cases some other sentiment or affection ought to concur, and have a principal influence' (TMS III.6.1). TMS considers the degree of applicability of moral rules and finds them limited to specific cases. First is considered the extent to which moral action can proceed from a rule rather than from the affection itself, and this is found only to a somewhat limited extent; benevolent actions, it is argued, should by their nature proceed from the affections concerned rather than from a rule: 'All those graceful and admired actions, to which the benevolent affections would prompt us, ought to proceed as much from the passions themselves, as from any regard to the general rules of conduct' (TMS III.6.4). The contrary maxim applies with regard to the unsocial passions, such as meting out punishment, where it is better to be rule-directed than personally vengeful; and the selfish passions lie somewhere in between with ordinary cases of private interest being rule-governed and the extraordinary cases being directly subject to the (properly directed) passion of self-interest itself (TMS III.6.5–7). Next, TMS considers the extent to which it is possible to translate moral issues into a general rule with any degree of precision or exactness. Here, as argued in chapter 2 above, a sharp contrast is drawn between justice which can be formulated in terms of precise rules, and the other virtues which cannot:

> The general rules of almost all the virtues, the general rules which determine what are the offices of prudence, of charity, of generosity, of gratitude, of friendship, are in many respects loose and inaccurate, admit of many exceptions, and require so many modifications, that it is scarce posssible to regulate our conduct entirely by a regard to them.
> (TMS III.6.9; also III.6.11)

The common proverbial maxims of prudence are 'perhaps the best general rules which can be given about it' but none the less to affect 'a very strict and literal adherence to them would evidently be the most absurd and ridiculous pedantry'. In the case of gratitude, perhaps, the rules are 'the most precise, and admit of the fewest exceptions', but even here:

> Upon the most superficial examination, however, this rule will appear to be in the highest degree loose and inaccurate, and to admit of ten thousand exceptions . . . It is evident, that no general rule can be laid down, by which a precise answer can, in all cases, be given to any of these questions.
> (TMS III.6.9)

The rules which provide guidance in the case of friendship, humanity, hospitality and generosity are even less helpful, being 'still more vague and indeterminate'. In the practice of these virtues, therefore, 'our conduct should rather be directed by a certain idea of propriety, by a certain taste for a particular tenor of conduct, than by any regard to a precise maxim or rule; and we should consider the end and foundation of the rule, more than the rule itself' (TMS III.6.10).14[14]

---

[14] Smith argued against the casuists that 'they attempted, to no purpose, to direct by precise rules what it belongs to feeling and sentiment only to judge of' (TMS VII.iv.33).

Thus, the account of general moral rules in TMS, Part III, is one that presents them as an inferior substitute for the mechanism of the impartial spectator. Their inferiority derives both from their inappropriateness to certain forms of moral judgment which should derive from the passions concerned rather than from adherence to rules, and from their inability to offer guidance that is either precise enough or accurate enough to determine appropriate moral behaviour. But this is to judge these rules according to the standards of the impartial spectator. If they are judged according to another standard, then they will be seen to be useful guides to decent behaviour for those who are unable to make independent moral judgments as represented by the impartial spectator. It is the treatise on these 'general rules' of behaviour that is later designated as the 'science of ethics' in Part VII, section iv,[15] and included within this science is the work of the ancient moralists who have provided a loose and general[16] description of the different vices and virtues and an account of the general ways of acting in various circumstances (TMS VII.iv.1–6).[17] Cicero's *De Officiis* is placed within this domain of these general and loose rules of morality:

> It is impossible by language to express, if I may say so, the invisible features of all the different modifications of passion as they show themselves within. There is no other way of marking and distinguishing them from one another, but by describing the effects which they produce without, the alterations which they occasion in the countenance, in the air and external behaviour, the resolutions they suggest, the actions they prompt to. It is thus that Cicero, in the first book of his Offices, endeavours to direct us to the practice of the four cardinal virtues . . .
>
> (TMS VII.iv.5)

Thus, it is the 'general rules' of morality in TMS that correspond to the Stoic *officia* or *kathekonta*. As argued in the earlier part of this chapter, the

---

15 The first sentence of TMS VII.iv refers the reader back to the earlier discussion in Part III: 'It was observed in the third part of this discourse, that the rules of justice are the only rules of morality which are precise and accurate: that those of all the other virtues are loose, vague, and indeterminate . . .' (TMS VII.iv.1).

16 Their work is compared to the work of the critics whose rules relate to the 'attainment of what is sublime and elegant in composition, and which present us rather with a general idea of the perfection we ought to aim at, than afford us any certain and infallible directions for acquiring it' (TMS VII.iv.1).

17 The ancient moralists in providing general rules were sharply differentiated from the casuists, whom Smith compares with the grammarians laying down hard and fast rules. Smith scorns the casuists for encouraging moral chicanery by attempting to lay down exact and precise rules where such are impossible (TMS VII.iv.7–34): 'casuistry ought to be rejected altogether; and the ancient moralists appear to have judged much better, who, in treating of the same subjects, did not affect any such nice exactness, but contented themselves with describing, in a general manner, what is the sentiment upon which justice,

main distinguishing features of Cicero's *officia* are their reliance upon rules/ precepts to guide external behaviour and their second-order level as a form of moral activity. Both these characteristics of Cicero's *officia* are evident in the treatment of the general rules of morality in TMS which are both rule-governed in order to direct external behaviour, and a second-order level of moral discourse.[18]

3

The implication for TMS of the existence of a large portion of humanity standing outside the purview of the process of moral judgment represented by the impartial spectator can be discerned by examining the comments of TMS on mankind generally, the 'great mob of mankind', where the language becomes fiercely denunciative. The account of the disposition of the 'great mob of mankind' to admire the rich and the great is conducted in the fallen voice of humanity:

> upon coming into the world, we soon find that wisdom and virtue are by no means the sole objects of respect; nor vice and folly, of contempt. We frequently see the respectful attentions of the world more strongly directed towards the rich and the great, than towards the wise and the virtuous.
>
> (TMS I.iii.3.2)

Accordingly, there are two different routes available to enjoy the respect and admiration of mankind, one which leads by the study of wisdom and the practice of virtue, and one which leads by the pursuit of wealth and greatness: 'Two different characters are presented to our emulation; the one, of proud ambition and ostentatious avidity; the other, of humble modesty and equitable justice.' The one is gaudy and glittering, the other is correct and more exquisitely beautiful. Which character is chosen by the bulk of humanity? The voice switches to that of the detached didactic voice:

> They are the wise and the virtuous chiefly, a select, though, I am afraid, but a small party, who are the real and steady admirers of wisdom and virtue. The great mob of mankind are the admirers and worshippers, and, what may seem more extraordinary, most fre-

---

modesty, and veracity are founded, and what is the ordinary way of acting to which those virtues would commonly prompt us' (TMS VII.iv.34).

18 Waszek (1984) provides a Stoic analysis of TMS where Smith's equivalent of the *officia* is provided by the propriety of the multitude as determined by the impartial spectator according to the second standard of moral judgment; this, however, collapses the distinction between self-direction and rule-governed behaviour in Stoic thinking which is reworked in TMS.

quently the disinterested admirers and worshippers, of wealth and greatness.

(TMS I.iii.3.2)

The great mob of mankind admire those who are not worthy of their admiration, and it is this that constitutes 'the great and most universal cause of the corruption of our moral sentiments' and the 'complaint of moralists in all ages' (TMS I.iii.3.1). The adulation of the mob is easily secured for those who can provide dazzling displays of excessive presumption and excessive self-admiration (TMS VI.iii.27), or for those who appear to be mighty conquerors, even though their course to glory has been marred by injustice and brutality (TMS VI.iii.30).[19]

In contrast to the adulation of the multitude for the wealthy and the great, the judgments of TMS on the powerful, the ambitious and the successful, were invariably punitive, displaying a deep contempt for the low moral and intellectual standards deemed appropriate for persons of eminent public position. Of the aristocrats and princes who governed the world, TMS states that it is not 'by knowledge, by industry, by patience, by self-denial, or by virtue of any kind' that such a person is esteemed but by 'his air, his manner, his deportment', and his 'elegant and graceful sense of his own superiority' (TMS I.iii.2.4). Of the dangers of a career at court, it warns:

> Are you in earnest resolved never to barter your liberty for the lordly servitude of a court, but to live free, fearless, and independent? There seems to be one way to continue in that virtuous resolution; and perhaps but one. Never enter the place from whence so few have been able to return; never come within the circle of ambition; nor ever bring yourself into comparison with those masters of the earth who have already engrossed the attention of half mankind before you.
>
> (TMS I.iii.2.7)

Also: 'the candidates for fortune too frequently abandon the paths of virtue; for unhappily, the road which leads to the one, and that which leads to the other, lie sometimes in very opposite directions' (TMS I.iii.3.8). And of the political conduct between states:

> The ambassador who dupes the minister of a foreign nation, is admired and applauded. The just man who disdains either to take or to give any advantage, but who would think it less dishonourable to give than to take one; the man who, in all private transactions, would be the most beloved and the most esteemed; in those public transactions is regarded as a fool and an idiot, who does not understand his

---

19 Smith, however, remarks on the social utility of these aberrations of moral judgment.

business; and he incurs always the contempt, and sometimes even the detestation of his fellow-citizens.

(TMS III.3.42)

TMS also displays a consistent disdain for wealth and greatness, arguing that they are:

> mere trinkets of frivolous utility, no more adapted for procuring ease of body or tranquillity of mind than the tweezer-cases of the lover of toys; and like them too, more troublesome to the person who carries them about with him than all the advantages they can afford him are commodious.
>
> (TMS IV.1.8)[20]

Similarly, power and riches are really:

> enormous and operose machines contrived to produce a few trifling conveniencies to the body, consisting of springs the most nice and delicate, which must be kept in order with the most anxious attention, and which in spite of all our care are ready every moment to burst into pieces, and to crush in their ruins their unfortunate possessor.
>
> (TMS IV.1.8)[21]

Wealth and greatness are mere trinkets of frivolous utility, and power and riches produce a few trifling conveniencies: the context for these passages is that of the classic Stoic disdain for things indifferent which do not contribute to a person's mental tranquillity and moral worth,[22] and the voice of the text here is that of the didactic voice. The Stoic conception of the highest moral worth is one that is available to everyone, irrespective of social position; indeed those in a lower position are not only as eligible but may even find such mental tranquillity more easily obtainable than those distracted by an excess of worldly goods. But this Stoic view of the emptiness of wealth and greatness is apparent to men only in times of illness, low

---

20 The reference to 'toys' here is to the growing Birmingham metal 'toy trades' of adult trinkets and knick-knacks such as buttons, buckles, jewellery, cosmetic and writing accessories, etc.

21 The passage continues: 'They are immense fabrics, which it requires the labour of a life to raise, which threaten every moment to overwhelm the person that dwells in them, and which while they stand, though they may save him from some smaller inconveniencies, can protect him from none of the severer inclemencies of the season. They keep off the summer shower, not the winter storm, but leave him always as much, and sometimes more exposed than before, to anxiety, to fear, and to sorrow; to diseases, to danger, and to death' (TMS IV.1.8).

22 Cf. 'The never-failing certainty with which all men, sooner or later, accommodate themselves to whatever becomes their permanent situation, may, perhaps, induce us to think that the Stoics were, at least, thus far very nearly in the right; that, between one permanent situation and another, there was, with regard to real happiness, no essential difference: or that, if there were any difference, it was no more than just sufficient to render some of them

spirits, and the weariness of old age. In men's normal condition, the power of the imagination is irresistible in representing the attractions of wealth and greatness, and at this moment the text switches to the first person plural:

> But though this splenetic philosophy, which in time of sickness or low spirits is familiar to every man, thus entirely depreciates those great objects of human desire, when in better health and in better humour, we never fail to regard them under a more agreeable aspect. Our imagination, which in pain and sorrow seems to be confined and cooped up within our own persons, in times of ease and prosperity expands itself to every thing around us. We are then charmed with the beauty of that accommodation which reigns in the palaces and œconomy of the great . . .
>
> (TMS IV.1.9)

The didactic voice which concluded the Stoic sentiments of the preceding paragraph, gives way to the plural voice of deluded humanity at just that moment when the text moves to consider the way in which mankind normally views the pleasures of wealth and greatness which appear in the imagination as objects to be esteemed and emulated.[23]

This Stoic conception of things indifferent that do not contribute to moral worth also provides the moral context for the statements on the distribution of material goods, including the much-quoted passage referring to the invisible hand:

> They [i.e. the rich] are led by an invisible hand to make nearly the same distribution of the necessaries of life, which would have been made, had the earth been divided into equal portions among all its inhabitants, and thus without intending it, without knowing it, advance the interest of the society, and afford means to the multiplication of the species. When Providence divided the earth among a few lordly masters, it neither forgot nor abandoned those who seemed to have been left out in the partition. These last too enjoy their share of all that it produces. In what constitutes the real happiness of human life, they are in no respect inferior to those who would seem so much above them. In ease of body and peace of mind, all the different ranks of life are nearly upon a level, and the beggar, who suns himself by the side of the highway, possesses that security which kings are fighting for.
>
> (TMS IV.1.10)

---

the objects of simple choice or preference; but not of any earnest or anxious desire . . . Happiness consists in tranquillity and enjoyment' (TMS III.3.30).

23 This paragraph continues: 'If we consider the real satisfaction which all these things are capable of affording, by itself and separated from the beauty of that arrangement which is

The import of this passage has traditionally been interpreted as an *economic* statement on the distribution of material goods, and so it has been understood as a statement of a blind acceptance of a natural economic harmony.[24] As a *moral* statement, however, it endorses the central Stoic argument that material goods do not contribute to the *summum bonum* and therefore do not affect a person's happiness; it follows, therefore, that the existing distribution of worldly goods does not undermine or prevent the pursuit of the moral end of man, the *telos* of man's nature, which alone constitutes the objective of a truly moral life. Elsewhere it is reiterated that from a moral point of view, from the point of view of a man's happiness,[25] the level of material goods required is rudimentary and can be supplied even by the wages of the meanest labourer, wages which cover not only the necessities of nature but occasionally some conveniencies and items of vanity (TMS I.iii.2.1). In this case there is no reason why every man, including the meanest labourer, should not aspire to the true happiness that derives from a moral life:

> What can be added to the happiness of the man who is in health, who is out of debt, and has a clear conscience? To one in this situation, all accessions of fortune may properly be said to be superfluous; and if he is much elevated upon account of them, it must be the effect of the most frivolous levity.
>
> (TMS I.iii.1.7)

If material possessions and positions of power do not contribute towards happiness and tranquillity, why do men aspire to them? This question and the answer to it are delivered in the plural voice of fallen humanity. Emulation and the desire to 'better our condition'[26] arise from our vanity: 'To be observed, to be attended to, to be taken notice of with sympathy, complacency, and approbation, are all the advantages which we can propose to derive from it. It is the vanity, not the ease, or the pleasure, which interests us' (TMS I.iii.2.1). It is the spectator model of sympathy, based on the imagination, that underlies the common approbation of wealth and

---

fitted to promote it, it will always appear in the highest degree contemptible and trifling. But we rarely view it in this abstract and philosophical light' (TMS IV.1.9).

24 Viner's classic article (Viner 1966) has led to much discussion as to whether WN retreats from an allegedly 'optimistic' view presented in TMS.

25 It should be emphasised that the concept of happiness in TMS is a *moral* not an *economic* concept, deriving from the ancient notion that only the virtuous can be happy; Stoic happiness is equivalent to moral worth, the *agathon* or the *summum bonum*, and has nothing at all to do with the later economic notion of utility or consumer satisfaction.

26 Taking the clause 'that great purpose of human life which we call bettering our condition' (TMS I.iii.2.1) out of the context of the structure of the extended argument of this long paragraph, and without being sensitive to the changes in tone and voice within this paragraph, has led many commentators to misinterpret it as a commendation of 'the desire to better our condition' as 'natural and proper'; cf. the Editors' Introduction to TMS, p. 9.

greatness: 'When we consider the condition of the great, in those delusive colours in which the imagination is apt to paint it, it seems to be almost the abstract idea of a perfect and happy state. It is the very state which, in all our waking dreams and idle reveries, we had sketched out to ourselves as the final object of all our desires. We feel, therefore, a peculiar sympathy with the satisfaction of those who are in it' (TMS I.iii.2.3). And again: 'Of such mighty importance does it appear to be, in the imaginations of men, to stand in that situation which sets them most in the view of general sympathy and attention' (TMS I.iii.2.8). But, as argued in chapter 2 above, the didactic voice rebukes the 'prejudices of the imagination' for elevating the great in this way, and counterposes 'reason and experience' against the imagination. Rejecting the vanity fuelled by these fond imaginations of superior position and approbation, it is only the man 'confirmed in wisdom and real philosophy' who can rest satisfied that 'while the propriety of his conduct renders him the just object of approbation, it is of little consequence though he be neither attended to, nor approved of' (TMS I.iii.2.8). Thus, it is the imagination and the desire for sympathy that operate against reason and experience, and so contribute towards the corruption of moral sentiments so much lamented by moralists. This again illustrates how imagination and sympathy play an ambiguous role in TMS, as they provide the fundamental mechanisms both of moral judgment and of the corruption of moral judgment.

This same argument illustrating the moral ambiguity of imagination and sympathy reappears in a later chapter which explains the effect of utility on the sentiment of approbation. TMS argued that the pleasure yielded by the utility ascribed to objects is an aesthetic pleasure deriving from the fitness of the means for attaining a given conveniency, rather than the conveniency itself (TMS IV.1.1), and the account of the impartial spectator here supports this account of the aesthetic pleasure afforded by the utility of objects:

> If we examine, however, why the spectator distinguishes with such admiration the condition of the rich and the great, we shall find that it is not so much upon account of the superior ease or pleasure which they are supposed to enjoy, as of the numberless artificial and elegant contrivances for promoting this ease or pleasure. He does not even imagine that they are really happier than other people: but he imagines that they possess more means of happiness.
>
> (TMS IV.1.8)

But although it is this aesthetic pleasure that is the source of approbation, the imagination is misled into thinking that the owners of these conveniencies really are happier than others:

> If we consider the real satisfaction which all these things are capable of affording, by itself and separated from the beauty of that arrangement

which is fitted to promote it, it will always appear in the highest degree contemptible and trifling. But we rarely view it in this abstract and philosophical light. We naturally confound it in our imagination with the order, the regular and harmonious movement of the system, the machine or œconomy by means of which it is produced. The pleasures of wealth and greatness, when considered in this complex view, strike the imagination as something grand and beautiful and noble, of which the attainment is well worth all the toil and anxiety which we are so apt to bestow upon it.

(TMS IV.1.9)

Thus, here again, TMS counterposes the imagination and philosophy where the former is the source of delusion and the corruption of moral sentiments, whereas the latter is the still small voice of Stoic reason. This section continues by attempting to retrieve this highly charged moral ambivalence by arguing that nature's deception is just as well as it 'rouses and keeps in continual motion the industry of mankind' which has led to the development of agriculture, house-building, cities and commonwealths, science and art, all the arts indeed that have contributed towards ennobling and embellishing human life and maintaining 'a greater multitude of inhabitants'. But, so unconvincing is this section as a eulogy to an increase in the productive arts,[27] that the paragraph concludes by retreating from this celebration of nature's moral artifice and reiterating the argument of abstract philosophy that 'in ease of body and peace of mind, all the different ranks of life are nearly upon a level' and that, as cited above, the beggar upon the highway 'possesses that security which kings are fighting for' (TMS IV.1.10). The poor man's son 'whom heaven in its anger has visited with ambition' is, thus, truly held out as a lesson to all on the vanity of ambition as 'he sacrifices a real tranquillity that is at all times in his power' only to find that 'wealth and greatness are mere trinkets of frivolous utility' (TMS IV.1.8). Once again, the text of TMS is polarised between a nature which is identified with the frailties and weaknesses of human nature, and reason or philosophy which from a moral standpoint is savagely critical of nature which then has to be redeemed in some way by calling upon a larger view of social harmony. But, in this passage, the moral redemption of nature's purpose is undermined from within; nature's deception may well have acted as a stimulus to human ingenuity and creativity, but the ultimate moral judgment that the text offers is the Stoic one that all these creations and artefacts are merely things indifferent.[28]

---

27 It is noteworthy that manufacture is omitted from this list and commerce is referred to only obliquely.
28 The editors of TMS (TMS, pp. 183–4, n. 5) point out a possible connection between TMS IV.1.10 and Rousseau's *Discourse on the Origin of Inequality*, especially in view of Smith's

4

Although the man of excellence is the man of perfect virtue and wisdom, the ideal of moral perfection achieved only by the philosophical sage, many of the qualities admired in TMS are attainable by persons of a less elevated moral character, qualities such as modest demeanour and plain attire, superior knowledge of one's profession and superior industry in the exercise of it, patience in labour, resolution in danger, firmness in distress, good judgment, probity, prudence, temperate and just conduct, generosity and frankness. These are the qualities associated with the industrious members of the middle and inferior ranks who excel in society by the application of an unsullied and honest endeavour, and it is here that the second-order virtues find a fertile soil in which to flourish (TMS I.iii.2.5; I.iii.3.5). But it would be anachronistic to read into this celebration of honest pursuit an endorsement of the morals, the behaviour, or the aspirations of what later came to be seen as the middle classes in an economic or entrepreneurial sense. Chapters 7 and 8 below will examine the place of the manufacturing and mercantile classes in the discourse of WN. In TMS, however, it is the word 'rank' not 'class' that is used, and the chapter heading refers to the 'distinction of ranks'. The concept of the middling and inferior ranks is therefore not an economic concept in the sense in which class has since come to be understood. In TMS, the man from the middle and inferior ranks is described in contrast to the great, the rich, the eminent, and the powerful; he is described as a 'private man', the opposite of a man who has a public presence in the eyes of the world. This 'private man' may have a private income and may indeed be highly educated; the crucial point about him is that if he wishes to 'distinguish himself', that is, to change his standing from that of a private man to that of a person of public eminence, he must 'acquire dependents to balance the dependents of the great, and he has no other fund to pay them from, but the labour of his body, and the activity of his mind' (TMS I.iii.2.5). Thus, men from the middling and inferior ranks of society can become great men of public standing only by the vigorous application of their own labour and intellect, but such men may well choose not to enter that great scramble for wealth and honours, and so may remain 'private men'.

It is a mistake, therefore, to think that in commending prudence as a lower-order virtue, TMS is praising either economic activity in general or

---

'Letter to the Editors of the *Edinburgh Review*' (reprinted in Smith 1980) which contained translated passages from Rousseau's *Discourse*. See also West (1971). Ignatieff (1986) argues that Smith's Stoicism enabled him to argue a relatively optimistic case against Rousseauian vanity (*amour propre*) in that self-command and self-detachment as represented by the impartial spectator could make possible a virtuous, if austere, market society. The interpretation offered here in this chapter argues that the mechanism of the impartial spectator is a problematic solution to Rousseauian vanity, in that it relies upon the

the economic activities associated with what later became known as the middle classes, as a close examination of the descriptions of self-love and the virtue of prudence shows. It is often assumed by commentators that the expression 'self-love' in TMS is simply an unproblematic eighteenth-century synonym for self-interest,[29] but this overlooks the Stoic context for the sympathetic account of self-love in Parts VI and VII of TMS. In earlier sections of TMS, the 'arrogance' and 'natural misrepresentations' of self-love are presented as obstacles to virtuous behaviour and have to be brought down to a level which the impartial spectator can go along with (TMS II.ii.2.1; III.3.4). For those unable to enter into the dialogic moral debate that this requires, the general rules of morality are proposed as an alternative means of countering the 'delusions of self-love' and the 'too partial views which self-love might otherwise suggest' (TMS III.4.7,12). In these sections, self-love is akin to *amour propre* or vanity, and is presented negatively as a moral quality. In Parts VI and VII, however, a softer and more accommodating tone of voice presents an account of self-love in terms of the Stoic view of the requirements of self-preservation. Here self-love is akin to *amour de soi*, a caring of the self that is entirely consistent with moral behaviour.[30]

In Part VI, sections i and ii, nature recommends each individual person to take proper care of himself: 'Every man, as the Stoics used to say, is first and principally recommended to his own care . . .' (TMS VI.ii.1.1), and in Part VII's summary of the Stoic doctrine, every animal is endowed with self-love in order to preserve itself as fully as possible:

> According to Zeno, the founder of the Stoical doctrine, every animal was by nature recommended to its own care, and was endowed with the principle of self-love, that it might endeavour to preserve, not only its existence, but all the different parts of its nature, in the best and most perfect state of which they were capable.
> (TMS VII.ii.1.15)

Whatever tended to promote this best state of existence was to be chosen and whatever undermined it was to be rejected; virtue and propriety therefore entailed 'choosing and rejecting all different objects and circumstances according as they were by nature rendered more or less the objects

---

operation of imagination whose own defective workings are constitutive in creating vanity. See note 30 below on *amour de soi* as self-love.

29 TMS Introduction, p. 22. Ferguson (1767) argues against the popular use of self-love as a synonym for self-interest (1966, pp. 12–13).

30 Stoic self-love has been identified as *amour de soi* (Edelstein 1966, p. 35), but this is far from Rousseau's *amour de soi* of the state of nature. Rousseau's *amour de soi* pertains to the individual needs of an asocial and amoral being who has no moral relations with others (Rousseau 1973a, pp. 70–1); such a being could not become sociable without also becoming 'wicked' (p. 82). By contrast, the Stoic *amour de soi* is premised on the notion that

of choice or rejection' (TMS VII.ii.1.16). This is a classic statement of the Stoic doctrine concerning goods to be preferred or rejected, but the text continues to elaborate the other half of the Stoic doctrine that having arranged one's affairs in the best way possible, a person should then accept with equanimity whatever Providence should arrange. If all went well, a man may offer thanks to God and live happily, but if all went ill, then similarly he should offer thanks and rest in perfect tranquillity of mind, never straining himself or fretting against the order of Providence, but acknowledging the indifferent character of all things of this world (TMS VII.ii.1.18–24). Although TMS rejected the Stoic argument that all external pleasures were morally indifferent, it was still operating within a discursive space mapped out by Stoic moral philosophy, and this is also the case for the concept of self-love.

The Stoic concept of self-love falls under the doctrine of *oikeiosis*, which provides an account of the process of moral and psychological development from the early stages of childhood to that of the mature moral agent, a process during which first the child and then the adult comes to recognise and appreciate its own self and rational nature.[31] Within this doctrine, the fact of self-love is the starting-point in the child's development, and it is this which provides the rationale for the natural instinct of both child and adult towards those things that tend towards preservation, and away from those things that might cause harm. The fact of self-love is adduced by the Stoics both on deductive grounds from the benevolent intentionality of nature, and on inductive grounds from observation of a child's instinctive behaviour. What is loved is the 'self'; this means that as the child develops into an adult and comes to understand its own rational nature, it is this rational nature which comes to be loved and preserved. Thus, the Stoic concept of self-love is not egoistical in a material sense, but describes nature's mechanism for motivating the development of moral awareness in the individual agent. And it is this moral concept of self-love that is evident in TMS in Part VII where, according to Zeno, self-love is directed to preserve not only the person's existence, but 'all the different parts of its nature, in the best and most perfect state of which they were capable'. Thus, according to the Stoic philosophy, a person's attachment to himself includes the furtherance of his own moral and intellectual state, and does not imply any prioritisation of physical or material concerns. Similarly, within the Stoic philosophy, the pursuit of *eudaimonia*, or happiness, is identical with a perfectly moral life as it was believed that moral virtue alone is happiness, and this emphasis is

---

individuals are inherently both sociable and moral. On *amour de soi*, TMS is therefore decidedly Stoic rather than Rousseauian.

31 See references in note 10 above. The word *oikeiosis* conveys a range of meanings including the process of making something one's own and making something dear to oneself.

apparent throughout TMS where the general presupposition is that only the wise and virtuous are truly happy.

As a person's relation to himself can be described under the doctrine of *oikeiosis*, so can his relation with others; indeed this must be the case as relations with others must also be in conformity with that same nature. In this way, the doctrine of *oikeiosis* is seen as having two aspects, an inward-looking aspect and an outward-looking aspect. This latter aspect, dealing with a person's relations with others, is founded on the natural love of parents for their offspring and on their consequential fellow-feeling for others. This doctrine gave rise to the view of such relations with others as a set of concentric circles enclosing a person at its centre, beginning with the person's immediate family, extending outwards beyond distant kin to social and political groupings, and eventually encompassing the entire world.[32] The doctrine of *oikeiosis* includes a well-developed notion of people's natural sociability and fellow-feeling based on their mutual recognition as rational beings living according to nature. In its most elevated form, this leads to the global cosmopolitanism of the 'dear city of Zeus' in which all (men) are fellow-citizens of the world. Thus, Stoic self-love becomes the basis for love of the fellowship of others, and cannot be construed as an individualistic concern with one's own well-being to the exclusion of a concern with others. Significantly, this outward-looking aspect of Stoic self-love is also evident in TMS in Part VI which reproduces the classic structure of the Stoic argument. Chapters 1 to 3 of Part VI, section ii, are structured according to these concentric circles, where chapter 1 considers the order in which individuals are recommended by nature to our care; chapter 2 considers the order in which societies are so recommended; and chapter 3 considers the ultimate case of universal benevolence. As shown above, self-love is introduced in the conventional Stoic way at the beginning of chapter 1: 'Every man, as the Stoics used to say, is first and principally recommended to his own care . . .' (TMS VI.ii.1.1), and the following paragraph reproduces the standard Stoic progression by moving from a person's caring for himself to his caring for his family: 'After himself, the members of his own family, those who usually live in the same house with him, his parents, his children, his brothers and sisters, are naturally the objects of his warmest affections' (TMS VI.ii.1.2). The chapter then proceeds with a discussion of other degrees of affection and of the nature of family affection. The beginning of chapter 2 makes reference back to this Stoic context for situating its subject matter: 'The same principles that direct the order in which individuals are recommended to our beneficence, direct that likewise in which societies are recommended to it' (TMS VI.ii.2.1), and the chapter goes on to discuss love of country and public spirit.

---

32 This was considered as the foundation of justice and is considered again below in chapter 5.

Thus, the concept of self-love in Parts VI and VII of TMS is deployed within a discursive space mapped out by the Stoic doctrine of *oikeiosis*. This does not mean that this doctrine is simply reproduced in TMS as, at a number of points, TMS distances itself from Stoic conclusions. It does mean, however, that where 'self-love' is approved of, it includes a moral dimension denoting a process of moral maturation for an agent to whom nature recommends certain forms of behaviour, and for this reason it cannot be equated with modern conceptions of self-interest, individualism, or egocentric behaviour.[33]

Similarly, the concept of prudence in TMS has a specific range of application and is not to be construed as having a particularly economic provenance. Prudence comprises 'care of the health, of the fortune, of the rank and reputation of the individual, the objects upon which his comfort and happiness in this life are supposed principally to depend' (TMS VI.i.5). This list of the items of care subject to prudence may appear a motley collection to a twentieth-century mind as it spans fortune, an intangible such as reputation, health, which to some degree lies in the hands of Providence, and rank which derives from a combination of inheritance, good luck, ambition, adroit judgment in the public affairs of the world and, sometimes, personal excellence. The unifying coherence of this category is provided by the Stoic notion of things to be preferred yet indifferent, the intermediates or the *kathekonta*. All items in such a category lie outside the control of the individual person; health may deteriorate, fortune may be lost, and rank and reputation may be subject to calumnies, but all these events lie outside the sphere of the moral purpose and so should be accepted with equanimity by the wise man. For this reason, prudence cannot be deemed a specifically 'economic' virtue, as it is no more associated with commerce, manufacturing or any of the other activities that have since come to be identified with economic behaviour, than it is with a general solicitous care for the matters which tend to the self-preservation of a person in his 'best and most perfect state'. Health, rank and reputation are constituent parts of prudence but are entirely non-economic in their objectives. A man's fortune is more of an economic category, but even here a man's fortune in eighteenth-century Britain was subject to a range of factors such as marriage settlements and political preferment. Crucially it would also be determined for many by proper management of a landed estate which, though including an economic dimension, would not normally figure in a list of typical entrepreneurial or middle-class economic activities.

It has been emphasised that all animals are expected to take proper care of

---

33 Further, the reference to self-love at TMS VII.ii.3.15–16, should be read in the context of a refutation of the moral system of benevolence which denied that regard to a person's own private happiness could ever be a laudable principle of action (even, for example, in the case

themselves and a regard to a person's own 'private happiness and interest' is approved of, just as a lack of care is disapproved of, but prudence itself is clearly denoted an inferior virtue (TMS VII.ii.3.15–16). TMS had earlier distinguished between 'virtue and mere propriety; between those qualities and actions which deserve to be admired and celebrated, and those which simply deserve to be approved of' (TMS I.i.5.7). Thus, to eat when hungry is 'right and proper' and is approved of, but yet it would be absurd to regard it as virtuous. Similarly, the habits of economy and such like may well be approved of, but this does not imply that they are virtues that are comparable with first-order, moral virtues. Further, as argued in chapter 2 above, the virtue of prudence as such is approved of largely for its self-command, a pre-eminently Stoic virtue. Thus, spectatorial approbation of prudence cannot be construed as an endorsement of an ultimate objective of amassing a fortune. Further, this prudent man is not a man of great ambition and is certainly not something later called an entrepreneur. In the account of the circumscribed limits of his interests, the prudent man's very moderate ambition is descibed with reference to public as well as private affairs, showing once again that the concepts of ambition and self-advancement in TMS have a distinctly eighteenth-century and pre-capitalist connotation: the prudent man

> would be much better pleased that the public business were well managed by some other person, than that he himself should have the trouble, and incur the responsibility, of managing it. In the bottom of his heart he would prefer the undisturbed enjoyment of secure tranquillity, not only to all the vain splendour of successful ambition, but to the real and solid glory of performing the greatest and most magnanimous actions.
>
> (TMS VI.i.13)

The merely prudent man was not likely to be a great leader of men nor to seek any kind of prominent position in the world, and for this reason too prudence is considered neither an endearing nor an ennobling virtue, but commands only a 'cold esteem' (TMS VI.i.14). The lack of any straightforward correspondence in TMS between prudence and the economic sphere is further illustrated by the examples provided of the more elevated version of the good qualities associated with prudence. When these are combined with wise and judicious conduct directed to greater and nobler purposes than merely health, fortune, rank and reputation, then there is the 'superior prudence' associated with the great general, the great statesman and the great legislator, notably not the 'great entrepreneur', the 'great

---

of deserved self-approbation). In arguing that it could, TMS was simply reinstating self-preservation as a laudable, though inferior, virtue; cf. also TMS VII.ii.4.8.

employer of labour', or the 'great merchant or manufacturer' (TMS VI.i.15).[34]

5

Attention to the moral hierarchy at work in TMS, together with its Stoic foundations, cautions against reading it as a text that may be transcribed into the instrumentalist language of commercial discourse. At significant moments, the text's stylistic devices underline its own distancing from the conventional mores of a commercial society, and the presence of the detached didactic voice provides a punitive commentary on eighteenth-century social aspirations. This chapter and the previous one have argued that the discursive structure of TMS is marked by a dependence on Stoic moral discourse, and that this is also evident in the stylistic features of the interplay of voices in the text. For these reasons, it is hazardous to read TMS in search of moral categories that can be used as validating devices for the economic development of a commercial society.

---

[34] The inclusion of such terms here underlines just how inappropriate it is to translate the terms of TMS into the economic categories deployed in WN.

5

JUSTICE AND JURISPRUDENCE

1

It was argued in chapter 2 that the form of LJ differs from that of TMS; whereas the style of TMS is a dialogic one epitomising the dialogic nature of moral judgment, LJ is characterised by a style that is more akin to that of WN. The monologic style of LJ epitomises the lower moral status and rule-bound nature of the virtue of justice which is the other lower-order virtue that lies outside moral activity proper. Justice is rule-governed, not subject to individual sensibility, as here the man who 'adheres with the most obstinate steadfastness to the general rules themselves, is the most commendable, and the most to be depended upon' (TMS III.6.10).[1] The rules of justice are compared with the rules of grammar which are 'precise, accurate, and indispensable' (TMS III.6.11; also VII.iv.1–2), and agents must adhere to the rules of justice because to question these rules soon leads to chicanery. The rules themselves are the subject of the 'science of jurisprudence' (TMS VI.ii.Intro 1; VII.iv.37) which are covered in LJ. But how does this affect the natural jurisprudence of LJ? How does the lower-order moral status of justice accord with the natural jurisprudential basis of LJ? This chapter will address this issue by presenting a reading of LJ which shows how the jurisprudence of LJ evinces an erosion of the traditional moral basis of natural law leaving its positive law manifestation in sharper relief.

LJ locates its subject matter of justice, police, revenue and arms firmly within the mainstream west European tradition of natural law jurisprudence. This has generated a copious secondary literature identifying the various links and changes within the natural law tradition emanating from Grotius's *The Rights of War and Peace* (first published 1625) and handed down in modified form to Adam Smith through such works as Pufendorf's *Of the Law of Nature and Nations* (first published 1672) and *The Whole Duty of Man According to the Law of Nature* (first published 1673), John

---

[1] Also TMS II.ii.1–2; III.6.5; VII.iv.7.

Locke's *Second Treatise on Government* (first published 1690), and Francis Hutcheson's *A Short Introduction to Moral Philosophy* (1747). Interpretations of LJ have emphasised the importance of jurisprudential debates concerning a subjective right to property (*ius*) for the historical account of law and government in which the stadial progress of society through the four stages of hunting, pasturage, agriculture and commerce is connected with different forms of property.[2] LJ's jurisprudential focus is also seen by some commentators as an important element in the conquest of the new market-orientated commercialism of Smith's own day, which provides the ideological motor for the liberal market economics of WN;[3] and it has also been seen as providing a moral framework for WN by those who wish to retrieve a moral dimension for Smith's economic analysis.[4] The significance of LJ for interpretations of Adam Smith's overall project is that it is thought to provide an interpretative 'bridge' for linking the analysis of TMS and WN by focusing on the discussions of law and civil government, a significance captured for some commentators in the expression 'the science of a legislator'.[5] The appeal of the civil jurisprudential approach for many commentators is that it appears to have opened up a space for understanding Adam Smith's works within a broader interpretative matrix of political, social, historical as well as jurisprudential writings of the eighteenth century, thus contributing to a properly historical understanding of Smith's intentions and achievements within the broader intellectual context of the Enlightenment in both its Scottish and continental manifestations.

The central importance of the jurisprudential *ius* for understanding Adam Smith's works has, however, been challenged by the civic humanist paradigm which emphasises the importance of the classical concept of virtue (*virtus*) in organising political debates in the seventeenth and eighteenth centuries.[6] In spite of overlaps and a shared historiographical commitment to the recovery of intended authorial meanings, it has been argued that the civil jurisprudential and civic humanist paradigms offer different and non-commensurate methods of interpretation in that the concepts of *ius* and *virtus* are thought to be irreconcilable: 'The basic concept in republican thinking is *virtus*; the basic concept of all jurisprudence is necessarily *ius*; and there is no known way of representing virtue as a right' (Pocock 1983, p. 248). Thus, the language of rights and markets seems to lie uneasily beside the language of virtue and corruption in spite of a number of

---

2 See, for example, Meek (1967b, 1976, 1977), Skinner (1975, 1979, 1982), Stein (1979) and Pesciarelli (1986).
3 See, for example, Hont and Ignatieff (1983a).
4 See, for example, Lindgren (1973), Billet (1976), Samuels (1976), Skinner (1986), McNally (1988) and Winch (1992).
5 See, for example, Winch (1978, 1983b), and Haakonssen (1981).
6 Pocock (1975, 1985).

attempts to straddle both interpretative paradigms and offer a unified interpretation that spans the major works of Adam Smith.[7]

This chapter will examine the foundations of natural law in the Stoic philosophy where, it will be argued, there is no discursive incompatibility between *ius* and *virtus*. The distance between these Stoic foundations and the natural jurisprudence of LJ, however, is presented as evidence of the way in which jurisprudential categories have become detached from moral foundations in Smith's discourse. In view of this, the chapter will argue against the notion that there is a pervasive discursive unity underlying Adam Smith's works which can be signified by the notion the 'science of a legislator' and which is subtended by LJ acting as a kind of 'bridge' linking together the different discourses of TMS and WN.

2

The discursive context for LJ is that of the natural law tradition, but a tradition that spans the period from Cicero through the medieval scholastics to the post-Renaissance Europe of the eighteenth-century Enlightenment is one that defies any simple history.[8] Scholars are not in agreement over the precise place of natural law in either ancient Greek or Hellenistic philosophy, nor on its emergence from its scholastic integument and subsequent modern rehabilitation within humanist philosophy. By the time of the eighteenth century, discussions of justice and jurisprudence were being reworked within the discourses of the Enlightenment, and here the names of writers as disparate as Hutcheson, Hume, Kames and Montesquieu are sufficient to register the subtleties of range and nuance that such discussions underwent. Within these discourses, the notion of the 'natural', whether natural law or natural rights, was subject to very different constructions, being divinely sanctioned (where the divine itself ranged from pagan deism to Catholic or Protestant orthodoxy), in harmony with man's essential being (variously construed), or as practical responses to the changing social circumstances of the time.

Thus, describing the subject matter of LJ as 'natural jurisprudence' does not by itself provide a key which will make its meaning self-evident. The structure of the argument of LJ has itself to be placed within this larger tradition of natural law thinking and its specific eighteenth-century inflexions. As already noted, writers such as Grotius and Pufendorf have figured

---

7 This issue is addressed by many of the articles in Hont and Ignatieff (eds) (1983a), especially those by Pocock (1983, pp. 235–52), and Winch (1983a, pp. 253–69).
8 Histories of natural law include D'Entreves (1970), Watson (1971), Tuck (1979, 1987), Forbes (1982), MacCormick (1982), Striker (1987), Inwood (1987) and Tully (1991).

prominently in the secondary literature as initiators of modern natural law.[9] This has helped to situate natural jurisprudence as the discourse that produced the notions of subjective individual rights as private property rights *par excellence*, thus contributing a language of subjective rights – of *ius* – which was of crucial importance in the political debates from Hobbes to Locke and beyond concerning property rights and political obligation in a modern political and, in some interpretations, modern capitalist order. But this discussion has not provided a systematic account of the Stoic and Ciceronian character of much natural law writing, and it also overlooks the importance of Stoicism, as distinct from civic humanism, in the intellectual universe of eighteenth-century Europe.[10]

The moral basis for law in Cicero's writings was the Stoic equivalence of reason and nature which underpinned the Stoic system of ethics. *De Legibus* investigates the nature and origins of justice and argues that 'Law is the highest reason, implanted in Nature, which commands what ought to be done and forbids the opposite' (Cicero 1928, I.18).[11] Here, the account of justice and law deploys the classic Stoic insistence on the coincidence of reason and nature in establishing what is just behaviour. In this account, reason and nature provide divinely ordained ethical guarantees for justice, and they also constitute the means by which just behaviour is actually known. The passage continues by explaining that law is a natural force for the man who is *prudens*, as 'the origin of Justice is to be found in Law, for Law is a natural force; it is the mind and reason of the intelligent man [*mens ratioque prudentis*], the standard by which Justice and Injustice are measured' (Cicero 1928, I.19). Thus, the man who is *prudens* here is the man for whom

---

9 'Grotius seems to have been the first who attempted to give the world any thing like a regular system of natural jurisprudence, and his treatise on the laws of war and peace, with all its imperfections, is perhaps at this day the most compleat work on this subject' (LJB 1).
10 For example, Francis Hutcheson published a translation of the *Meditations* of Marcus Aurelius Antoninus in 1742. The early eighteenth-century appeal of Cato's Stoicism for both Whigs and Tories is discussed in Dwyer (1987, pp. 46–51) and Stewart (1991). Cf. 'The various sects of philosophy among the ancients could be considered as kinds of religion. There has never been one whose principles were more worthy of men and more appropriate for forming good men than that of the Stoics, and, if I could for a moment cease to think that I am a Christian, I would not be able to keep myself from numbering the destruction of Zeno's sect among the misfortunes of human kind' (Montesquieu 1989, 5.24.10, pp. 465–6).
11 Again man's possession of reason unites him with God and provides the basis for the commonwealth of all men: 'Therefore, since there is nothing better than reason, and since it exists both in man and God, the first common possession of man and God is reason. But those who have reason in common must also have right reason in common. And since right reason is Law, we must believe that men have Law also in common with the Gods. Further, those who share Law must also share Justice; and those who share these are to be regarded as members of the same commonwealth. If indeed they obey the same authorities and powers, this is true in a far greater degree; but as a matter of fact they do obey this celestial system, the divine mind, and the God of transcendent power. Hence we must now conceive of this whole universe as one commonwealth of which both gods and men are members' (Cicero 1928, I.23).

reason and nature are as one, and for him the precepts of justice are known as a natural force. The passage then goes on to refer to the general populace's need for legal codification and written decrees as the crowd's definition of law, thus reproducing the Stoic argument that the generality of the people require external rules to guide them in the *officia* or *kathekonta* of life, within which are included the legal decrees of that society, but the text still insists that all may know justice because it is based upon nature: 'surely there comes nothing more valuable than the full realisation that we are born for Justice, and that right [*ius*] is based, not upon men's opinions, but upon Nature. This fact will immediately be plain if you once get a clear conception of man's fellowship and union with his fellow-men' (Cicero 1928, I.28).

The Stoic concept of justice is derived from the outward-looking aspect of the concept of *oikeiosis*, which denotes the process by which a person comes to recognise the bands of fellowship uniting all men.[12] Using the analogy of the concentric circles, it was argued that a person comes to love and esteem not only close kin but larger social groupings and ultimately all mankind. This notion of the benevolence and brotherhood of all men (the gender was always masculine), was subject to attacks from other schools at the time which argued that people will always naturally prefer themselves and close kin, and that the notion of a universal brotherhood was patently against the facts of human nature. Against this criticism, the Stoics argued that as a person worked through the stages of moral development and came to love his own nature as an instance of a higher all-pervading Reason, such a person would come to realise that human fellowship was implicit in the laws of nature. In Cicero's hands, this Stoic doctrine received a Roman civic twist such that this sense of union was strengthened for those within the same nation or city state, but it was still emphasised that it is this bond of fellowship that unites all men and which provides the basis for the *ius gentium* or natural law.[13] According to this law, no man was allowed to injure another in the hope of securing his own private gain.[14] Thus, the fundamental axiom of justice, that 'the first office of justice is to keep one man from doing harm to another, unless provoked by wrong' (Cicero 1913, I.20), was based on the notion of a universal fellowship or commonwealth among all men, which included not only fellow-citizens but foreigners too:

> Others again who say that regard should be had for the rights of fellow-citizens, but not of foreigners, would destroy the universal brotherhood of mankind; and, when this is annihilated, kindness, generosity, goodness, and justice must utterly perish; and those who

---

12 On *oikeiosis*, see chapter 4, note 10 and pp. 96–7.
13 Cicero 1913, I. 12, 22, 50, 157–9; III. 28, 69.
14 For example, Cicero 1913, III. 22–7.

work all this destruction must be considered as wickedly rebelling against the immortal gods. For they uproot the fellowship which the gods have established between human beings, and the closest bond of this fellowship is the conviction that it is more repugnant to Nature for man to rob a fellow-man for his own gain than to endure all possible loss, whether to his property or to his person . . . or even to his very soul . . .

(Cicero 1913, III.28)

Nature prohibits injury to others because this would demolish the universal brotherhood of man which was based on the acknowledgement of human reason as the spark of the divine element in all men. Thus, the first duty of justice is to refrain from hurting others. The second duty of justice is to 'lead men to use common possessions for the common interests, private property for their own' (Cicero 1913, I.20); this refers to acts of kindness and generosity (Cicero 1913, I.42–5). Corresponding to these two aspects of justice, there are also two kinds of injustice, one which refers to inflicting wrong and the other to withholding help from those on whom wrong is being inflicted (Cicero 1913, I.23).

Thus, the notion of justice was premised upon a particular view of *societas* construed in both a moral and a social sense. Man is a sociable creature who needs the society of others for reasons that are independent of his obvious material dependence on them: 'And it is not true, as certain people maintain, that the bonds of union in human society were instituted in order to provide for the needs of daily life' because 'if all that is essential to our wants and comfort were supplied by some magic wand, as in the stories, then every man of first rate ability . . . would seek to escape from his lonelines and to find someone to share his studies' (Cicero 1913, I.158). This account of human fellowship and natural human sociability independent of any material needs formed the basis of the virtue of justice: 'For these virtues [i.e. generosity, love of country, service to others and gratitude] originate in our natural inclination to love our fellow-men, and this is the foundation of Justice' (Cicero 1928, I.43). This rooting of justice in natural human sociability rather than self-preservation or self-interest (in their narrow senses), continued in the later natural law tradition and constitutes one of the reasons why the natural law tradition's emphasis on individual moral responsibilities and individual legal rights should not be interpreted as a form of modern individualism *tout court*. Certainly, the fact of man's natural sociability was entirely coincident with his material needs; life within society was not only morally and socially essential for man, but also practically and materially superior. This coincidence of moral, social and material requirements is a classic example of the work of Providence, and is a recurrent feature of later natural law theories which were grounded simultaneously on that which is morally superior, that which is in agreement with man's nature, and that which is practically most appropriate for fulfilling man's material needs. It is a coincidence which has proved fruitful of different emphases, however, as later writers reworked these doctrines in changing economic circumstances and with different religious and philosophical inflexions.

Part of the power and appeal of the natural law tradition lay in its continued attempt to ground justice and law in the fundamental characteristics of human life. As this tradition was reworked over the centuries, it became a mark of its resilience that different views of human nature and of its relation with God could facilitate a range of different inflexions and innovations whilst still keeping within the discursive parameters of natural law and natural justice. A highy influential restatement of this tradition for the eighteenth century which affirms the crucial importance of Stoicism in general and Cicero's texts in particular, is Jean Barbeyrac's *An Historical and Critical Account of the Science of Morality*, first published as a Preface to Pufendorf's *The Law of Nature and Nations* in 1709. The section on Stoic philosophy argues that the Stoic doctrine 'That we ought to live conformable to Nature' (Pufendorf 1729, p. 71) is to be lauded, in spite of specific criticisms that can be levelled against aspects of Stoic doctrine and some of the more paradoxical Stoic dogmas:

> However, bating some certain Things, nothing can be more beautiful than their Morality, consider'd in itself; which, by only correcting a few of its Maxims, with some small Difference in their Explanation; might be easily reduc'd to a system of Morality, very near approaching to that of the Gospel; to that, I say, which alone is entirely conformable to the Dictates of right Reason.
> (Barbeyrac 1729, p. 71)[15]

Here, Barbeyrac reinterprets the 'heathen' philosophy of the Stoics within a Protestant frame, where the Providential God of the Hellenistic world becomes the Christian God of the Gospels.[16] Barbeyrac's essay opens in section 1 by referring to the Stoic argument that knowledge of the practical science of morality is not the exclusive preserve of erudite philosophers or theologians, but is attainable by every person through the use of reason:

> We shall scarce have occasion to carry our Thoughts beyond our-

---

15 'of all the Philosophers of Antiquity, they [i.e. the Stoics] are the Men, who have gone the farthest into the Particulars of Morality; and have best apply'd its general Precepts to the several States of Life; and the different Exigences of humane Affairs' (Barbeyrac 1729, p. 73); further, Cicero's *De Officiis* 'is without Dispute the best Treatise of Morality, that all Antiquity has furnish'd us with' (Barbeyrac 1729, p. 75), although here the eclecticism of *De Officiis* is being noted, rather than its Stoicism.
16 In view of the direct input of Stoicism during the first centuries of Christianity, this appropriation could be readily effected.

selves, or consult any other Master besides our own Heart. The most common Experience of Life; and a little Reflection on ourselves, and the Objects that surround us on every Side; are sufficient to furnish even the most ordinary Capacities with general Ideas of the Law of Nature; and the true Grounds of all our moral Duties. Who does but ever so little examine his own Nature; and contemplate that wonderful Order of the Universe, which on all sides presents itself to the View of every one capable of any Degree of Reflection; will immediately be rais'd to the Knowledge of that Almighty, All-wise, and All-good Creator, *in whom we live, and move, and have our Being* . . .
(Barbeyrac 1729, p. 2, original emphasis)

Here the Stoic doctrine of natural law is given a Protestant twist, but the emphasis is still that morality and the laws of nature are available to anyone simply on the basis of some rudimentary reflection and introspection.[17] As in Cicero's writings, pride of place is given to 'Nature' as the source of virtue, morality and law, and in a later section on the Stoic philosophy (section 17), some of the different Stoic nuances attaching to this notion are outlined:

for, say they [i.e. the Stoics], *Nature leads us to Virtue.* By this *Nature*, some of 'em meant directly the Constitution of the humane Nature; or that Light of Reason, by the Help of which we discern what is truly sutable to our State and Condition; others meant, universal Reason, or the Will of God; which forbids us every Thing, that is contrary to our natural Constitution; and prescribes to us every Thing that is agreeable thereto; and others again, meant both these join'd together.
(Barbeyrac 1729, p. 71, original emphasis)

The classic Stoic coincidence of nature and reason underpins the discussion of nature as the source of morality. Whether the emphasis is on the constitution of human nature, human reason, or right Reason, as the guiding force of a providential universe, nature as rationality provides the keystone to the discussion. Hence natural law is based on Stoic moral categories deriving from the moral awareness of the individual moral agent.

This account then becomes crucial for the explanation of natural jurisprudence: 'Justice, as such, is not from the Institution of Men, but from its own Nature; as is also Law and right Reason . . .' (Barbeyrac 1729, p. 71). Justice derives its moral imperative from being natural; this means that it is also self-evident to reason.[18] Again, Cicero's writings are acknowledged as

---

17 This argument is used to counter the claims of contemporary scepticism in sections 3 and 4.
18 As long as reason is uncorrupted, that is. Barbeyrac's answer both to the sceptics and to those propounding innate ideas, is that justice is evident to those who use their reason. This means that justice is not an innate idea, and that corrupted reason will not result in justice.

pre-eminent in defining natural law as independent of human institutions, although interpreted from a Christian viewpoint:

> His Discourse of *Laws* [i.e. Cicero's *De Legibus*], which we yet have, though imperfect; contains many excellent Things. *Cicero* there particularly applies himself to prove at large, that there is a natural Law, independent of any humane Institution; and which derives its obligatory Force from the Will of *God*. This he proves to be the Foundation of all just and reasonable Laws.
>
> (Barbeyrac 1729, p. 76)

Barbeyrac also acknowledges the Stoic foundation of natural law[19] in the moral interdependence of men in that they are 'born, not every one for himself alone; but for the Good of humane Society' (p. 71), together with the importance of this for Cicero who 'follows the grand Principle of the *Stoicks*, that Man is born for Society; and from thence deduces all the reciprocal Duties of Mankind' (p. 76),[20] thus showing that neither Stoicism nor the natural law tradition can simply be appropriated wholesale in the service of a later individualist view of the moral and legal relations pertaining to civil society.

Barbeyrac's *Historical Account* foregrounded the Stoic basis of natural law for an eighteenth-century readership. In doing this, it also served to emphasise particular aspects of Stoic and natural law doctrine which can be identified in the earlier works of Grotius and Pufendorf. First, Barbeyrac's account emphasised the Stoic basis of justice in the social interdependence of men in that they are all 'born for society'. In Grotius's Preliminary Discourse to *The Rights of War and Peace*, the fountain of right (*ius*) is *oikeiosis*:

> Now amongst the Things peculiar to Man, is his Desire of Society, that is, a certain Inclination to live with those of his own Kind, not in any manner whatever, but peaceably, and in a Community regulated according to the best of his Understanding; which Disposition the *Stoicks* termed *oikeiosis*. Therefore the Saying that every Creature is led by Nature to seek its own private Advantage, expressed thus universally, must not be granted.
>
> (Grotius 1738, para. VI, pp. xv–xvi)

Thus Barbeyrac was able to explain the diversity of moral and legal practices in different societies, as well as the existence of palpable cases of injustice and wrongdoing.

19 Barbeyrac also recognised the Stoic contribution to Roman Law and natural jurisprudence: 'The *Roman Lawyers*, of whom the greatest Part were *Stoicks*, contributed very much to the perfecting that Part of Morality, which may be call'd *Natural Jurisprudence*' (Barbeyrac 1729, p. 77).

20 They [i.e. the Stoics] believ'd, they were born, not every one for himself alone; but for the Good of humane Society ... There was never any Sect of Philosophers, who so well

According to this approach, therefore, justice was the cement which reinforced men's natural human fellowship, rather than a bridle intended to rein in their individual rapaciousness. Pufendorf's *The Law of Nature and Nations* based justice on *socialitas*, but this was founded not on men's love for each other but on their joint material interdependence (i.e. on their interests) (Pufendorf 1729, II.III.XV). In *The Whole Duty of Man*, the laws of nature are 'The Rules then of this Fellowship, which are the Laws of *Human Society*, whereby men are directed how to render themselves useful Members thereof, and without which it falls to pieces' (Pufendorf 1716, I.III.VIII), but this is based on the material and security aspects of self-preservation, rather than on a sense of human fellowship: 'in order to his Preservation, 'tis absolutely necessary, that he be *sociable*, that is, that he *joyn* with those of his kind, and that he so *behave* himself towards them, that they may have no justifiable cause to do him *Harm*, but rather to *promote* and *secure* to him all his Interests' (Pufendorf 1716, I.III.VII; also II.I.VIII–XI).[21]

Second, following the emphasis on human fellowship, Barbeyrac's account emphasised the reciprocal duties of mankind which provide the grounding of natural law in the moral obligations of individual moral agents: Cicero, he says, 'follows the grand Principle of the *Stoicks*, that Man is born for Society; and from thence deduces all the reciprocal Duties of Mankind' (Barbeyrac 1729, p. 76). A fundamental aspect of justice thus concerns the 'moral duties' owed to others. A primary function of *ius* is therefore to refer to the negative duty of not harming others. In the *Preliminary Discourse*, for example, 'This Sociability . . . is the Fountain of Right [*ius*], properly so called; to which belongs the Abstaining from that which is another's . . .' (Grotius 1738, para. VIII, p. xvii). In the first chapter of the *Rights of War and Peace*, various meanings of the word 'right' are presented. The first meaning is the objective sense of right as 'that which is just', which turns out to be in the negative sense of 'that which may be done without injustice' (Grotius 1738, I.I.3). The first authority cited is Cicero's *De Officiis* (III.v), which argues that it is 'unnatural to take from another to enrich one's self'; this principle of justice had been introduced earlier on where 'the first office/duty (*primum munus*) of justice is to keep one man from doing harm to another, unless provoked by wrong' (Cicero 1913, I.20). Thus, justice in this sense corresponds to the duty not to harm others. Similarly, Pufendorf's *Whole Duty of Man* is constructed around a series of

---

understood, and so strongly press'd those indispensable Duties of Humanity, which Men, precisely consider'd as such, owe to one another' (Barbeyrac 1729, pp. 71–2).
21 For a discussion on the extent to which Grotius's and Pufendorf's works may be thought to fall properly within a Stoic or a Hobbesian view of the grounding of justice, see Tuck (1987) and the summary discussion in Tully (1991, pp. xix, xxvii–xxix).

duties: to God, to oneself, to every other man, and as a citizen.[22] Of the three main duties owed by every man to every other man, the first one is the negative duty not to harm others and this constitutes the first duty of natural law:

> Among those Duties we acount *Absolute*, or those of every man towards every man, this has the first place, that *one do no wrong to the other*; and this is the *amplest* Duty of all, comprehending *all men* as such, and it is at the same time the *most easie*, as consisting only in an *Omission* of acting, unless now and then when unreasonable Desires and Lusts are to be *curb'd*. It is also the *most necessary*, because without it *Human Society* cannot be preserv'd.
>
> (Pufendorf 1716, I.VI.II)

Following on from this primary duty not to harm others, is the subjective right to one's life, liberty and property; this claim right, however, is properly derivative upon the first meaning of right as it presupposes a correlative duty to abstain on the part of others.[23] The second and third duties owed by men to all other men are the duty that 'every man esteem and treat another, as *naturally* equal to himself, or as one who is a Man as well as he' (Pufendorf 1716, I.VII.I), and that 'every man ought to promote the good of another, as far as conveniently he may' (Pufendorf 1716, I.VIII.I). Here the *Whole Duty of Man* moves beyond the notion of negative duty to include positive duties to others which are owed for the sake of common sociality, and here the discussion includes distributive justice and benevolence.

Finally, Barbeyrac's account endorses the view that natural law is self-evident to reason. In the Preliminary Discourse to Grotius's *The Rights of War and Peace*, man is endowed not only with a social faculty, but

> likewise with Judgment to discern Things pleasant or hurtful, and those not only present but future, and such as may prove to be so in their Consequences; it must therefore be agreeable to human Nature, that according to the Measure of our Understanding we should in these Things follow the Dictates of a right and sound Judgment, and not be corrupted either by Fear, or the Allurements of present Pleasure, nor be carried away violently by blind Passion. And whatso-

---

22 Although the Latin word for duty here is *officium*, by this is meant not proper function as understood by the Stoics (see chapter 4 above), but duty in the sense of obligatory action, i.e. 'That *Action* of a Man, which is regularly order'd according to some prescrib'd *Law*, which he is oblig'd to obey' (Pufendorf 1716, I.I.1); see note at I.I.1.

23 The second meaning of right in Grotius's *The Rights of War and Peace*, arising from the first, is that of a subjective right and this includes (a) a power either over oneself (i.e. liberty) or over others; (b) the right of property; (c) the right to demand what is due (Grotius 1738, I.I.4–5). For the importance of this subjective right for the development of theories of property rights, see Tuck (1979).

ever is contrary to such a Judgment is likewise understood to be contrary to Natural Right, that is, the Laws of our Nature.

(Grotius 1738, Preliminary Discourse, para. IX)

In Pufendorf's *Whole Duty of Man*, natural law is known by the light of reason:

> But Nature is said thus to teach us, partly because the knowledge of this Law may be attain'd by the help of the *Light* of *Reason*; and partly because the general and most useful points thereof are so *plain* and *clear*, that they at first sight force the Assent, and get such root in the minds of men, that nothing can eradicate them afterwards; let wicked men take never so much pains to blunt the edge and stupifie themselves against the Stings of their *Consciences*.
>
> (Pufendorf 1716, I.III.XII)

Thus, natural law may be known solely by the use of reason and is available as a form of natural moral knowledge for all men. In this it is entirely independent of revealed religion, although its precepts will always be found to be in conformity with the precepts of the Christian religion. Although independent of moral theology,[24] the law of nature is still premised on the notion of individual moral agency and, thus, still functions powerfully as a form of moral discourse.

Barbeyrac's account foregrounded the Stoic foundations of natural law by emphasising the equivalence of reason and nature, and this portrayal included the three fundamental Stoic arguments that justice is based on human fellowship, that justice is denominated in terms of moral duties to others, and that natural law is self-evident to reason and so can be known by all men. Crucially, this means that Barbeyrac's account of natural law is reconstituting the moral categories of Stoic philosophy. In starting from the standpoint of the individual moral agent and his relation with the moral universe, natural law's origins in Stoic moral philosophy were being reaffirmed. Once detached from its Stoic basis, however, these origins assume a more individualistic form where the individual was conceived not as an integral part of a moral and social universe, but as standing apart and outside it. In this process, the notion of objective right based on a shared understanding of reciprocal duties became transformed into its correlate, a subjective right implying claims on society. The question for political philosophy then becomes one of how to reintroduce man back into a social and political arena; to this end the doctrine of the social contract became necessary in order to solve the fundamental problem of how this asocial bearer of subjective rights could be conceptualised as the constitutive basis of a political and social order.

---

24 Cf. Pufendorf's Preface to *The Whole Duty of Man*.

3

The jurisprudence of LJ and TMS represents a major departure from this natural law tradition in that it has become detached from the Stoic moral foundation that informed natural law.

Whereas the natural law tradition grounded law in the moral potentialities of individual moral agents, LJ and TMS separate moral judgment from the virtue of justice. Whereas moral judgment crucially involves the dialogic moral capabilities and individual judgment of moral agents, justice and jurisprudence are concerned with the observance and generation of rules. The function of jurisprudence in TMS and LJ is to generate a system of rules in order to guide authority, not to provide an inner juridical code for individual agents: 'It is the end of jurisprudence to prescribe rules for the decisions of judges and arbiters' (TMS VII.iv.8; also VII.iv.36), and the virtue of justice involves only that agents adhere to these rules of justice that have been laid down for them:

> there is no pedantry in sticking fast by the rules of justice. On the contrary, the most sacred regard is due to them; and the actions which this virtue requires are never so properly performed, as when the chief motive for performing them is a reverential and religious regard to those general rules which require them.
>
> (TMS III.6.10)

The primary perspective here in TMS thus becomes one of law enforcement as a system of legal rules,[25] and this standpoint is reflected in the concern of LJ with the requirement of civil governments for a system of laws rather than with individual moral judgments or the requirements of a moral being.[26] In LJA, jurisprudence is 'the theory of the rules by which civil governments ought to be directed' (LJA i.1) and in LJB it is 'the theory of the general principles of law and government' (LJB 5). Thus, justice is based not on *oikeiosis* or moral interdependence, but on the requirements for civil order and the protection of private property:

> The first and chief design of every system of government is to maintain justice; to prevent the members of a society from incroaching on one anothers property, or seizing what is not their own. The

---

25 Cf. 'It is essential to human laws, that they be clear, plain, and readily applicable to particular cases; without which, judges would be arbitrary, and law made a handle for oppression. For this reason, none of our actions can be the object of positive law, but what are reducible to a precise rule' (Kames 1751, p. 134).

26 'Jurisprudence is concerned not with what the good man should be disposed to do, but with what a judge should compel him to do . . . Concentration on the method of enforcement in delimiting law and morals led Smith and his friends to look at law from the point of view of the judge . . .' (Stein 1957, pp. 14–15).

design here is to give each one the secure and peacable possession of his own property.

(LJA i.1)

In TMS, the virtue of justice is presented as a duty in that the adherence to the rules of justice is itself a duty, but this duty is an impoverished form of obligation compared with the duties that underwrote the natural law approach. In Pufendorf's *Whole Duty of Man*, for example, a person's duties covered a wide range of moral and just actions, including the duties of distributive justice and benevolence (I.VI–VIII), but in both TMS and LJ, natural justice basically amounts to no more than the negative duty not to harm others: 'Mere justice is, upon most occasions, but a negative virtue, and only hinders us from hurting our neighbour' (TMS II.ii.1.9). Natural justice thus covers only commutative justice (i.e. the perfect rights) and excludes distributive justice (i.e. the imperfect rights) (TMS VII.ii.1.10). This again links up with the argument that jurisprudence concerns only those duties which can be enforced by the power of positive law (TMS II.ii.1.5, 9; VII.ii.1.10). It also serves to underline the separation of natural justice from morality. In explaining the distinction between perfect and imperfect rights (and between commutative and distributive justice), LJA states that perfect rights only are to be considered as 'the latter not belonging properly to jurisprudence, but rather to a system of moralls as they do not fall under the jurisdiction of the laws' (LJA i.15). Here the issue of morals is again kept entirely separate from natural justice: morals are a private and voluntary affair, whereas natural justice concerns those rules that may be enforced by the positive laws of a country and whose violation is liable to legally administered punishment.[27]

In natural law writings, natural reason is a self-evident guide to just and moral individual behaviour. As argued in chapter 3 above, TMS rejected the Stoic equivalence of nature and reason and substituted the impartial spectator as the process by which moral judgments are made. In LJ, it is accepted that natural rights 'need not be explained' as they are normally 'evident to reason, without any explanation' (LJA i.24; also LJB 149); they are 'evident' such that 'no body doubts' (LJB 11). Acquired rights, by contrast, require explanation. In LJ, natural rights with respect to a person's body and reputation are deemed self-evident; in the case of personal injury and restraints on liberty, natural rights 'need not be explained' because they

---

[27] A similar view was later put forward by John Millar: 'A more material defect in most of the writers on jurisprudence is their not marking sufficiently the boundaries between strict law and mere morality. They seem to consider, what a good man, from the utmost propriety of feelings and scruples of conscience, would be disposed to do, rather than what an upright judge would compel him to perform; and are thus led frequently to confound what is properly called justice (which requires that we should avoid hurting our neighbours) with generosity or benevolence, which prompts us to increase their positive happiness' (Millar

are 'evident to reason' (LJA i.24). But, the case for natural rights to estate is not so straightforward as here 'the origin of naturall rights is not altogether plain' (LJA i.25). For this reason, the impartial spectator is introduced in order to provide a foundation to property rights based on occupation (LJA i.35–8, 42–4). In the case reported in LJ, the issue concerns exclusive property rights over an apple plucked in the forest, and whether an injury was done to the possessor by taking the fruit away from him. This is an instance of possession over the fruit with the substance of the thing left behind, a case which in the natural law literature had been regarded as a natural right as it did not involve prejudicing others' rights to the fruits. Thus, in this case, the impartial spectator is required to provide a justification for a natural right as reason alone is not sufficient to make it self-evident.

The impartial spectator is further introduced in the case of prescriptive property rights (LJA i.77), contracts (LJA ii.43–5), and punishment in the case of criminal injury (LJA v.18).[28] What all these cases have in common is the issue of injury as the impartial spectator is called upon to settle the question as to whether an injury has in fact occurred.[29] The centrality of the question of injury relates to the defining character of natural justice as the negative duty not to hurt others; once the fact of injury has been established, this is then taken to be clear evidence that the agent has indeed been hurt and that, therefore, an injustice has been committed. The importance of this negative duty for the natural law tradition has already been noted, although there it formed only a part and not the sole content of natural justice. But, in deploying the impartial spectator to establish whether the central fact of injury has been committed, LJ is departing from the natural law tradition in which natural justice was self-evident to moral agents and required no further explanation.

The function of the impartial spectator in LJ in establishing the presence of injury differs from its function in TMS in illustrating the dialogic process of conscience. The context for the impartial spectator in TMS is the process of moral judgment for the individual moral agent. Here, the impartial spectator illustrates the dialogic process by which agents come to function as truly moral agents by engaging in moral deliberation about their own and others' actions. The virtue of justice requires only that agents adhere to the rules of justice in the most scrupulous manner without chicanery; knowledge of justice or the making of judgments about what constitutes just behaviour do not therefore require the involvement of the

---

An Historical View of the English Government, 1803, vol. iv, essay VII; excerpts in Lehmann 1960, pp. 346–7).
28 LJB 150, 154, 181–2.
29 See chapter 2, above.

impartial spectator. An example of this contrast is provided in the passage where commutative justice is compared with distributive justice. Commutative justice is where 'we are said to do justice to our neighbour when we abstain from doing him any positive harm' (TMS VII.ii.1.10). In this case, the observance of justice may be compelled by force and the violation of it incurs liability for punishment. Here there is no mention of the impartial spectator. Distributive justice, by contrast, implies that 'we are said to do injustice to a man of merit who is connected with us, though we abstain from hurting him in every respect, if we do not exert ourselves to serve him and to place him in that situation in which the impartial spectator would be pleased to see him' (TMS VII.ii.1.10). In describing distributive justice, the text includes the impartial spectator as an integral part of the process by which just behaviour is ascertained in the particular circumstances of the case.

The issue that does involve the impartial spectator in TMS, however, is that of the obligatory force of the rules of justice and the consequent approval of punishment for acts of injustice. An unnamed acknowledgment is made to Kames for the distinction between justice and all the other virtues in that

> we feel ourselves to be under a stricter obligation to act according to justice, than agreeably to friendship, charity, or generosity . . . somehow or other, we feel ourselves to be in a peculiar manner tied, bound, and obliged to the observation of justice. We feel, that is to say, that force may, with the utmost propriety, and with the approbation of all mankind, be made use of to constrain us to observe the rules of the one, but not to follow the precepts of the other.
>
> (TMS II.ii.1.5)[30]

Acts of injustice will be followed by the resentment of the injured and the disapprobation of mankind, and it is this disapproval on the part of others that provides the greatest discouragement to acts of crime. The withdrawal of approbation by mankind is the greatest torment for the violators of the laws of justice, and is the cause of their remorse and ultimate desire to be accepted back into society (TMS II.ii.2–3). In retrospect, the criminal comes to view his crimes as society and the impartial spectator view them, and so he comes to repent of the crime and seek readmission into society. The impartial spectator mechanism here provides an account of the torments of conscience in the guilty soul, but it does not provide a way of determining

---

[30] See Kames's *Of the Foundation and Principles of the Law of Nature* 1751, chapters III–IV, especially pp. 72–4 where it is argued that as 'pain is a stronger motive to action than pleasure, the remorse which attends a breach of strict duty is, with the bulk of mankind, a more powerful incitement to honesty, than praise and self-approbation are to generosity';

what it is that constitutes injustice; it provides a means whereby agents come to feel the force of the laws of justice, but not to ascertain what those laws ought to be.

The standpoint of LJ is not that of the individual moral agent, but the requirements of a civil and legal system which needs legal rules for its operation. Within this context, the impartial spectator establishes moral credentials for those legal rules that cannot be deemed as self-evidently just without further explanation; here the impartial spectator device provides the explanation that is redundant in the case of self-evident natural rights. The result is that the jurisprudential basis of existing codified laws is provided by arguments which have recourse to the impartial spectator, but this is not a description of the process of legal deliberation that is required of either individual agents or judges. The impartial spectator mechanism thus functions in LJ as a retroactive jurisprudential justification for certain laws and is not a description of how agents make decisions, whether individual agents who follow the rules of justice without chicanery, or judges who administer the law without arbitrary interventions.[31]

In LJ, the impartial spectator is introduced not only to vouchsafe the moral standing of acquired rights such as contract, but also to provide jurisprudential guarantees for the natural right to property in LJA as well as the acquired rights to property in LJB. But, once the natural right to property has been justified by using the impartial spectator in LJA, the significance of denoting property as a natural right loses its force; what happens is that there is a shift between LJA and LJB in which the natural as a moral category loses even more of its explanatory power.

In LJB, the reliance upon natural law assumptions about natural rights is reduced by treating the rights to estate as adventitious rights (LJB 7–8, 11, 149). In LJA, they were designated as natural rights in two separate passages (LJA i.12, 25), but then later they were described as acquired rights (LJA ii.93). Commentaries on LJ assume that this switch must be the result of faulty reporting by the student who got it wrong on the first two occasions, but no evidence is adduced to provide support for this assumption, which is based simply on the unexamined postulate of authorial unity.[32] There is, however, some internal textual evidence to suggest that the student notes may well be correct and that, at the beginning of LJA, the rights to estate are

---

also p. 88, where the needs of preservation require that 'pain is in a greater degree the object of aversion, than pleasure is of desire'.

31 'I had observed an other thing which greatly confirms the liberty of the subjects in England. – This was the little power of the judges in explaining, altering, or extending or correcting the meaning of the laws, and the great exactness with which they must be observed according to the literall meaning of the words . . .' (LJA v.15).

32 'In the first two places in LJ(A) the student has obviously been confused, taking Smith to be saying that natural rights were identical with the whole area of private law, including

indeed natural rights. In the discussion on inheritance and other exclusive privileges, it is argued that some exclusive privileges are natural rights but that most are creatures of the civil law. The substantive division between these two categories remains unchanged across LJA and LJB, but the presentation of the argument differs: in LJA privileges as acquired rights are presented as the exception to the general rule that property is a natural right, whereas in LJB this is reversed and privileges as natural rights are presented as the exception to the general case of acquired rights. Thus, in LJA the text states:

> Some of them [i.e. exclusive privileges] are founded on natural reason, and others are intirely the creatures of the civil constitutions of states. This of inheritance is evidently founded on natural reason and equity ... The greatest part however of exclusive priviledges are the creatures of the civil constitutions of the country.
>
> (LJA ii.28,30)

In LJB, however, the argument is presented as follows:

> Exclusive priviledges are the last division of real rights. Among these is the right of inheritance, which is not a creature of the civil law but arises from nature ... Tho' these and some other exclusive priviledges arise from nature, they are generaly the creatures of the civil law.
>
> (LJB 174–5)

The wording of these two passages indicates that the background supposition of the basis of property rights is not the same in the two cases. In LJA, the presupposition is that property rights are natural rights, which means that most exclusive privileges are exceptions; as a natural right, inheritance needs no special marker or explanation, whilst the civil origins of the greatest part of exclusive privileges are marked as exceptions by the use of the word 'however'. In LJB, the presupposition is that property rights are acquired rights, which means that it is the right of inheritance that has to be signalled as an exception to the general case. This is precisely what happens as the right of inheritance is presented as an exception to the general case ('the right of inheritance, which is not a creature of the civil law but arises from nature'), and the privileges as acquired rights are presented as the general case ('they are generaly the creatures of the civil law') not the exceptional case.

This suggests that in the early sections of LJA, property rights are indeed

---

property law. But at ii,93 he has got it right, and the student writing LJ(B) seems to have had no difficulties with the distinction' (Haakonssen 1981, p. 205, note 10).

denominated as natural rights. Certainly there is no independent textual reason to doubt the veracity of LJA notes at just those moments where it is explained that property is a natural right. By the time of LJA ii.93, it is stated that property is an acquired right. If the texts of LJ are accepted as they stand, this means that at some point during the delivery of LJA, between LJA ii.30 and LJA ii.93, there is a switch from seeing property rights as natural, to seeing them as acquired rights. If this is the case, and there is no textual reason to doubt it, this would provide an explanation for the changed order of topics in the later LJB version. In LJA, the order of presentation is first private law, then domestic law, and finally public jurisprudence, whereas in LJB the order is first public jurisprudence, then domestic law, and finally private law. The assumption that the changed order is of no substantive significance[33] has resulted in disregarding the evidence that there is a shift from a natural rights basis for property in LJA to a conventional basis for property in LJB. It also neglects the point that in LJB the explanation for the order of the topics is explicitly related to the issue of the character of property rights:

> The origin of natural rights is quite evident. That a person has a right to have his body free from injury, and his liberty free from infringement unless there be a proper cause, no body doubts. But acquired rights such as property require more explanation. Property and civil government very much depend on one another. The preservation of property and the inequality of possession first formed it, and the state of property must always vary with the form of government. The civilians begin with considering government and then treat of property and other rights. Others who have written on this subject begin with the latter and then consider family and civil government. There are several advantages peculiar to each of these methods, tho' that of the civil law seems upon the whole preferable.
>
> (LJB 11)

As property rights are acquired rights depending on civil government, the text follows the practice of the civil law and treats public jurisprudence before private law.[34] Once it is accepted that property rights are acquired rights dependent on civil government, the argument in favour of presenting public jurisprudence first and private law last becomes compelling, as LJB acknowledges. Correspondingly, the presentation of LJA, where private law is placed before either domestic law or public law, had derived its rationale from the natural rights status of the basis of property rights, even

---

33 As argued for example by Haakonssen (1981, p. 104).
34 John Millar starting teaching civil law in the University of Glasgow from 1761; see Lehmann (1961, 1970).

though the regulations concerning such rights are held to vary along with the mode of subsistence of society (LJA i.27).

Thus, in spite of the similarities in the descriptive and historical passages of LJ, the theoretical structure of these lectures is in the process of shifting between LJA and LJB. This means that the practice of reading LJ as a discursive unity loses its foundation and it is no longer possible to read the two sets of lecture notes as alternative versions of the same text. Other close readings of these lectures reveal further differences. The passages already cited on exclusive privileges also provide an account of the differences between natural and acquired rights that supplement the bald statements provided at the beginning of the lectures,[35] and here there is a marked difference between the definitions provided in the two sets of lecture notes. In LJA the contrast between natural and acquired rights is that natural rights are founded in natural reason and acquired rights are the creatures of the civil law or the civil constitution (LJA i.20; ii.28, 30, 32); this distinction thus draws on the standard natural law emphasis on the identity of reason and nature.[36] LJB, however, makes no reference to reason or natural reason, but instead describes natural rights as those which 'arise from nature' (LJB 174, 175), or 'as in a state of hunters even before the origin of civil government' (LJB 10). Thus, in LJB natural rights are no longer described with reference to reason or natural reason but are presented as those rights which are simply pre-civil; here the Ciceronian natural law identity of nature and reason has simply been discarded. Not only is the division of rights between natural and acquired rights not held constant between LJA and LJB, but the definitions of these crucial terms are also not uniform across the two sets of lecture notes.[37] These changes signify a reduced dependence on the traditional forms of argument of natural jurisprudence with its moral privileging of nature as reason by which all agents may know what is just. Again the emphasis is put on the definition of justice as provided by civil governments rather than the ways in which individuals may have direct access to a self-evident knowledge of justice.

The result of this for LJ is a more sociological and historical approach to justice and changing forms of property than had previously been apparent

---

35 In LJA it had been stated that natural rights are those that antecede human actions (LJA i.12), whereas in LJB it simply states that natural rights are *iura hominum naturalia* (LJB 8).
36 In LJA it is stated that jurisprudence attempts to show how far different systems of government 'are founded in reason' (LJA i.1).
37 A consequence for LJ is that the arguments explaining the origin of property rights become problematic. Abandoning the identification of 'natural' with natural reason, and identifying 'natural' with the pre-civil age of hunters, means that although the introduction to LJB criticises state of nature arguments on the grounds that there is no such state existing (LJB 3), yet the pre-civil society of the age of hunters is now designated as a state of nature: 'Thus among hunters there is no regular government; they live according to the laws of nature' (LJB 19). Notwithstanding this, the age of hunters is then used to illustrate both the

in the natural law writings. In spite of the claim at the end of TMS that jurisprudence should be based on 'an inquiry into what were the natural rules of justice independent of all positive institution' (TMS VII.iv.37), and in spite of the function of the impartial spectator in LJ in providing a historically transcendent set of moral underpinnings for certain fundamental legal categories such as exclusive property rights, contractual promises and legal punishment, the theory of law delivered in LJ serves to undermine this claim. The overall emphasis of LJ relates more to the ways in which the changing historical circumstances of society are connected with changes in laws and government than in the ways in which 'natural rules of justice' hold sway throughout very different historical epochs and positive institutions. Such an account highlights the gradualness and the contingencies involved in the processes of legal and constitutional change. According to such a scheme, natural rules of justice must inevitably play a relatively minor role in the processes of history.

4

Such a focus on the contingencies of historical change draws attention back to the role of 'judges and arbiters' in the historical process of legal adaptation, as the legal rules of jurisprudence are intended for them and not for legislators. This focus is entirely in accord with the emphasis of the Scottish historical school of jurisprudence regarding the importance of judge-made law rather than statute law as the main vehicle for introducing legal change as part of the process of historical development.[38] It is also in accord with the prevailing legal viewpoint in both England and Scotland at the time which stressed the general superiority of judge-made common law over statute law and the role of the legislator.[39] The focus of LJ is, therefore, entirely congruent with the legal writing of the time, which accepted the superiority of judicial practice over the work of the legislator[40] and even actively mistrusted the legends and myths of the legislator.

---

paradigm case of occupation as an acquired property right, as well as the right to pursue a wild animal as a natural right.
38 'In this manner, by the successive litigation of individuals, and by the continued experience and observation of judges, the science of law grows up in society, and advances more and more to a regular system. Particular decisions become the foundation of general rules, which are afterwards limited by particular exceptions . . . But though the rules of justice derive their origin from the business of the world, and are introduced by the actual decisions of judges, their extensive utility is likely to attract the notice of speculative reasoners, and to render them the subject of criticism and philosophical discussion' (Millar *Historical View of the English Government*, vol. iv, Essay VII; in Lehmann 1960, pp. 345–6). On Kames's championing of common law over legislation, see Lieberman (1983).
39 See Lieberman (1989).
40 This argument was later attacked in the work of Jeremy Bentham, which attempted to set up a science of legislation to supersede judge-made common law. Comparing Kames with

These legends and myths were still pervasive in the eighteenth century.[41] Their roots lay in admiration for the founders of states and architects of constitutions such as Romulus, Lycurgus and Solon, and in reverence for classical political discourses such as Aristotle's *Politics*. In keeping with this classical discourse, the civic humanism of Machiavelli's writings had served to perpetuate the role of the legislator/statesman as the guiding source of prudence and virtue for a republic struggling to preserve its *virtù* in the face of the contingencies and corrupting influences of historical time (Machiavelli 1975; see especially I.9). By the eighteenth century, the figure of the wise legislator/statesman can still be seen as a commanding if controversial input into some of the political and economic discourses of the time.[42] Montesquieu's *Spirit of the Laws*, first published in 1748, introduced a more materialist account of law which explained legal differences in terms of social and economic factors and this proved hugely influential with the Scottish legal philosophers of the mid-eighteenth century,[43] but Montesquieu's account is positioned within a discourse that allocated a pre-eminent role to the legislator in fashioning the laws. Rousseau's *Social Contract*, published in 1762, is famously based on the legislative vision of a political prime mover who actively frames the original constitution (Rousseau 1973c, especially II.9). Each in its different way, these accounts have in common a view of society which privileges the statutory legal framework in determining or encapsulating the moral as well as political character of society. The legislative function thus includes as one of its concerns the political personality of its citizens together with those moral attributes that are considered to be politically relevant. In overseeing citizens' virtue, such an approach to some degree therefore effects a politicisation of moral behaviour and of the notion of virtue itself as public virtue. Rousseau, for example, argues that in addition to the three kinds of law as public law, civil law and criminal law, there is also a fourth, moral law, which forms the 'real constitution of the state' and 'with this the great legislator concerns himself in secret';[44] whereas particular regulations make

---

Bentham, Lieberman (1989, pp. 174–5) writes: 'For Kames, no less than for Bentham, utility featured as a critical principle of legal modernization. But, the reformers to whom Kames directed the principle were enlightened judges and not scientific legislators . . . Indeed, for Kames as for so many of his English contemporaries, the most important and recently confirmed lesson of English law was the clear superiority of the courts over the legislature in orchestrating legal development'.

41 Burns (1967) provides a brief history of different concepts of the legislator.
42 The importance of the legislator may also be gauged by the inclusion of the article 'Législateur' in volume IX of the *Encyclopédie* (1765).
43 See, for example, Stein (1980, pp. 15–19, 23–50).
44 Also cf. Rousseau *A Discourse on Political Economy*, first published 1755 (Rousseau 1973b, especially pp. 139–44) on the 'reign of virtue': 'If it is good to know how to deal with men as they are, it is much better to make them what there is need that they should be. The most absolute authority is that which penetrates into a man's inmost being, and concerns itself no less with his will than with his actions' (p. 139).

only the arch, a society's manners and morals 'form in the end its immovable keystone' (Rousseau 1973c, p. 228).[45] In the works of Adam Smith, however, the concept of public virtue is hardly present at all, and there is great reticence in promoting statute law as the guardian of public morals or public virtue. With private morality epitomised by the dialogism of the impartial spectator, the public virtue of justice is reduced to a separate and lower-order form of rule-governed behaviour, while the civic humanist virtues entailing political personality and active citizenship are hard put to be accommodated at all within such a framework. In TMS there is a reference to the role of the civil magistrate/law-giver in going beyond restraining injustice and promoting prosperity by establishing good discipline and discouraging vice, but this possibility is broached with the greatest caution and without reference to specifically civic virtues (TMS II.ii.1.8).

The legislator/statesman also played a determining role in certain mercantilist and state regulationist economic discourses, functioning actively in superintending the economic interests of the nation as a whole. *Discourses on the Public Revenues* by Charles Davenant, (first published 1698), applies a civic humanist analysis to post-Revolution Britain,[46] and here the legislator/statesman is required to assume responsibility for the political, moral and economic health of the nation. The good legislator/statesman needs to know the real wealth of the nation and its taxable capacity as it is this ultimately which provides the resources for a country's foreign policy and its ability to conduct wars. He also needs to have a detailed knowledge of the balance of trade as the trade surplus is the source of a nation's increasing wealth and the direct means by which a war may be financed. This kind of economic and political judgment is made possible by 'the art of reasoning by figures, upon things relating to government' (Davenant 1967a, vol. I, p. 128), that is, by the newly developing art of political arithmetic:

> A great statesman, by consulting all sort of men, and by contemplating the universal posture of the nation, its power, strength, trade, wealth and revenues, in any counsel he is to offer, by summing up the difficulties on either side, and by computing upon the whole, shall be able to form a sound judgment, and to give a right advice: and this is what we mean by Political Arithmetic.
>
> (Davenant 1967a, vol. I, p. 135)

Thus, political arithmetic was conceived not as an abstract statistical skill

---

45 In a variation on the architectural metaphor, TMS argues that beneficence, the truly moral virtue, 'is the ornament which embellishes, not the foundation which supports the building' whereas justice, a negative virtue, is the 'main pillar that upholds the whole edifice. If it is removed, the great, the immense fabric of human society . . . must in a moment crumble into atoms' (TMS II.ii.3.4).

46 See, for example, Pocock 1975, pp. 436–46.

divorced from the world of politics, but as rooted in the perceived requirements of the nation state and in the notion of the legislator/statesman as a source of active superintendence in the interests of the polity.[47] Here it was also based on a mercantilist view of the primacy of foreign trade and the trade surplus, and the need for detailed regulation and direction of manufactures and international and colonial trade in order to meet the political as well as economic objectives relating to the national interest. Similarly, although promoting agricultural interests, Arthur Young's *Political Arithmetic* (1774) was directed towards legislators and statesmen in order to rebut what were seen as the harmful policy implications of writers such as the Économistes, and so it was presented as advice to legislators and statesmen on how best to promote agriculture (Young 1774, pp. vi, 198, 200, 206, 208, 227, 287, 298). Although a policy of liberalising agriculture was proposed along with improved husbandry, this did not exclude mercantilist arguments concerning the Corn Laws, the Navigation Acts, the harmful consequences of free trade, and the need for high prices to stimulate production, and it accepted without question the centrality of the statesman's role in overseeing the implementation of policy. It also located itself with respect to 'political oeconomy': 'The great encouragement which agriculture at present meets with in *Europe* has been either the cause or effect (probably both) of many publications upon that part of political oeconomy which concerns the culture of the earth' (Young 1774, Preface, p. v).

In 1767, just nine years before *The Wealth of Nations* was published, Sir James Steuart's *Inquiry into the Principles of Political Oeconomy* presented an account of political oeconomy which is also premised on the pervasive directing hand of the legislator/statesman in directing the economy: 'In treating every question of political oeconomy, I constantly suppose a statesman at the head of government, systematically conducting every part of it . . .' (Steuart 1966, I.XIX, p. 122). Throughout the *Inquiry*, the statesman is required at all times to steer and guide the economy, especially through the stormy waters of international competition:

> the abilities of a statesman are discovered, in directing and conducting what I call the delicacy of national competition . . . The trading nations of Europe represent a fleet of ships, every one striving who shall get first to a certain port. The statesman of each is the master . . . the master who sails his ship with the greatest dexterity, and he who can lay his rivals under the lee of his sails, will, *caeteris paribus*, undoubtedly get before them, and maintain his advantage.
> (Steuart 1966, II.XII, p. 203)

---

47 Endres (1985) explores ways in which political arithmetic was constructed as advice and warnings to statesmen regarding political and economic issues. See also Tribe (1978, p. 86), and Deane (1987).

Reviews of the first edition of the *Inquiry* objected to its dependence on the statesman;[48] the Preface to the second edition replied to these criticisms, but the reliance on the statesman was not reduced.[49] The reviews were particularly sceptical about the illiberal implications of such a reliance on the statesman/legislator, and argued against both the economic and political implications of investing so much power in a single person. The *Monthly Review*, for example, contested the argument of the *Inquiry* that the statesman should not be judged according to the standards of private morality:[50] these were 'poisonous sentiments', it responded, which were entirely opposed to the British constitution and the 'free and manly spirit of the nation', and would inevitably lead 'either to slavish despotism, or mad democracy' (*Monthly Review* 1767, vol. 36, pp. 464–5). The *Monthly Review* also castigates the *Inquiry* for promoting the idea that the statesman should work upon the spirit of a people:

> Blush and tremble ye multitudes at this mortifying likeness! . . . Those who can lead you *blindly* to *good*, can lead you as *blindly* to *evil*. – If you are such tractable cattle, as you are represented to be, it depends upon the *characters* of your *masters* and owners, whether they shall drive you to safety or destruction . . .
> (*Monthly Review* 1767, vol. 36, p. 368, original emphasis)[51]

Entrenched in contemporary discourses pertaining both to the polity and the economy, the legislator/statesman symbolised so much of what Smith's writings and lectures were arguing against that it becomes implausible to identify Smith's own intellectual project as the 'science of a legislator'.[52] Commentaries that interpret Smith's works in terms of the 'science of a legislator' argue that the legislator here is not the omniscient or innovatory

---

48 See *Monthly Review* 1767, vol. 36, pp. 282, 367–8, 464–66 and vol. 37, p. 125; *Critical Review* vol. 23, pp. 411–12. See editor's note, Steuart's *Inquiry* 1966, p. 4, n. 2.
49 Steuart 1966, p. 4.
50 Machiavelli's *Discourses* (Machiavelli 1975, I.9) had argued that for the legislator, the ends justified the means, and so had provided an argument that the legislator's actions are beyond conventional morality.
51 See note 62 below for the reviewers' response to the praise of Lycurgus and the Spartan system.
52 Haakonssen (1981, p. 97) argues that Smith's use of 'that legendary figure, the "legislator" ' supports his reading of the normative function of the natural jurisprudence in LJ where the legislator is 'clearly the man of public spirit who will strike the perfect Smithian balance between the enlightenment of "Some general, and even systematical, idea of the perfection of policy and law", and the piecemeal action to alleviate the concrete evils'; also pp. 188–9. Winch (1978, pp. 9, 12–13, 159–60, 170–3; 1983a; 1983b) argues that the notion of 'the science of a legislator' situates LJ within the normative concerns of natural jurisprudence and that this underscores the political (rather than the materialist/economic) dimensions of Smith's overall vision where 'political economy' itself is seen as just one branch of the science of the legislator. See also Lindgren (1973, p. 122). McNally (1988, especially pp. 208, 252–4) and Evensky (1989) draw on the work of both Haakonssen and Winch.

legislator of ancient myth, but rather one who is attuned to opinions and habits already existing and who acts in the knowledge of what is right.[53] But by the mid-eighteenth century, the concept of the legislator/statesman was so saturated by its immersion in these other discourses that it is questionable as to whether it could be conceived as a feasible project to try to reposition the semantic and discursive resonances of this term in such a way.

Certainly, other members of the Scottish historical school explicitly repudiated what to them was the myth of an originating legislator. Arguing that a country's laws and customs develop historically in accordance with the larger social and economic needs of society, it follows that it is misplaced to attribute natural historical developments to the commanding genius or foresight of individual men.[54] In John Millar's Introduction to *The Origin and Distinction of Ranks*, first published in 1771,[55] it is argued that any reforms associated with such statesmen must have been due very largely to the historical needs of that society at that particular time:

> But, notwithstanding the concurring testimony of historians, concerning the great political changes introduced by the lawgivers of a remote age, there may be reason to doubt, whether the effect of their interpositions has ever been so extensive as is generally supposed . . . It is even extremely probable, that those patriotic statesmen, whose existence is well ascertained, and whose laws have been justly celebrated, were at great pains to accommodate their regulations to the situation of the people for whom they were intended; and that, instead of being actuated by a projecting spirit, or attempting from visionary speculations of remote utility, to produce any violent reformation, they confined themselves to such moderate improvements as, by deviating little from the former usage, were in some measure supported by experience, and coincided with the prevailing opinions of the country.
>
> (Millar 1960, pp. 177–8; see also p. 357)

Even where the historical authenticity of such legislators is supported by evidence, the empirical experience that laws and customs are attendant upon the requirements of society suggests that the innovatory potential of any

---

53 For example, Winch (1978, p. 172; 1988, p. 90) and Haakonssen (1985b, pp. 48–9).
54 Forbes (1954, p. 659) refers to the 'de-rationalization by Ferguson, Smith and followers, of the work of Lycurgus and other great legislators'. In the Introduction to Ferguson 1966, Forbes writes: 'Ferguson, like Smith, Millar, and others (but not Hume), has dispensed with the "Legislators and Founders of States" . . . The Legislator myth flourished in the eighteenth century, for a variety of reasons, and its destruction was perhaps the most original and daring *coup* of the social science of the Scottish Enlightenment. Ferguson himself seems, at a later stage, to have had momentary doubts about its validity' (p. xxiv).
55 This Introduction was first published in the third edition, 1779.

specific set of intended legislation must be very slight. This view was also put forward in Adam Ferguson's *Essay on the History of Civil Society*, 1767:

> We are therefore to receive, with caution, the traditionary histories of ancient legislators, and founders of states. Their names have long been celebrated; their supposed plans have been admired; and what were probably the consequences of an early situation, is, in every instance, considered as an effect of design.
> (Ferguson 1966, p. 123; see also pp. 124, 134)

Here is enunciated the argument associated with the Scottish Enlightenment that human institutions are the unintended consequences of human action but not human design. According to this historical and empirical scheme of social progress, individual legislators of whatever stage of society cannot be responsible for the general regulation of its laws and customs.[56] In spite of this hostility towards the idea of a founding legislator, however, Ferguson's *Essay* is still sufficiently close to the discourse of civic humanism for there to be an active place for the traditional virtues of the statesman in the governance of a state.

Ultimately, however, evidence for the significance and place of the legislator/statesman in Smith's works must be sought in the texts themselves. If LJ formed the core component of the 'science of a legislator', then the textual evidence for this must be available in these lectures. The expression 'science of a legislator', however, does not appear in LJ. At the beginning of both LJA and LJB, the general subject matter of the lectures is clearly and consistently signalled, and it might be thought that this would be the appropriate place for such an important description, but a definition is offered without reference to the 'science of a legislator' or even to the legislator.[57] As the expression the 'science of a legislator' is absent from LJ, its meaning and therefore its significance in relation to the supposed intentionality behind LJ has been adduced from its appearance elsewhere in Smith's works but in making these transpositions, the distinctiveness of those primary discursive contexts has been neglected. The term 'legislator' does occur in LJ, but the legislator here does not refer to someone of public spirit or exemplary juridical or political virtues, and is used simply to refer to various subordinate aspects of a detailed exposition of the law. For example, the term 'legislator' refers to the law of the Visigoths (LJA ii.5); legislators have not neglected the blind and foolish resentment at even inanimate objects which have occasioned someone's

---

56 Meek (1973, pp. 6–7) argues that Turgot's discourse delivered at the Sorbonne in July 1750 contained 'a diatribe against great legislators'.
57 Jurisprudence is described as 'the theory of the rules by which civil governments ought to be directed' (LJA i.1), and 'Jurisprudence is that science which inquires into the general

death (LJA ii.177); as men are the legislators, they curb women as much as possible and give themselves greater freedom (LJA iii.16); democratic governments are unlikely to abolish slavery as here the legislators are themselves masters of slaves (LJA iii.114); and legislators have made servitudes into real rights (rather than personal rights) in order to reduce the number of lawsuits required to get possession of them (LJB 9). This motley collection of detailed legal points shows that the term 'legislator' is not performing any organisational or theoretical function in LJ, neither is it signalling any normative framework that can be called upon to interpret the meaning of the overall jurisprudential arguments being offered.

There are two main places in Smith's works which do refer to the legislator/statesman, and these are WN, Book IV, and TMS, Part VI, (added in the sixth edition 1790).[58] The expression 'the science of a legislator' occurs twice only, appearing on both occasions in WN, Book IV. This part of WN is directed to a sustained criticism of the mercantile and agricultural systems; the references to the 'science of a legislator' are therefore to be understood within this discursive context of opposition to certain prevailing theories and practices. The first time that the expression occurs is in the Introduction to Book IV:

> Political œconomy, considered as a branch of the science of a statesman or legislator, proposes two distinct objects; first, to provide a plentiful revenue or subsistence for the people, or more properly to enable them to provide such a revenue or subsistence for themselves; and secondly, to supply the state or commonwealth with a revenue sufficient for the publick services. It proposes to enrich both the people and the sovereign.
>
> The different progress of opulence in different ages and nations, has given occasion to two different systems of political œconomy, with regard to enriching the people. The one may be called the system of commerce, the other that of agriculture. I shall endeavour to explain both as fully and distinctly as I can, and shall begin with the system of commerce. It is the modern system, and is best understood in our own country and in our own times.
>
> (WN IV, Introduction, 1–2)

---

principles which ought to be the foundation of the laws of all nations' (LJB 1); also (LJB 5). This is consistent with the definition provided in TMS VII.iv.37.

58 In a paper drawn up by Adam Smith in 1755, statesmen and projectors are criticised together: 'Man is generally considered by statesmen and projectors as the materials of a sort of political mechanics. Projectors disturb nature in the course of her operations in human affairs; and it requires no more than to let her alone, and give her fair play in the pursuit of her ends, that she may establish her own designs' (quoted in Stewart 1980, p. 322). Ferguson sometimes identifies legislators with 'projectors' and a projecting spirit, for example: 'Although free constitutions of government seldom or never take their rise from

This reference to political oeconomy as a branch of the science of a legislator/statesman is generally taken to provide a self-description of WN itself.[59] But in this passage it is only the mercantile and agricultural systems which are identified as systems of political oeconomy; it is not stated that WN itself constitutes a distinct or third system of political oeconomy. This is the case throughout WN: the expression 'political oeconomy' consistently refers to those systems of economic policy and analysis which are being opposed and criticised, and not to the arguments and analysis that are presented in WN. The *Introduction and Plan of the Work* is the first place where the term is used, and here it refers exclusively to the mercantile and agricultural systems:

> those different plans . . . have given occasion to very different theories of political œconomy; of which some magnify the importance of that industry which is carried on in towns, others of that which is carried on in the country . . . I have endeavoured, in the Fourth Book, to explain, as fully and distinctly as I can, those different theories . . .
> (WN, Introduction, 8)

Most of the references to 'political oeconomy' in WN are of this sort, where either one or both of these two systems are being signified: 'This notion is connected with the system of political œconomy which represents national wealth as consisting in the abundance, and national poverty in the scarcity of gold and silver; a system whch I shall endeavour to explain and examine at great length in the fourth book of this enquiry' (WN I.xi.n.1); 'Gold and silver, therefore, are, according to him [i.e. John Locke], the most solid and substantial part of the moveable wealth of a nation, and to multiply those metals ought, he thinks, upon that account, to be the great object of its political œconomy' (WN IV.i.3); 'The title of Mun's book, *England's Treasure by Forraign Trade*, became a fundamental maxim in the political œconomy, not of England only, but of all other commercial nations' (WN IV.i.10); 'it necessarily became the great object of political œconomy to diminish as much as possible the importation of foreign goods for home-consumption, and to increase as much as possible the exportation of the produce of domestick industry' (WN IV.i.35); 'The agricultural systems of political œconomy . . .' (WN IV.ix.1); Quesnay 'seems not to have considered that on the political body, the natural effort which every man is continually making to bettter his own condition, is a principle of preservation capable of preventing and correcting, in many respects, the bad effects of a political œconomy, in some degree, both partial and oppressive. Such a

---

the scheme of any single projector . . .' (Ferguson 1966, p. 134; also p. 124). Cf. also Millar 1960, p. 357.
59 For different accounts of WN as 'political oeconomy', see Cannan (1950, p. xviii), Tribe (1978, p. 107), Winch (1983a, 1983b), Blaug (1985, p. 57) and Letwin (1988).

political œconomy . . .' (WN IV.ix.28); 'This system [i.e. the agricultural system], however, with all its imperfections is, perhaps, the nearest approximation to the truth that has yet been published upon the subject of political œconomy, and is upon that account well worth the consideration of every man who wishes to examine with attention the principles of that very important science' (WN IV.ix.38); and 'As the political œconomy of the nations of modern Europe, has been more favourable to manufactures and foreign trade, the industry of the towns, than to agriculture, the industry of the country; so that of other nations has followed a different plan, and has been more favourable to agriculture than to manufactures and foreign trade' (WN IV.ix.39). In each of these cases 'political oeconomy' refers not to the argument of WN, but to the system that the argument of WN is counterposing; it is 'that science' not 'this science'. But how can this be reconciled with the one statement in WN that has been taken as direct evidence that Smith conceived of WN as a form of political oeconomy? This passage occurs as part of the discussion of the agricultural system: 'This sect [i.e. the French Économistes], in their works, which are very numerous, and which treat not only of what is properly called Political Oeconomy, or of the nature and causes of the wealth of nations, but of every other branch of the system of civil government . . .' (WN IV.ix.38). Here the placing of the word 'of' before 'the nature and causes of the wealth of nations' suggests that the title of WN is to be differentiated from the area of 'political oeconomy'; though both descriptors may be applied to the agricultural system, the presence of the word 'of' shows that they are not synonymous.

In the remaining references, the oppositional inflection of 'political oeconomy' is apparent from the terms of the argument. Where the expression occurs in Book II, chapter v, this is in the context of a criticism of the policy of encouraging the carrying trade and the foreign trade of consumption above the home-trade; here it is argued that, even accepting the objective of political oeconomy (riches and power), the mercantile policy is wrong:

> But the great object of the political œconomy of every country, is to increase the riches and power of that country. It ought, therefore, to give no preference nor superior encouragement to the foreign trade of consumption above the home-trade, nor to the carrying trade above either of the other two. It ought neither to force nor to allure into either of those two channels, a greater share of the capital of the country than what would naturally flow into them of its own accord.
> (WN, II.v.31)

In Book V, in the context of a discussion of the East India Company, it is stated that: 'The miserable effects of which the company complained, were the cheapness of consumption and the encouragement given to production, precisely the two effects which it is the great business of political œconomy to promote' (WN V.i.e.26). Thus, the East India Company was complaining about those very effects, i.e. cheapness and the encouragement of production, which the political oeconomy of mercantilism was intended to promote. It was, however, part of the argument of WN to oppose the view that 'cheapness' and 'production' should be 'promoted' as specific policy objectives; in this context here, the expression 'the great business of political œconomy' therefore has an ironic and contemptuous inflexion.[60]

Thus, in exclusively signifying the mercantile and agricultural systems, the reference to 'political oeconomy' in the Introduction to Book IV is consistent with references elsewhere in WN. In signifying the systems to which the arguments of WN are opposed, this term cannot be taken as a self-description of the arguments of WN, nor as the inclusive name of a science within which WN may be located. Just as the legislator/statesman and 'the science of a statesman or legislator' are derogated notions in WN, so too is the term 'political oeconomy'. In WN the discursive context for the legislator/statesman is the body of writings on the overall regulation of the economy by the statesman. Charles Davenant's *Discourses on the Public Revenues* (1698) has already been cited. But further, by the mid-eighteenth century, the term political oeconomy itself was being directly connected with a more statist conception of economic and political supervision, and here the role of the legislator/statesman is significant. Rousseau's *Discourse on Political Economy*, published in the *Encyclopédie* 1755, provided an account of the civic humanist conception of the moral, political and economic guiding role of the legislator/statesman together with an account of familiar mercantilist doctrines presented under the rubric of a 'political economy' explained by the analogy of state government and household management. Joseph Harris's *Essay upon Money and Coins* (1757) identifies political oeconomy as the province of a more extended discourse which includes the political as well as economic aspects of commercial regulation, and this is categorised as relating particularly to the role of the statesman (p. 25 note). Steuart's *Inquiry*, it was argued above, also harnesses the guiding hand of the legislator/statesman to the science of political oeconomy. The Introduction to Book I of the *Inquiry* states that 'The principal object of this science [i.e. political oeconomy] is to secure a certain fund of subsistence for all the inhabitants' (Steuart 1966, p. 17), a declaration which is similar to the description of political oeconomy presented in the Introduction to Book IV of WN. Thus, when read in terms of this discursive context, the significance of the legislator/statesman in the Introduction to WN, Book IV, is that it performs a rhetorical function in referring to a central organising concept of the entire system of state control proposed by mercantilist and

---

60 A further reference to 'political oeconomy' is at V.i.e.31 where the Abbé Morrelet is referred to as 'An eminent French author, of great knowledge in matters of political œconomy . . .'.

civic humanist discourses on 'political oeconomy',[61] and as such was not to be endorsed by the argument of WN.[62]

The agricultural system of the French Économistes was a reaction against the mercantilist preferences accorded to manufacturing industry, but it was no less dependent than the mercantilist system on the discursive importance of the state as a central organising category both in their economics and in their wider social theory.[63] The agricultural system was based on an understanding of a determinate natural law in which social laws were simply the instanciation of natural laws. This necessary social order allowed no space for the moral initiatives of the civic humanist legislator/statesman in moulding society to a preconceived moral and political order, but instead the centrality of the legal framework derived from the need to impose these natural laws on society by means of absolute positive laws. The favoured constitutional form is therefore one of 'legal despotism', which abjures any element of pluralist or decentred powers. China's despotism was seen as a model of 'legal despotism' for Europe, in which the sovereign would lay down positive laws enacting the natural laws which would be absolutely binding for all. In this model of legal despotism, the legislator was transformed from that of political prime mover to one whose recognition of the inevitability of the natural order would play an essential part in the governance of society:

> All the positive laws that have to do with the general economic order of the nation, influence the physical progress of the annual repro-

---

[61] Similarly, WN turns one of the state regulationist literature's own metaphors against itself where the metaphor of the prudent master of a family is deployed to criticise the regulation of external trade. The immediate context is that of an argument against restraints on imports: 'It is the maxim of every prudent master of a family, never to attempt to make at home what it will cost him more to make than to buy . . . What is prudence in the conduct of every private family, can scarce be folly in that of a great kingdom' (WN IV.ii.11–12). Cf. Steuart 1966, vol. I, Introduction, p. 16.

[62] Davenant's *Essay upon the . . . Balance of Trade* (Davenant 1771, vol. II, p. 275), and Steuart's *Inquiry* (Steuart 1966, II.XIV, p. 218), both extol Lycurgus, one of the heroes in the civic humanist canon, as an exemplary legislator. In reviewing Steuart's *Inquiry*, both the *Monthly Review* and the *Critical Review* took exception to the praise of the Spartan system and criticised the illiberal implications of lauding Lycurgus: 'That it should have been the fashion of late years to revive the ideas of this slavish government, and that repeated attempts should be made to familiarise them to the minds of Britons, is a circumstance which we have beheld with astonishment, and which cannot fail to raise the indignation of every intelligent friend to the liberties of mankind' (*Monthly Review* 1767, vol. 36, p. 465); and 'We have more than once, in the course of this Review, disapproved of all the system of Spartan government, no part of which, we think, is appropriate to social life. They were a nation of brutes, and appear the more so, the more we are conversant with their history' (*Critical Review* 1767, vol. 23, p. 413). See also editor's note 1 at Steuart's *Inquiry* (Steuart 1966, p. 218). WN simply scorns Lycurgus' reforms as unfeasible (WN IV.i.13). Anderson and Tollison (1984) stress Smith's opposition to the anti-liberalism of Steuart's *Inquiry*.

[63] For different treatments of the statist element in physiocratic writings, see Samuels (1961, 1962), Fox-Genovese (1976) and Tribe (1978, ch. 5).

duction of the wealth of the kingdom; these laws require on the part of the legislator and of those who enforce them, a very extensive knowledge and elaborate calculations, the results of which must present, with proof, the advantages to the sovereign and to the nation, especially the advantages to the sovereign, for he must be induced by self-interest to do the right thing.

(Quesnay 1946, pp. 270–1)

Thus, the legislator plays a part in the necessary framework of positive legal enactments which are required both to recognise and enforce the essential and natural order. In particular, the legislator displays a systematic knowledge of the fundamental laws governing the production of revenue, a knowledge that is embodied in the 'tableau économique'.

Thus, when the Introduction to Book IV of WN is read in terms of the discursive context of its own time, the legislator/statesman is seen to be a familiar and active figure in the discourses of state management of the oeconomy against which the arguments of WN were directed. The rhetorical function of the use of this expression in WN is, thus, to reinforce the distance between WN and the discourses of state management to which WN was opposed. As WN argues, the individual is better placed to direct his own capital than any statesman or lawgiver: 'What is the species of domestick industry which his capital can employ, and of which the produce is likely to be of the greatest value, every individual, it is evident, can, in his local situation, judge much better than any statesman or lawgiver can do for him' (WN IV.ii.10); and 'But the law ought always to trust people with the care of their own interest, as in their local situations they must generally be able to judge better of it than the legislator can do' (WN IV.v.b.16).

The statesman or legislator is very often referred to as the instigator or perpetrator of the harmful practices deriving from the mercantile system and the colonial monopoly, and so such references carry an oppositional, ironic or sardonic tone: 'The affected anxiety of the law-giver . . .' (WN I.x.c.12); 'Those statesmen who have been disposed to favour it [i.e. the carrying trade] with particular encouragements, seem to have mistaken the effect and symptom for the cause' (WN II.v.35); 'the exchangeable value of its annual produce, instead of being increased, according to the intention of the lawgiver, must necessarily be diminished by every such regulation' (WN IV.ii.12); 'They are the projects [i.e. the quest for gold], therefore, to which of all others a prudent law-giver, who desired to increase the capital of his nation, would least chuse . . .' (WN IV.vii.a.18); and 'To found a great empire for the sole purpose of raising up a people of customers, may at first sight appear a project fit only for a nation of shopkeepers. It is, however, a project altogether unfit for a nation of shopkeepers; but extremely fit for a nation whose government is influenced by shopkeepers. Such statesmen, and such statesmen only . . .' (WN IV.vii.c.63). The harmful effects of the colonial monopoly are so widespread that the process even of dismantling it will involve problems, and so WN sardonically concludes: 'In what manner, therefore, the colony trade ought gradually to be opened; what are the restraints which ought first, and what are those which ought last to be taken away; or in what manner the natural system of perfect liberty and justice ought gradually to be restored, we must leave to the wisdom of future statesmen and legislators to determine' (WN IV.vii.c.44).

It is hard to find a reference to the legislator/statesman that carries an unambiguously positive commendatory meaning. The one that comes closest to this occurs not in the economic criticisms of Book IV but in the final Book's well-known discussion of the mutilating effects of the division of labour in manufacturing, where the discursive reference is not the erroneous political oeconomy of modern Europe but the undifferentiated personality of barbarous societies: 'In those barbarous societies, as they are called, every man, it has already been observed, is a warrior. Every man too is in some measure a statesman, and can form a tolerable judgment concerning the interest of the society, and the conduct of those who govern it' (WN V.i.f.51). In the discussion of the colonial disturbances, by contrast, the aspirations of the leading colonists are described in somewhat sarcastic terms noting the power of ambition: 'From shopkeepers, tradesmen, and attornies, they are become statesmen and legislators, and are employed in contriving a new form of government for an extensive empire, which, they flatter themselves, will become, and which, indeed, seems very likely to become, one of the greatest and most formidable that ever was in the world' (WN IV.vii.c.75).[64]

With this clarification, it is also possible to make sense of the other reference to the term 'the science of a legislator' at WN IV.ii.39. The general context here is a long discussion on restraints on imports, but the specific and immediate context is the issue of retaliation in the face of high duties imposed by a competitor country, and whether such retaliations will induce the rival country to repeal its high duties. The reference to the science of a legislator at this point relates to this specific issue as to whether a retaliation will result in a reduction in the high duties in the other country, but WN argues that this is a political issue not an economic one: 'To judge whether such retaliations are likely to produce such an effect, does not, perhaps, belong so much to the science of a legislator, whose deliberations ought to be governed by general principles which are always the same, as to the skill of that insidious and crafty animal, vulgarly called a statesman or politician' (WN IV.ii.39). The science of a legislator refers to the steering of the ship of

---

[64] At WN III.ii.3,16 proprietors of land were anciently the legislators of their country, and at WN V.i.g.6 a long passage from Hume is cited which includes a reference to the 'wise legislator'.

state which ought to be based on certain general principles of political oeconomy according to which certain retaliatory restraints on imports are levied for direct economic reasons; the issue of the effects of that retaliation on the competitor country, however, requires a political judgment about the response of the competitor country, and this political judgment is not subject to general principles but is dependent on political skills which, by their nature, are insidious and crafty. It has been suggested that this passage is displaying 'a specific eighteenth-century semantic pattern' with two patterns of usage, one of them belonging to vulgar discourse and the other to learned or cultivated discourse.[65] If this is so, then the point of this passage is not to compare the 'statesman' unfavourably with the 'legislator',[66] but to differentiate between judgments based on general (though faulty) economic principles and judgments based on political strategy, where the 'statesman' had been wrongly identified in the 'vulgar' mind with the latter type of political judgment. In this case, as elsewhere in WN including the Introduction to Book IV, the terms 'statesman' and 'legislator' are used synonymously with no particular derogation attached to the statesman compared with the legislator.

As the references to 'the science of the legislator/statesman' in WN carry negative connotations, revealing the theoretical and policy distance that exists between WN and those discourses proposing state control, it is no accident that the only two references to this science occur in Book IV of WN, which is addressed to the task of directly confronting those erroneous systems. If WN were proposing itself as part of the discourse of the science of a legislator, then it would be expected that such a central expression would find its way into other sections of the book, especially those sections that present its own theoretical contribution. It is also no accident that this expression is not used in the economic sections on 'police' in LJ. As this expression presupposes an interventionist economic policy stance that LJ did not accept, it would have been out of place there as a self-description. Further, of course, Smith's lectures on jurisprudence were delivered at the University of Glasgow before Steuart published the *Inquiry* and before the physiocratic doctrines were widely promulgated, which means that this frame of reference would not have functioned so powerfully within contemporary economic discourse when the lectures were presented.

The legislator and statesman also appear in TMS, and here too they are to be found mainly in one part of the book, in Part VI which was added to the sixth edition of 1790, the final edition published within Smith's lifetime. Prior to this final edition, there are a few references to the legislator/statesman but they do not perform any organising function for the text as a

---

65 Viner (1965, pp. 30–1).
66 Cf. Winch (1978, p. 159) and Haakonssen (1981, p. 97).

whole. There is a passing reference to Peter the Great as a celebrated legislator in the context of a passage on public police (TMS IV.1.11), but the other references are largely of a general nature signifying little about the nature of government policy, legislation or justice. These references form part of a general discourse on heroes, great men and a miscellaneous assortment of benefactors to mankind. In Part III of TMS, as part of a criticism of the notion that Christian virtue is composed predominantly of religious worship, it is argued that it is absurd that the 'futile mortifications of a monastery' should have more merit than an active life as a member of the lay community:

> It is this spirit, however, which, while it has reserved the celestial regions for monks and friars, has condemned to the infernal all the heroes, all the statesmen and lawgivers, all the poets and philosophers of former ages; all those who have invented, improved, or excelled in the arts which contribute to the subsistence, to the conveniency, or to the ornament of human life; all the great protectors, instructors, and benefactors of mankind; all those to whom our natural sense of praise-worthiness forces us to ascribe the highest merit and most exalted virtue.
>
> (TMS III.2.35)

In Part VII's discussion of the Stoic attitude to suicide and the contentious issue as to whether Zeno the Stoic had committed suicide, reference is made to the fact that as relatively little is known of men of letters (such as Zeno) compared with great princes or statesmen, details of their death come to be fabricated in the course of time in order to satisfy public curiosity. Here the contrast is between the obscurity of men of letters compared with the public nature of the lives of great princes and statesmen (TMS VII.ii.1.31), but again this says nothing about the political or judicial role of the statesman. Until the sixth edition, that is from 1759 to 1790, this is basically all that TMS had to say on legislators and statesmen.[67] Nothing in the structure of the argument of TMS or in its moral theory is dependent on the notion of the legislator/statesman which simply takes its place in a pantheon of great men and heroes in history.

In the sixth edition of TMS a new section was included as Part VI, which contains a number of references to legislators and statesmen.[68] Part VI is structured in terms of a discussion of the character of the virtues of prudence, beneficence and self-command. The Stoic framework of Part VI

---

67 Apart from the reference to the law-giver at TMS II.ii.1.8 discussed above.
68 There has been some discussion in the secondary literature concerning the extent to which Part VI presents its own problems of interpretation, whether it should it be read as Smith's personal response to the political issues thrown up by the French Revolution or whether it

has been discussed above in chapter 4: prudence is presented from a Stoic standpoint which emphasises self-command; the discussion of beneficence is based on the Stoic concept of *oikeiosis*; and the discussion of self-command is rooted in Stoicism. It is within this structured Stoic discussion that the scattered references to legislators and statesmen are inserted as illustrations alongside other heroes such as warriors, generals and poets. Thus, whereas the presence of the legislator/statesman in Book IV of WN was constructed with reference to the discourses of economic state regulation and carried negative connotations, in TMS the presence of the legislator/statesman is constructed with reference to the moral discourse of Stoic philosophy together with a wider classical and historical discourse of great men and heroes. Within this discourse, legislators and statesmen appear alongside other heroes such as warriors, generals and poets; they are identified by the generic qualities of the 'hero' defined by reference to certain outstanding personal qualities, which are used as illustrations for the general portrayal of the virtues, but this remains rooted in a moral discourse pertaining to personal attributes rather than a political or juridical discourse.

Prudence, beneficence and self-command are the three virtues which are the subject of Part VI. In the chapter on prudence, the great general, the great statesman and the great legislator are provided as illustrations of 'superior prudence', which includes valour, strong benevolence, a 'sacred regard to the rules of justice' and a 'proper degree of self-command'. Further, 'when carried to the highest degree of perfection', superior prudence

> necessarily presupposes the art, the talent, and the habit or disposition of acting with the most perfect propriety in every possible circumstance and situation. It necessarily supposes the utmost perfection of all the intellectual and of all the moral virtues. It is the best head joined to the best heart. It is the most perfect wisdom combined with the most perfect virtue.
>
> (TMS VI.i.15)

This is a classic statement of the general virtues appropriate to a class of great men – generals, legislators and statesmen. But even this rarefied excellence only 'constitutes very nearly the character of the Academical or Peripatetic sage', not fully such a sage nor indeed the Stoic sage. This distance from the full and complete state of virtuosity represented by the Stoic sage is partly a recognition that such a person was something of an unattainable ideal even by philosophical standards, but it also follows from the predominant characteristic of these heroic men that they were men of

---

reflects the heightened Stoicism of a man at the very end of his life. See, for example, Rothschild (1992).

action rather than men of contemplation and, given the cynicism evident in TMS concerning the standards of probity in public life, there is a presumption that it is unlikely that a sage would ever become a national hero. Thus, here, superior prudence is related to those who are active in moulding the course of history, men such as the general, the statesman and the legislator.

The second section of Part VI is devoted to beneficence and is constructed in terms of the Stoic discussion of the order in which others are recommended by nature. This is an aspect of the Stoic doctrine of *oikeiosis*, discussed in chapter 4 and above, where moral development is traced through a number of stages, and where personal and social relationships are seen as a series of 'concentric circles' enclosing the moral agent. The thrust of the Stoic doctrine involved the contraction of these circles towards the centre as a person's heightened sense of humanity and benevolence come to encompass wider and wider circles and the moral agent becomes a citizen of the world. The first and third chapters of this section of TMS deal with the inner and outer circles and contain no references to the legislator/statesman. The second chapter considers the intermediate circles of this concentric scheme, that is, it considers the order in which societies are by nature recommended to our beneficence, and it is in this chapter that the references to the legislator/statesman occur. Thus, the chapter addresses political issues under the general rubric of beneficence, a moral category relating to individual moral characteristics.

This chapter on beneficence as a moral virtue opens by including legislators/statesmen along with other national heroes such as warriors, poets, philosophers and men of letters (TMS VI.ii.2.2), but the chapter later becomes more politically focused by considering the character of citizenship and political leadership. The public spirit of the good citizen who loves his country involves respecting existing institutions and desiring to promote the welfare of society (para. 11) and so is 'founded upon the love of humanity, upon a real fellow-feeling with the inconveniencies and distresses to which some of our fellow-citizens may be exposed' (TMS VI.ii.2.15). Thus, public spirit is founded upon the love of humanity; instead of being constructed as a political characteristic, public spirit is here presented in terms of the Stoic moral categories of *oikeiosis* and beneficence. Within this moral framework, in times of civil faction, the leader of the successful party may 'assume the greatest and noblest of all characters, that of the reformer and legislator of a great state' if he manages to 're-establish and improve the constitution' (TMS VI.ii.2.14). Here the main threat to moral excellence and public-spirited behaviour is the 'spirit of system', which may infect the leader's public spirit and induce him to attempt to 'new-model the constitution' (TMS VI.ii.2.15) rather than 're-establish and improve' it. The chapter reaches the cautious political conclusion that the 'man whose public spirit is prompted altogether by humanity and benevolence, will respect the established powers and privileges' but this conclusion is based on a moral rather than political analysis of the ideal character of the legislator/statesman as a person characterised by 'humanity and benevolence'. Such a person will distrust political visions of an ideal political system and so will readily settle for second-best political solutions; 'like Solon, when he cannot establish the best system of laws, he will endeavour to establish the best that the people can bear' (TMS VI.ii.2.16).

Although the text of TMS is drawing on the classical discourse of legislators/statesmen, it is largely subsumed within the moral discourse of TMS as examples of heroes and great men who are distinguished by their personal moral qualities. Legislators/statesmen are used at various moments in Part VI to illustrate specific virtues rather than any juridical or political qualities; here in section ii, chapter 2, they are used to illustrate 'humanity and benevolence'. In this way, the character of the legislator/statesman is largely depoliticised by the moral discourse of TMS. The concluding paragraph of this chapter grudgingly recognises that the statesman must inevitably have recourse to 'some general, and even systematical, idea of the perfection of policy and law' (TMS VI.ii.2.18) but the text distrusts such ideals as a guide to action. Comparing political society with a game of chess, TMS argues that the legislator/statesman errs if he thinks that he can control the pieces on the 'great chess-board of human society' and it castigates the man of system as the prime perpetrator of this error (TMS VI.ii.2.17). But, this analogy also reveals the moral rather than political conception of society that is at work in TMS. In a game of chess, the pieces have 'no other principle of motion' than that which the chess-player determines, but in human society every chess-piece is an autonomous agent having 'a principle of motion of its own'. This underlying conception of autonomous human agency in TMS is a moral conception deriving from the moral autonomy of the person and exemplified by the dialogism of conscience and moral judgment. It stands entirely apart from political discourses dominated by the legislator/statesman in which individual human agency is subordinated to political organisation and objectives.[69]

This means that the text's engagement with the legislator/statesman in TMS is predominantly a moral engagement, where moral judgments are offered on the individual behaviour of these acknowledgedly great men. In section iii, which considers the third virtue, self-command, the text offers direct moral judgment on the legislator/statesman. Here it is argued that outstanding success in the world is seldom achieved without a degree of excessive self-admiration, and legislators/statesmen are included within the ranks of the vainglorious: 'the most successful warriors, the greatest

---

69 Cf. 'It is a misfortune of the human condition that legislators are obliged to make laws that oppose even natural feelings . . . This is because the statutes of legislators regard the society more than the citizen, and the citizen more than the man' (Montesquieu 1989, 6.27, p. 528).

statesmen and legislators, the eloquent founders and leaders of the most numerous and most successful sects and parties; have many of them been, not more distinguished for their very great merit, than for a degree of presumption and self-admiration altogether disproportioned even to that very great merit'. For those who became successful, 'this presumption has often betrayed them into a vanity that approached almost to insanity and folly' (TMS VI.iii.28). To the wise man, such excessive self-estimation and popular adulation must always appear shallow; 'To a real wise man the judicious and well-weighed approbation of a single wise man, gives more heartfelt satisfaction than all the noisy applauses of ten thousand ignorant though enthusiastic admirers' (TMS VI.iii.31).[70]

The one virtue that is absent from this systematic discussion of the virtues in Part VI is that of justice. A passing reference to justice is provided in just one paragraph in the Introduction to section ii of Part VI, but it is explained that this is the subject of natural jurisprudence, 'concerning which it belongs not to our present subject to enter into any detail' (para. 2). This paragraph continues with some remarks on the 'perfectly innocent and just man', but there is no mention of the legislator/statesman. The entire omission of any discussion of the importance of justice as one of the virtues relevant to the legislator/statesman, or of any discussion of jurisprudence in relation to the activities of the legislator/statesman, further underlines the extent of the depoliticisation of this category that is taking place in this Part of TMS. The scattered references to the legislator/statesman in Part VI of TMS cannot therefore provide textual support for interpretations of the jurisprudence underlying LJ.

The reading presented here points to the distinct discursive specificity of both the expression 'the science of a legislator' in WN and the references to the legislator/statesman in TMS. In both cases, the meaning of Smith's texts has been explored in terms of their own specific discursive conditions which structure the argument and place limits on what is being said at any time. According to this reading, the meaning of the legislator/statesman is different in WN and in TMS, and neither of them can legitimately be used to provide support for an interpretation of LJ. This itself casts doubt on the extent to which LJ can be used as a 'bridge' between TMS and WN. Such an ascription by other commentators has been based on a privileging of the concept of justice in Adam Smith's writings, which is then used to effect a

---

[70] Earlier in section ii, chapter 2, it is argued that statesmen are more likely to be motivated by national interests rather than by public benevolence. Although the 'most extensive public benevolence which can commonly be exerted' is that of statesmen who maintain the balance of power among neighbouring countries and preserve 'peace and tranquillity', the text hastens to assure the reader that generally the statesmen 'who plan and execute such treaties, have seldom any thing in view, but the interest of their respective countries' (TMS VI.ii.2.6).

reading across the disparate discursive structures of TMS, LJ and WN. It has been argued above, however, that justice in TMS plays a subordinate role and is designated a second-order moral virtue. Thus, justice does not have the discursive power to unify the three texts and situate them all on the same plane of moral discourse. This conclusion also casts doubt on the politicisation of Adam Smith's writings implied by the general descriptor of the 'science of a statesman or legislator'.[71] Instead of stressing the discursive priority of politics (broadly conceived) for Adam Smith's discourse, the reading offered in this chapter has emphasised the need to read each of Smith's texts within its own discursive framework.

5

The Stoicism of natural jurisprudence had traditionally focused upon the individual moral agent's reason as the source of knowledge about natural law and what is just behaviour. Given the moral foundations of this natural law in the individual agent's use of reason, it could truly be said that justice was one of the virtues; this holds both in terms of the moral character of justice as the obligation not to harm others, and also in the moral basis of justice itself founded in *oikeiosis* and benevolence. In this sense, there is no divergence between the moral vocabulary of Stoicism and the natural law jurisprudential vocabulary of just behaviour, or between *virtus* and *ius*. TMS and LJ rejected this notion of natural jurisprudence in so far as it was grounded in individual moral judgment, although these texts accepted the natural law primacy of the individual agent as the constitutive element of civil society. The negative duty of not injuring others remains central but, corresponding with the shift from a moral to a legal conception of law, the import of this injunction changes from a moral injunction to perform duties for others to a legalistic conception that the good order of society strictly forbids certain forms of behaviour. This shift in Smith's discourse amounts to a decoupling of moral and jurisprudential discourses which had been fused in earlier natural law writing. The move in Hutcheson's moral philosophy in presenting the ethics separately from the law of nature prepared the way for the separation of TMS from LJ, but in Hutcheson's work the consistency of the moral basis of the ethics and of the law of nature is achieved by the role of reason working alongside that of the moral sense in the configuration of conscience.[72] In Smith's discourse, the lower-order moral status accorded to the rule-governed nature of the virtue of justice

---

71 Stimson (1989) presents a criticism of attempts to recover a systematic theory of politics in Smith's writings.
72 Hutcheson 1747, II.1–3: 'That inward power called *Conscience*, so much talked of, is either this very moral sense or faculty we have explained, or includes it as its most essential part; since without this sense we could discern no moral qualities. But when this is presupposed,

meant that the account of moral philosophy became structurally detached from the account of jurisprudence. Following the importance of individual moral judgment in the areas of beneficence (the imperfect rights) and self-command as represented by the dialogic model of the impartial spectator, the negative virtue of justice for the individual moral agent became demoted in a moral sense, as it simply required obedience to the positive laws of the country. In terms of maintaining the order and security of society, however, justice is the most important of the virtues and must be secured at all costs by the positive system of laws of the country, and could not be left to the uncertainties of the operation of the impartial spectator mechanism with its troubled relation between nature and reason.

In TMS and LJ, justice is construed as the duty not to harm others, and individual subjective claim rights are derivative of this prior obligation. Though the moral basis of the laws of a country are deduced from their congruence with the response of the impartial spectator, this is presented in the form of a moral defence of original legal principles rather than as the means by which day-to-day legal decisions are made. The general principles underlying the laws of a country are ideally congruent with the impartial spectator's views, but the laws themselves will evolve gradually in response to changing historical conditions. The province of the legislator as the guardian of the political and moral order, or as the initiator or embodiment of statute law, is thus greatly diminished in this scheme of things. TMS is deeply suspicious of the moral probity and wisdom of the political leaders of men, and its framework of analysis is denominated in terms of an individual moral autonomy that is resistant to the imposition of political and moral schemes from above or beyond that domain of autonomous moral action. LJ's theoretical framework also resists a role for a guiding legislator; the emphasis on the historical parameters of different forms of civil government, and the gradualness and contingency of historical experience, belie an active function for the legislator.

The programme for economic reform made famous by *The Wealth of Nations* raises questions about the need for changes at the level of statute law, but in order to consider this, it is first necessary to examine the economic arguments presented in LJ and in WN. The following two chapters will examine these arguments, and in the course of this they will also consider the terms of the economic debates within which criticisms of the role of statute law and the legislator/statesman could be articulated.

---

our reason will show what external actions are laudable or censurable according as they evidence good or evil affections of soul' (II.3.I; p. 125).

6
THE EMERGENCE OF *THE WEALTH OF NATIONS*

1

The relationship between the economic analysis in LJ and WN has been extensively discussed in the secondary literature. The consensus now is that there is a continuity of analysis and concern to be found in the two accounts, a view summarised in the editors' Introduction to WN:

> It will be obvious that that section of the lectures [i.e. LJ] which deals with 'cheapness and plenty' does in fact contain many of the subjects which were to figure in the WN. It also appears that many of his central ideas were already present in a relatively sophisticated form: ideas such as equilibrium price, the working of the allocative mechanism, and the associated concept of the 'natural balance' of industry.
>
> (WN, Introduction, p. 22)[1]

Thus the consensus now amongst economists is that the evidence of the early works (including the *Early Draft* (ED) of WN[2]) reveals that Smith's analysis of natural liberty was based on an account of the competitive market and was developed in its essentials prior to his visit to France and the writing of WN.[3] Smith himself was apparently anxious to establish priority

---

1 The Introduction goes on to point out that in spite of this common core, significant sections in WN were entirely absent from LJ but there is no suggestion that these additional sections in any way affect the interpretation of the material that can be seen in embryo form in the early works, pp. 22–34.

2 Published as Appendix to LJ, pp. 562–81; hereafter referred to as ED.

3 Earlier Schumpeter (1954) and Kauder (1953) had argued that the analysis of WN was inferior to that of LJ with its more explicit emphasis on utility and scarcity as determinants of price. Cannan's adamant contention that nothing of central significance in WN could be attributed to Smith's knowledge of physiocratic theories has also contributed to this consensus interpretation of a basic continuity between LJ and WN (Cannan 1950, p. xxx). The current editors, however, emphasise the importance of physiocratic influence (Introduction, pp. 31–3), as do A.S. Skinner (1979, pp. 114–29) and Winch (1965, pp. 11–12). The presence of an agricultural bias has been noted in a number of commentaries (e.g. Koebner 1959, p. 390; Lindgren 1973, pp. 127–8; Caton 1985; Persky 1989), but the significance of this for the overall economic argument of WN has not been extensively addressed in the secondary

for his economic arguments,[4] and this sign of authorial intentionality has been taken as additional evidence of the basic continuity of analysis from LJ through ED to WN. This view of an underlying continuity is also accepted by other intellectual historians who have endeavoured to place WN in its wider political setting, but who have read these three texts as alternative versions of the same set of economic arguments.[5]

Though a concern with economic liberty may be present in both LJ and WN, this does not mean that the theoretical structure of the economic arguments is the same across both texts, nor even that the relation between the state and the economy remains unchanged in the two texts. This chapter will examine these issues and will argue that the discursive structures of the economic analysis in the two texts diverge markedly, and that neither can straightforwardly be construed as an anticipation of the modern analysis of the competitive market based on a scarcity of resources.

2

The economic sections of LJ occur under the heading 'police' (or 'policy'), a key term in the interventionist discourses of the eighteenth century. Here, LJ is concerned with what is denoted 'opulence', arguing against the view that opulence consists of money or a favourable balance of trade. This corresponds to the familiar view of Smith's writings as the opponent of mercantilism in all its forms,[6] but the terms and theoretical basis of this opposition deserve scrutiny.

Opulence is presented as the 'object' of police, but this usage echoes the language deployed in state interventionist discourses. Describing opulence as the state's 'object' reveals that the state in question takes responsibility for 'promoting' or 'introducing' opulence; the government is 'desirous of promoting the opulence of the state. This produces what we call police. Whatever regulations are made with respect to the trade, commerce, agriculture, manufactures of the country are considered as belonging to the police' (LJA i.2; also LJB 5), and 'The third thing which is the object of police is the proper means of introducing plenty and abundance into the

---

literature; an exception is McNally (1988, esp. pp. 228–50), which emphasises the agrarian bias of WN which, it is argued, derives from the physiocrats and from classical republicanism in its analysis of agrarian capitalism.

4 Dugald Stewart 'Account of the life and writings of Adam Smith', p. 322, in Adam Smith (1980); first read to the Royal Society of Edinburgh, 1793.

5 For example, Hont and Ignatieff (1983b) and Hont (1983), which focus not on the allocative role of the competitive market, but on the potential of an internationally competitive market economy to provide a relatively high standard of living for its labouring classes in spite of the unequal distribution of property within society.

6 The coherence of the term 'mercantilism' has been much disputed, along with the issue of the extent to which Adam Smith's account of it amounts to a gross distortion. See, for

country . . .' (LJA vi.7). Thus, the language of LJ does not challenge the state's right and duty to promote opulence; what it does is challenge 'the proper means to produce opulence', and so the concept of opulence in LJ still has something of a statist connotation. The opulence of a state, however, consists not in foreign treasure or money, but in 'plenty and abundance':

> That state is opulent where the necessaries and conveniencies of life are easily come at, whatever otherwise be its condition, and nothing else can deserve the name of opulence but this comeattibleness. That is, a state is opulent when by no great pains and a proper application of industry these things may be easily obtained; and this whether money or other things of that sort abound or not.
>
> (LJA vi.33–4)

Thus, by stressing at the outset the place of police with respect to the design of government, LJ is still situated to some degree within a traditional discourse that discussed opulence or economic well-being as an attribute of a state whose duty it was to 'promote' the desired end by an appropriate 'police'. The challenge of LJ to the orthodox view of a state's object was to redefine the nature of opulence as 'cheapness and plenty' rather than a favourable balance on foreign trade,[7] but the preparedness to engage within the terms of the old discourse about national viability in trade is evidenced by the argument that it is the state that is opulent in these terms that will maintain its foreign commerce and not be undersold by foreign rivals:

> And if it ever happens that of two states, whereof, one is opulent and the other poor, the former loses any branch of its trade by being undersold by the other who can afford it at a less price, the opulence of the former can never be the cause of it . . . As a rich merchant can always afford to under-sell a poor one, so can a rich nation one of less wealth.
>
> (LJA vi.34)[8]

Here, LJ may be viewed in terms of an economic debate of the times which revolved around the question as to whether advanced commercial societies could maintain their international trading advantage over poorer countries whose costs of production were thought to be lower. A longstanding issue within the mercantilist literature had concerned the extent to which prosperity itself contained the seeds of its own decay. Partly

---

example, Viner (1937, chapters 1, 2); Letwin (1963); Coleman (1969, 1980); Rashid (1980b, 1987).

[7] 'For it is not this money which makes the opulence of a nation, but the plenty of food, cloaths, and lodging which is circulated' (LJA vi.127).

[8] LJB even appears to accept the mercantilist policy conclusion concerning the need to export manufactured goods and import rude produce (LJB 319–20). It is largely in relation to the monetary form of the mercantilist argument that LJB objects to this prescription.

THE EMERGENCE OF *THE WEALTH OF NATIONS*

this had to do with the monetary consequences of a prolonged balance of trade surplus which, it was recognised, would tend to increase prices, thus rendering the nation less competitive on international markets with the long-term result that the balance of trade would deteriorate.[9] It also had to do with the ever-recurrent fear of 'luxury', that is, the consumption and importation of foreign goods which would harm both the balance of trade and the nation's morals.[10]

In the mid-eighteenth century, debate focused on whether the position of any individual country in the international trading system was inherently unstable, in that increasing national wealth and a balance of trade surplus would set in motion a series of economic and moral effects that would reverse this process.[11] Thus, national economic prosperity, together with the political power that accompanied it, was seen by some writers as an inherently fragile and temporary state of affairs which required astute state management – or specifically a legislator – to postpone or avert the process of decline that would otherwise occur. This debate partly connects up with classical and Machiavellian notions of the inevitable decline and decay of civilisations and trading republics,[12] but it was also lodged securely within a mercantilist discourse which examined the extent to which individual nations could consistently pursue increased national wealth within an international arena in which foreign trade was privileged as the source of increasing wealth.[13] Hutcheson's *Short Introduction to Moral Philosophy* (first published 1747) argued that the effects of luxury would be higher wages and therefore higher prices, which would reduce exports and so harm the balance of trade (Hutcheson 1969, III.8, p.322). In Cantillon's *Essay on the Nature of Trade in General*, probably written in the late 1720s but not published until 1755, the trading ascendancy of a nation was seen as naturally ephemeral. A positive balance of trade, the object of policy, would secure an influx of precious metals but, in stimulating economic activity and raising prices, this would inevitably lead in time to a loss of competitiveness and hence a reversal of the process of prosperity into its opposite of a period of decline: 'When a State has arrived at the highest point of wealth (I assume always that the comparative wealth of States consists principally in the respective quantities of money which they possess) it will inevitably fall into poverty by the ordinary course of things' (Cantillon 1931, p. 185). The

---

9 For example, see Mun (1967, p. 17; first published 1664). This enabled Mun to argue that the export of money would be beneficial as it would reduce the inflationary consequences of a favourable balance of trade. Viner (1937, pp. 49–51, 85), discusses a range of other expedients suggested in the mercantilist literature, such as hoarding and turning money into plate.
10 For example, see Mun (1967, pp. 26, 72–3).
11 Accounts of this debate may be found in Low (1952), Rotwein (1970, pp. lviii–lix), and Hont (1983).
12 Pocock (1975), Hont (1983).
13 Viner (1937, pp. 83–7).

influx of money stimulates 'a habit of spending' and it is this 'luxury' that precipitates the eventual decline: increased spending has the beneficial effect of increasing employment, but it produces the rise in prices which eventually leads to the reversal into economic decline. The inevitable cycle of economic activity is thus linked with the debates on 'luxury' as a cause of national economic decline: 'When money becomes too plentiful in the State, Luxury will instal itself and the State will fall into decay' (Cantillon 1931, p. 193).[14]

David Hume's essays 'Of commerce' and 'Of money' in his *Political Discourses* (1752, 1758) argued that the high price of labour, as well as the plenty of money, would increase the price of exports from rich nations and so put them at a disadvantage in foreign trade. 'Of commerce' expresses the unmercantilist view that a nation may yet continue great and powerful even though its foreign trade may be lost: 'When the affairs of the society are once brought to this situation, a nation may lose most of its foreign trade, and yet continue a great and powerful people' (Hume 1970, p. 14).[15] The orthodoxy of the day, however, still identified foreign trade as a vital source of wealth; in this case it was of paramount importance for a country to maintain its international trading viability by a series of measures designed to control the domestic price level, encourage export trades, and discourage imports.[16] The later essay 'Of money' presents as a benign outcome, a 'happy concurrence of causes in human affairs', that trading wealth should not ultimately be monopolised by a single nation (Hume 1970, p. 34). It has been argued that this may be understood in terms of Hume's Scottish identification with the poor country as opposed to a rich country such as England, in so far as the relatively underdeveloped Scotland of his day would stand to gain long-term benefits from its greater absorption into foreign trade following the Act of Union in 1707.[17] But from the perspective of the rich country, a sanguine response to this outcome is based on Hume's breaking with the mercantilist presupposition that foreign trade was the main (or indeed only) source of wealth.

---

14 Cantillon considers whether the prince or 'legislator' (la législature) should withdraw some money from circulation in order to prevent prices from rising too much, or whether he should take political advantage of the short-term strength of the state by a policy of national aggrandisement: 'And all things considered they do not perhaps so badly in working to perpetuate the glory of their reigns and administrations, and to leave monuments of their power and wealth; for since, according to the natural course of humanity, the State must collapse of itself they do but accelerate its fall a little' (Cantillon 1931, pp. 185–6).
15 Postlethwayt (1757, pp. 350–4) argued that the monetary consequences of a balance of trade surplus would ultimately check foreign trade whereas Wallace (1758, pp. 34–8) argued against Hume on the grounds that a rich country can always undersell a poorer one. Both these texts endorse the possibility that a state's prosperity may be maintained in the event of a cessation of foreign trade.
16 Steuart's *Inquiry* (first published 1767) represented this viewpoint and saw as harmful the inevitable deterioration in foreign competitiveness for the rich country.
17 See Hont (1983).

Just as the jurisprudential argument of LJ made redundant the moral and political supervision of the legislator, so too the economic analysis detached itself from this discourse pertaining to the cycle of decline of trading nations. First, LJ argued that the balance of trade whether favourable or not was irrelevant as an object of policy, and that what was important was the balance of consumption and production (LJA vi.135–71), an argument that was carried over into WN (WN IV.i–ii). Second, it denied that a rich country would suffer from high prices compared with a poor country. LJ argues that the rich country, by definition a producer of plenty and low-price abundance, can always produce goods for sale at a lower price than a poor country, unless it is hampered by inappropriate taxes or other burdens laid on by the state. The argument here is partly definitional and partly substantive. On the definitional aspect, the opulent state is defined to be one where goods are cheap as 'these terms plenty and cheapness are in a manner synonymous, as cheapness is a necessary consequence of plenty' (LJA vi.7; also LJB 205).[18] It is in this context that the famous reference to water and diamonds was introduced where water 'by its abundance costs nothing but the uptaking' and diamonds 'give an immense price' (LJA vi.8; also LJB 206). The substantive aspect concerns the ways in which the development of the arts and businesses of a developed society conduce to a greater productiveness which, together with the benefits deriving from the division of labour and invention of machines, ensures a standard of living even for the poor labourer that is far in excess of that enjoyed even by a savage prince. For this reason, 'the price of labour comes to be dear while at the same time work is cheap, and these two things, which in the eyes of the vulgar appear altogether incompatible, are in this evidently very consistent, as the improvement of arts renders things so much easier done that a great wage can be afforded to the artizan and the goods still be at a low price' (LJA vi.33; LJB 214–15).[19] Thus, opulence is defined as a low-price, high-wage situation where the necessaries of life are easily affordable by the working population. As the division of labour is dependent on the extent of the market, commerce is unambiguously advantageous because it provides for an extension of the market far beyond the confines of the local market and so contributes to the provision of low-price opulence: 'Hence also we may see the great benefit of commerce, not as it brings in money into the country, which is but a fancifull advantage, but as it promotes industry, manufactures, and opulence and plenty made by it at home' (LJA vi.66; LJB 222–3). Thus, by defining wealth as low-price opulence, LJ reinterprets the significance of foreign trade as a means of extending the market and encouraging the division of labour.

---

18 'For plenty and cheapness are one and the same' (LJA vi.76).
19 It was not the money price of labour that was relevant, but its real price in terms of the ease or difficulty with which the necessaries of life could be earned (LJA ii.33); alternatively 'the

Crucially, it is this argument based on a specific definition of opulence which is used in the later section that criticises any police that causes the market price to diverge from the natural price: 'Whatever policy tends to raise the market price above the naturall one diminishes publick opulence and naturall wealth of the state. For dearness and scarcity, abundance and cheapness, are we may say synonimous terms' (LJA vi.84; LJB 230). It is for this reason that taxes and monopolies were deemed harmful as, by raising the price of commodities, they diminished opulence: 'all taxes on industry must diminish the national opulence as they raise the market price of the commodities' (LJA vi.85; LJB 230–1).[20] The case against taxes and monopolies is, therefore, that they are detrimental because they raise prices and this is inimical to low-price opulence. But any police which *reduces* the market price of any particular good below the natural price is also detrimental on the grounds that the artificial abundance caused for this one good will be more than offset by the artificial scarcity implied for other related goods whose price will therefore be higher than they would otherwise be (LJA vi.91–7; LJB 232). Taxes or bounties also upset the 'natural balance of industry' where the 'industrious people naturally apply themselves to the different branches of trade just in proportion to the demand that is for those commodities. Whatever breaks this naturall balance by giving either an extraordinary discouragement by taxes and duties, or an extraordinary encouragement by bounties or otherwise, tends to hurt the national opulence' (LJA vi.92; LJB 233).[21] The natural balance of industry is, thus, defined as the composition of industry where the supply of goods is equal to the demand for them. Its importance for the national opulence, however, derives from its effect on prices; as opulence is defined as low-price plenty, anything which puts up prices is deemed injurious to opulence, and this is just as true for bounties as it is for taxes: 'Whenever therefore you call more hands than are naturally engaged in it to any particular business, you sink indeed the price of that commodity to the foreign merchant, but you raise the price or perhaps of all others proportionably at home . . . The price of that commodity falls, but those of all or some others rises' (LJA vi.94–5). A bounty may improve prospects for the foreign merchant but at the cost of increased prices at home and must therefore be injurious to the object of police which is to promote low-price opulence. The example provided is of the corn bounty which reduces the price of corn but raises the price of

---

opulence of a state depends on the proportion betwixt the moneyd price of labour and that of the commodities to be purchased by it. If it can purchase a great quantity then it is opulent; if a small then it is poor' (LJA vi.52).

20 'as all monopolies raise the price of commodities they must be detrimental to the opulence of the nation' (LJA vi.87).

21 In the text of LJA the penultimate word given is 'naturall' but the editors suggest in a note that it should probably read 'national'.

butchers' meat, horses and transportation, and reduces the extent of the inland commerce (LJA vi.95–7; LJB 234–5).

The analysis of LJ is substantially unchanged in ED. The first chapter is missing in ED but the second chapter, headed 'Of the nature and causes of public opulence', reproduces the analysis of LJ in its concern with opulence where labour is dear but the product of labour is cheap,[22] and here it is argued that the opulence of a rich country can never be the cause of its being undersold by a poorer one (ED 12–13). Again the relation between the natural price and the market price is explained, together with its connection with public opulence and the natural balance of industry, such that any interference with the natural balance results in increased prices, even in the case of bounties (ED 31–3).

This discourse based on opulence as low-price plenty is absent from WN. At the end of Book I, chapter iv, in introducing the subsequent three chapters dealing with different aspects of value, the distinction between value in use and value in exchange is referred to in passing. It is stated that goods which have the greatest value in use, such as water, frequently have little value in exchange, and that goods that have a high exchange value such as diamonds, may have little value in use. This is not presented as a paradox or as a problem to be solved; more importantly still, it does not refer to the desirability of low-price abundance as the object of police.

The account of opulence in LJ had hinged on the analysis of the relation between market price and natural price. Although the recompense for labour is the only component of the natural price in LJ, whereas wages, profits and rent enter into the analysis of WN, the formal similarities between the analysis in LJ and WN have been regarded as evidence of a similar underlying analytical structure in the two texts. WN is commended for its greater sophistication in handling a more comprehensive list of individual revenues, and for recognising the significance of profit for the emerging capitalist economy of the eighteenth century.[23] Some commentators have identified a de-emphasis on utility and scarcity as determinants of price in WN,[24] whilst others have argued that these important analytical concepts are fully implicit in the later work.[25] In LJ, this market analysis was linked to the account of opulence which itself formed the basis for the argument against regulations or monopoly practices. Thus, in LJ, the

---

22 In ED, however, the references to the opulence of the 'state' are beginning to be replaced to some degree by references to an 'opulent and commercial society' and 'opulence of society'; for example cf. LJA vi.33–4 with ED 11–12. Further ED here directly links the national opulence with the opulence of the people (e.g. 'National opulence is the opulence of the whole people' (ED 12); this was not stated in this way in LJA).
23 Meek (1967a).
24 Kauder (1953), Schumpeter (1954), Robertson and Taylor (1957), O'Brien (1975, pp. 78–84), and Hutchison (1988, pp. 363–6, 377–8).
25 Bowley (1973, pp. 133–42), Kaushil (1973), Hollander (1973, ch. 4; 1987, ch. 4).

market analysis was closely linked to the prescriptive policy arguments, but this is not the case in WN. Competitive prices are the subject of Book I, chapter vii, perhaps one of the best-known chapters in the whole of WN as it is the one that economists most admire from a technical viewpoint as the clearest anticipation of modern price theory. This chapter analyses the relation between the natural price of commodities and their market price where there are three main forms of revenue, viz. wages, profit and rent, and it analyses the movement of market price around the natural price showing how the market price 'gravitates' as it were to the natural price. It is this chapter which many economists have understood to contain the analytical core of the system of natural liberty as it describes the technical operation of what is thought to be a competitive market. Analytically, the interest of this chapter has been seen to lie in its explanation of market equilibrium where the natural price is the equilibrium price where demand is equal to supply. Seen in this way, it is easy to conclude that the function of this chapter is to demonstrate the efficiency property of competition and to provide the analytical foundation for the system of natural liberty, especially when it is read through the perspective provided by LJ and ED, where the corresponding passages on the relation between market and natural price contain the argument that public opulence is secured where the natural and market prices are equal and the natural balance of industry is not disturbed.

The origin of Book I, chapter vii, in the earlier passages in LJ and ED is striking, but so is the absence of any reference to opulence, cheapness and plenty, or to the natural balance of industry; in other words, the crucial theoretical concepts underpinning the efficiency arguments which had earlier led to the conclusion that economic regulations were harmful, are absent from the parallel passages in WN. It was argued above that the concept of opulence was central to the economic argument of LJ and ED; there, any regulations such as taxes, monopolies, bounties and corporations which prevented the market price from settling at the level of the natural price were harmful on the grounds that they raised domestic prices (relative to wages) higher than would otherwise have been the case, and in this way led to a diminution of opulence. Without a definition of opulence of some sort against which the various outcomes in chaper vii can be assessed, it is impossible to make any judgment on the efficiency of the potential outcomes of the competitive market process.[26] In LJ and ED, the concept of opulence had supplied this element, but it is absent from chapter vii.

---

26 The contrast with Léon Walras' *Elements of Pure Economics* with which Smith's chapter vii in Book I is frequently compared, is instructive. In part II, lesson 8 (Walras 1954), where welfare claims about the competitive outcome are advanced, the concept of effective utility (i.e. total utility) is used as that which is maximised under certain conditions.

Chapter vii does include the argument, however, that the natural price or the price of free competition is 'the lowest which can be taken, not upon every occasion, indeed, but for any considerable time together' (WN I.vii.27; also para. 6), and so it might perhaps be thought that this low-price argument constitutes the efficiency claim in favour of competitive market outcomes. In LJ and ED it had been argued that plenty and abundance were an object of police, and that low prices were synonymous with abundance, and it might be thought that this emphasis on low prices persists into WN. But, the point to notice here is that in spite of the prominence of such arguments in LJ and ED, these arguments again are absent from WN. These references linking cheapness with opulence, the object of police in the earlier works, are missing from WN, and in chapter vii itself, the crucial chapter on the market, there are no efficiency statements of the kind that feature so prominently in the earlier works. As shown above, LJ had discussed the harmful effects of artificial devices to increase prices (LJA vi.84; LJB 230), but in chapter vii there are no arguments of this sort linking the natural price to public opulence and wealth, or linking abundance or wealth with cheapness. The same marked absence applies to the other efficiency criterion of LJ and ED, the natural balance of industry, which is linked to the notion of opulence as the lowest possible price regime; in WN these earlier arguments linking the natural balance with public opulence are not repeated.[27]

The absence from chapter vii of the key terms opulence, natural balance, cheapness and abundance, provides a striking contrast with LJ and ED, and suggests that a close examination of the texts cannot sustain the interpretation that the allocative implications of WN I.vii derive from the analysis of LJ and ED. Even more remarkable is the absence of any alternative efficiency concepts in chapter vii which could sustain the standard interpretation that this chapter provides the core of the argument in favour of natural liberty. Although later commentators have concluded that this chapter shows that the competitive price mechanism leads to an optimal allocation of resources or some other such optimal outcome, there is nothing in the chapter which actually attempts to demonstrate this.

Further, nowhere in the analysis of the market in LJ and WN is there an understanding of the later neoclassical concept of scarcity, a concept which is essential for the analysis of the price mechanism as allocation analysis. It is often argued that Smith's analysis of the market as an allocative mechanism shows a firm if at times 'implicit' understanding of the significance of scarcity,[28] but the presence of the word 'scarcity' does not by itself denote

---

27 Further, when the concept of a 'natural balance of industry' is applied later in WN, it refers not to the balance of demand and supply across industries, but to the balance of sectors. This is discussed below in chapter 7 (note 37).
28 Kaushil (1973), Hollander (1973, ch. 4; 1987, ch. 4). Dissenting voices have been Schumpeter (1954, pp 308–9), Kauder (1953), and Robertson and Taylor (1957).

the presence of the later neoclassical concept of generalised scarcity which pertains to all positively priced goods in a competitive market, and which underlies the need for an efficient allocative mechanism. There is, of course, an awareness in Smith's work that goods in short supply relative to demand will command a high price significantly above the normal or natural price, and this had long been recognised and had indeed been commonplace in the literature for some time.[29] It is to this restricted class of goods that the term 'scarce' was applied, and it is in this narrow sense (i.e. 'specific scarcity') that it was argued that 'scarcity' gives value to a good or contributes to its high price.[30] In this pre-neoclassical discourse, these references to 'scarcity' (i.e. specific scarcity) are regularly contrasted with abundant, low-priced goods which may or may not include the limiting case of a zero-priced good such as water. Thus in Smith's writings on the market, references to 'scarcity' denote a local not a general analysis: 'The scarcity on the other hand raises the price immoderately' (LJA vi.71) and 'If the commodity be scarce, the price is raised, but if the quantity be more than is sufficient to supply the demand, the price falls' (LJB 227–8). In WN, the word 'scarcity' denotes the same concept as in LJ, for example: 'The scarcity of hands occasions a competition among masters, who bid against one another, in order to get workmen . . .' (WN I.viii.17, also para. 24), and 'A produce of which the value is principally derived from its scarcity, is necessarily degraded by its abundance' (WN.I.xi.c.34). Sometimes the word 'scarcity' refers to the state of the harvest where it refers specifically to grain: 'Both in years of plenty and in years of scarcity, therefore, the bounty . . .' (WN I.xi.g.14).

Thus in WN, the later neoclassical concept of scarcity as the defining characteristic of 'the economic problem' is absent. But, even in its restricted meaning of scarcity as specific or local scarcity, the word 'scarcity' is absent from Book I, chapter vii, the obvious place for it. The absence of the word 'scarcity' from chapter vii has generated a good deal of discussion; at one time it was thought that Smith had abandoned the utility/scarcity approach of the natural lawyers, but the consensus now is that the concept of scarcity is implicitly present in chapter vii even though the word itself is absent.[31] But this constitutes a double misreading: first, it construes the word 'scarcity' in LJ to be the same as the later concept of generalised scarcity; second, it imputes the presence of the later concept of generalised scarcity to chapter vii, which contains neither the word nor the concept. But, this still leaves unexplained the absence of the word 'scarcity' (i.e. the concept of specific

---

29 The early utility/scarcity approach is associated with the natural law writings of Grotius, Pufendorf and Hutcheson. Scholars have also found it in earlier scholastic literature; cf. de Roover (1955, 1967) and Langholm (1979).
30 The neoclassical concept of generalised scarcity is differentiated from specific scarcity in Brown (1987).
31 In so far as the allocative mechanism presupposes the existence of scarcity.

scarcity) from chapter vii of WN in view of its prominence in LJ in the account of natural price. In LJ, scarcity and abundance were synonymous with high prices and low prices respectively, and this was part of the argument that the primary object of police was to secure opulence, that is, cheapness and plenty. But this 'object of police' was not argued for in WN. Further, in LJ, this argument was also associated with the distinction between water and diamonds as an illustration of the necessary relation between abundance and low prices on the one hand and scarcity and high prices on the other.[32] In WN, the analysis of natural liberty was no longer based on the analysis of cheapness and opulence, and this meant that the earlier analysis linking scarcity with high price, as in the case of diamonds, no longer had a special place in the market analysis.[33] But this also signals that chapter vii has a different theoretical orientation from the sections on price in LJ.

The argument of LJ concerning the importance of low-price abundance as an object of police was applied to the contemporary debate concerning the longer-term trajectory and viability of rich trading nations. LJ accepted unquestioningly the view that foreign commerce was beneficial, although not for reasons connected with the balance of trade or the desirability of importing precious metals into the country. During the 1750s and 1760s, however, Quesnay published a number of articles in which the notion of a low-price abundance was criticised. The theoretical basis for Quesnay's arguments was the priority accorded to agriculture for a landed nation wishing to exchange its agricultural products for manufactured products. Quesnay argued that the key to opulence lay in abundance plus dearness: 'Valuelessness plus abundance does not at all equal wealth. Dearness plus dearth equals poverty. Abundance plus dearness equals opulence' ('Corn', in Meek 1963a, p. 84; also 'The General Maxims', ibid., p. 235). Abundance itself denoted poverty if it was accompanied by low prices, and so Quesnay, in his essay, 'Men' (Meek 1963a, p. 94) emphasised the importance of *bon prix*, the good price or the proper price that would support this opulence, rather than *bon marché*, or cheapness of goods which would undermine it.[34] WN argued that artificially high prices were harmful and distorted the pattern of productive activity, and also that the natural price was the lowest price that could be viable in the

---

32 'In the following part of this discourse we are to confine ourselves to the consideration of cheapness or plenty, or, which is the same thing, the most proper way of procuring wealth and abundance. Cheapness is in fact the same with plenty. It is only on account of the plenty of water that it is so cheap as to be got for the lifting, and on account of the scarcity of diamonds (for their real use seems not yet to be discovered) that they are so dear' (LJB 205–6; also LJA vi.7–8).
33 This distinction is referred to at WN I.iv.13.
34 'That people do not believe that cheapness [bon marché] of produce is profitable to the lower classes; for a low price of produce causes a fall in their wages, reduces their well-being, makes less work or remunerative occupations available for them, and reduces the

long run, but the overall theoretical structure of WN was not based on the identity of opulence with low-price abundance as LJ had been.

3

WN argues against both the mercantile system and the agricultural system. Its opposition both to the mercantilist notion that a surplus on the balance of trade is a source of wealth, and the physiocratic notion that agriculture is the only productive sector, is well recognised. But, in mounting a critical attack that would be effective against both these systems, WN reconceptualised them in such a way that they could both be designated as occupying the same theoretical space, but one from which WN could then detach itself. Accordingly, these two systems are characterised in terms that apply to each the mirror-image error of the other; by casting these two systems as promulgating opposite errors, WN constructs them as joint occupants of a theoretical space subject to critical attack from a position that is external to it. A crucial theoretical concept that is used to effect this transformation is that of 'police'. It was argued above that the frame of reference for the 'police' of LJ was the proper provenance of a state's duties with respect to promoting the 'opulence' of a country; this provenance was defined as the area of 'police', that is, the promotion of cheapness and plenty. But, in WN the word 'police' is no longer used in this sense, nor as a general self-description, but as a term referring to those systems of state economic regulation to which WN is opposed. These systems of state regulation are characterised as sharing the same fault of not treating all sectors of the economy equally, but of favouring a privileged sector at the expense of the others. In the 'Introduction and Plan of the Work', it is explained that the 'policy' of Europe is the subject of the third book which considers the plans followed by different nations, and it is here that WN signals its symmetrical characterisation of the mercantile and agricultural systems: 'The policy of some nations has given extraordinary encouragement to the industry of the country; that of others to the industry of the towns. Scarce any nation has dealt equally and impartially with every sort of industry' (para. 7). Thus, whereas the mercantile system had favoured towns and the agricultural system had favoured agriculture, WN is to promulgate a system that treats each sector impartially. Hence, the word 'police' in WN is not used as a self-description as it had been in LJ. In WN, the word 'police' denotes systems of economic state regulations that favour the industry either of the towns or of the country. As WN is generically opposed to such systems, the term 'police' comes to acquire a derogatory sense that was entirely absent in LJ. It

---

nation's revenue' (Quesnay 'Remarks on the tableau oeconomique', in Meek 1963a, pp. 112–13; also p. 122).

is in this derogatory sense that the word 'police' is used in the context of the 'regulations of police' (WN I.vii.20, 29; xi.p. 8), the 'rules of police' (WN I.x.c.9), and the 'policy of Europe' (WN Intro. 7; I.x.a.2; x.b.8; x.c.1, 3, 32, 33, 41). It is also used to denote agricultural policy in the context of the policy of named countries (China at WN IV.ix.40; ancient Egypt and Indostan at WN IV.ix.42, the ancient republics of Greece and Rome at WN IV.ix.47; Asia at V.i.d.17) and to denote the police 'of a particular town' (WN V.i.i.3). Thus whereas in LJ, the word 'police' denoted the general heading under which its own discussion of economic topics could be organised, in WN this is no longer the case as the word 'police' is used negatively to denote systems of state regulation to which WN is opposed.

This different use of the word 'police' in WN signals a different discursive structure for WN, where the state is no longer assigned the responsibility for pursuing any 'object of police', whether that object is constituted by the cheapness and plenty of provisions, or by the promotion of towns or agriculture.[35] This does not mean that there is no economic or social role for the state. Commentators have exhaustively listed the different areas in which the state should be involved in addition to the basic trio of 'maintenance of inter-individual justice; defense; and essential "public works," including education' (Viner 1960, p. 59).[36] What it does mean is that WN does not employ that discourse on the economy which included a regulatory role for the state as part of the sphere of operation of the economy. Within the terms of that discourse, the state was conceived as a regulatory state not simply in the sense that it had a political interest in the pursuit of national wealth, or that its intervention was required in the case of specific market failure, but because the proper development of the economy could not be conceptualised independently of the state and its police; in the mercantile and agricultural systems, the state fulfilled a necessary role providing guidance and direction without which the economy was sure to degenerate. WN, however, reconceptualises the economy in such a way that neither

---

35 In TMS, 'police' also carries a regulatory statist meaning, and its celebration there is at odds with the argument of WN. The following statement, for example, could not have occurred in WN: 'When the legislature establishes premiums and other encouragements to advance the linen or woollen manufactures, its conduct seldom proceeds from pure sympathy with the wearer of cheap or fine cloth, and much less from that with the manufacturer or merchant. The perfection of police, the extension of trade and manufactures, are noble and magnificent objects. The contemplation of them pleases us, and we are interested in whatever can tend to advance them' (TMS IV.1.11). Recognising the regulatory dimension of 'police' in TMS also allows a more discriminating interpretation of the passage linking the 'perfection of policy' with the 'statesman': 'Some general, and even systematical, idea of the perfection of policy and law, may no doubt be necessary for directing the views of the statesman. But . . .' (TMS VI.ii.2.18). Such an interpretation would point to the sardonic and ironic tone of this sentence.
36 Viner's article is the classic piece here. Also A.S. Skinner (1979, ch. 9; 1986, pp. 25–8) and Letwin (1988).

the state nor its police is a necessary element in the development of the economy. The question of the extent of state activity is then seen as the degree of state involvement or intervention in something beyond itself, a contingent involvement which may or may not be justified according to certain arguments and practices. Thus the different use of the word 'police' in WN signals the different discursive structure for WN as well as its different policy conclusions.

This discursive shift explains why WN was effectively left without a generic name. The title of WN avoids any generic self-reference referring to itself simply as 'An Inquiry into . . . the Wealth of Nations'; the significant point being that a nation's wealth was now being conceptualised independently of the state and the old policy implications attaching to that, and so LJ's designation of 'police' was no longer appropriate. For the same reason, WN could not be named as an inquiry in 'political oeconomy'. It was argued in chapter 5 that designating the subject-matter of WN as 'political oeconomy' disregards the textual evidence that the term is reserved for the theoretical systems that WN is opposing. The Introduction to Book IV of WN refers to political oeconomy 'as a branch of the science of a statesman or legislator' which 'proposes two distinct objects; first, to provide a plentiful revenue or subsistence for the people, or more properly to enable them to provide such a revenue or subsistence for themselves; and secondly, to supply the state or commonwealth with a revenue sufficient for the publick services'. This statement cannot be taken as a description of the objectives of WN, as WN was arguing *against* all systems that 'propose' or 'enable' forms of enrichment. WN was formulating an alternative system, the system of natural liberty, that was not premised on the directing hand of a legislator/statesman to oversee economic development. Chapter 5 argued that the political resonances of the legislator/statesman were incompatible with the moral theory of TMS and the jurisprudence of LJ but, in addition to this, the economic resonances of the legislator/statesman were incompatible with the argument of WN.

The systems which are unambiguously designated as political oeconomy in WN are the systems of commerce and agriculture, and it was their shared approval of the state's/statesman's duty to oversee the direction of sectoral activity that Book IV was opposing at some length.[37] It was argued above that an issue in mid-eighteenth-century debates was the instability of national economic growth based on foreign trade. Only nine years before the publication of WN, the *Inquiry into the Principles of Political Oeconomy*

---

37 Political economics was 'the art of managing a state' (Letwin 1963, p. 217); see King (1948, pp. 230–1) and Groenewegen (1987) on 'political economy'. Cf. 'Political Oeconomy is concerned with the administration of an aggregated polity by a "sovereign" or "statesman", whose presence is essential to the discourse in providing a unity which is otherwise dispersed among the instances of the economy or the categories that articulate these

was published by Sir James Steuart, in which the account of political oeconomy was premised on the pervasive directing presence of the legislator/statesman. The Introduction to Book IV of WN constitutes a clear reference to Steuart's *Inquiry* which stated that 'The principal object of this science [i.e. political oeconomy] is to secure a certain fund of subsistence for all the inhabitants' (Steuart 1966, vol. I, Intro. p. 17).[38] Steuart's *Inquiry* was based on the importance of a series of balances: for example, the balance between work and demand, and the balance on foreign trade. The significant point about these balances is that they would inevitably deteriorate in the course of progress unless the statesman controlled them. It was thus imperative that the statesman should continually attend to these balances and, if he did not, then his negligence would harm the country. For example, it is argued that the balance between work and demand will not be stable as a country progresses and that the statesman must plan accordingly to subvert the harmful results of this:

> While this gradual increase of people is in proportion to the growing demand for hands, the balance between work and demand is exactly kept up: but as all augmentations must at last come to a stop, when this happens, inconveniences must ensue, greater or less, according to the negligence or attention of the statesman . . .
> (Steuart 1966, II.X, p. 196)

In the case of the balance of trade, the course of wealth and prosperity would raise prices which would entail the loss of foreign markets and so again here 'the statesman should be constantly on his guard to prevent the *subversion of the balance*' (Steuart 1966, II.XVI, p. 240; original emphasis). Thus, the statesman had to exercise constant vigilance in order to provide a series of countermeasures that would prevent the balances from deteriorating.

The other system of political oeconomy referred to in WN is the system of agriculture,[39] and this also included the state as part of its conception of the proper pursuit of wealth. Although the Économistes advocated freedom of trade, this did not signify a passive role for the state. The *tableau économique* was a representation of the economy which privileged the generation of net revenue as a source of taxation for the state, and the conception of the economy as a self-sustaining and progressive system was based on the

---

instances' (Tribe 1978, p. 85). It is thus ironic that modern commentators who wish to retrieve what is thought of as a political dimension to Smith's *œuvre* should foist upon WN the very term that it rejects as a self-description.

38 Also 'In treating every question of political oeconomy, I constantly suppose a statesman at the head of government, systematically conducting every part of it, so as to prevent the vicissitudes of manners, and innovations, by their natural and immediate effects or consequences, from hurting any interest within the commonwealth' (Steuart 1966, I.XIX, p. 122).

39 WN IV.ix.1, 28, 38.

necessary presence of the state in directing economic activities and ensuring the observance of natural law. Not only is the state required to direct activities into agriculture as the only sector which produces a revenue or net product, but movements in this revenue are held to be the outcome and therefore the responsibility of the state: 'Thus a kingdom's population increases or diminishes in the proportion that its revenue increases or diminishes. This diminution or increase does not depend on the people: it is always the result of the policy of the government of a state' (Quesnay's 'Men', in Meek 1963a, p. 96).[40] The importance of state direction may also be seen in the conception of the economy as one where the proper course of development could not be assured unless the state undertook responsibility for directing resources from other sectors into agriculture.[41]

WN entirely distanced itself from these contemporary discourses of state management, of police, and of the statesman as an active agent in the economy. In their place, WN offered a different conception of the economy, one that could function independently of state regulation. The 'system of natural liberty' was opposed to the systems of commerce and agriculture on precisely this ground that the unassisted development and 'natural' progress towards wealth was not only feasible but also the most advantageous, and in formulating this WN challenged conventional views about the place of the state and the statesman in taking responsibility for the overall direction of private industry. Steuart had argued that the statesman would be negligent if he allowed the natural course of events: 'If a statesman should be negligent on this occasion; if he should allow natural consequences to follow upon one another, just as circumstances shall determine . . .' (Steuart 1966, II.X, p. 191).[42] Cantillon had argued that the 'state must collapse of itself' 'according to the natural course of humanity' (Cantillon 1931, pp. 185–7). WN reversed this ordering of natural consequences and state-managed consequences by arguing that natural consequences were

---

[40] 'even the sovereign and his ministers contribute directly and generally to the increase of wealth through their economic government of the state. It is on this, indeed, that the prosperity of the nation depends: but the administration must never lose sight of the true source of the kingdom's revenue' (Quesnay 'Men', in Meek 1963a, p. 98).

[41] The Introduction to Say's *Treatise on Political Economy* criticises earlier 'political economy' for confounding the science of politics with political economy, and it specifically mentions the first chapter in Steuart's *Inquiry*, the sect of the Économistes, and Rousseau's article *Political Economy*. It continues: 'Since the time of Adam Smith, it appears to me, these two very distinct inquiries have been uniformly separated, the term *political economy* being now confined to the science which treats of wealth, and that of *politics*, to designate the relations existing between a government and its people, and the relations of different states to each other' (Say 1971, pp. xv–xvi, original emphasis; this edition first published 1880).

[42] 'Let us now examine what may be the reason why, in a trading and industrious nation, time necessarily destroys the perfect balance between work and demand. We have already pointed out one general cause, to wit, the natural stop which must at last be put to augmentations of every kind. Let us now apply this to circumstances, in order to discover in what manner natural causes operate this stop, either by preventing the increase of work,

beneficial and should not be prevented by a regulating state or statesman. Thus a considerable part of the analysis of WN was directed towards explaining how it was that natural outcomes could be beneficial. In particular, this applies to the 'system of natural liberty', which was counterposed to the mercantile and agricultural systems. At the conclusion of WN, Book IV, a summary of the system of natural liberty is provided in opposition to the systems of commerce and agriculture:

> Every man, as long as he does not violate the laws of justice, is left perfectly free to pursue his own interest his own way, and to bring both his industry and capital into competition with those of any other man, or order of men. The sovereign is completely discharged from a duty, in the attempting to perform which he must always be exposed to innumerable delusions, and for the proper performance of which no human wisdom or knowledge could ever be sufficient; the duty of superintending the industry of private people, and of directing it towards the employments most suitable to the interest of the society.
> (WN IV.ix.51)

Here again the view of the sovereign's duty which Smith is opposing is that of 'superintending the industry of private people' and 'directing it' in the 'interest of society'. It is this conception of regulatory necessity that WN is opposing, not the contingent possibilities for *ad hoc* intervention that have been widely cited in the literature. Thus it is not simply arguments about 'market failure' that WN is contending, but rather well-established arguments based on the supposition of 'system failure' leading to inevitable decay and decline, loss of international markets, or the imbalance of sectors of the economy.[43] An example of what was involved in this regulatory view of the sovereign or statesman is provided in Steuart's *Inquiry*, where it is shown how a statesman might avert system failure by preventing the balance of trade turning against the country; there it is argued that it is the duty of the statesman to direct the output, prices and profits of each branch of industry, together with the habits of industriousness, frugality and luxury of the people. Reversing contemporary providential metaphors, Steuart's *Inquiry* compares a modern state to a watch which is 'continually going wrong' and which needs to be set right by the statesman (Steuart 1966, II.XIII, p. 217), although even Steuart baulks at the phenomenal degree of knowledge required for the statesman to achieve this.[44] WN is

---

on one side of the balance, or the increase of demand, on the other' (Steuart 1966, II.XI, pp. 196–7); cf. also pp. 122, 194, 198).

43 Cf. A.S. Skinner (1989), which points to Steuart's emphasis on market failure.

44 'The mechanism of his administration becomes more complex, and . . . he finds himself so bound up by the laws of his political oeconomy, that every transgression of them runs him into new difficulties' (Steuart 1966, II.XIII, p. 217).

entirely sceptical that any person would have the wisdom or knowledge required for the task, but it argues further that the task is itself misconceived as it is based on the erroneous conception of endemic system failure.

The passage at WN IV.ix.51 also makes reference to the way in which, under a system of natural liberty, every man is free to pursue his own interest. The novelty of the argument of WN however does not hinge on its recognition of the role of self-interest, as opposed to institutional incentives or other-regarding personal virtues such as benevolence. Both systems that WN is opposing also assumed that private action would be determined by the pursuit of private interest. Even Steuart, with his battery of duties and powers for the statesman, argued that this principle of action must be presupposed for a free people: 'The principle of self-interest will serve as a general key to this inquiry . . . This is the main spring, and only motive which a statesman should make use of, to engage a free people to concur in the plans which he lays down for their government' (Steuart 1966, II.Introduction, p. 142, also p. 143). Similarly, in the physiocratic literature it is accepted that individuals will be motivated by self-interest:

> The whole magic of a well-ordered society is that each man works for others, while believing that he is working for himself. This magic, the general character and effects of which are revealed by the subject we are studying, shows us that the Supreme Being bestowed upon us as a father the principles of economic harmony, when he condescended to announce and prescribe them to us, as God, in the form of religious laws.
>
> (Mirabeau 'Rural philosophy', in Meek 1963a, p. 70)

In this conception of economic harmony, the state is the agent responsible for ensuring that society is 'well ordered', so here the role of the state is actually enhanced by the acceptance of the postulate of a harmony of economic interests between the individual and society. Thus, it is not a difference over the importance of self-interest which separates WN from the regulationist texts, or over a belief in the resulting harmony between the pursuit of individual interest and the interest of the state. The crucial difference lies instead in the autonomy of the conception of progress to be found in WN, an autonomy that makes economic progress a self-regulating and independent process.

4

In constituting this new concept of the economic domain, WN refers to every man as free to 'bring both his industry and capital into competition with those of any other man'. This statement highlights the importance of free competition in WN but, in this summary account at the end of Book IV, there is no reference either to competitive *markets* or competitive *prices*, features of WN which have been thought to be central to the core analysis of the system of natural liberty. This may well suggest that these aspects of competition, though central to later understandings of competition, were not central to the innovations of WN and that the system of natural liberty is far removed from modern economic theory. If so, this means that the system of natural liberty needs to be re-examined. This is the subject of the following chapter.

7
THE SYSTEM OF NATURAL LIBERTY

1

It was argued in chapter 2 that WN is characterised by a monologic style in the Bakhtinian sense that there is a single voice at work in the text controlling and structuring the argument. It was also argued that WN operates as a non-moral or amoral discourse in that its arguments and assumptions do not require that economic agents function as moral agents. For this reason, market outcomes are divorced from the operation and oversight of the impartial spectator who is, therefore, absent from WN. This does not mean, however, that market outcomes are unconnected with the issue of justice. One of the points to be examined in the course of this and the final chapter is the relation between justice and market outcomes, but justice here denotes not a truly moral virtue in the dialogic sense, but a lower-order virtue, a rule-governed activity necessary for the orderly material reproduction of society.

This absence of ethical or truly moral concerns from WN is entirely consonant with its monologic style which is pre-eminently well suited to discourses that are rule-governed and systematic, both in the sense that the virtue of justice is a rule-governed activity and in the sense that economic activity and, hence, economic discourse is rule-governed. Both the mercantile system and the agricultural system were based on statist assumptions about the economy as neither of these systems could envisage the notion of an ordered, autonomous process of growth that could function independently of the state's overall economic governance. WN, in putting forward the notion of a system of natural liberty, counterposed political oeconomy with the idea of a rule-govered economic system whose outcome would be beneficial and self-sustaining.

Later sections of this chapter will provide an account of the analytic basis of the system of natural liberty, a system which is delivered in a detached and commanding tone of the authorial voice. But, in the course of WN, this voice adopts a range of different devices. While some parts of WN are analytic, others take the form of a historical narrative, empirical investigations, polemic, or declamations. These different approaches are interwoven throughout the course of WN in the construction of an argument in favour of the system of natural liberty and against systems of police. For this reason, as argued above in chapter 1, the distinction made in LRBL between didactic and persuasive discourse is not a helpful one for reading WN.[1] Didactic discourse is where 'the design is to set the case in the clearest light; to give every argument its due force, and by this means persuade us no farther than our unbiased judgment is convinced' (LRBL ii.13),[2] and rhetorical discourse is where 'we propose to persuade at all events, and for this purpose adduce those arguments that make for the side we have espoused, and magnify these to the utmost of our power; and on the other hand make light of and extenuate all those which may be brought on the other side' (LRBL ii.13), but it is not clear which of these terms should be applied to WN. For example, Book I is generally regarded by commentators as analytical, and would therefore be a form of didactic as opposed to rhetorical writing, but it does not 'give every argument its due force'. The three chapters on value, that is Book I, chapters v–vii, may be taken as an example. These chapters present an analysis of exchangeable value first by looking at the measure of value (in chapter v), then by analysing the three revenue components of the prices of commodities (chapter vi), and then by presenting an analysis of the relation between the natural and market price of commodities in terms of deviations in the market rates of wages, profits and rents from their natural rates. But these chapters omit any discussion of other approaches to exchangeable value as they simply argue for the one point of view. Thus, these chapters do not argue their case according to the 'didactic' manner of presenting counterarguments according to their due force; counterarguments are not even recognised in these chapters, let alone presented fairly in an unbiased way. According to a strict application of the distinction in LRBL between didactic and rhetorical forms of discourse, the three chapters on exchangeable value are a prime example of rhetorical discourse.[3]

Such a result seems clearly absurd in view of the serious analytical content of the three chapters on value, but it does underline the difficulties involved in distinguishing between didactic and rhetorical discourse as defined in LRBL. If it is possible to show that the analytic parts of WN are actually rhetorical according to the categories of LRBL, it is also possible to wonder whether the abuse hurled at merchants and manufacturers might qualify as being didactic. To take a single example, also from Book I: in chapter x it is

---

1 Lindgren (1973) and Endres (1991) use this distinction in their reading of WN.
2 'didactical discourse attempts to prove a proposition by putting *both* sides of an argument to an audience and by allowing each side its due degree of influence' (Endres 1991, p. 79).
3 LRBL also suggests another distinction between didactic and rhetorical discourse based on the distinction between reason and passion (LRBL ii.14). But reason itself presupposes an

stated that the 'clamour and sophistry of merchants and manufacturers easily persuade them [i.e. landlords, farmers and labourers] that the private interest of a part, and a subordinate part of the society, is the greatest interest of the whole' (WN I.x.c.25). This may be thought to be typical of the polemical abuse delivered against merchants and manufacturers in WN, and as such is clearly rhetorical as it does not present the other side of the argument, and indicates passion rather than reason. But, this statement occurs in an extended passage criticising the inequalities occasioned by the police of Europe, in particular, at this point, the fundamental inequality between the towns and the country. If the statement were construed as a straight inference from this lengthy criticism, then it might be considered as part of a didactic discourse, or as a polemical restatement of it. On the other hand, the entire section which is criticising the police of favouring towns at the expense of the countryside strictly fails to qualify as a piece of didactic discourse for the same reason that the chapters on value also fail, that is, the passages do not include a reasoned consideration of possible counterarguments. Indeed, as most of WN may be regarded as a sustained attack on the police of Europe without a comprehensive account of the arguments in favour of that police, it could be said that WN as a whole is an example of rhetorical discourse.

WN is a text that argues for the superiority of the system of natural liberty, and conviction and/or persuasion may be secured in a number of different ways using a range of stylistic devices, analytical techniques, polemics, figurative language, irony, conjectural history, empirical evidence or the lack of it, and so on. For this reason, as chapter 1 argued above, the distinction between didactic and rhetorical discourse is not helpful as a means of reading Adam Smith's works. Discourse achieves conviction/persuasion, if it does so, by a number of means depending on the circumstances and the readership. In this sense, any piece of discourse is susceptible to a rhetorical reading which examines the means by which that particular piece may be persuasive, and this holds for serious, reasoned, and analytical discourse. According to this usage, rhetoric is not 'mere' rhetoric, the opposite of reasoned discourse, but inhabits all discourse. This means that an examination of WN must include an account of its rhetoric as well as its analytical structure.

2

The distinctive and characteristic thesis of WN is its argument in favour of 'the system of natural liberty'. The challenge for the reader is to know how

---

unbiased account of an argument, and this cannot include the presentation of only one side of the argument.

to interpret the analytical structure and juridical/political resonances denoted by this term. Most commentators have interpreted the system of natural liberty as an argument in favour of *laissez-faire* commercial capitalism, and so have seen it as a prescient ideological statement for a new economic age waiting in the wings.[4] It is, of course, fully recognised that WN is not opposed to all forms of state intervention but endorses the importance of a range of forms of state economic action.[5] The trend of contemporary economic scholarship acknowledges the importance of state intervention in WN and regards as a caricature the popular view sometimes presented of Adam Smith as the arch-opponent of all forms of government activity. Even so, the general assessment of the overall *economic* content of WN is still largely that it represents an ideological stance that was highly conducive towards, if not entirely uncritical of, the emergence and consolidation of the liberal commercial and industrial capitalism which later emerged in nineteenth-century Britain.

The pervasiveness of this view of the ideological significance of WN has been challenged by the work of some intellectual historians who have attempted to place Adam Smith's *œuvre* within the context of a broader philosophical and political matrix of eighteenth-century writings, and who stress the significance of the political and social dimensions of WN. One implication of this approach, for example, is that WN records the losses as well as the gains deriving from the coming of commercial society.[6] But, in retrieving the politics of WN by paying due regard to its philosophical and political context, the *economic* analysis is treated as largely unproblematic and as providing no new interpretative challenges.[7] This, however, serves only to reinforce the methods of reading associated with the view that the economic analysis of WN functions ultimately as an ideological defence of commercial capitalism, a method of reading in which modern economic concepts are foisted upon the text of WN. The result is that no effective

---

[4] Taken from a vast literature, the following judgments from different standpoints are not unrepresentative: 'The *Wealth of Nations* was adopted as the ideology of early liberal capitalism and its popularity may have been due as much to the way in which it accorded with the economic and political prejudices of the emergent bourgeoisie as to its intrinsic merits as a scholarly work' (Campbell 1971, p. 15); Adam Smith was 'so eloquent a spokesman for capitalism and *laissez-faire*' (Rosenberg 1975, p. 378); and in a social history of the eighteenth century, Adam Smith is referred to as 'that high priest of capitalism' (Porter 1990, p. 87).

[5] See, for example, Viner (1960), A.S. Skinner (1979, ch. 9; 1986, pp. 25–8) and Letwin (1988).

[6] For example, see Winch (1983a, p. 266) and Horne (1981).

[7] 'Finally, there is the *economic* analysis of the *Wealth of Nations*, which has a shadowy existence in recent discussions on civic humanism or moralism and its bearings on Smith, and which I have also ignored here. By emphasizing that political economy was merely a branch of the science of the legislator, I have, by implication, treated it as unproblematic – as not requiring any special effort to explain its presence or form. This is a fair reflection of my present position . . .' (Winch 1983a, p. 268).

challenge is made to the view that the economic analysis of WN is primarily concerned with the equilibrating mechanism of competitive markets and the efficient allocation of resources in achieving maximum rates of economic growth; all that can be contended is that this is an overly economistic interpretation of WN that leaves out its moral and political aspects.[8]

At the level of economic theory, the analysis of WN is still largely characterised in terms of a system of competitive markets which efficiently allocate economic resources in both a static sense and a long-run growth sense. The analysis of competitive prices and the competitive market is, thus, seen as the theoretical linchpin underlying the arguments for *laissez-faire* and free trade, a linchpin figuratively illustrated by the metaphor of the invisible hand. There are different versions of this interpretation to be found in the economics literature, partly reflecting different modern approaches to economic theory but, in spite of their differences, they are united by a shared view that the theoretical core of the economic analysis of the system of natural liberty lies in its analysis of the competitive market and competitive market prices as presented in Book I, chapter vii.[9] Whether

---

[8] Winch (1992) insists that WN's significance lies in its attempt to reposition economic discourse within the field of Scottish moral philosophy, yet it still accepts that the economics of WN does constitute a 'post-Newtonian attempt to expose the equilibrating mechanisms at work in commercial society' (Winch 1992, p. 93), although it argues that this is not what is really important about WN.

[9] Robbins provides an early statement: 'the central achievement of his book was his demonstration of the mode in which the division of labour tended to be kept in equilibrium by the mechanism of relative prices – a demonstration which . . . is in harmony with the most refined apparatus of the modern School of Lausanne. The theory of value and distribution was really the central core of the analysis of the Classics, try as they might to conceal their objects under other names' (Robbins 1935, pp. 68–9). Another influential statement of this position is to be found in Kaushil (1973) where it is argued that the analysis of Book I, chapter vii, shows that Smith's perception is 'almost Walrasian' (Kaushil 1973, p. 68). Hollander (1973) argues that WN I.vii must be read in conjunction with the later 'applied' chapters on growth in order to understand that Smith's 'objective was to demonstrate that reliance upon the free operation of the competitive mechanisms of resource allocation would assure the maximisation at any time of the national income generated by the community's given resources' (Hollander 1973, p. 308). Another classic statement is to be found in Stigler (1977) that: 'Smith's attack on protectionism in all its forms . . . rested squarely on his theory of competitive prices. The crucial argument for unfettered individual choice in public policy was the efficiency property of competition' (Stigler 1977, p. 5). More recently Evensky (1987) has argued that WN contains 'a framework similar to neoclassical general competitive analysis. Given appropriate behaviour guided by appropriate rules, society will achieve a Pareto optimal general equilibrium and therefore the greatest possible wealth for the nation' (Evensky 1987, p. 466).

Non-neoclassical interpretations of WN also agree that the theoretical core of the economics of WN is the analysis of competitive prices. For example, although Rosenberg (1960) argues for the importance of the institutional analysis of WN, it is still accepted that: 'Smith's *Wealth of Nations* provided the first systematic guide to the manner in which the price mechanism allocated resources in a free market economy, and the book has been justly celebrated for this unique achievement' (Rosenberg 1960, pp. 569–70). From a neoRicardian position, Eatwell (1982) examines different conceptions of competition, but this too remains within the accepted discourse on competition as regulator of prices: 'The culmination of the

the ideological position of the commentator conduces towards a view of WN as benign prophet of the progressive liberal economic order that was to follow, or as apologist for the exploitative regime that it signalled, most interpretations of the economic analysis of WN have identified it as a competitive market analysis appropriate to the commercial needs of a developing liberal capitalist society. This understanding of the economic significance of WN has itself become a central part of twentieth-century perceptions of the development of economic thought. As argued above, this view of the economic analysis of WN has not been dislodged by the work of intellectual historians examining the wider political and moral resonances of WN.

This chapter will argue that when WN is situated within the discursive context of its own time, a different picture emerges of the economic analysis of WN, and that this inevitably has implications for the political and jurisprudential content of WN as well. In particular, the chapter will argue that the analysis of competitive prices and competitive markets was not the primary analytical feature of the system of natural liberty, nor was it even so very novel in its own time. Further, far from being a book promoting manufactures and commerce,[10] WN argued on the contrary that the manufacturing and trading sectors had grown too fast and that this had been detrimental to the growth of opulence. Thus, neither the detailed economic argument nor the overall structure of the system of natural liberty lends itself as herald for a newly dawning era of liberal commercial capitalism of whatever hue or political complexion. On the contrary, a reading that attempts to understand the theoretical structure of the economics of WN

---

search for a coherent abstract characterisation of markets, and hence the foundation of modern economic analysis, is to be found in chapter 7 of Book I of Adam Smith's *Wealth of Nations* – "Of the natural and market price of commodities". In this chapter Smith presented the first satisfactory formulation of the regularity inherent in price formation' (Eatwell 1982, p. 204). Myint (1948) has argued that Smith was less concerned with the 'allocative efficiency' of the competitive market than with the 'problem of increasing the total physical output' (Myint 1948, p. 12), and so draws attention to the importance of the growth theory of Book III rather than the analysis of Book I, but even this challenge to the 'allocative' reading is circumscribed by the acceptance of the view that Book I, chapters vii and ix, do present an allocative analysis: Smith 'succeeded in showing that the equilibrium process of the competitive market will lead to an optimum allocation of resources among different industries, whether or not we share his metaphysical optimism concerning the working of the "invisible hand" ' (Myint 1948, p. 12). Tribe (1978) argues against interpreting WN from the vantage point of neoclassical economics, but even here it is accepted that 'Books I and II can support a neoclassical construction' although 'only at the cost of ignoring almost completely the existence of three further books' (Tribe 1978, p. 102). Accounts which emphasise the importance of justice for the argument of WN, argue that the significance of competitive prices lies in their congruence with just outcomes; for example, Lindgren (1973, p. 99), and Young (1986).

10 Again, the opposite view is legion in the secondary literature, e.g. 'a man given freedom to pursue his own gain is "led by an invisible hand" to promote the growth of commerce and industry' (Teichgraeber 1986, p. 167).

must pose the opposite question of how such a text later came to be seen as the ideological flagship of a new economic era.

One route into exploring the structure of the economic argument of WN is to examine it in terms of the discursive space that marks it off from the sections on 'police' in LJ. It was argued in chapter 6 above that the identification of 'opulence' with low-price abundance, which had featured so prominently in the sections on 'police' in LJ, was not present in WN.[11] But, without a definition of some sort of the wealth of a nation, it would be difficult for WN to argue that the system of natural liberty was superior to the systems of political oeconomy, as to do this it needs to show that national wealth, according to its own definition, is greater under the one system than under the others. In WN, a new definition of wealth is introduced and is used consistently throughout the work. The new definition of wealth is provided in Book I and it is clarified in Book II which shows how this wealth grows in the normal course of a country's development. Book III shows how the normal course of development had been inverted by the police of Europe, and Book IV argues that the mercantile and agricultural systems retard the growth of wealth according to this definition.

The new definition of wealth which in WN superseded LJ's concept of abundance as low-price opulence, is presented in Book I, chapter vi. In this chapter it is first argued that the price of any individual commodity comprises the three revenues of rent, wages and profits:

> the whole price of any commodity must still finally resolve itself into some one or other, or all of those three parts; as whatever part of it remains after paying the rent of the land, and the price of the whole labour employed in raising, manufacturing, and bringing it to market, must necessarily be profit to somebody.
>
> (WN I.vi.16)

This account of the revenue components of price is presented in the context of a historical account of changing property relations, where the extent of existing property relations is determined by the mode of subsistence of society, an argument also to be found in WN V.i.b.2.[12] This means that the change in the rule for value determination after the private ownership of land and the accumulation of stock, is caused by the change in the

---

11 Further, in WN high real wages were no longer associated with the rich country as they had been in LJ. In WN, it is the increase in national wealth which results in a high real wage, whereas the country that has long been wealthy will have low wages (WN I.viii.22–7; xi.p.9). The example provided of the stationary rich country is China, a country which has attained its full complement of riches, but where real wages are low.

12 Also in LJ where it has been the subject of a considerable secondary literature: LJA i.27–35, 64–6; LJB 149–51; see Meek (1967b, 1976, 1977), A.S. Skinner (1975, 1982), and Stein (1979, 1980, pp. 33–50).

mode of subsistence as land and stock became integrated into the production process, providing rent and profit as original sources of revenue alongside labour, thus contributing directly to the exchangeable value of commodities which comprised wages, profit and rent: 'Wages, profit, and rent, are the three original sources of all revenue as well as of all exchangeable value. All other revenue is ultimately derived from some one or other of these' (WN I.vi.17). In this way, the issue of the *minority* ownership of land and capital is irrelevant to the issue of the generation of the original sources of revenue. The significance of minority ownership lies in determining the recipients of these revenues, but it is not itself the factor that generates those original revenues. Although, historically, the development of private property as minority ownership meant that the receipt of rent and profit developed as forms of class revenues, yet, analytically, rent and profit are received as revenues irrespective of the particular pattern of private ownership in existence. A number of examples are provided to demonstrate this point, examples including gentleman farmers, common farmers, independent manufacturers, and gardeners cultivating their own garden where the pattern of ownership does not correspond to class ownership (WN I.vi.19–23); in each case the appropriate original revenue, whether wages, rent or profit, is generated independently of the issue of the minority ownership of land and capital.

The second stage of the argument in this chapter takes place when the new concept of wealth is constructed by means of aggregating the exchangeable value of all commodities to provide a valuation of the whole annual produce of the country:

> As the price or exchangeable value of every particular commodity, taken separately, resolves itself into some one or other or all of those three parts; so that of all the commodities which compose the whole annual produce of the labour of every country, taken complexly, must resolve itself into the same three parts, and be parcelled out among different inhabitants of the country, either as the wages of their labour, the profits of their stock, or the rent of their land.
>
> (WN I.vi.17)

The annual produce of the country is, thus, identical to the annual revenue, taken as the sum of all wages, profits and rent. Throughout WN, the new terms 'annual produce', 'exchangeable value of the annual produce of the land and labour', and 'annual revenue' are used synonymously to refer to the wealth of a nation, and this new definition is used consistently as a benchmark against which the progress of a country's development may be assessed. This new concept of wealth is not, however, presented as an object of police. Further, it is argued that the police of Europe has reduced the annual produce/annual revenue to a level lower than it would otherwise have been, and that a system of natural liberty would result in its highest possible level given the existing material conditions of the country.

A consequence of this new definition of wealth is that it provides a theoretical link between the interests of individual property owners and the interest of society, as it is the pursuit of high wages, profits and rent that motivates individual property owners. This may be seen in Book I, chapter vii, which shows how the interest of all property owners (i.e. landlords, labourers and employers) will prompt them to move their land, labour or stock if the market rate of rent, wages or profits falls above or below their natural rates (WN I.vii.13–14). This model of individual interest underlies the concept of natural liberty where landlords, employers and labourers are unconstrained in symmetrically seeking the highest return for themselves independently of any wider social or political considerations.[13] The significance of the conceptualisation of capital and profit as the return on capital has been emphasised as reflecting the development of capitalist social relations,[14] but its recognition to the exclusion of the significance of land and rent has led to the problem of explaining Smith's apparent emphasis on capital and profits at a time when industrial capitalism was a thing of the future.[15] But land and labour are also treated as property to be used in pursuit of the highest revenue. When WN states that 'the interest of the landlords will immediately prompt them to withdraw a part of their land' or 'prepare more land' in response to changing rentals, it is signalling the demise of the traditional approach to the landed estate where rents were not fixed simply according to market criteria and where leases were not purely a contractual arrangement between a farmer and landlord. Similarly, the labourer no longer simply responds to windfall gains and losses as he did in LJ, but is now actively seeking out the highest revenue.

Thus, chapter vii shows how the natural rates of wages, profit and rent will be established in the markets for final output; the significance of the distinction between natural and market price thus lies in the revenue components theory of the exchangeable value of commodities, not in a model of resource allocation. The notion of a going rate of return is important in later chapters where movement from one industry to another and from one sector to another is achieved by the responses of individual property owners to changes in the market rates of rent, wages and profits. This emphasis on the three revenues structures the remaining chapters in Book I which examine how the natural rates of rent, wages and profits are linked to the changing historical circumstances of society. This provides the

---

13 cf. 'Dominium, or the full right of property. By this a man has the sole claim to a subject, exclusive of all others, but can use it himself as he thinks fit, and if he pleases abuse or destroy it . . . Property is to be considered as an exclusive right . . .' (LJA i.17).
14 For example, Meek (1967a).
15 For example, see Koebner (1959), Kindleberger (1976), Crafts (1985) and Jackson (1990).

opportunity for a considerable amount of analytical, historical, conjectural, and polemical material delivered in opposition to the police of Europe, but the benchmark concept of the annual revenue underlies the entire account. For example, the historical account of the relative development of towns and country is conducted in terms of the revenue components theory which is used to show the process by which the towns secured an unmerited advantage over the country (WN I.x.c.19). The unfair advantage of the towns over the country is a persistent theme throughout WN and is used as evidence to show how the police of Europe has distorted the proper order of development of Europe. Another example occurs at the end of Book I, where the effects of the progress of improvement upon the three great orders of society is considered. Here, the relative position of landlords, labourers and employers is analysed with direct reference to the new concept of the annual produce (WN I.xi.p. 7). It is argued that the interests of landlords and labourers are 'strictly connected with the interest of the society' (WN I.xi.p. 10) as their revenues rise or decline with the rise or decline of society. This is contrasted with the interests of the third order of society of employers, merchants and manufacturers, which are 'always in some respects different from, and even opposite to, that of the publick' (WN I.xi.p.10) because profits move inversely with the progress of society, falling when society progresses. This is the context for one of the periodic attacks on the merchants and manufacturers that occur regularly throughout the pages of WN, castigating them as an order of men 'whose interest is never exactly the same with that of the publick, who have generally an interest to deceive and even to oppress the publick, and who accordingly have, upon many occasions, both deceived and oppressed it' (WN I.xi.p.10). These two themes – the unfair advantage that towns have secured over the country and the rapacious spirit of the commercial classes – are raised here in Book I and are developed and pursued in later Books of WN.

This first Book of WN is also preparing the foundations of an analytical structure that is already revealing its dependence on the writings of the Économistes in France. The complaint that the towns of Europe had benefited disproportionately from mercantilist policies was a common complaint among the Économistes, who disputed the mercantilist claim that foreign trade is the source of wealth for a nation. Further, the definition of the nation's annual wealth as the annual produce/annual revenue was also derived from their writings. In Quesnay's *Encyclopédie* article 'Men', the annual wealth of a nation is identified with the annual product and revenue of the nation (Meek 1963a, pp. 88, 96, 100). This corresponds to the *produit net* which comprised just one form of revenue, that of rent. WN argued that this conception was mistaken, and that profits and wages also contribute towards the net revenue of society, but in formulating this argument against the Économistes' notion of the *produit net*, WN was dependent on their identification of the annual wealth with annual product and annual revenue.[16]

The insistence of WN that all three forms of revenue contribute to the annual revenue of society might be thought to forge a very direct link between the interest of the individual property owner and the society as a whole, and for some commentators this identity of individual interests with national interests is regarded as so self-evident as to be entirely unproblematic. But in WN, the individual and the society were not to enjoy such a simple and unmediated relation, as later analysis was to demonstrate. In this larger story, the market dynamics of Book I, chapter vii, were to have a relatively small role to play in establishing evidence of the harmful effects of police on the annual produce/annual revenue of society. This kind of market analysis was not unfamiliar in the contemporary literature of the mid-eighteenth century. It was widely agreed upon by a number of writers, but it did not lend itself to addressing questions concerning the historical progress of development of a society that WN was investigating.

The analysis of Book II on capital is also structured in terms of the revenue components theory of value. Capital is defined as that portion of a person's stock from which a revenue or profit may be derived. At the beginning of chapter ii of this Book, explicit reference is made to the revenue components theory of value (WN II.ii.1, 2) and this forms the basis of the chapter's argument that money forms no part of the annual revenue of society. By thus excluding the stock of money from the definition of wealth, the chapter provides a counterargument to the view that national wealth is constituted by money. This chapter also differentiates between net revenue and gross revenue; it argues that it is net revenue and not gross revenue that is significant, thus excluding the maintenance costs of fixed capital and of the money stock from the measure of annual revenue (WN II.ii.1–15). The account of the accumulation of capital in chapter iii is also dependent on the concept of the annual revenue/annual produce. Here, it is argued that the wages of unproductive labour are excluded from the net revenue (WN II.iii.1–8).[17] Capital accumulation takes place when revenue is used to add to capital (WN II.iii.13–42).[18] WN redefines the notions of prodigality and frugality, and argues that the annual produce can be increased only by frugality, that is, by increasing the amount of capital employed.[19] But the theoretical climax of this Book occurs in chapter v,

---

16 Book I also argues that the abundance of food gives value to other goods by creating a demand for them (WN I.xi.c.36).
17 WN's celebrated distinction between productive and unproductive labour derived from the physiocratic argument that only agricultural labour was productive of the *produit net*.
18 The similarity between this argument and Turgot's analysis of capital has been discussed by many commentators (Turgot 1963; first published 1770).
19 Prodigality and frugality had previously been defined with respect to luxury expenditure on consumer goods, especially imported luxuries. The economic effects of luxury were seen to

THE SYSTEM OF NATURAL LIBERTY

where it is argued that different employments of capitals do not equally contribute towards increasing the annual produce of society. It is here that WN argues that individual interests and the public interest are not linked in terms of a simple summation; a sectoral wedge is interposed between the interests of individual property owners acting in response to expected revenues, and the overall effect on the annual revenue of society.

Book II, chapter v, considers the relative contributions of different sectors in increasing the annual produce of society. A hierarchy of sectoral activities is presented, based on the contribution of that sector towards the annual revenue of society. The sectors are ranked according to how many of the three basic forms of revenue (rent, wages and profits) are contributed towards the annual revenue of society (WN II.v.8–12, 19, 23, 37).[20] In this scheme, agriculture is ranked first because it contributes all three forms of revenue:

> The labourers and labouring cattle, therefore, employed in agriculture, not only occasion, like the workmen in manufactures, the reproduction of a value equal to their own consumption, or to the capital which employs them, together with its owners profits; but of a much greater value. Over and above the capital of the farmer and all its profits, they regularly occasion the reproduction of the rent of the landlord. This rent may be considered as the produce of those powers of nature, the use of which the landlord lends to the farmer.
>
> (WN II.v.12)

In this passage, agriculture produces not only wages and profit, but rent as well, and so it is the only form of activity that raises all three forms of revenue. Rent, it is argued, is the produce of the powers of nature and pertains only in the sphere of agriculture where production involves the use of land. Manufacturing is placed second because it contributes two forms of revenue (wages and profits); wholesaling is placed third because it contributes mainly profits and only the limited wages derived from transporting the goods; and retailing is placed last because it contributes profits only.[21]

---

be a deterioration of the balance of trade and upward pressure on wages, while the moral effects were seen as effeminacy, vice and political venality.

20 These sectoral divisions are not present in LJ. In LJB it is stated that 'Agriculture is of all other arts the most beneficent to society, and whatever tends to retard its improvement is extremely prejudicial to the public interest' but the reason for this is simply its size: 'The produce of agriculture is much greater than that of any other manufacture' (LJB 289).

21 When WN argues that a certain employment of capital leads to a greater increase in the annual revenue, it sometimes also argues that this will put into motion a greater quantity of productive labour. For example, in the case of agriculture, it is argued that: 'The capital employed in agriculture, therefore, not only puts into motion a greater quantity of productive labour than any equal capital employed in manufactures, but in proportion too to the quantity of productive labour which it employs, it adds a much greater value to the annual produce of the land and labour of the country, to the real wealth and revenue of its

Wholesaling activity is further ranked into the home trade, the foreign trade of consumption, and the carrying trade in declining order of importance according to their indirect effects on the annual revenue in replacing domestic capitals and in the speediness of returns.[22] The chapter argues that a country that has insufficient capital to invest in all branches of employment should first direct its capitals to those branches that will contribute the greatest increase to the annual produce (WN II.v.18–20). Thus, the order of a country's historical development that will generate the greatest annual revenue is one where capital is first directed to agriculture, then to manufactures, and then to the wholesaling and retail trades. These crucial sectoral distinctions and categories are then put to work in the discussion of the progress of opulence in Book III,

---

inhabitants' (WN II.v.12). This has led some commentators to infer that a particular employment of capital is beneficial because it will support a larger quantity of productive labour; see Hollander (1973, ch. 10, p. 294), and A.S. Skinner (1979, pp. 178–80). But it is the latter criterion in the passage above that is crucial. The reason for this is that whenever the two criteria diverge, it is the contribution to the annual revenue that is determinant. Comparing agriculture and manufactures, for example, the criterion of employment by itself provides no reason for preferring one rather than the other, as WN does not say that more people are employed in agriculture than in manufacturing. What WN does say is that agriculture puts into motion a greater quantity of productive labour if the labouring cattle are included as labourers: 'No equal capital puts into motion a greater quantity of productive labour than that of the farmer. Not only his labouring servants, but his labouring cattle, are productive labourers. In agriculture too nature labours along with man; and though her labour costs no expence, its produce has its value, as well as that of the most expensive workmen . . . The labourers and labouring cattle, therefore, employed in agriculture, not only occasion, like the workmen in manufactures, the reproduction of a value equal to their own consumption, or to the capital which employs them, together with its owners profits; but of a much greater value. Over and above the capital of the farmer and all its profits, they regularly occasion the reproduction of the rent of the landlord. This rent may be considered as the produce of those powers of nature, the use of which the landlord lends to the farmer' (WN II.v.12). The claim that the capital employed in agriculture puts into motion a greater quantity of labour must therefore be understood in a figurative sense, where the labouring cattle generate the landlord's rent, and this undermines the analytical significance of any employment effect for labour of different kinds of investments. Similarly, the retailer is referred to as a productive labourer, but in this case the only addition to the annual produce is in the form of profits (WN II.v.9). Further, at crucial moments in WN, it is the criterion of revenue-generation alone that is used, not that of employment-generation. For example: 'The capital of all the individuals of a nation is increased in the same manner as that of a single individual, by their continually accumulating and adding to it whatever they save out of their revenue. It is likely to increase the fastest, therefore, when it is employed in the way that affords the greatest revenue to all the inhabitants of the country, as they will thus be enabled to make the greatest savings. But the revenue of all the inhabitants of the country is necessarily in proportion to the value of the annual produce of their land and labour' (WN II.v.20). Also IV.i.45 (which summarises the structure of the argument for the remaining chapters on the mercantile system in Book IV): '. . . I shall examine chiefly what are likely to be the effects of each of them [i.e. restraints/encouragements] upon the annual produce of its industry. According as they tend either to increase or diminish the value of this annual produce, they must evidently tend either to increase or diminish the real wealth and revenue of the country.'

22 WN II.v.23–8, 31–7.

and in the critical discussion of the mercantile system and the agricultural system in Book IV.[23]

Most commentators are agreed that this sectoral analysis derives to some degree from the Économistes.[24] But, although the analytical conception of different sectors, the recognition of their relative importance, and the attempt to rank them, were a response to the Économistes and their writings, the theoretical basis of the ranking itself is not the same. The ranking of WN was grounded in the revenue components theory of value of Book I, chapter vi, where rent, profit and wages all carry equal status as original revenues contributing to the annual revenue of society, whereas the Économistes privileged the concept of a gratuitous surplus and identified rent as the only source of revenue or net product.[25] The ranking in WN, however, was based on how many of the three original sources of revenue are generated by the employment of capital; agriculture was accorded priority as it generates all three revenues, manufactures comes next generating two revenues, and commerce is placed last as it generates one only. In praising agriculture as the most productive, the references in WN to nature's gratuitous contribution echo the writings of the Économistes, but the structure of the argument does not depend on their conception of the surplus product and this can be seen by the ranking of the remaining sectors.

Later commentators were to criticise this ranking scheme as inconsistently derivative of physiocratic thinking, but the basis of this symmetric treatment of land, labour and capital as forms of revenue-generating property is to be found in the account of the stadial development of society and property (WN V.i.b.2),[26] where it is argued that the extent of existing property relations depends on the mode of subsistence of society. This means that the changed rule for value determination after the accumulation of stock and the private ownership of land is not caused simply by the changes in property relations, as they are themselves the result of changes in the mode of subsistence. When society became more advanced, and stock

---

23 The final sentence of Book II reads: 'What circumstances in the policy of Europe have given the trades which are carried on in towns so great an advantage over that which is carried on in the country, that private persons frequently find it more for their advantage to employ their capitals in the most distant carrying trades of Asia and America, than in the improvement and cultivation of the most fertile fields in their own neighbourhood, I shall endeavour to explain at full length in the two following books' (WN II.v.37).
24 Smith met members of the school while in Paris during 1764–6. Cannan (1964, pp. xxii–iv; 1950, pp. xxx–xxxiii), Winch (1965, pp. 11–12), Groenewegen (1969) and A.S. Skinner (1979, pp. 114–29) discuss the influence of physiocracy for WN. See also references provided in note 3 to chapter 6 above.
25 'The proposition, then, remains unshaken that there is no revenue save the net produce of lands, and that all other annual profit is either paid by the revenue, or forms part of the expenditure which serves to produce the revenue' (Turgot 1963, p. 96).
26 And in LJA i.27–35, 64–6; LJB 149–51.

and land both came to be used as productive factors, these factors necessarily contributed to the exchangeable value of commodities, irrespective of who actually owned them (WN I.vi.19–23). In this way, the revenue components theory of value was a challenge to the view that agriculture alone is productive.[27]

The analysis of the employment of capitals in Book II, chapter v, argues that the best order of historical development for any country lies first in agriculture, then in manufactures, and finally wholesaling and the export trades (WN II.v.19–23). The fundamental point about the system of natural liberty is that it postulates a natural order of development, entirely undirected by politics or state intervention, which perfectly mirrors the ideal sequence of development. In the absence of restrictions, the natural course of development will also be from agriculture, to manufactures, to foreign trade. This course of development is a a naturalistic one, deriving partly from the stadial theory of history, where societies progress in a linear sequence through the stages of hunting, pasturage, agriculture and finally commerce. It also derives from a notion of a natural division of labour between the country and the town, in which agricultural activity is prior to and proportioning of the manufacturing activity of the towns. Just as a surplus of agricultural goods can be exchanged for manufactures from the town, so a surplus of manufactured goods over and above this exchange with the countryside will be required before foreign trade becomes feasible. This naturalistic order is also promoted by the 'natural inclinations of man', who prefers to employ capital in just this order (WN III.i.3, 7).

The *economic* mechanism here, however, can be understood only in terms of the revenue model presented in Books I and II. In the case of agriculture, the most clearly delineated case, the argument is that the natural financial incentives inducing capital into agriculture had been eroded by the system of landownership, including primogeniture and entails, which had resulted in the engrossing of land by large proprietors who were not equipped to improve the land. The presence of this class of large landowners had prevented small proprietors from developing land in the combined role of landlord and farmer, receiving both rent and profit which could be reinvested in the land.[28] WN repeatedly points to the instance of the superior profitability of the North American colonies as an example of the greater advantages of agriculture;[29] there the colonist functions as both landlord and farmer, receiving large profits that include an unacknowledged rental element: 'In Carolina, where the planters, as in other British colonies, are generally both farmers and landlords, and where rent consequently is confounded with profit . . .' (WN I.xi.b.37).

---

27 In WN the work of the Économistes is criticised at IV.ix.29–38, 49–50.
28 WN I.vi.20; III.ii.20; IV.vii.b.2.
29 WN I.vi.20, II.v.21; III.i.5; III.iv.19; IV.vii.b.1–3,16–19, 56.

The other sectoral sequences are less well developed and tend to rely on what is seen as the natural preference for employing capital nearer home and the greater security of doing so, together with the speedier replacement of domestic capitals (WN III.i.7–8). In this natural scheme, it is only when one stage in the sequence becomes saturated with stock, and profits and wages tend to fall, that the surplus capital will then be employed in the next sector in the sequence in order to boost these falling revenues (WN II.v.32–6; IV.vii.c.87).

Within the system of natural liberty, therefore, the order of development will naturally correspond to the optimal order. This constitutes the core of WN's criticism of the policy of Europe (including the colonial monopoly) and the agricultural system, as it pinpoints their disruption of this natural order and the consequent reduction of the annual revenue. In doing this, WN was turning conventional wisdom on its head. The conventional mercantile argument of the time held that foreign trade was the source of wealth,[30] and that the best commodities to export were manufactured goods.[31] Against this WN argues, first, that foreign trade should be placed last of all activities in terms of its contribution to the annual revenue, thus challenging the major policy programme of the time which was to encourage foreign trade. Second, WN argues that agricultural activity is more productive than manufacturing activity, thus reversing the conventional ranking of agriculture and manufactures, and challenging the very basis of the various state measures taken to promote manufactures. Third, WN stresses the importance of the home trade above foreign trade, whereas contemporary wisdom generally saw it as inferior to foreign trade. The agricultural system had also challenged these conventional wisdoms, but WN's response here was to deny that non-agricultural forms of activity were non-productive of annual revenue.

The analysis of the system of natural liberty postulates a homology between the natural progress of opulence of a country and the order deriving from the sectoral ranking scheme laid out in Book II, chapter v. The primary criticism of the police of Europe and the colonial monopoly then centred on their disruption of this natural order, with its consequent reduction of the annual revenue below what it would have been. The notion of the natural progress of opulence is laid out in Book III and connects up with the stadial theory of history based on the stages of hunting, pasturage, agriculture, and commerce. This natural sequence is argued to have been

---

[30] Even in spite of misgivings about the possibility of any coherent characterisation of 'mercantilism', it is argued in Coleman (1980) that overseas trade was widely seen as the main source of wealth and that the internal trade was largely dismissed as being of little economic significance.
[31] LJB accepts that it is better to import unmanufactured and rude goods rather than manufactured goods as they provide greater employment and maintenance (LJB 320).

disrupted by the policy of Europe which favoured the industry of the towns over the industry of the countryside:

> According to the natural course of things, therefore, the greater part of the capital of every growing society is, first, directed to agriculture, afterwards to manufactures, and last of all to foreign commerce. This order of things is so very natural, that in every society that had any territory, it has always, I believe, been in some degree observed. Some of their lands must have been cultivated before any considerable towns could be established, and some sort of coarse industry of the manufacturing kind must have been carried on in those towns, before they could well think of employing themselves in foreign commerce.
>
> But though this natural order of things must have taken place in some degree in every such society, it has, in all the modern states of Europe, been, in many respects, entirely inverted. The foreign commerce of some of their cities has introduced all their finer manufactures, or such as were fit for distant sale; and manufactures and foreign commerce together, have given birth to the principal improvements of agriculture. The manners and customs which the nature of their original government introduced, and which remained after that government was greatly altered, necessarily forced them into this unnatural and retrograde order.
>
> (WN III.i.8–9)[32]

The analytical context for Book III's historical account of the distortions and 'unnatural and retrograde order' introduced by the police of Europe is, thus, provided by the sectoral hierarchy of Book II, chapter v. It is in the context of the superior productiveness of agriculture that the criticisms of great proprietors and the laws of primogeniture and entail are presented at WN III.ii. It is in this context too that the historical account of the rise and progress of cities and towns is delivered in the following chapter (III.iii). As the history of Europe had been contrary to the natural course of things, its progress had been slow and uncertain (WN III.iv.19).

Thus, the natural progress of opulence during the commercial stage of society is also presented as the best form of progress in the sense that it ensures the greatest increase in the annual revenue of society. Significantly, the word 'opulence' is used in WN to refer to this natural progress in which the annual revenue is increasing. It is this view of the proper course of economic progress and the place of trade within it that is then put to work in Book IV, where the systems of political oeconomy are criticised for taking the opposing view that the best course of progress requires the regulating hand of the statesman to direct the industry and capital of private

---

32 Also WN III.i.1–4; iii.12; iv.2, 18–19.

persons into the preferred sectors. WN is sympathetic to the objective of the Économistes in promoting agriculture, but it argued that it was counterproductive in achieving it, and WN was completely opposed to the mercantile system's attempt to direct resources into commerce and manufactures.[33] It is sometimes argued that the major point of criticism made in WN against the system of commerce is that it confused money for wealth and that, in making this criticism, WN misunderstood the nature of mercantilism. But, in describing the commercial system, the argument of WN at this point does address some of the wider issues, such as the effect of the amount of currency on the state of trade and the need of a nation for foreign currency to pay for wars (WN IV.i.11–33). Further, WN's criticism is not restricted to a discussion of the nature of wealth or the status of the balance of trade, but applies an external criterion, the new measure of the annual revenue developed analytically in the earlier books. Thus, the main arguments brought to bear against the commercial system are based on the new criterion of the annual revenue that was being proposed by WN. Throughout Book IV, the standard against which the systems of political oeconomy are being evaluated is that of the 'annual revenue of society' or the 'value of its annual produce', thus making it clear that the analytical model developed in the previous three Books is providing the theoretical basis for these comparisons and evaluations.[34] For example, the final paragraph of Book IV, chapter i, signals that the regulations of the commercial system are to be examined, not in terms of their supposed effect on the balance of trade, but in terms of their impact on the annual revenue: 'I shall examine chiefly what are likely to be the effects of each of them upon the annual produce of its industry. According as they tend either to increase or diminish the value of this annual produce, they must evidently tend either to increase or diminish the real wealth and revenue of the country' (WN IV.i.45). The criticisms of the mercantile system and the agricultural system in Book IV are, therefore, directed towards showing how the inversion of

---

[33] 'Those systems, therefore, which preferring agriculture to all other employments, in order to promote it, impose restraints upon manufactures and foreign trade, act contrary to the very end which they propose, and indirectly discourage that very species of industry which they mean to promote. They are so far, perhaps, more inconsistent than even the mercantile system. That system, by encouraging manufactures and foreign trade more than agriculture, turns a certain portion of the capital of the society from supporting a more advantageous, to support a less advantageous species of industry. But still it really and in the end encourages that species of industry which it means to promote. Those agricultural systems, on the contrary, really and in the end discourage their own favourite species of industry. It is thus that every system that endeavours, either, by extraordinary encouragements . . . or, by extraordinary restraints . . . is in reality subversive of the great purpose which it means to promote. It retards instead of accelerating, the progress of the society towards real wealth and greatness; and diminishes, instead of increasing, the real value of the annual produce of its land and labour' (WN IV.ix.49–50).
[34] WN IV.Intro; IV.i.20, 31, 32, 33, 45; IV.ii.9, 12, 13, 14; IV.iii.c.3, 4, 7, 15; IV.v.a.23; IV.v.b.32; IV.vii.c.57–60, 102; IV.ix.2, 32, 33, 34, 36, 37, 50, 52.

the natural progress of opulence forces capital into less advantageous channels and reduces the annual revenue below what it would otherwise have been.[35]

In the long chapter on colonies in Book IV, the core of the argument is that the colonial policy has upset the natural balance of industry and has forced capital from more advantageous channels into less advantageous channels.[36] In LJ, as argued above, the 'natural balance' concerned the market balance, but in WN the natural balance takes on a new meaning as the sectoral balance of industry.[37] First, it is argued that the 'unnaturally' high levels of profits in the colony trade have diverted mercantile capital into less advantageous channels,[38] and here the argument draws on the hierarchy of wholesale trade outlined in WN II.v. But, second and more crucially, it is argued that the increased rate of mercantile profit has diverted capital away from agriculture and manufactures into the colonial trade, and that this too has reduced the annual revenue. But, if the colonial monopoly really has raised the rate of mercantile profit, does this not undercut the argument that the annual revenue has been reduced below the level that it would otherwise have been? This is a crucial moment for the system of natural liberty as it raises starkly the nature of the theoretical basis of the argument against the mercantile system.

In WN, the pursuit of individual profit is held to increase the annual revenue only if the employment of that capital has been decided upon in the absence of preferences and restraints. The argument against the case where the rate of mercantile profit has been raised as a result of the mercantile policy is constructed in terms of the sectoral hierarchy of capitals. The mercantile system has reduced the annual revenue because it has deranged the employment of capital compared with the proper sectoral sequence: 'That system, by encouraging manufactures and foreign trade more than agriculture, turns a certain portion of the capital of the society from supporting a more advantageous, to support a less advantageous species of

---

35 For example, WN IV.ii.1–12; v.a.3; vi.2.
36 'The dazzling splendour of the object, however, the immense greatness of the commerce, is the very quality which renders the monopoly of it hurtful, or which makes one employment, in its own nature necessarily less advantageous to the country than the greater part of other employments, absorb a much greater proportion of the capital of the country than what would otherwise have gone into it. The mercantile stock of every country, it has been shewn in the second book [II.v], naturally seeks, if one may say so, the employment most advantageous to that country' (WN IV.vii.c.85–6).
37 'The monopoly of the colony trade besides, by forcing towards it a much greater proportion of the capital of Great Britain than what would naturally have gone to it, seems to have broken altogether that natural balance which would otherwise have taken place among all the different branches of British industry' (WN IV.vii.c.43). In the chapter on the commercial system, there is a reference to the relation between the quantity of a commodity and the effectual demand for it, and this account does follow the approach of Book I, chapter vii, but this is not referred to as the 'natural balance' (WN IV.i.12).
38 WN IV.vii.c.19–22, 24–8, 34–46, 86.

industry' (WN IV.ix.49), and this must hold true, it is argued, even if we concede (which WN accepts) that the rate of mercantile profit has increased and has pulled up the general rate of profit. The argument here is that by diverting capital from agriculture, manufactures and the home trade,[39] the other original sources of revenue such as wages,[40] rent,[41] and non-mercantile profit,[42] must have been reduced by an amount greater than any increase in profits accruing to the mercantile sector. The net effect must entail a reduction in the annual revenue:

> All the original sources of revenue, the wages of labour, the rent of land, and the profits of stock, the monopoly renders much less abundant than they otherwise would be. To promote the little interest of one little order of men in one country, it hurts the interest of all other orders of men in that country, and of all men in all other countries.
>
> (WN IV.vii.c.60)[43]

Thus, the argument demonstrating that the colonial monopoly reduces the annual revenue in spite of the increased rate of profit resulting from the monopoly, is one that is premised on the model of revenue sources and the sectoral hierarchy. If capital has been diverted from agriculture, manufactures and the home trade into the colonial trade, then the annual revenue must have been reduced overall; the other original sources of revenue such as wages, rent and non-mercantile profit must therefore have fallen by an amount greater than the increase in mercantile profits.

---

39 'Its [i.e. the colonial monopoly's] effect has consequently been to turn a part of the capital of Great Britain from an employment in which it would have maintained a greater quantity of manufacturing industry, to one in which it maintains a much smaller, and thereby to diminish, instead of increasing, the whole quantity of manufacturing industry maintained in Great Britain' (WN IV.vii.c. 55).

40 'The monopoly hinders the capital of that country, whatever may at any particular time be the extent of that capital, from maintaining so great a quantity of productive labour as it would otherwise maintain, and from affording so great a revenue to the industrious inhabitants as it would otherwise afford . . . One great original source of revenue, therefore, the wages of labour, the monopoly must necessarily have rendered at all times less abundant than it otherwise would have been' (WN IV.vii.c.57).

41 'By raising the rate of mercantile profit, the monopoly discourages the improvement of land . . . But by discouraging improvement, the monopoly necessarily retards the natural increase of another great original source of revenue, the rent of land' (WN IV.vii.c.58).

42 'The monopoly indeed, raises the rate of mercantile profit, and thereby augments somewhat the gain of our merchants. But as it obstructs the natural increase of capital, it tends rather to diminish than to increase the sum total of the revenue which the inhabitants of the country derive from the profits of stock; a small profit upon a great capital generally affording a greater revenue than a great profit upon a small one. The monopoly raises the rate of profit, but it hinders the sum of profit from rising so high as it otherwise would do' (WN IV.vii.c.59).

43 WN goes on to argue that an even more harmful consequence of the forced increase in the ordinary rate of profit is 'perhaps' that it seems 'to destroy that parsimony which in other circumstances is natural to the character of the merchant' (WN IV.vii.c.61).

3

By understanding that the system of natural liberty is based on the theory of sectoral revenue sources, it is also easier to make sense of the famous reference to the invisible hand at WN IV.ii.9. It has sometimes puzzled commentators that the invisible hand should make its appearance in what is regarded as a relatively obscure passage in the Book on systems of political oeconomy, but this puzzlement is caused by misconstruing the metaphor of the invisible hand as a reference to the operation of competitive markets. The chapter that includes the invisible hand metaphor is the one concerning restraints on imports; it argues that the pursuit of individual gain by the employer of mercantile capital naturally leads him to support domestic rather than foreign industry, and that this will therefore result in the greatest annual revenue to society (WN IV.ii.4–9). The clear theoretical context for this argument is the proper sequence for the employment of capitals and the necessary identity of the annual revenue with the exchangeable value of the whole annual produce, the identity first put forward in Book I, chapter vi:

> But the annual revenue of every society is always precisely equal to the exchangeable value of the whole annual produce of its industry, or rather is precisely the same thing with that exchangeable value. As every individual, therefore, endeavours as much as he can both to employ his capital in the support of domestick industry, and so to direct that industry that its produce may be of the greatest value; every individual necessarily labours to render the annual revenue of society as great as he can. He generally, indeed, neither intends to promote the publick interest, nor knows how much he is promoting it. By preferring the support of domestick to that of foreign industry, he intends his own security; and by directing that industry in such a manner as its produce may be of the greatest value, he intends only his own gain, and he is in this, as in many other cases, led by an invisible hand to promote an end which was no part of his intention.
>
> (WN IV.ii.9)

The metaphor of the invisible hand refers to the unintended consequences of individual human behaviour, but this metaphor is constructed within a discourse on the hierarchy of capitals. In the particular case here, it is argued that domestic industry rather than foreign industry is naturally preferred and is also more advantageous to the public interest. This is a classic instance of the homology between the 'natural' progress of a society and that progress which most enhances the annual revenue; it is therefore both unnecessary and inappropriate to encourage domestic industry by restraints on imports. The argument is, therefore, an epitome of the system of natural liberty, where the natural order of sectoral development is the one that will lead to the greatest increase in the annual revenue; and that in this natural order, agriculture, domestic manufactures and the inland trade are of greater importance than foreign industry and foreign trade.

This chapter and the previous one have argued that the analysis of the system of natural liberty is not based on the efficiency property of competitive markets as that is now understood by economists, but on an approach which located individual contributions to the annual revenue within the context of a sectoral view of the economy. The attachment to a stadial conception of the development of society, both leading up to the commercial society and within that society, facilitated an argument associating property ownership with productive activity, such that each person's use of property was deemed inherently productive from the point of view of society as a whole. This then enabled a classification of the different employments of capital according to how many of the three basic forms of productive property were being put to work and how many of the three original sources of revenues were being generated. The economic relation between the individual and society was, thus, not a simple one of aggregation or disaggregation, but was mediated through a sectoral view of the composition of revenues. Within the system of natural liberty, therefore, competition secures the greatest annual revenue, not by promoting market equilibrium, but by means of facilitating the proper course of sectoral development which underlies the natural progress of opulence.

In the mid-eighteenth century, many writers supported both some forms of free markets and some forms of state regulation, and to some degree the so-called mercantilist and free trade literatures merged.[44] It was also widely argued that market price was determined by the interaction of influences on both the demand and supply side. Much of the so-called mercantilist literature provided an account of the competitive market mechanism, but argued that market outcomes would not always be in the best interest of the nation as a whole. For example, Francis Hutcheson's *Short Introduction to Moral Philosophy* (first published 1747) presents the mercantilist view that national wealth will be 'drained by our buying foreign manufactures' (Hutcheson 1969, III.8, p. 323), but it also provides an account of the determination of market price according to the natural law tradition of the demand for goods and the difficulty of supplying them (Hutcheson 1969,

---

[44] 'But the most serious conflict in interpretations seems to have been brought about by an excessively rigid and exclusivist use of the categories "mercantilist", and support of *laissez-faire*; or by too sharply black-and-white definitions of the supporters thereof. There is nothing necessarily contradictory in recognizing, generally, the efficacy and beneficence of free market forces, or *laissez-faire*, over wide areas of the economy, while, at the same time, supporting government intervention with regard to this or that issue or sector – even in respect of the closely linked problems of foreign trade and the money supply' (Hutchison 1988, p. 125).

II.12, pp. 209–12).[45] Cantillon's *Essay* promulgated mercantilist views about the desirability of a favourable balance of trade and the need to export manufactured goods (Cantillon 1931, pp. 191–3, 233–5), but yet it also explained the process of bargaining by which the market price matches the intrinsic value (Cantillon 1931, pp. 117–21). Sir James Steuart's *Inquiry* (first published 1767) displayed an understanding of market dynamics (Steuart 1966, II.ii, iv, vii, x), but it insisted throughout that free market or natural outcomes were to be prevented by the statesman. Lord Kames's *Sketches on the History of Man* presented an analysis conducted in terms of a version of the mercantilist emphasis on money and the balance of trade with its characteristic battery of trade regulations, but it also included a precise analysis of market price according to demand and quantity (Kames 1774, vol. I, pp. 71–84, 488–519). After describing the providential nature of international trade according to which 'all nations should benefit by commerce as by sunshine' (p. 81), it concludes that the best policy for individual countries is to maintain a balance of trade equilibrium by a series of regulatory measures, including export bounties designed to prevent either deficit or surplus on the external balance (Kames 1774, vol. I, pp. 77–84).

Thus mercantilist-type debates about the proper use of bounties and duties to encourage or discourage the production and consumption of particular goods, demonstrate that individual market outcomes were distrusted rather than not understood. A policy of encouraging the export of certain manufactured goods involved state manipulation of excess supply over domestic consumption which would allow a surplus for export; within the framework of thinking of the time, such policies generating excess supply were based on arguments concerning national monetary requirements, the need to promote domestic employment, and the protection of vital industries including shipping. The main point to note, however, is that such thinking was not necessarily based on a lack of understanding of market processes at the micro level, but rather on the view that market outcomes were unable to achieve certain national economic and political objectives.

Whereas protectionist and mercantilist literature could provide coherent accounts of the market mechanism, the more free trade literature of the mid-eighteenth century could also show signs of mercantilist or protectionist tendencies. For example, Jacob Vanderlint's *Money Answers All Things* (1734) explained price in terms of demand and quantity supplied (Vanderlint 1734, p. 6), provided an account of the automatic specie-flow mechanism (pp. 46–7) and proposed a general freedom of international

---

[45] The discussion of price occurs in Book II on the Law of Nature as part of an extended account of contracts, whereas the reference to foreign trade occurs in Book III on civil laws under Principles of Oeconomicks and Politicks.

trade (pp. 43–7), but yet it still privileged the balance of trade as evidence of a nation's prosperity and as a source of money for a nation without mines (e.g. pp. 30, 38). David Hume's essay 'Of the jealousy of trade' (1758) argued for the mutually beneficial qualities of international trade (Hume 1970, pp. 78–82), and the essay 'Of the balance of trade' (1752) is credited with the first fully systematic statement of the international specie-flow mechanism (Hume 1970, pp. 60–77), and yet this latter work also displays some protectionist features. Arthur Young's *Political Arithmetic* (1774) espoused a liberalisation of domestic agriculture and argued that price changes will effectively shift resources between different uses, but yet it supported the Corn Laws and the Navigation Acts and was opposed to free trade: 'A general free trade, as there has been no example of it in history, so it is contrary to reason' (Young 1774, p. 262). Thus, accounts of market dynamics were given widespread assent amongst disparate writings with different theoretical and policy leanings, but they were not always regarded as relevant with respect to the issue of freedom of internal and external trade.

One widely held view, however, was that foreign trade constituted the major source of wealth, and this was challenged by WN's insistence that foreign trade had been vastly overrated as a source of wealth or revenue for the nation. The more rigorously mercantilist literature had located the source of the benefit in the positive balance of trade. Thomas Mun's *England's Treasure by Forraign Trade* (first published 1664) had argued the classic mercantilist case that 'The ordinary means therefore to increase our wealth and treasure is by *Forraign Trade*, wherein we must ever observe this rule; to sell more to strangers yearly than we consume of theirs in value' (Mun 1967, p. 5). Charles Davenant's *Discourses on the Public Revenues* (first published 1698) and *Essay upon . . . the Balance of Trade* (first published 1699) identified increases in national wealth (and hence the source of increasing state wartime expenditure) with the balance of trade surplus; the influx of precious metals were the measure of this surplus although its foundation lay in the real productive capacity of the country. Joshua Gee's *The Trade and Navigation of Great Britain Considered* (first published 1729), contained a clear statement of the mercantilist and colonial policies later criticised in Book IV of WN, and argued that trade was the chief source of a nation's wealth and power; by furthering the export of manufactured goods (and also corn) and restricting imports except those of necessary raw materials, it was argued that a favourable balance of trade could be maintained and the poor at home could be provided with employment. In writings such as Vanderlint's *Money Answers All Things* (1734) and Kames's *Sketches* (1774), versions of an automatic specie-flow mechanism are outlined. However, as money stimulates productive activity and trade, concern with the level of specie inflow was still seen as vitally important.

By the mid-eighteenth century, though, some writings were offering the view that foreign trade was no longer essential for the economic well-being of a nation once it had reached its full development. Hume's essay 'Of commerce' (1752) had broached this as a possibility (Hume 1970, pp. 14–15), and Wallace's *Characteristics* had argued that a nation's prosperity was not dependent on foreign trade although it was inconceivable that a rich and industrious nation would not engage successfully in foreign trade (Wallace 1758, pp. 35–40, 141). WN countered this emphasis on foreign trade by arguing not only that the balance of trade was irrelevant, but also that foreign trade was the least productive form of economic activity. By inverting the conventional sectoral hierarchy and by placing commerce last in the historical order of development, WN was attacking the view that commerce and manufactures are the main source of wealth for a developing economy.

In addition, WN needed to address the system of agriculture with its rival claims that agriculture provided the source of wealth for a nation. The argument of WN was formulated in such a way that these two theories could simultaneously be differentiated from each other but yet indicted of the same mirror-image error of favouring specific sectors at the expense of others. A theory of resource allocation based on competitive price movements was unable to do this as it could not provide a framework in which different kinds of market activities could be compared; it could analyse outcomes within a market, but it had no mechanism for comparing outcomes across markets and hence across different sectors. It was unable to do this because a theory of competitive market dynamics had no overall definition of national wealth or measure of overall economic well-being which could be used to assess the aggregate impact of diverse activities across many markets.[46] And it was precisely this that the system of natural liberty was able to achieve.

One result of the tendency to interpret the system of natural liberty largely as a model of the equilibrating market mechanism, is that the non-economic aspects have largely been filtered out from what is seen as the economic core of the book; these aspects then have to be reimported into WN in order to emphasise the historical and juridical aspects of economic progress. But the system of natural liberty is itself a model of how the general progress of opulence can cohere and subsist through time without the guiding hand of the statesman, and so already includes within itself a concept of 'progress' or 'development' that contains historical, jurisprudential, political and social as well as economic dimensions. Indeed, in spite of the prevalence of mechanical analogies in the commentaries and the well-known reference to the way in which the market price 'gravitates' towards the natural price, at crucial moments WN itself uses organic and biological

---

[46] The theoretical difficulties of achieving this may be appreciated by noting that it was not until Léon Walras developed the concept of 'effective utility' (i.e. total utility) as a welfare

metaphors which epitomise its fundamental concern with the process of historical development. For example, in criticising the agricultural system's emphasis on a precise regimen, WN argues that the political body, like the human body, contains a principle of preservation which enables it to prosper in spite of maladroit human interference (WN IV.ix.28; II.iii.31).[47] The notion of stadial development through time, which supported the notion of a specific sectoral order of development for commercial society, included an account of the civil law and government of a nation. Part of the argument of WN was that the laws of a nation often continue long after the material circumstances that first gave rise to them have passed away and been replaced by others that then come into conflict with those outmoded laws (WN III.ii.4). It was argued that the commercial stage of society was associated with an increase in liberty and a reduction in dependence; the towns first secured a number of liberties from the crown when the countryside was still subjected to forms of feudal bondage, but in time some of these liberties were secured in the countryside as well (WN III.iii). The overwhelming message of WN, however, was that this historical process of increasing liberty was incomplete. The citizens of Great Britain enjoyed a high degree of civil liberty and enjoyed security under the law, but this still fell far short of 'perfect liberty', where the economic use of property would not be constrained by the state regulations against which WN was arguing.[48] The existing degree of liberty also bore the marks of its specific origins in the original freedom of the towns and cities which, however, came to take on a regulationist and restrictive character as the 'freedoms' of the mercantile practices of the towns came to form the basis of the unfreedoms of those who were excluded.

This multidimensionality of the *economic* progress of opulence and the system of natural liberty is lost sight of when the argument of WN is construed primarily in terms of the mechanics of self-equilibrating markets. It is not just that the economic theory of WN needs to be read alongside the other broader aspects of WN, but rather that the core theoretical structure of WN already includes these other aspects which have since been subtracted from it by misconstruing its core element as market analysis. Book

---

measure, that claims about the efficiency of the competitive outcome could properly be made. See chapter 6, n. 26 above.
47 Also, manufactures 'grow up naturally' and are even 'the offspring of agriculture' (WN III.iii.20). The effects of the monopoly trade are described in terms of an unwholesome body with swollen blood vessels (WN IV.vii.c.43). The movement of stock from the town to the countryside is described in terms of a fluid metaphor where stock 'overflows' from the towns and 'spreads itself . . . over the face of the land' (WN I.x.c.26), and the notion of fluidity is continued elsewhere as wages and prices sink, labour is circulated, and commerce runs in a number of channels.
48 It is widely agreed amongst commentators that civil liberty in WN was to some degree independent of political liberty: see Forbes (1975) and Letwin (1988).

I, chapter vii, of WN explained the role of the three revenues of rent, profit and wages in terms of an analysis of the competitive market that would not be unfamiliar to contemporaries. But the natural price outcome itself was not related in any direct way to the new definition of wealth as the annual revenue/annual produce of society. The function of competition within the system of natural liberty was to show how the order of sectoral development that would occur naturally, that is, in the absence of state regulations, would also be the same order of development that would result in the largest annual revenue. When one sector had absorbed all the capital investment that it could, competition would lead to a fall in the rates of return in that sector, and capital would then naturally move to the next sector in the sequence.[49] Thus, the primary economic significance of competition is that it leads to the proper sequence of sectoral development, thereby promoting the greatest possible annual revenue. By interpreting Book I as a form of allocation analysis, rather than as laying the revenue foundations for the analysis of the growth of the annual revenue in the process of a nation's progress of opulence, the theoretical basis of the system of natural liberty has been largely bypassed by modern commentators.

The prevalence of the more economistic readings of WN has, however, prompted other commentators to redress the balance by integrating into WN the ethical concerns of TMS and the juridical concerns of LJ. Chapter 2 above argued that the monologic style of WN is entirely congruent with the absence from it of the ethical concerns of TMS. It was argued that the impartial spectator is truly absent from WN; neither the higgling of the market nor the equilibrium outcome can be construed as falling under the domain of the impartial spectator, and to emphasise these aspects of the economic argument of WN is to misconstrue the analytical framework of the system of natural liberty. But chapter 2 also argued that the monologism of WN is entirely in accord with the lower-order moral status accorded to justice and prudence, the second-rank virtues associated with the public sphere of a person's role in civil society.

In WN, the system of liberty is presented as being the only system whose rules are fully in accordance with the rules of justice. At the end of Book IV, it is argued that under the system of natural liberty, 'Every man, as long as he does not violate the laws of justice, is left perfectly free to pursue his own interest in his own way, and to bring both his industry and capital into competition with those of any other man, or order of men' (WN IV.ix.51). Here, a person may freely pursue his own interest and exercise his own industry and capital, subject only to the proviso that he does not violate the laws of justice. The mercantile system, however, is presented as an 'unjust' system which 'violates' natural liberty, justice, and the most 'sacred rights

---

49 WN II.v.32–7; IV.vii.c.86–8.

THE SYSTEM OF NATURAL LIBERTY

of mankind' (WN I.x.c.59; IV.v.b.16; IV.vii.b.44), and which does not leave things at perfect liberty (WN I.x.a.2; I.x.c.1). But there is no reference to the impartial spectator or to 'natural justice' as the substantiation of the impartial spectator's decisions. So what can be said about the justice that underlies the system of natural liberty? Book IV states that 'To hurt in any degree the interest of any one order of citizens, for no other purpose but to promote that of some other, is evidently contrary to that justice and equality of treatment which the sovereign owes to all the different orders of his subjects' (WN IV.viii.30). In jurisprudential terms, such a rule falls within public law, not private law, the arena in which the impartial spectator had made his appearances in LJ. In this concluding chapter on the mercantile system, justice is described with respect to the different orders of society. Justice requires that all orders of citizens are treated equally; this is the rule and the sovereign should abide by it. All privileges, bounties or restrictions that treat different orders of citizens differently are to be regarded as unjust and, therefore, should be abolished. By definition, this means that all the measures of the mercantile system that give such advantages to merchants and manufacturers are unjust and ought to be abolished. Similarly, all the measures of the agricultural system that attempt (although unsuccessfully) to promote agriculture are also unjust. What would remain if all these restrictions were to be removed would be the system of natural liberty; here sectional interests are removed and justice can be described in terms of individual persons, not the different orders of society. Here, every person would be unconstrained by law from employing his industry in any place or in any way as long as this did not infringe any one else's right to do the same (WN I.x.c.12, 59; IV.ii.42; IV.ix.51). To ensure this, the duty of the sovereign with respect to justice is described as 'the duty of protecting, as far as possible, every member of the society from the injustice or oppression of every other member of it, or the duty of establishing an exact administration of justice' (WN IV.ix.51).

The rules of justice thus show why the regulations of any system that proposes either preferences or restraints are a violation of justice and natural liberty. WN does not, however, propose that the system of natural liberty either could or should be instituted immediately in their place. It recognises that the political opposition to such sweeping changes would make such a project impossible to achieve, and in this respect it compares the introduction of freedom of trade with idealistic impossibilistic schemes from the republican lexicon, such as Oceana and Utopia (WN IV.ii.43). Further, natural liberty is not absolute even in the system of natural liberty propounded in WN. Legal restrictions on banking and building practices are specifically mentioned as examples of the need to curb individual freedoms where the security of the whole society might be endangered:

Such regulations [e.g. banking regulations or building regulations] may, no doubt, be considered as in some respect a violation of natural liberty. But those exertions of the natural liberty of a few individuals, which might endanger the security of the whole society, are, and ought to be, restrained by the laws of all governments; of the most free, as well as of the most despotical.

(WN II.ii.94)[50]

If the tone of WN in places becomes warm with indignation at the mercantile violations of natural liberty, it is also deeply sceptical and cautious when discussing even piecemeal legislative changes. WN recognises that any changes will result in hardships for some groups, and for this reason it argues that any changes should be introduced slowly and cautiously:

> Humanity may in this case require that the freedom of trade should be restored only by slow gradations, and with a good deal of reserve and circumspection. Were those high duties and prohibitions taken away all at once, cheaper foreign goods of the same kind might be poured so fast into the home market, as to deprive all at once many thousands of our people of their ordinary employment and means of subsistence.
>
> (WN IV.ii.40)[51]

It also recognises that to rectify one injustice may simply create an even greater injustice elsewhere, and so here too great caution is required:

> Such are the unfortunate effects of all the regulations of the mercantile system! They not only introduce very dangerous disorders into the state of the body politick, but disorders which it is often difficult to remedy, without occasioning, for a time at least, still greater disorders.
>
> (WN IV.vii.c.44)[52]

The reduction of the system of natural liberty to a view of justice

---

50 Also, the building of party walls was to be enforced in order to prevent the spread of fire. In addition, the rate of interest was to be legally fixed (WN II.iv.13–17).

51 The argument then goes on to claim that the resulting disorder may however be less than might be imagined. Concern is also expressed for the undertakers of a great manufacture, a group of people not normally treated very sympathetically in WN: 'The undertaker of a great manufacture who, by the home markets being suddenly laid open to the competition of foreigners, should be obliged to abandon his trade, would no doubt suffer very considerably ... The equitable regard, therefore, to his interest requires that changes of this kind should never be introduced suddenly, but slowly, gradually, and after a very long warning' (WN IV.ii.44).

52 A similar caution was shown in the discussion of the grain trade, where it is argued that 'The very bad policy of one country may thus render it in some measure dangerous and imprudent to establish what would otherwise be the best policy in another', but this argument is applied only to small states not to 'great countries such as France or England' (WN IV.v.b.39).

associated with an almost unqualified use of private property has become a familiar story.[53] But the inclusion of labourers along with landlords and employers in the triadic analysis of property owners responding to changes in the market rates of return, together with the argument that the mercantile system had benefited the rich and powerful amongst the merchants and manufacturers rather than their poor labourers,[54] seems to emphasise the point that most sections of society were expected to benefit materially from the improved justice that the system of natural liberty seemed to offer, including even the labouring classes.[55] Thus, the emphasis on the superior justice of the system of natural liberty can be seen as backing up its claims to superior material prospects for society. In this sense, juridical claims and material claims worked in parallel in providing support for the system of natural liberty.

4

It was emphasised in the introduction to this chapter that the monologic style of WN does not mean that it can be viewed as a didactic text in the sense that excludes a rhetorical dimension. The theoretical structure presented in section 2 above constitutes the analytical frame that supports the large and leisurely discourse of WN. This discourse includes historical, comparative, empirical and conjectural material interspersed with juridical claims and a sustained criticism of the mercantile system. The intellectual pace for the reader who starts with Book I and continues right to the end is therefore highly variable; some passages and chapters are tightly constructed theoretically, others digress magnificently, while others range widely through illustrative material. But, this heterogeneous reading experience stands in contrast with the constancy of the voice of the text. As a monologic text in Bakhtin's sense, WN discloses a space over which the controlling voice is confidently asserting its authority. Analytically, this is pursued by the gradual unfolding of the theoretical argument across the first four Books of WN. Rhetorically, a number of devices are deployed.

---

53 See, for example, Thompson (1991a, 1991b) for an account as to how debates about the inland grain trade were linked to the power of WN's arguments regarding the unconstrained use of private property. Also Hont and Ignatieff (1983b). The concept of 'liberty' in WN is discussed in the following chapter.
54 'It is the industry which is carried on for the benefit of the rich and the powerful, that is principally encouraged by our mercantile system. That which is carried on for the benefit of the poor and the indigent, is too often, either neglected, or oppressed' (WN IV.viii.4).
55 Taking into account the increased annual revenue that would have accrued in the absence of the mercantile system, together with the argument that the wages of labour are highest in the progressive state, it might be inferred that manufacturing labourers would be better off in a system of natural liberty. But this is not an argument that WN actually advances. Certainly, WN recognises that the actual distribution of the annual revenue would be very different under an alternative system, with a larger agricultural sector and a smaller

The focus of criticism of WN is on the systems of political oeconomy, or systems of police, where the meddling legislator/statesman attempts to direct the industry of private persons. This means that the attack is directed at both the system of commerce and the system of agriculture. It was argued above that the sectoral distinctions of the Économistes were of fundamental importance in shaping the theoretical categories of WN, but the main fire is directed at the system of commerce. It was this system that was the prevalent one and commanded the most support, and it was against this system that the argument of WN was most directly targeted.

The polemic directed at the merchants and manufacturers, the alleged architects of this system, is well known. Hardly a reference to these groups passes without a barrage of negative terms: 'the clamour and sophistry of merchants and manufacturers' (WN I.x.c.25); 'the sophistry of merchants and manufacturers' (WN IV.ii.38); 'the impertinent jealousy of merchants and manufacturers . . . the mean rapacity, the monopolizing spirit of merchants and manufacturers' (IV.iii.c.9); 'the interested sophistry of merchants and manufacturers' (IV.iii.c.10); 'with all the passionate confidence of interested falsehood' (WN IV.iii.c.13).

WN also denies the mercantile system any standing as a coherent or credible intellectual position that could reasonably attract any serious, informed support; it is a system based on sophistry. The doctrine concerning the balance of trade, for example, is repeatedly presented as 'absurd' or 'ridiculous': 'Among all the absurd speculations that have been propagated concerning the balance of trade . . .' (WN III.i.1); 'It would be too ridiculous to go about seriously to prove, that wealth does not consist in money, or in gold and silver' (WN IV.i.17);[56] 'even they, who are convinced of its absurdity, are very apt to forget their own principles . . .' (WN IV.i.34); 'Nothing, however, can be more absurd than this whole doctrine of the balance of trade . . .' (WN IV.iii.c.2). Similarly, on entails: 'entails . . . are founded upon the most absurd of all suppositions . . .' (WN III.ii.6). And the laws against regrators: 'the absurd laws against engrossers, regrators, and forestallers . . .' (WN III.ii.21). Allied to this kind of denigration is the presentation of fundamental mercantile tenets as mere 'popular notions' or 'vulgar prejudices': 'the popular notion, that as the quantity of silver naturally increases in every country with the increase of wealth . . .' (WN I.xi.e.15); 'Such slight observations, however, upon the prices either of corn or of other commodities, would not probably have misled so many intelligent

---

mercantile sector, and with a lower average rate of profit on capital in all sectors. This would result in losses as well as gains across different sectors and within the labouring class.

56 Although this is precisely what WN then goes on to do (WN IV.i.17–34); the end of this section concludes: 'I thought it necessary, though at the hazard of being tedious, to examine at full length this popular notion that wealth consists in money, or in gold and silver' (WN IV.i.34).

authors, had they not been influenced, at the same time, by the popular notion, that . . .' (WN I.xi.e.30; I.xi.i.1); 'That wealth consists in money, or in gold and silver, is a popular notion . . .' (WN IV.i.1); 'In consequence of these popular notions, all the different nations of Europe have studied, though to little purpose, every possible means of accumulating gold and silver in their respective countries' (WN IV.i.5); 'I thought it necessary, though at the hazard of being tedious, to examine at full length this popular notion that wealth consists in money . . .' (WN IV.i.34; also para. 33); 'the law for the encouragement of coinage derives its origin from those vulgar prejudices which have been introduced by the mercantile system' (WN IV.vi.32). These passages are not just arguing that the mercantile system is wrong or ill-conceived; a system may be wrong but may still be recognised as deserving intellectual respect. What these passages show is that WN not only argues analytically against the mercantile system, but further denies it any credibility as an informed system; intelligent men can only have been drawn to it as a result of being misled by mere popular notions propagated by the sophistry of the merchant class. Its widespread influence on policy and on popular opinion can, therefore, only be due to the interested chicanery of merchants and manufacturers who hoodwinked others into accepting their nostrums; as a system it could not possibly have influenced policy on account of the inherent persuasiveness of its doctrines. Further, WN even purports to disdain rebutting these popular notions which are thus placed outside the pale of serious discussion. When it does rebut them, it does so with a protestation of how demeaning it is to confute such vulgar notions.

As argued above, WN claims that the actual order of development of Europe is an inversion of the proper order of sectoral development as a result of the influence of the mercantile system. Instead of agriculture being developed first, followed by the manufactures of the towns, and finally by foreign trade, the actual order of development in Europe had been based on the prior development of the towns and foreign trade with agricultural development lagging behind. Again here, the terms used by WN in describing this development are entirely negative. Such development is characterised as an 'unnatural and retrograde order' (WN III.i.9) and 'contrary to the order of nature and of reason' (WN I.x.c.26). In obstructing the free circulation of labour, the corporation laws have produced 'disorder, the greatest perhaps of any in the police of England' (WN I.x.c.45) and the colonial regulations are 'impertinent badges of slavery imposed without any sufficient reason' (WN IV.vii.b.44).

The key terms used to denote the mercantile system are, thus, terms such as 'absurd', 'sophistry', 'popular notions', 'vulgar prejudices', 'unnatural', 'disorder' and 'contrary to the order of reason'. These key terms are then reversed in the presentation of the system of natural liberty, which is put forward as the opposite of the mercantile system. The system of natural liberty epitomises 'reason' and the working out of the 'natural order of things'. It is 'plain reason' as opposed to 'vulgar prejudice':

> Whatever, therefore, we may imagine the real wealth and revenue of a country to consist in, whether in the value of the annual produce of its land and labour, as plain reason seems to dictate; or in the quantity of the precious metals which circulate within it, as vulgar prejudices suppose; in either view of the matter . . .
>
> (WN II.iii.25)

Further, the system of natural liberty is 'manifest', 'obvious', 'self-evident' and based securely on 'common-sense': 'It is the ambiguity of language only which can make this proposition [i.e. concerning money] appear either doubtful or paradoxical. When properly explained and understood, it is almost self-evident' (WN II.ii.15); 'The proposition [i.e. relating to free trade] is so very manifest, that it seems ridiculous to take any pains to prove it; nor could it ever have been called in question, had not the interested sophistry of merchants and manufacturers confounded the common sense of mankind' (WN IV.iii.c.10); 'The maxim [i.e. that consumption is the sole end of production] is so perfectly self-evident, that it would be absurd to attempt to prove it. But in the mercantile system . . .' (WN IV.viii.49); and 'the obvious and simple system of natural liberty' (WN IV.ix.51). Thus, in the series of binary opposites deployed in these comparisons, it is the derogated term that is systematically applied to the mercantile system. Pairs such as prejudice/reason, sophistry/commonsense, disorder/order, and unnatural/natural, map out a discursive space in which the system of natural liberty is presented as reasonable and self-evidently superior to all those who are not blinded by prejudice. In the section above, the juridical pairs unjust/just and violated natural liberty/system of natural liberty were identified, and these too function in the same way. Within this system of binary opposites, the mercantile system is constructed as the 'other' of the system of natural liberty. Rhetorically, the effect of this is to heighten the distinguishing characteristics of the system of natural liberty and to set them into sharper focus compared with the main rival system. But further, the meaning of these terms is to some degree constructed by means of this antithetical positioning: reason and prejudice are defined by their functioning as antithetical terms; sophistry and commonsense are defined by their functioning as antithetical terms, and so on. In an analogous way, the system of natural liberty and the mercantile system are constructed as antithetical systems. It is not so much that the independently conceived systems of commerce and natural liberty are compared with each other, but that the characterisation of each is to some degree dependent on the characterisation of the other. In a discursive sense, the presentation of WN is dependent on its representation of the mercantile system.

The absorption of both the mercantile system and the system of natural liberty within the one discursive space is achieved by the overriding presence of the controlling voice of the text. It was argued in chapter 2 that the dialogic interplay of voices characteristic of TMS is absent from WN. The text of WN occasionally uses the first person singular to refer to illustrations or observations, or to signpost the direction of the text (WN I.vii.32–7). Very rarely it uses the first person singular to provide an answer or response to the false claims of the mercantile system (WN IV.iii.c.3, 8; v.a.8). Sometimes it uses a first person plural as a pedagogic device where the teacher carries his readers along with him on some point (WN I.viii.13). But the characteristic style of WN is the detached voice speaking with authoritative jurisdiction over the domain of the text. It was argued in chapter 3 above, that a source of the ethical dialogism of TMS is provided by the discourse of conscience in which a moral agent debates with himself. It was also argued that a source of the dialogism of the text of TMS is provided by the framing context of Stoicism and the irresolvable conflicts this posed for TMS between the claims of nature and of reason. In the Stoic philosophy, the claims of nature and reason act in unison, but TMS was unable to accept this, and so it is the irreconcilability of the claims of nature and of reason that underlies the dialogism of conscience. In the amoral monologism of WN, however, there is no tension between nature and reason; in contrast to the mercantile system which satisfies neither nature nor reason, the system of natural liberty is presented as satisfying both together. This, again, underlines the different discursive space occupied by these two texts. The categories of TMS are derived from Stoic categories and so there 'nature' and 'reason' derive from a predominantly moral register of meanings. In WN, 'nature' and 'reason' no longer refer to this moral universe, but rather to a systematic inquiry into the objective phenomena of the world.

As the system of natural liberty accords with reason and nature, and is practically self-evident once it has been properly explained, all may come to understand it and appreciate its benefits. The dialogism of the text of TMS bears the signs of the moral fragmentation of humanity; the sage and the philosopher who are able to enter into the dialogism of moral discourse are differentiated from other moral agents, but the rest of humanity, the mob of mankind, can at best hope to live a merely decent life according to given rules. As the discourse of WN is not a moral discourse, but a scientific or monologic discourse, the readership is not fragmented in this way. At a number of points, the text directly includes the reader. Sometimes this is achieved by means of the inclusive first person plural voice. In TMS the use of this voice frequently signified the degenerate norms of a fallen humanity, but in WN this voice is used to enlist the reader in the advancement of the argument by appeals to what is ordinarily and generally known: 'In order to satisfy ourselves upon this point it will not be necessary to enter into any tedious or doubtful calculation of what may be the lowest sum upon which it is possible to do this. There are many plain symptoms that the wages of labour . . .' (WN I.viii.28); 'That the industry which is carried on in towns is, every-where in Europe, more advantageous than that which is carried on in the country, without entering into any very nice computations, we may satisfy ourselves by one very simple and obvious observation' (WN I.x.c.21); 'Without entering into any particular discussion of their calculations, a very simple observation may satisfy us that the result of them must be false. We see every day . . .' (WN II.v.37).

An implication of the simple and obvious nature of the system of natural liberty is that it requires no abstruse or refined knowledge to understand and accept it. This conveniently obviates the need for WN itself to collect this information and present it to its readers. But further, in calling upon common observation, the text is including all its readers in a shared understanding of the system of natural liberty, as well as legitimising the common knowledge of society that anyone may lay claim to. Thus, the voice of WN is able to include its readership by addressing it directly and calling upon it to furnish those observations that the text requires to demonstrate its point: 'Observe the accommodation of the most common artificer or day-labourer in a civilized and thriving country, and you will perceive that . . .' (WN I.i.11); 'Compare the cultivation of the lands in the neighbourhood of any considerable town, with that of those which lie at some distance from it, and you will easily satisfy yourself how much . . .' (WN III.i.1); 'Compare the present condition of those estates with the possessions of the small proprietors in their neighbourhood, and you will require no other argument to convince you . . .' (WN III.ii.7); 'Compare the slow progress of those European countries of which the wealth depends very much upon their commerce and manufactures, with the rapid advances of our North American colonies, of which the wealth is founded altogether in agriculture' (WN III.iv.19); 'Compare the mercantile manners of Cadiz and Lisbon with those of Amsterdam, and you will be sensible how . . .' (WN IV.vii.c.61). Here the text is directly addressing the reader and requiring him to furnish the common knowledge of the day in support of the system of natural liberty, but in doing this the text is at the same time constructing for the reader what it requires that common knowledge to be. In including the reader as an active participant in the text and also, therefore, as a fully responsible member of a scientific community, the text is at the same time controlling the reader's contribution in order to further its own argument.

5

The rhetoric of WN presents its own argument as manifest to reason and available to commonsense: the system of natural liberty is 'simple and obvious' to anyone who is not blinded by prejudice, sophistry or interested falsehood. But yet WN is a complex work of nearly a thousand pages. The reading experience of WN is far from simple, a complaint even of Smith's own friends and admirers. Further, the theoretical arguments underlying the system of natural liberty are unravelled at a leisurely pace over the course of the first three Books and are then put to work over the course of the lengthy fourth Book. Relying on a theoretical structure of this sort, the sectoral argument in favour of the system of natural liberty is highly complex and abstract. It has also come to be lost from sight. In this, the rhetorical claims of WN have triumphed over the analytical argument: the appeal to commonsense understandings and the 'obvious' superiority of a system of liberty contributed to the easy absorption of the rhetoric of WN. By disregarding the sectoral analysis of WN, the public interest came to be seen as no more than the simple summation of individual interests, and WN came to be interpreted as a straightforward defence of the untrammelled use of private property.

This transformation of the argument of WN, and the triumph of the rhetorical claims over the analytical content, did not happen immediately. There were two aspects to this transformation. The first concerned the assessment of the validity of the sectoral hierarchy, and the second concerned the way in which the sectoral hierarchy was detached from the argument for natural liberty. Early commentators were well aware of the sectoral hierarchy, and this led to a discussion of the validity of the doctrines of the Économistes, whose influence on WN was widely recognised. The theoretical implication of the sectoral hierarchy for the relation between individual self-seeking and the public interest was keenly debated, and the issue of whether the pursuit of individual interest was always conducive to the public interest was widely discussed. In the final section of this chapter, these early debates will be briefly reviewed in order to demonstrate how the meaning of WN came to be constructed and hence appropriated during the early part of the nineteenth century in terms of a set of concerns which have since become paradigmatic for most readings of WN. It was during this period that the sectoral argument supporting the system of natural liberty came to be abandoned, while the preference for natural liberty was maintained.

Governor Thomas Pownall wrote a public letter to Adam Smith in 1776[57] in which he opposed just about all of the main policy conclusions of WN, but he did not criticise its basic theoretical argument.[58] Pownall

---

57 *A Letter from Governor Pownall to Adam Smith*, London 1776, reprinted as Appendix A in *The Correspondence of Adam Smith* (1987), pp. 337–76.
58 Proposals advanced against WN's conclusions relating to commercial policy include infant industry protection (pp. 358–9), restraints on the importation of live cattle and corn (pp. 359–61), and a corn bounty to protect land workers and landlords against the secular fall in the value of corn (pp. 341–6, 361–6). This last proposal related to a criticism of the

accepted the main structure of the analysis relating to the hierarchy of capitals and he also recognised that this underlay the analysis of Book IV, but he made a number of criticisms of this. A minor criticism relies upon an elaboration of the categories of WN. It is argued that WN does not distinguish between circuitous and round-about foreign trade as alternative forms of non-direct foreign trade. The *Letter* agrees that round-about foreign trade proper, trade by 'Tom-Long the carrier', is an unprofitable use of capital, but that circuitous trade (i.e. multilateral trade) is profitable and produces what is called a 'superlucration of profit' as each leg of the journey contributes to overall profits (Pownall 1977, pp. 355–8). Although this point is stressed against WN, it is only an amendment of the hierarchy of capitals analysis and not a challenge to it. Its main effect was to underline the point that the colonial trade, even when circuitous, could generate increased profit for mercantile capital, but as the argument of WN accepted that the colonial trading profit rate was increased, it did nothing to damage the more fundamental argument that the increased profitability of the colony trade harmed the annual revenue by deflecting capital away from agriculture, manufactures and the home trade.

The major criticism levelled at the argument of WN against the colonial monopoly was also based on an acceptance of the sectoral hierarchy (with its own amendment). What the *Letter* challenged was the view that this hierarchy would be coincident with the long-term historical order of the employment of capitals; the *Letter* accepts that the national interest requires a greater development of domestic agriculture and industry but it argues that this will best be promoted in the long term by the increased demand for domestic output arising from the colonial monopoly (Pownall 1977, pp. 371–4). The *Letter* even accepted the argument of WN that the colonial monopoly would draw capital away from the land, but this is immediately qualified by the argument that this would happen only in the 'first instance' and that in the longer term the increased trade would provide a stimulus to agriculture (p. 374). In this way, the *Letter* argued that WN was out of touch with the needs of a commercial society where commerce was seen as a long-run stimulant to domestic output rather than as a rival claim on a given capital stock, but its argument was based on a general acceptance and adaptation of the theoretical structure of the book and its sectoral hierarchy, rather than a wholesale challenge to it.

For nearly half a century, debate focused on the extent to which the different sectors could be ranked in order of importance and whether the system of the Économistes was correct in ascribing a superior productiveness to agriculture. This was also closely linked to the question of whether

---

invariable real corn price in WN which formed the basis of the argument against the corn bounty.

the national interest could be seen simply as the summation of individual interests, where individuals are unconstrained in the use of their own property. The posthumous lectures on political economy delivered by Dugald Stewart[59] concur with WN that the commercial policy of Europe had promoted manufactures and commerce at the expense of agriculture, the more productive activity, but it adopts the argument of the Économistes that only the land produces a net produce arising from the bounty of nature (Stewart 1968, II.I.i, pp. 253–308). Although sympathetic to the economic analysis of the Économistes, Stewart's lectures offer a warning against the political absolutism and 'unmixed despotism' of their writings (Stewart 1968, pp. 307–8). Dugald Stewart's intellectual influence among the new generation interested in political economy guaranteed a wide forum in which these issues would be discussed. In particular, the question of the nature of public wealth and the means by which it might be increased were seriously debated, together with the twin issues of the relative productiveness of different sectoral investments and the congruence of the individual and national interest.[60]

Francis Horner wrestled with the issues of productive and unproductive labour in private notes, but his articles in *The Edinburgh Review* inclined towards the physiocratic view that agriculture constitutes the source of national wealth (*The Edinburgh Review*, vol. 1, Jan. 1803, pp. 446–7; 1957 reprint, pp. 72–3), and were sympathetic towards the treatment of different employment of capitals in WN whilst acknowledging that 'we are not yet in possession of a complete theory' (*The Edinburgh Review*, vol. 5, Oct. 1804, p. 205; 1957 reprint, p. 111). Henry Brougham, on the other hand, was breaking away from Dugald Stewart and what he saw as the physiocratic bias of WN. Brougham's *Inquiry into the Colonial Policy of the European Powers* (1803) criticised the privileging of agricultural activity, but its arguments concerning the benefits of the colonial monopoly show that other aspects of WN's ranking scheme which were thought to be independent of the Économistes were not rejected.[61] Although less critical of the colonial monopoly than WN, Brougham's *Inquiry* does, however, severely circum-

---

59 *Lectures on Political Economy*, vols 8 and 9 of *Collected Works of Dugald Stewart* (1855); reprinted 1968.
60 Meek (1963b) argues that the physiocratic influence was still much in evidence during this period. Fontana (1985) examines the early contributors to *The Edinburgh Review*, especially pp. 46–68.
61 This work accepted WN's threefold hierarchy of mercantile capital together with the attendant notions of the replacement of domestic capitals and the issue of speedy returns, but it amended the conclusion by arguing that the colonial trade was a branch of the home trade, not the foreign trade, and this enabled the various kinds of colonial trade to be ranked somewhat higher than in WN (Brougham 1803, I.II.I.1, 2, 6 to p. 175; I.II. II., pp. 231ff.). It is not accepted that the colonial monopoly could lead to overinvestment in the colony trade relative to domestic agriculture; instead a notion of a natural division of labour amongst capital is proposed such that different sizes and availabilities of capital are naturally

scribe the conclusion of WN that individual investing behaviour is always conducive to the national good. In commending Book III of WN, it seems to concur that the relative underdevelopment of European agriculture had not been in the best interest of overall economic development, but it inclines to the view that this was partly the result of individual preferences, and so cannot be entirely attributed to the policy of Europe (Brougham 1803, pp.143–5). It also argues that the country's interest is not advanced by the large traders (such as colonial traders and some domestic traders in an advanced country) who favour great profits but with slow returns (Brougham 1803, pp. 254–6).[62]

Lauderdale's *Inquiry into the Nature and Origin of Public Wealth* (1804a) argues that the pursuit of individual gain (parsimony) does not necessarily lead to an increase in public wealth: 'But popular prejudice, which has ever regarded the sum-total of individual riches to be synonymous with public wealth, and which has conceived every means of increasing the riches of individuals to be a means of increasing public wealth, has pointed out parsimony or accumulation . . . as the most active means of increasing public wealth' (Lauderdale 1804a, pp.208–9). Brougham's review in *The Edinburgh Review* responded sharply to this and argued that 'the riches of a nation, and the sum of the riches of all its inhabitants, are expressions completely synonymous' (*The Edinburgh Review*, vol. 4, July 1804, p. 353).[63] This review also attacked the work of the Économistes along with what it sees as WN's inconsistently derivative position (pp. 354–64). In emphatic refutation of what its sees as the Économistes' privileging of nature as the source of surplus in WN's ranking scheme, it stresses the importance of the interdependence of all forms of labour in a developed system of the division of labour where 'nature work[s] with man, in manufacture as well as in agriculture' (p. 359) and where the profit of stock is as much the 'wages of nature' as the rent of land is.

The controversy surrounding the publication of William Spence's pamphlet *Britain Independent of Commerce* in 1807 reveals a greater sympathy for the doctrine of WN than was evident in Brougham's *The Edinburgh Review* article on Lauderdale's *Inquiry*. Spence's pamphlet assures the public that they need not fear the economic consequences of Napoleon's commercial blockade of Britain. Agriculture is the only source of wealth, it argues,

---

suited for different types of sectoral investment (I.II.I.7), and in this way the *Inquiry* limits the scope for any imbalance in sectoral investment caused by the colonial monopoly which acts rather as a 'vent for surplus' for overflowing capital funds (I.II.I.8) and as a source of increasing demand for domestic manufactures (I.II.I.4).

62 'The interests of traders, in the employment of their capitals, are by no means the same, in all cases, with the interests of the community to which they belong' (Brougham 1803, I.II.II, p. 254).

63 This point was taken up in Lauderdale's reply (1804b, pp. 23ff.), and responded to in Brougham (1805, pp. 66–9).

because only agriculture 'creates' wealth whereas manufactures and commerce (i.e. foreign trade), though necessary to stimulate the development of agriculture, only 'transfer' wealth already created and so may suffer some reduction without significantly threatening the economic well-being of the nation. The third edition of the pamphlet acknowledges that this emphasis on the absolute superiority of agriculture differs from WN's sectoral ranking, but it inclines to the view earlier expressed by *The Edinburgh Review*'s review of Lauderdale's *Inquiry* that WN's ranking is merely an inconsistent derivation of the Économistes' theory: 'The principles of Dr. Smith clearly carry him to the theory of the Economistes; and in order to be consistent, he ought, unquestionably, to have reckoned Agriculture the *only* productive employment of capital or labour' (Brougham, *The Edinburgh Review*, vol. 4, July 1804, p. 357; cited by Spence 1808a, note p. 12). On this occasion, however, the Edinburgh Reviewer (probably T.R. Malthus) is more sympathetic to WN and defends its 'middle doctrine' between the mercantile and the agriculture sects (*The Edinburgh Review*, vol. 11, Jan. 1808, p. 430) which postulated that manufacturing and commerce each contribute to national wealth, implying that the physiocratic definition of national wealth should be extended from the narrow notion of agricultural surplus to that of the real revenue of society which would include the value of all food and commodities, i.e. all consumption (pp. 429–48). Traces of WN's sectoral ranking surface at the end of this review which claims not to be a 'blind admirer' of foreign trade: 'Every rational political economist considers it [i.e. foreign trade] as greatly inferior, both in magnitude and importance, to the internal trade of a country; and always places it below its two elder sisters, agriculture and manufactures' (p. 446).[64]

Traces of WN's ranking of investment sectors are present even in James Mill's response to Spence's pamphlet as *Commerce Defended* (first published 1808) adverts to the superior productiveness of land as a source of wealth:

> In the praises which the *Économistes*, together with Mr Spence and Mr Cobbett, bestow upon land as a source of wealth, absolutely considered, the intelligent reader will not hesitate to join. Of all species of labour, that which is bestowed upon the soil, is in general rewarded by the most abundant product. In the present circumstances of the greater part of Europe, the cultivation of the soil not only pays the

---

[64] If the Reviewer in this case were really Malthus (Fetter (1953, p. 246) thinks it 'probably' was Malthus; Semmel (1963, pp. 14–15) thinks it was probably authored by Brougham), then it is ironic that Spence's reply to his Reviewers cites approvingly from Malthus's *Essay on Population* (2nd edn 1803, pp. 433, 435, 441) in support of its arguments for the priority of agriculture (Spence 1808b, pp. 36–9), claiming that 'the testimony of this gentleman is entitled to greater attention, when it is understood that he is far from being a *blind follower* of the Economists' (Spence 1808b, p. 37, emphasis added).

wages of labour, and the profit of stock employed in it, the sole return of other species of industry, but over and above this affords a share of the produce payable, as rent to the landlord. On this point, therefore, no controversy strictly exists . . .

(Mill 1966, pp. 94–5)

In spite of the reference to the Économistes, the reason adduced here is that given by WN relating to the three forms of revenue (wages, profit and rent) generated by agricultural activity compared with only two forms of revenue (wages and profit) generated by other kinds of industry, rather than the Économistes' argument that rent constitutes the only form of surplus. *Commerce Defended* also agrees with Spence's pamphlet that the present state of agriculture in Europe is one of relative underinvestment, and again the language derives from WN.[65]

It goes on to ascribe the general opulence of society to the operation of the division of labour, a process more advanced in manufacturing than in agriculture (Mill 1966, pp. 103–5), but concludes by conceding a part of Spence's conclusion (though not the arguments used to derive it), that the importance of commerce is 'in general greatly overrated' (p. 150). This conclusion is based partly on the priority accorded to agriculture, and partly on the statement of what has come to be known as Say's Law, which is used here to counter the 'vent for surplus' explanation of trade. Spence's (1808) reply to critics reiterates the main points including the distinction between the creation and transfer of wealth/revenue, and it claims Malthus's authority for the argument (Malthus 1973, p. 433). This stimulated a short response from *The Edinburgh Review* (vol. 14, April 1809, pp. 50–60)[66] which repeated Brougham's 1804 uncompromising argument that 'man never creates' and that in this sense manufacture is no different from agriculture. According to this view, the advantage of trade is that it promotes the division of labour and, in such a system of interdependent activities, it is otiose to ascribe a greater inherent productivity to any single sector.

During this period, Say's *Treatise on Political Economy* was published (1803), and this too put forward the argument of WN that the capital which earned the largest profit and was the most beneficial to the owner of the capital, may not be the most beneficial to society (Say 1971, II.VIII.iii). The argument given is that, in addition to generating profit, capital provides the means by which land and labour also yield a revenue. For this reason, capital is most beneficially employed first in agriculture, then in manufacture and internal commerce, and finally in foreign trade and the carrying trade. In addition to rehearsing the arguments for the sectoral hierarchy,

---

65 'a greater share of the industry and capital of every nation than consisted with its interests, was thus forcibly diverted into the commercial channel' (Mill 1966, p. 95).
66 This time possibly authored by Buchanan and Jeffrey, see Fetter (1953, p. 247).

Say's *Treatise* also repeats the argument of WN that the natural course of events will result in just this order of investment:

> It is very fortunate, that the natural course of things impels capital rather into those channels, which are the most beneficial to the community, than into those, which afford the largest ratio of profit. The investments generally preferred are those that are nearest home; whereof the first and foremost is the improvement of the soil, which is justly considered the most safe and permanent; the next, manufacture and internal commerce; and the last of all, external commerce, the trade of transport, and the commerce with distant nations.
>
> (Say 1971, II.VIII.iii)

Thus, during this period, the sectoral hierarchy of WN received considerable discussion and some influential proponents, but in the course of time it came under greater attack. The increasingly hostile response of *The Edinburgh Review* has already been noted, and this is also evident in the various editions of WN. William Playfair's edition (1805) disagreed with the notion of superior agricultural productiveness (vol. I, p. 64), but yet thought it would be 'wise policy' to encourage internal industry over foreign trade (vol. I, p. 70). David Buchanan's edition (1814) roundly condemned both the sectoral hierarchy (vol. II, p. 55) and the notion that the higher rate of profit in the monopoly trade could be harmful for the national revenue (vol. II, pp. 450–1).[67] But, even though the sectoral hierarchy was condemned, this did not lead to a rejection of the system of natural liberty, which came to be seen as a general statement in favour of the harmony of interest between individuals and society, and on the beneficial effects of individual profit-seeking behaviour. Thus, the policy conclusion of WN was retained even though the economic argument supporting it was rejected. So powerful was the rhetoric of WN that its celebration of economic freedom was accepted in spite of the agreed fallaciousness of the argument which had supported it, and in spite of the absence of other theoretical arguments to sustain the contention that individual profit-seeking would secure the greatest benefit for society as a whole.

This may be illustrated by the nature of the rejection of WN's arguments for natural liberty in McCulloch's *Principles of Political Economy* (1825a) (also *Discourse on Political Economy* (1825b) and 'Introductory Discourse' (1828)) where the hierarchy of investment sectors is criticised in the following terms:

---

[67] Later on, Edward Gibbon Wakefield's edition of WN (1835–9) also criticised these passages in WN. Say's *Treatise* was also later criticised by its editors; cf. editor's note to *Treatise* II.VIII.iii in Prinsep's edition (1821) and in Biddle's edition (1880 reprinted 1971).

> He [i.e. Smith] considered agriculture, though not the only productive employment, as the most productive of any; and he considered the home trade as more productive than a direct foreign trade, and the latter than the carrying trade. It is clear, however, that all these distinctions are fundamentally erroneous.
>
> (McCulloch 1825a, p. 55)

This passage dismisses WN's sectoral hierarchy as a self-evidently erroneous aberration deriving from the Économistes. In McCulloch's edition of WN, a note is inserted at WN II.v.12 which states: 'This is perhaps the most objectionable passage in the Wealth of Nations . . .' (WN 1828, vol. 2, p. 150). The central importance of the sectoral analysis for the structure of WN's argument against the monopoly of the colonial trade in Book IV is fully recognised. In McCulloch's edition of WN it is argued that it was wrong for WN to claim that the colonial monopoly raised the rate of mercantile profit, but it is recognised how dependent WN was on this position:

> Dr Smith justly maintains that the monopoly of the colony trade is productive of no real advantage to the mother country. But if it had really raised the rate of profit, as he contends it did, it would have been advantageous. Having once admitted that it had that effect, he had no other means of proving that it was disadvantageous, except by resorting to his theory with respect to the comparative advantageousness of the capital invested in different businesses . . .
>
> (WN 1828, vol. 3, note pp. 25–6)

Adopting a free trade position, it is argued here that the colonial monopoly could not be advantageous. But it is taken for granted that the level of the private rate of profit is a reliable indicator as to what really is advantageous for the nation; therefore it could not possibly be the case that the monopoly resulted in raising the colonial rate of profit. But, it is fully understood that the argument of WN against the colonial monopoly did accept that the monopoly had raised the rate of profit; its only argument against it therefore was the sectoral hierarchy argument that commercial trade *ipso facto* is less advantageous to the nation even if the rate of profit is increased.

The argument presented against WN here by McCulloch denies any validity to the sectoral ranking system or to the system of the Économistes upon which it is based. Having demolished the theoretical core of the system of natural liberty in WN, it might be thought that McCulloch would now reconsider how useful WN could be for advancing the new science of political economy. But instead of considering how much of WN might still be valid after this onslaught, both McCulloch's *Principles of Political Economy* and his edition of WN reclaim the text of WN by arguing that the sectoral hierarchy argument is actually opposed to Smith's own system. Immediately following the passage last cited, McCulloch's edition of WN continues: 'except by resorting to his theory with respect to the comparative advantageousness of the capital invested in different businesses; a theory which, I flatter myself, I have shown, is equally at variance with Dr Smith's own system and with the real principles of the science' (WN 1828, vol. 3, note p. 26). Here it is argued that the sectoral approach is at variance with 'Smith's own system' and with true scientific principles. Similarly, in the *Principles*, the sentence preceding the passage cited above reads: 'His [i.e. Smith's] leaning to the Economists – a leaning perceptible in every part of his work – made him so far swerve from the principles of his own system, as to admit that individual advantage is not always a *true test* of the public advantageousness of different employments' (McCulloch 1825a, p. 54, original emphasis). Here we see an early example of a truly retrospective reading of WN. The text of WN is appropriated for the emerging science of political economy but, in order to do this, its unacceptable elements are shorn from it on the grounds that they are at variance with what is really held to be the 'essential' message of WN that individual interest is identical with the public interest. WN had tried to formulate an argument to substantiate this proposition, but in McCulloch's *Principles* it was simply asserted:

> A state being nothing more than an aggregate collection of individuals, it necessarily follows, that whatever is most advantageous to them must be most advantageous to the state; and it is obvious, that the self-interest of those concerned will always prevent them from engaging in manufacturing and commercial undertakings, unless when they yield as large profits, and are, consequently, as publicly beneficial as agriculture.
>
> (McCulloch 1825a, p. 55)

Here a direct statement is made of the necessary identity between a state's interest and the aggregate of the individual interests that are deemed to comprise it. The problems generated by WN's attempts to demonstrate the identity of economic interest between the individual and the society are sidestepped by simply asserting that such an identity must necessarily exist.[68] This repeats Brougham's criticism of Lauderdale's *Inquiry* that the interest of the nation is necessarily synonymous with the aggregate of

---

68 This identity of interest had been earlier challenged in the first edition of Malthus's *Essay* (1798): 'A capital employed upon land may be unproductive to the individual that employs it and yet be highly productive to the society. A capital employed in trade, on the contrary, may be highly productive to the individual, and yet be almost totally unproductive to the society . . .' (Malthus 1970, p. 194). Malthus's writings had followed WN in arguing that in the 'natural progress of a state towards riches, manufactures, and foreign commerce would follow, in their order, the high cultivation of the soil', and that this 'natural order of things' had been inverted in Europe (p. 195), but it argued this not with respect to increasing the exchangeable value of the annual produce, but on the provision

individual interests (Brougham 1805, p. 66). WN's attempt to explain the identity of the individual and the public interest by way of the natural order of opulence, where individual behaviour would be shown to coincide with the natural progress of opulence, was abandoned but, in the process, the meaning of WN was reconstructed and appropriated by the political economy of the early nineteenth century. The authority of WN was such that it could not be simply discarded; it had to be reinterpreted and assimilated as part of the new economic thinking of the day.

6

WN came to be read unreservedly as a text tht argues that there is a direct congruence between private and public interests. In its narrow economic formulation, this came to mean that the pursuit of individual profits would best secure the public interest, but this economic argument has come to be interpreted in a wider frame of reference that extols the economic exercise of individual liberty. The economic analysis of WN thus came to be seen as paradigmatic of a more general argument concerning a harmony of economic interests. According to this broader argument, WN epitomises the moral as well as the economic superiority of a free system of market relations, and this interpretation has come to be buttressed by those readings that emphasise the congruence of Smith's moral philosophy and jurisprudence with the economic argument in favour of natural liberty. The following and final chapter will examine the moral assessment of commercial society that is to be found in Adam Smith's works.

---

of subsistence argument that Europe 'might undoubtedly have been much more populous than at present, and yet not be more incumbered by its population' (p. 196).

8
CONCLUSION
Commerce and conscience

1

In the Introduction above, the question was posed as to how Smith's works may be read. The range of existing interpretations of Smith's works shows that there is no single or simple answer to this question as his texts continue to stimulate quite different and sometimes conflicting interpretations. Two broad approaches may be identified in the existing secondary literature. The first approach tends to select a particular text, or combination of texts, and disregards the issue of the ways in which these texts relate to Smith's output as a whole. This approach results in highlighting particular aspects of Smith's works, and is the one that has produced the familiar picture of Smith as primarily an 'economist'. The other approach attempts to provide an account of the totality of Smith's intellectual output by integrating his moral philosophy, jurisprudence, politics, economics and methodological disquisitions. In this case, as the unifying element of this diverse collection of texts is constituted by the identity of their author, the interpretative project has been understood as the retrieval of the author's intentions. But, as it accepts without question the presumption that Smith's diverse writings constitute an *œuvre* in the sense of a unified intellectual programme, it thus sets itself the task of explaining what this *œuvre* might be, without first enquiring what kind of textual entity is meant by the term. It has been one of the arguments of this book that such a principle of exegesis assumes what it sets out to demonstrate in that it makes assumptions about the relation between the various texts which can only be known as a result of such an exegetical exercise. This, in turn, raises some very large issues concerning the language, literariness and rhetorical strategies at work in a text, and how these are put into play during the process of reading.

In the preceding chapters, each of the major works associated with Adam Smith has been the subject of a reading that attempts to take acount of these literary and rhetorical aspects. In each case, the text has been read in terms of its own discursive frame and without recourse to interpretative strategies that rely on an assumption of authorial unity. Having established a reading for the texts separately, it is now possible to consider them together as constituting a wider discourse about society.

2

It was argued in chapters 2 to 4 that the account of the virtues in TMS is a hierarchically ordered system that stems from the categories of Stoic philosophy. The truly moral virtues of beneficence and self-command in TMS are those that define the moral agent as engaged in a dialogic encounter with the self, a moral process of internal debate that is represented by the metaphor of the impartial spectator. The other virtues of justice and prudence are therefore denominated as second-order attributes; they elicit a certain esteem and are necessary for the material reproduction of society, but they do not qualify as truly moral virtues. This account of moral judgment as an essentially dialogic process of deliberation is also deeply pessimistic about the moral potential of the 'great mob of mankind', who are either incapable or unwilling to enter into the dialogic process of moral deliberation. Such people may behave quite decently from society's point of view, however, by following the various rules of morality which are handed down to them as moral duties. In this way, a society may cohere and its people may live decently, in spite of the moral failure of mankind at large. Similarly, a society may be a just society without requiring individuals to enter into an internal moral debate; all that is required is that the rules of justice are followed and this may be achieved even by complete inaction. Thus, justice as a virtue, without which no society can subsist for any period of time, is not dependent on moral judgment but on established rules of decency and the positive laws of a country.

Lodged in the interior recesses of a person's deliberative faculties, morality has become fundamentally privatised. The dialogic model of conscience as the epitome of moral engagement is presented as an essentially private form of moral activity. This does not mean that the moral agent is to be regarded as socially isolated or somehow living apart from society. The operation of the impartial spectator is the product of social existence; moral norms and expectations are learnt as part of the process of living as a member of society, and the desire to be praiseworthy is related to the natural desire to be loved and to be worthy of being loved. Further, the dialogic process of moral judgment embodies a form of internal debate that presupposes linguistic skills which are themselves a product of living in society. Thus, although the impartial spectator represents a private moral domain, this is premised upon the social existence of the moral agent. Given that social context, however, moral excellence is an intensely private form of behaviour, both in the sense that it refers to the private rather than the public sphere of a person's daily life, and in the sense that moral judgment itself denotes an inner dialogism. By contrast, the lower-order virtues of justice and prudence are the public virtues. This means that public virtue is not only uncoupled from private moral activity; it is also denoted as inferior to it in a moral sense. This means that WN is an amoral text in that it is not concerned with the dialogic experience of conscience, although it presupposes the basic rules of justice.

It follows from this that the overall structure of Smith's discourse reproduces the Stoic moral hierarchy. Moral worth, the inner state of mind, is the locus of greatest interest for Stoic philosophy as it is here that the moral agent seeks to achieve that dispassionate view of his present position which the divine Being has of it. In TMS, the impartial spectator functions as the analogue of the divine Being, but here the point of distance and objectivity is rooted in a more socialised view of human nature rather than in the detached infinitude of the Stoic moral universe. The domain of the lower-order virtues is equivalent to the indifferent acts (or proper functions) of the Stoic philosophy, and which are presented in Cicero's *De Officiis* as the four cardinal virtues of courage, wisdom, justice and prudence. This domain of the lower-order virtues is the terrain of LJ and WN with their primary attention directed to justice and prudence. Thus, the moral relation of WN to TMS is neither quite one of opposition, as the old Adam Smith problem had it, nor one of overall unity of purpose, as the recent revisionist literature has it, but is structured in terms of the moral hierarchy laid out in TMS itself. The discourse of WN (and LJ) is concerned not with the high ground of moral philosophy, but with decent behaviour in the public conduct of everyday life, in which it is recognised that people have interests in their material well-being that are both reasonable and credit-worthy to some degree; in this sense, WN (and LJ) comprise the *officia* of Adam Smith's discourse.[1] The correspondence of the structure of Smith's discourse with that of Stoic moral philosophy also ties in with the stylistic characteristics of Smith's texts. The dialogism of TMS accords with the dialogism of moral judgment and the model of conscience. By contrast, LJ and WN evince a more monologic style which is appropriate to rule-governed activities.

Deriving from the intensely private and internalised morality of the Stoics, the account of morality in TMS diverges widely from the public *virtus* of civic humanism (or classical republicanism). Following Aristotle and Machiavelli, it has been argued that civic humanist virtue is inseparable from political engagement and the practice of citizenship, whether this civic participation is conceived in an Aristotelian sense as an end in itself, or whether it is conceived in a Machiavellian sense as the means to the greater

---

1 Cf. 'As it is by treaty, by barter, and by purchase, that we obtain from one another the greater part of those mutual good offices which we stand in need of . . .' (WN I.ii.3).

end of civic and personal liberty.[2] Here it is the cardinal virtues that are most revered, where Cicero's account of them has been interpreted as a description of the morally excellent man, even though *De Officiis* refers to them as only a 'sort of second-grade moral goodness' (Cicero 1913, III.15, p. 283). By contrast with the civic humanist attachment to *virtus*, the virtues of TMS are decidedly apolitical; the truly moral virtues of beneficence and self-command do not carry any public or political resonances, while the lower-order virtues of justice and prudence, the public virtues pertaining to civil society, do not embody a political participatory dimension. The moral agent of TMS is thus not well endowed with a civic or political personality.[3]

This attenuation of a political personality accords with the treatment of civil government in LJ and WN, where the state is conceived in un-Aristotelian terms primarily as a constitutional arrangement for preventing injustice and protecting individual rights.[4] This contrast may be illustrated by comparison with Aristotle's argument that a state cannot be said to exist on the mere basis of preventing injustice and safeguarding exchange:

> It is clear then that a state is not a mere society, having a common place, established for the prevention of mutual crime and for the sake of exchange. These are conditions without which a state cannot exist; but all of them together do not constitute a state, which is a community of families and aggregations of families in well-being, for the sake of a perfect and self-sufficing life.
>
> (Aristotle 1988, 1280b30–35)

In Aristotle's *The Politics*, it is inconceivable that the state could be divorced from questions concerning virtuous activity and political participation for its citizens as the state is necessary for the sake of a perfect and self-sufficing life. This is not the case for TMS and LJ, where the state's activities are not integral to the realisation of a truly moral life as distinct from a merely just life conducted within a framework of civil liberty and security from arbitrary government.

The absence of a concept of public virtue or of the genuine motivation of striving for the 'public good' is also congruent with this displacement of the political realm in LJ and WN. So too is the elimination of the legislator/statesman, discussed in chapters 5 and 6, as a guiding force in setting up the constitution, establishing an ongoing programme of legislation, managing

---

[2] These two positions have been argued, respectively, by Pocock (1975, 1981, 1983, 1985) and by Q. Skinner (1984, 1990).

[3] See, for example, Edelstein (1966, pp. 85–7); also Schofield (1991, especially ch. 4), which provides a historical reading of the depoliticisation of certain Stoic categories from Zeno to the first century BC by which time Stoic political philosophy was 'bereft of virtually all interest in specifically political analysis – or, as one might say, depoliticised' (p. 97).

[4] WN IV.ix.51.

CONCLUSION: COMMERCE AND CONSCIENCE

the economy, or promoting public virtue. This is also congruent with the mistrust of rationalist schemes of law reform or a science of legislation, both of which were in various ways connected with the rationalism deriving from the legends of the legislator in the later part of the eighteenth century.[5] In Smith's texts, the emphasis is invariably placed on historical and institutional factors in safeguarding individual liberty and security under the law, rather than on the political and moral wisdom of legislators or on the affectations for the public good shown by any individuals or orders in society.[6] Thus the 'sceptical whiggism' of Smith's discourse is doubly sceptical, distancing itself not only from the more extravagant claims of vulgar whiggism and the lauded virtues of the British constitution, but also from political claims of almost any kind. The absence of the statesman as a guiding force is, thus, symptomatic of a larger distrust of political solutions in general. When justice is treated in LJ and WN, the marginalisation of political personality persists in that the emphasis on justice as a negative virtue presupposes nothing about a civic personality or public motivation. In this respect, these texts present only one part of Cicero's virtue of justice, the negative part, while omitting the positive part which emphasised beneficence or distributive justice. Commentaries on Smith's writings have made much of the ways in which the system of natural liberty in WN is embedded in a framework of law and justice, and this has sometimes been held as evidence that Smith regarded the system of natural liberty as a moral system. This conclusion is significantly weakened, however, as argued above, by the demotion of justice in TMS to the status of a second-order and negative virtue.

The diminution of a political dimension in Adam Smith's writings has sometimes been attributed to the submergence of politics as a result of the ascendence of a new discourse on the economy.[7] According to this view, the overwhelming priority accorded to the new commercial relations as heralded by WN caused the eclipse of an independent political sphere in Smith's writings. The argument that has been offered in the course of this book, however, suggests that the eclipse of polity was effected not by economy but by ethics; not by the superordinance of commerce (of which more below), but by the pre-eminence of the moral analysis of TMS which denied justice a place within a fully moral domain, excluded the development of a political personality, and accorded a lower moral status to the

---

[5] See Burns (1967) and Lieberman (1989). Also cf. Berlin (1969, pp. 143, 148).
[6] Forbes (1954, 1975) emphasises the constitutional and institutional aspects of Smith's politics, and Rosenberg (1960) emphasises the importance of institutional arrangements in the economic sphere.
[7] A classic statement of this view may be found in Cropsey (1957). Recent contributions include Stimson (1989) and Robertson (1990). This view has been challenged by Winch (1978, 1988), who reverses the order of priority arguing that the economy should properly be seen as falling within polity.

public as opposed to the private virtues. The separation of justice from the individual moral domain in LJ, and the movement away from the traditional Stoic emphasis on the conjunction of reason and nature, also contributed to this end. In keeping with other aspects of Stoic philosophy, however, this did not mean that the virtuous man could not have a public role in society, that *negotium* was entirely eclipsed by *otium*, but that public activities could not themselves be the defining source of virtue and, if anything, could well come into conflict with private moral judgments.

This does not imply that echoes and traces of other, more politically focused discourses are entirely absent from Smith's discourse. The texts of TMS and WN contain instances, for example, where concern is expressed over the impoverishing effects of commercial society in eroding standards of public decency as well as private morality. Much has been made of the censorious comments in WN on the impoverishment of the moral and martial personality of the labouring class in commercial society compared with barbarous societies, although WN also acknowledges that the undifferentiated lifestyle of those simpler societies means that hardly anyone there acquires an outstanding degree of knowledge or ingenuity (WN V.i.f.50–1). At such points in the texts, echoes of other discourses, such as a civic humanist discourse concerning active citizenship and a Christian discourse concerning sobriety and industriousness, can be discerned. However, these allusions, if not vestigial, are not systematic in the sense that they do not amount to a portrayal of political personality as a constitutive element in commercial society, nor do they provide an account of involvement in political activity as a form of self-expression or the pursuit of virtue.

Such instances also need to be read in terms of the analysis of commercial society and the arguments in favour of natural liberty presented in WN. Few commentators now interpret Smith's works as unreservedly in favour of the new commercial relations of the time, but the economic account of WN is still read as a treatise purportedly promoting the growth of commerce and manufactures, whether as a liberal capitalist argument in favour of free markets or as a more complex synthesis involving the language of virtue and rights. In chapter 7 above, however, it was argued that WN is not proposing an extension of commerce and manufactures: the case for free trade in WN does not espouse more foreign trade. Instead, WN argues that commerce and manufactures had been overdeveloped and that agriculture, the most beneficial activity, was underdeveloped as a result. This means that if the system of natural liberty were to prevail, the agricultural sector would be larger and the manufacturing and commercial sectors (including overseas trade) would be reduced. The frequent references to freedom of trade and to a person's liberty to employ his own capital where he wishes should, therefore, be seen as reversing the overexpansion of trade and manufactures.

This also facilitates a more precise reading of the critical attacks on aspects of commercial society, as it allows a recognition that these attacks are very often directed at the manufacturing and commercial sectors themselves rather than at the mercantile distortions of commercial society. The indictment that is levied upon the harmful effects of the division of labour on the labouring poor has been widely discussed in the secondary literature. As already noted, the character of the person whose life is spent performing the mindless drudgery necessitated by the division of labour is impoverished morally, mentally and martially (WN V.i.f.50). But this criticism of the effects of the division of labour applies only to the manufacturing sector and not to the agricultural sector. WN elsewhere argues that the division of labour cannot be so far extended in agriculture as in manufactures (WN I.i.4). In a section outlining the inequalities occasioned by the police of Europe in promoting the towns above the countryside, it is also argued that the arts of the farmer and the country labourer require far more skill and experience than the mechanical trades, and that the understanding even of the common ploughman is much superior to those who have to spend all their time performing a few simple operations (WN I.x.c.23–4). The attack on the effects of the division of labour is thus directed specifically against the manufacturing sector rather than against commercial society as a whole; and in the system of natural liberty with a larger agricultural sector and a smaller manufacturing sector, the absolute scale of this problem would be reduced.

Some commentators have found it puzzling that WN should have launched such a fierce attack on merchants and manufacturers who are thought to be the crucial agents of the economic system.[8] Others have resolved this apparent paradox by arguing that it is the system of competitive markets that keeps the greed and the profit levels of such men in check; thus it is the role played by merchants and manufacturers under a mercantile system that is being criticised in that they have usurped the nation's economic policy to further their own interests, not the role of merchants and manufacturers as the dynamic commercial classes.[9] But it is still the case that WN argues that the interests of such men are directly opposed to the interest of society. It may well be that the process of competition will help to bridle their greed; within the system of natural liberty, too, the decrease in the size of the manufacturing and trading sectors, relative to the agricultural sector, would diminish their influence. But WN still maintains that the interest of these two groups is 'never exactly the same with that of the publick, who have generally an interest to deceive and even to oppress the publick, and who accordingly have, upon many occasions, both deceived and oppressed it' (WN I.xi.p.10; also IV.iii.c.10), whereas this is not argued for the other two great orders of society, the landowners and the labouring

---

8 For example, Coleman (1988).
9 For example, Rosenberg (1975) and Winch (1992).

class, whose interests are held to be congruent with those of society.[10] But once WN is read as an argument that manufactures and commerce have been overdeveloped and are less beneficial than agriculture, the diatribes levied against merchants and manufacturers become less paradoxical. When merchants become country gentlemen, however, and turn their attention to improving their own land, WN argues that they are the best of all improvers, and here in the context of agricultural improvement their characteristic boldness of enterprise is highly commended (WN III.iv.3).[11]

WN offers recognition of the habits of 'order, œconomy and attention' (WN III.iv.3) associated with mercantile activities, although merchants and artificers are also sneeringly described as pursuing 'their own pedlar principle of turning a penny wherever a penny was to be got' (WN III.iv.17). In mercantile and manufacturing towns, the inferior ranks of people are 'industrious, sober, and thriving' compared with similar ranks living in towns supported by the residence of a court where they are in general 'idle, dissolute, and poor' (WN II.iii.12). The commercial virtue which is, however, universally esteemed in WN is that of frugality or parsimony, the denying of present pleasures in order to accumulate capital (WN II.iii.14–42), and it is this that leads to an increasing annual revenue over time. In spite of the maxim that 'consumption is the end of production' adumbrated elsewhere (WN IV.viii.49), and in spite of the emphasis on an increasing annual revenue as a measure of a society's economic progress, the crucial commercial virtue turns out to be based on the non-consumption of consumer goods. Although WN welcomes the better living standards made possible for the poor by a rising annual revenue, it shows little sympathy for consumerism and a clear disdain for the new consumer goods such as 'trinkets and baubles' (WN V.i.b.7) and the 'diamond buckles' (WN III.iv.10) that provide consumption expenditure for the rich landlords. Here the censorious tone provides echoes of TMS's disdain for things indifferent.[12] Frugality and parsimony arise from the desire to 'better one's condition', which provides the overriding motivation for economic activity in general and frugality in particular (WN I.viii.44; II.iii.28, 31, 36; III.iii.12; IV.v.b.43, ix.28). The 'uniform, constant, and uninterrupted effort of every man to better his condition' is the mainspring of economic endeavour; although the principle of expense and consumption prevails upon occasion, it is entirely swamped in its effects by the principle of frugality which prompts men to save.

Frugality is an element of prudence, and in terms of the moral hierarchy

---

10 Although these classes are defective in realising their own interests (WN I.xi.p.8–9, III.ii.7).
11 Elsewhere WN argues that small proprietors inspired by affection for their property are the most industrious, intelligent and successful of all improvers (WN III.iv.19).
12 Cf. Rosenberg (1968).

of TMS this is a second-order virtue. In spite of its undoubted economic advantages, any moral evaluation of frugality must rely on its element of self-denial of present pleasures, as this constitutes the commercial counterpart of the Stoic virtue of self-command which receives so much attention in TMS. The virtue of frugality may thus elicit a certain cold esteem, but it does not involve the fully dialogic model of conscience which represents the highest form of moral activity. Thus, the presence of even the overriding commercial virtue is not sufficient to counteract the amoral status of the discourse of WN and of the commercial activities that it analyses. Within such a discourse, there is an absence of the moral criticisms of vanity and the desire to better one's condition which were present in TMS, where the desire to better one's condition is itself the result of vanity and the desire to be observed (TMS I.iii.2.1). Delivered in a complex interplay of the first person voice of fallen humanity and the third person detached voice of philosophy and reason, many passages in TMS display a sustained contempt for consumer values and for the toys and trifling conveniencies of commercial society, and they also excoriate the vanity which promotes the conspicuous consumption of consumer society. It was argued in chapters 2 and 4 that attending to the dialogic interplay of voices in TMS shows how the didactic voice is sharply critical of these worldly vanities and is not condoning them. From a Stoic point of view, no matter how desirable these acquisitions may be for the great 'mob of mankind', they remain merely things indifferent to the wise and virtuous man.

The 'amoral' status of WN, however, sets it apart from TMS. Its analysis is concerned with the 'matters indifferent' of the Stoics; not the elevated pursuits of the wise and virtuous man, but the ordinary aspirations of mankind. Given the more monologic trajectory of WN and its rhetorical devices which include the generality of mankind within its readership, these ordinary aspirations are presented as a shared human experience from which neither the didactic voice nor the reader is excluded. Certainly the didactic voice inveighs against ruthless avidity and oppression,[13] but it does not criticise the desire for economic betterment itself. In this amoral context, the continual effort to 'better one's condition' is accepted as something entirely natural, and it is described as a 'natural' effort to better one's condition without any of the moral derogations which attended this term in TMS (WN IV.v.b.43; IV.ix.28).

3

The system of natural liberty is one where individuals may freely pursue their own interest in trying to better their own condition, and where the

---

13 For example, WN IV.vii.a.15–19.

pursuit of individual interest coincides with the public interest. This coincidence of private and public interest is not simply assumed by WN but, as argued in chapter 7, was the subject of a sustained account of the sectoral hierarchy of capitals in which WN attempted to show how individuals will contribute most to the annual revenue by pursuing their own interest. The sectoral hierarchy analysis stimulated considerable debate around the question whether all forms of individual investing behaviour were equally beneficial to society or whether domestic investment, particularly in agriculture, was more advantageous to society. Gradually, the sectoral hierarchy became increasingly criticised and eventually was abandoned altogether as an irremediable error deriving from the physiocratic system, an opinion that has persisted to the present.[14] Although WN's analysis in support of natural liberty was abandoned, the text itself was not rejected but was reinterpreted as a statement of the identity of economic interest between the individual and society. In the absence of the sectoral hierarchy analysis, this was sometimes interpreted as a statement whose obvious truism was beyond the necessity of proof, or as a profoundly intuitive insight which lacked only a formal proof, or else as a demonstration that only a competitive market system would ensure an equality of the market price and the natural price. In the course of time, not only was the importance of the sectoral hierarchy for the system of natural liberty entirely lost sight of, but commentators failed to note its presence or even denied its significance altogether.

Without the theoretical framework of analysis provided by the sectoral hierarchy and the composition of revenues, the structure of WN loses much of its rationale and reduces to a series of propositions against specific mercantilist measures or state regulations, and in favour of extensive economic freedom. Crucially important here is the rhetorical power of WN's argument that the system of perfect liberty was the only one which accorded with reason and commonsense. In this way, the abiding message of WN was taken to be its insistence on the importance of natural liberty and perfect freedom in the conduct of economic affairs. The mercantile system had involved violations of liberty in promoting the interest of one order of society above the other orders, but in the system of natural liberty all orders are treated equally. One of the benefits arising from the introduction of commerce – indeed the greatest benefit of all – is that of liberty and security, which were introduced along with order and good government (WN III.iv.4; LJA iv.168–v.43; LJB 61–75). The civil liberty deriving from

---

14 Cf. 'That Smith was in error is unequivocal. He allowed a system of financing to conceal the facts of economic life . . . If Smith had really incorporated this error into his theoretical system, the effects would have been disastrous: as one important example, the argument for private control over investment would have been damaged beyond repair' (Stigler 1977, p. 10).

CONCLUSION: COMMERCE AND CONSCIENCE

the 1688 Revolution is highly valued but, in the system of natural liberty, the scope for freedom of action would be greatly enlarged. Throughout WN, the repeated references to liberty, perfect liberty and natural liberty emphasise the difference between the civil liberty then existing and the radical increase in economic freedom that would pertain in the system of natural liberty, and in this way the liberty denoted as perfect liberty in WN goes far beyond contemporary Whiggish notions of civil liberty and security under the law.

In spite of the structural importance of the notion of perfect/natural liberty in WN, however, it is not argued for in WN, but assumed. It is to be defended by the laws of the country as it 'is the proper business of law, not to infringe, but to support' natural liberty (WN II.ii.94). Particular laws which circumscribe an individual's freedom in the use of property or in the freedom of movement or employment are presented as evident violations of natural liberty and are therefore unjust (e.g. WN I.x.c.12, IV.v.b.43), but WN does not actually present arguments to support this notion of perfect liberty. Sometimes commentators attribute this notion of natural liberty to the natural jurisprudence of LJ, and so attempt to ground it in a juristic and natural law foundation. It was argued in chapter 5, however, that by the time of LJB, the right to property is an acquired right (LJB 11), not a natural right. This means that the natural liberty of WN cannot be grounded in the natural jurisprudence of LJ. An alternative foundation for the natural liberty of WN might be thought to be the civic humanist/classical republican emphasis on liberty, but it was argued above that the classical notion of *virtus* as a political and participatory virtue is also absent from Adam Smith's discourse. Apart from the interpretative problems involved in making inferences across different texts, the absence of a developed notion of a political personality in Smith's discourse means that the notion of perfect liberty does not derive from arguments concerning either juristic rights, active citizenship or political liberty; and perfect liberty here is not derived from arguments concerning political freedoms such as the right to participate in political processes or forms of representative or republican democracy.

It was argued above that if the structure of Smith's overall discourse is seen as reproducing the structure of the Stoic hierarchy, then WN and LJ may be seen as inhabiting the domain of the *officia*, the 'proper functions' of individual agents in everyday activities. In this case, the liberty of action subtending these *officia* is derived from the notion of liberty in the Stoic philosophy itself. Thus the notion of perfect liberty in the economic argument of WN may be seen as one that derives from the Stoic autonomy of the individual as an independent moral agent. The dialogic model of conscience, where moral decisions are taken by independent moral agents, incorporates this notion of moral autonomy because truly moral decisions are those that are free and unconstrained in that they are the result of the exercise of individual conscience. This emphasis on freedom is fundamental to Stoic moral philosophy which 'took freedom to be a moral characteristic: the power of independent action' (Schofield 1991, pp. 48–9),[15] but crucially, within Stoicism, freedom is bounded by the power of reason to know what is right. This means that it is also bounded by the subordinate moral position accorded to the things indifferent which, being beyond any person's individual control and not being objects of any moral worth, are not desired as such. In the austere language of Epictetus, this implies that though 'He is free who lives as he wills, who is subject neither to compulsion, nor hindrance, nor force, whose choices are unhampered, whose desires attain their end, whose aversions do not fall into what they would avoid', this state of freedom is not a state of self-indulgence or self-assertion: 'For freedom is not acquired by satisfying yourself with what you desire, but by destroying your desire' (Epictetus 1925/8, IV.I: pp. 245, 305).[16] It was argued in chapters 2–4 that the extreme austerity of this philosophy was ultimately rejected in TMS, but that the tensions that this created were played out in the posited antithesis between nature and reason, and the switching between different voices in the text. That the fundamental priority accorded to freedom was not dislodged, however, is evident in the importance ascribed to it in the dialogic model of the impartial spectator, where the truly moral virtues were characterised as being freely determined and not subject to rules. The individual moral agent is, paradigmatically, one who freely enters into the process of moral judgment and freely orders his own actions.

Within the discourse of TMS, the freedom of the moral agent is a moral freedom as it is circumscribed by the dialogic requirements of individual conscience; moral judgments are made by reference to the impartial spectator and this is meant to provide moral bounds to the kind of decisions and actions that would be taken. Within WN, however, this moral dialogism is absent and individual freedom is unbounded by moral considerations although it is constrained by the positive laws of a country. Thus, what emerges in WN is a concept of individual freedom deployed within a basically amoral discourse. It was argued above that moral bounds on economic liberty are not provided by natural jurisprudence because the right to property is an acquired right, not a natural right. Further, as argued in chapter 6, the emphasis of the rules of justice as part of the legal machinery for establishing law and good order further detaches the individual agent from any need to make decisions concerning the requirements

---

15 Also Long (1971b, p. 175); Engberg-Pedersen (1990, chapter IX).
16 This is not the same concept of freedom as either the negative or positive freedom of political philosophy; see Berlin (1969), Taylor (1979, 1989), Pocock (1981), and Q. Skinner (1984, 1990). Berlin describes the Stoic concept of freedom as a sublime form of the 'doctrine of sour grapes' (Berlin 1969, p. 139).

CONCLUSION: COMMERCE AND CONSCIENCE

of just behaviour, thus reinforcing the distance travelled from the original natural law proposition that all agents may naturally know what is just. Most of the references to natural liberty in WN leave its moral limits and obligations entirely unspecified; the background assumption of a regular system of justice shows that natural liberty would be limited by the positive laws of justice, but this does not provide bounds for the proposed reforms of WN which are directed at increasing the freedoms allowed by the positive laws. LJ's transposition of natural jurisprudence from its foundations in Stoic moral philosophy where all moral agents may know what is just through the use of reason, to an account of the positive laws of a country which all must obey, amounts to the divorce of individual moral judgment from law-abiding behaviour – a divorce which is epitomised by the monologic treament of justice in Adam Smith's discourse.

The theoretical issue of the limits and constraints on this individual economic freedom in WN then becomes acute. The argument that the laws of the country should be changed in order to allow a greater degree of economic freedom is central to WN, but the moral and juristic limits to this process are left unspecified. The framework of laws that is proposed amounts to little more than a concern with commutative justice, which means that agents must abide by the laws of the country, but there are no grounds enabling them to make judgments concerning the moral or distributive implications of the freer use of property. For example, in the discussion of the corn laws in WN, the market is to be the sole means by which the corn supply is allocated, and so questions of the distributive implications of shortfalls or scarcity prices cannot be discussed as these lie beyond the parameters of commutative justice. Normally, judgments cannot be made beyond the existing laws as it is the business of law to support individual freedom. Legal restraints on natural liberty are, however, favoured where the exercise of such natural liberty might 'endanger the security of the whole society' (WN II.ii.94), but the grounds for determining what is meant by the security of the whole society or even what the 'whole society' might mean, remain undiscussed, with the result that such decisions remain theoretically arbitrary.[17]

Reclaiming autonomous action for the individual within a largely amoral discourse carries with it social and political implications that far transcend the theoretical resources of such a discourse. WN became a powerful ingredient in an ideology in which the Stoic context of Smith's discourse

---

17 The curious juxtaposition of the two examples of the obligation to build party walls to prevent the spread of fire, and the restriction of bank notes to sums not smaller than five pounds, illustrates this. The suggestion that the rate of interest should be fixed (WN II.iv.14–15) has appeared to some later commentators to be in opposition to the principles of natural liberty. The Navigation Acts were accepted by WN on the grounds of national defence.

became invisible. Freedom came to be seen as negative freedom and an end in itself, an ultimate moral and political good against which other claims would appear subordinate, whereas the Stoic concept of freedom was bounded by an insistence on the ultimate moral indifference of worldly outcomes. There are many ironies to note in the historical outcomes of Adam Smith's discourse and the canonisation of WN, as has been evidenced by the history of more than two centuries since WN was published. The argument of WN against the undue expansion of trade and manufactures has come to be interpreted as an argument in favour of such an expansion. The invective against merchants and manufacturers has been construed as an apologia for the new capitalist class that emerged in a later age. But one of the greatest ironies is that Adam Smith's discourse – indebted as it was to Stoic moral philosophy – has contributed centrally to the de-moralisation of economic and political categories and to the construction of an economics canon in which moral debate has virtually no place.

REFERENCES

KEY TO EDITIONS OF ADAM SMITH'S WORKS

TMS *The Theory of Moral Sentiments* (1976), edited by D.D. Raphael and A.L. Macfie as vol. I of *The Glasgow Edition of the Works and Correspondence of Adam Smith*, Oxford: Oxford University Press; reprinted by Liberty Press (1982).

WN *An Inquiry into the Nature and Causes of the Wealth of Nations* (1976), edited by R.H. Campbell and A.S. Skinner as vol. II of *The Glasgow Edition of the Works and Correspondence of Adam Smith*, Oxford: Oxford University Press; reprinted by Liberty Press (1981).

LJ *Lectures on Jurisprudence* (1978), edited by R.L. Meek, D.D. Raphael, and P.G. Stein as vol. V of *The Glasgow Edition of the Works and Correspondence of Adam Smith*, Oxford: Oxford University Press; reprinted by Liberty Press (1982).

LJA *Lectures on Jurisprudence*, Report dated 1762–3, printed in LJ.

LJB *Lectures on Jurisprudence*, Report dated 1766, printed in LJ.

ED 'Early Draft' of part of the *Wealth of Nations*, printed in LJ.

LRBL *Lectures on Rhetoric and Belles Lettres* (1983), edited by J.C. Bryce as vol. IV of *The Glasgow Edition of the Works and Correspondence of Adam Smith*, Oxford: Oxford University Press; reprinted by Liberty Press (1985).

PRIMARY SOURCES

Aristotle (1988) *The Politics*, Cambridge: Cambridge University Press.
Augustine (1990) *Soliloquies and Immortality of the Soul*, edited by G. Watson, Warminster: Aris and Phillips.
—— (1991) *Confessions*, edited by Henry Chadwick, Oxford: Oxford University Press.
Barbeyrac, Jean (1729) *An Historical and Critical Account of the Science of Morality*, published as a Prefatory Discourse to *The Law of Nature and Nations* by Samuel Pufendorf, London.
Brougham, Henry (Lord) (1803) *An Inquiry into the Colonial Policy of the European Powers*, Edinburgh.
—— (1804) review of *An Inquiry into the Nature and Origin of Public Wealth* by Lauderdale, in *The Edinburgh Review*, vol. 4, July, pp. 343–77.
—— (1805) *Thoughts, Suggested by Lord Lauderdale's Observations upon the Edinburgh Review*, London.
?Buchanan, D. and Jeffrey, F. (1809) review of *Agriculture, the Source of Wealth of Britain* by W. Spence, in *The Edinburgh Review*, vol. 14, April, pp. 50–60.

Butler, Joseph (1970) *Fifteen Sermons Preached at the Rolls Chapel*, edited by T.A. Roberts, London: SPCK.

Cantillon, Richard (1931) *Essay on the Nature of Trade in General*, edited and translated by Henry Higgs, London: Macmillan.

Cicero, Marcus Tullius (1913) *De Officiis*, translated by Walter Miller, Loeb Classical Library, vol. XXI of Cicero's works, Harvard University Press and Heinemann.

—— (1928) *De Legibus*, translated by C.W. Keyes, Loeb Classical Library, vol. XVI of Cicero's works, Harvard University Press and Heinemann.

—— (1931) *De Finibus*, translated by H. Rackman, Loeb Classical Library, vol. XVII of Cicero's works, Harvard University Press and Heinemann.

—— (1991) *On Duties*, edited by M.T. Griffin and E.M. Atkins, Cambridge: Cambridge University Press.

Davenant, Charles (1967a) 'Discourses on the public revenues, and on the trade of England', in *The Political and Commercial Works of Charles D'Avenant*, facsimile of 1771 edition collected and revised by Sir Charles Whitworth, Farnborough: Gregg Press Ltd.

—— (1967b) 'An essay upon the probable methods of making a people gainers in the balance of trade', in *The Political and Commercial Works of Charles D'Avenant*, facsimile of 1771 edition, collected and revised by Sir Charles Whitworth, Farnborough: Gregg Press Ltd.

Epictetus (1925/8) *The Discourses as reported by Arrian, The Manual and Fragments*, translated by W.A. Oldfather in two volumes, Loeb Classical Library, London: Heinemann.

Ferguson, Adam (1966) *An Essay on the History of Civil Society*, edited by Duncan Forbes, Edinburgh: Edinburgh University Press.

Gee, Joshua (1968) *The Trade and Navigation of Great Britain Considered*, Farnborough: Gregg International Publishers.

Grotius, Hugo (1738) *The Rights of War and Peace*, translated from *De Jure Belli et Pacis*, with the notes of J. Barbeyrac, London.

Harris, Joseph (1757) *An Essay upon Money and Coins*, London; facsimile edition, no date, Wakefield: S.R. Publishers Ltd.

Horner, Francis (1803) review of *Principes d'Economie Politique* by N.F. Canard, 1801, in *The Edinburgh Review*, vol. 1, January, pp. 431–50.

—— (1804) review of *An Act to Regulate the Importation and Exportation of Corn*, and *Cursory Observations of the Act for Ascertaining the Bounties*, in *The Edinburgh Review*, vol. 5, October, pp. 190–208.

—— (1957) *The Economic Writings of Francis Horner in* The Edinburgh Review, *1802–06*, edited by Frank Whitson Fetter, London.

Hume, David (1970) *Writings on Economics*, edited by Eugene Rotwein, Madison: The University of Wisconsin Press.

Hutcheson, Francis (1969) *A Short Introduction to Moral Philosophy*, Glasgow; vol. IV of the *Collected Works of Francis Hutcheson*, facsimile of 1747 edition, Hildesheim: Georg Olms Verlagsbuchhandlung.

—— (1971a) *An Inquiry into the Original of our Ideas of Beauty and Virtue*, London; vol. I of the *Collected Works of Francis Hutcheson*, facsimile of 1725 edition, Hildesheim: Georg Olms Verlagsbuchhandlung.

—— (1971b) *An Essay on the Nature and Conduct of the Passions and Affections*, London; vol. II of the *Collected Works of Francis Hutcheson*, facsimile of 1728 edition, Hildesheim: Georg Olms Verlagsbuchhandlung.

Kames, Lord (Henry Home) (1751) 'Of the foundation and principles of the Law of Nature', in *Essays on the Principles of Morality and Natural Religion*, Edinburgh, pp. 33–149.

REFERENCES

—— (1774) *Sketches of the History of Man*, Edinburgh and London.
Lauderdale (Eighth Earl) James Maitland (1804a) *An Inquiry into the Nature and Origin of Public Wealth*, Edinburgh.
—— (1804b) *Observations by the Earl of Lauderdale, on the Review of his Inquiry into the Nature and Origin of Public Wealth, published in the VIIIth number of the Edinburgh Review*, Edinburgh.
Locke, John (1959) *An Essay Concerning Human Understanding*, edited by Alexander Campbell Fraser, London: Dover Publications.
McCulloch, J.R. (1825a) *Principles of Political Economy*, Edinburgh.
—— (1825b) *A Discourse on the Rise, Progress, Peculiar Objects and Importance of Political Economy*, Edinburgh.
—— (1828) 'Introductory Discourse' to *An Inquiry into the Nature and Causes of the Wealth of Nations* by Adam Smith, Edinburgh.
Machiavelli, N. (1975) *The Discourses of Niccolò Machiavelli*, London and Boston: Routledge and Kegan Paul.
—— (1803) *An Essay on the Principle of Population* (2nd edition), London.
?Malthus, T.R. (1808) review of W. Spence's *Britain Independent of Commerce* (3rd edition), in *The Edinburgh Review*, vol. 11, January, pp. 429–48.
—— (1970) *An Essay on the Principle of Population*, Harmondsworth, UK: Penguin.
Marcus Aurelius (1964) *Meditations*, translated by M. Staniforth, Harmondsworth: Penguin.
Mill, James (1966) 'Commerce defended', in *James Mill: Selected Economic Writings*, edited by Donald Winch, Edinburgh and London: Oliver and Boyd, pp. 85–159.
Millar, John (1960) 'The origin of the distinction of ranks', in *John Millar of Glasgow 1735–1801*, edited by W. C. Lehmann, Cambridge: Cambridge University Press, pp. 165–322.
Montesquieu, Charles de Secondat (1989) *The Spirit of the Laws*, Cambridge: Cambridge University Press.
Mun, Thomas (1967) *England's Treasure by Forraign Trade*, Oxford: Basil Blackwell.
Plato (1960) *Georgias*, translated by Walter Hamilton, London: Penguin.
Postlethwayt, Malachy (1757) *Great Britain's True System*, London.
Pownall, Governor T. (1977) *A Letter from Governor Pownall to Adam Smith*, reprinted as Appendix A in *The Correspondence of Adam Smith*, pp. 337–76, edited by E.C. Mossner and I.S. Ross as vol. VI of *The Glasgow Edition of the Works and Correspondence of Adam Smith*, Oxford: Oxford University Press; reprinted by Liberty Press (1987).
Pufendorf, Samuel (1716) *The Whole Duty of Man According to the Law of Nature*, translated by Andrew Tooke from *De Officio Hominis et Civis Juxta Legem Naturalem*, with the notes of J. Barbeyrac, London.
—— (1729) *Of the Law of Nature and Nations*, translated by Basil Kennett from *De Jure naturae et gentium*, with the notes of J. Barbeyrac, London.
—— (1991) *On the Duty of Man and Citizen According to Natural Law*, edited by James Tully and translated by Michael Silverthorne from *De Officio Hominis et Civis Juxta Legem Naturalem*; Cambridge: Cambridge University Press.
Quesnay, François (1946) 'Despotism in China', in *China A Model for Europe*, edited by Lewis A. Maverick, San Antonio, Texas: Paul Anderson Company.
Rousseau, Jean-Jacques (1973a) *A Discourse on the Origin of Inequality*, edited and translated by G.D.H. Cole, in *The Social Contract and Discourses*, London: J.M. Dent, pp. 31–126.
—— (1973b) *A Discourse on Political Economy*, edited and translated by G.D.H. Cole, in *The Social Contract and Discourses*, London: J.M. Dent, pp. 127–68.
—— (1973c) *The Social Contract*, edited and translated by G.D.H. Cole, in *The Social Contract and Discourses*, London: J.M. Dent, pp. 179–309.

Say, Jean-Baptiste (1821) *A Treatise on Political Economy*, translated by C.R. Prinsep, London.
—— (1971) *A Treatise on Political Economy*, edited by C.C. Biddle, New York: Augustus M. Kelley.
Semmel, Bernard (ed.) (1963) *Occasional Papers of T.R. Malthus*, New York: Burt Franklin.
Shaftesbury, Third Earl of (Anthony Ashley Cooper) (1900) *The Life, Unpublished Letters, and Philosophical Regimen of Anthony, Earl of Shaftesbury*, edited by B. Rand, London: Swan Sonnenschein.
—— (1964) *Characteristics of Men, Manners, Opinions, Times*, edited by J.M. Robertson, NY: Bobbs Merrill.
Smith, Adam (1805) *An Inquiry into the Nature and Causes of the Wealth of Nations*, edited by William Playfair, London.
—— (1814) *An Inquiry into the Nature and Causes of the Wealth of Nations*, edited by David Buchanan, Edinburgh.
—— (1828) *An Inquiry into the Nature and Causes of the Wealth of Nations*, edited by J.R. McCulloch, Edinburgh.
—— (1835–9) *An Inquiry into the Nature and Causes of the Wealth of Nations*, edited by Edward Gibbon Wakefield, London.
—— (1963) *Lectures on Rhetoric and Belles Lettres*, edited by John M. Lothian, London and Edinburgh: Thomas Nelson.
—— (1976) *The Theory of Moral Sentiments*, edited by D.D. Raphael and A.L. Macfie as vol. I of *The Glasgow Edition of the Works and Correspondence of Adam Smith*, Oxford: Oxford University Press; reprinted by Liberty Press (1982).
—— (1976) *An Inquiry into the Nature and Causes of the Wealth of Nations*, edited by R.H. Campbell and A.S. Skinner as vol. II of *The Glasgow Edition of the Works and Correspondence of Adam Smith*, Oxford: Oxford University Press; reprinted by Liberty Press (1981).
—— (1978) *Lectures on Jurisprudence*, edited by R.L. Meek, D.D. Raphael, and P.G. Stein as vol. V of *The Glasgow Edition of the Works and Correspondence of Adam Smith*, Oxford: Oxford University Press; reprinted by Liberty Press (1982).
—— (1980) *Essays on Philosophical Subjects*, edited by W.P.D. Wightman and J.C. Bryce as vol. III of *The Glasgow Edition of the Works and Correspondence of Adam Smith*, Oxford: Oxford University Press; reprinted by Liberty Press (1982).
—— (1983) *Lectures on Rhetoric and Belles Lettres*, edited by J.C. Bryce as vol. IV of *The Glasgow Edition of the Works and Correspondence of Adam Smith*, Oxford: Oxford University Press; reprinted by Liberty Press (1985).
—— (1987) *The Correspondence of Adam Smith*, edited by E.C. Mossner and I.S. Ross, as vol. VI of *The Glasgow Edition of the Works and Correspondence of Adam Smith*, Oxford: Oxford University Press; reprinted by Liberty Press (1987).
Spence, William (1808a) *Britain Independent of Commerce*, 3rd edition, London.
—— (1808b) *Agriculture the Source of Wealth of Britain*, London.
Steuart, James (1966) *An Inquiry into the Principles of Political Oeconomy*, edited by Andrew S. Skinner, Edinburgh and London: Oliver and Boyd (for The Scottish Economic Society).
Stewart, Dugald (1968) *Lectures on Political Economy*, New York: Augustus M. Kelley.
—— (1980) 'Account of the life and writings of Adam Smith', in *Adam Smith Essays on Philosophical Subjects*, pp. 269–351, edited by W.P.D. Wightman and J.C. Bryce as vol. III of *The Glasgow Edition of the Works and Correspondence of Adam Smith*, Oxford: Oxford University Press; reprinted by Liberty Press (1982).
Turgot, A.M.J. (1963) *Reflections on the Formation and the Distribution of Riches*, facsimile of 1898 edition, edited by W.J. Ashley, New York: Augustus M. Kelley.

REFERENCES

Vanderlint, Jacob (1734) *Money Answers All Things*, facsimile edition, Wakefield: S.R. Publishers Limited, no date.
Wallace, Robert (1758) *Characteristics of the Present Political State of Great Britain* (2nd edition), London.
Walras, Léon (1954) *Elements of Pure Economics*, translated by W. Jaffé, London: George Allen & Unwin.
Young, Arthur (1774) *Political Arithmetic*, London.

SECONDARY SOURCES

Anderson, Gary M. and Tollison, Robert D. (1984) 'Sir James Steuart as the apotheosis of mercantilism and his relation to Adam Smith', *Southern Economic Journal* 60, pp. 456–68.
Anspach, Ralph (1972) 'The implications of the *Theory of Moral Sentiments* for Adam Smith's economic thought', *History of Political Economy* 9, pp. 176–206.
Bakhtin, M.M. (1981) *The Dialogic Imagination*, Austin TA: University of Texas.
—— (1984) *Problems of Dostoevsky's Poetics*, Manchester: Manchester University Press.
—— (1986) *Speech Genres and Other Late Essays*, Austin TA: University of Texas.
Barthes, Roland (1977) 'The death of the author' in *Image Music Text*, pp. 142–8, London: Fontana.
Berlin, Isaiah (1969) 'Two concepts of liberty' in *Four Essays on Liberty*, Oxford: Oxford University Press.
Bevilacqua, Vincent M. (1965) 'Adam Smith's Lectures on Rhetoric and Belles Lettres', *Studies in Scottish Literature* 3, pp. 41–60.
—— (1968) 'Adam Smith and some philosophical origins of eighteenth-century rhetorical theory', *Modern Language Review* 63, pp. 559–68.
Billet, Leonard (1976) 'The just economy: the moral basis of the *Wealth of Nations*', *Review of Social Economy* 34, pp. 295–314.
Blaug, Mark (1985) *Economic Theory in Retrospect*, 4th edition, Cambridge: Cambridge University Press.
Bowley, Marion (1973) *Studies in the History of Economic Theory before 1870*, London: Macmillan.
Brewer, Anthony (1988) 'Cantillon and mercantilism', *History of Political Economy* 20, pp. 447–60.
Brissenden, R.F. (1969) 'Authority, guilt, and anxiety in *The Theory of Moral Sentiments*', *Texas Studies in Literature and Languages*, 11, pp. 945–62.
Brown, Vivienne (1987) 'Value and property in the history of economic thought: an analysis of the emergence of scarcity', *Œconomia*, no. 7 Série P.E. de la revue, *Économies et Sociétés*, pp. 85–112.
—— (1993) 'Decanonizing discourses: textual analysis and the history of economic thought', in *Economics and Language*, edited by Willie Henderson, Tony Dudley-Evans and Roger Backhouse, London: Routledge, pp. 64–84.
—— (forthcoming) 'The moral self and ethical dialogism: three genres', *Philosophy and Rhetoric* 27.
Brunschwig, Jacques (1986) 'The cradle argument in Epicureanism and Stoicism', in *The Norms of Nature, Studies in Hellenistic Ethics*, edited by M. Schofield and G. Striker, Cambridge: Cambridge University Press, pp. 113–44.
Burns, J.H. (1967) *The Fabric of Felicity: the Legislator and the Human Condition*, an inaugural lecture delivered at University College London, March.
Campbell, Keith (1985) 'Self-mastery and Stoic ethics', *Philosophy* 60, pp. 327–40.
Campbell, T.D. (1971) *Adam Smith's Science of Morals*, London: Allen & Unwin.

Cannan, Edwin (1950) Introduction to *The Wealth of Nations* by Adam Smith, facsimile of 1904 edition, New York: Augustus M. Kelley.
—— (1964) Introduction to *Lectures on Justice, Policy, Revenue and Arms* by Adam Smith, facsimile of 1896 edition, New York: Augustus M. Kelley.
Caton, Hiram (1985) 'The preindustrial economics of Adam Smith', *Journal of Economic History* 45, pp. 833–53.
Clark, Katerina and Michael Holquist (1984) *Mikhail Bakhtin*, Cambridge MA: Harvard University Press.
Cleary, John J. (ed.) (1987) *Proceedings of the Boston Area Colloquium in Ancient Philosophy*, vol. II, Lanham MD and London: University Press of America.
Coleman, D.C. (ed.) (1969) *Revisions in Mercantilism*, London: Methuen.
—— (1980) 'Mercantilism Revisited', *Historical Journal* 23, pp. 773–91.
—— (1988) 'Adam Smith, businessmen, and the mercantile system in England', *History of European Ideas* 9, pp. 161–70.
Crafts, N.F.R. (1985) *British Economic Growth During the Industrial Revolution*, Oxford: Clarendon Press.
Cropsey, Joseph (1957) *Polity and Economy: An Interpretation of the Principles of Adam Smith*, The Hague: Martinus Nijhoff.
D'Entreves, A.P. (1970) *Natural Law*, London: Hutchinson.
De Marchi, Neil (ed.) (1988) *The Popperian Legacy in Economics*, Cambridge: Cambridge University Press.
De Roover, Raymond (1955) 'Scholastic economics: survival and lasting influence from the sixteenth century to Adam Smith', *The Quarterly Journal of Economics* 59, pp. 161–90.
—— (1967) *San Bernardino of Siena and Sant'Antonino of Florence*, Harvard Graduate Business School of Business Administration (Baker Library).
Deane, Phyllis (1987) 'Political arithmetic', in *The New Palgrave Dictionary of Economics*, vol. 3, London: Macmillan, pp. 900–3.
Dwyer, John (1987) *Virtuous Discourse: Sensibility and Community in Late Eighteenth-Century Scotland*, Edinburgh: John Donald.
Eatwell, John (1982) 'Competition', in *Classical and Marxian Political Economy*, edited by I. Bradley and M. Howard, London: Macmillan, pp. 203–28.
Edelstein, Ludwig (1966) *The Meaning of Stoicism*, Cambridge, MA: Harvard University Press.
Endres, A.M. (1985) 'The functions of numerical data in the writings of Graunt, Petty and Davenant', *History of Political Economy* 17, pp. 245–64.
—— (1991) 'Adam Smith's rhetoric of economics: an illustration using "Smithian" compositional rules', *Scottish Journal of Political Economy* 38, pp. 76–95.
Engberg-Pedersen, Troels (1986) 'Discovering the good: *oikeiosis* and *kathekonta* in Stoic ethics' in *The Norms of Nature, Studies in Hellenistic Ethics*, edited by M. Schofield and G. Striker, Cambridge: Cambridge University Press, pp. 145–83.
—— (1990) *The Stoic Theory of Oikeiosis*, Aarhus: Aarhus University Press.
Evensky, Jerry (1987) 'The two voices of Adam Smith: moral philosopher and social critic', *History of Political Economy* 19, pp. 447–68.
—— (1989) 'The evolution of Adam Smith's views on political economy', *History of Political Economy* 21, pp. 123–45.
Fetter, Frank Whitson (1953) 'The authorship of economic articles in *The Edinburgh Review*, 1802–47', *Journal of Political Economy* 61, pp. 232–59.
Fish, Stanley (1988) 'Comments from outside economics', in Klamer *et al.* (eds) *The Consequences of Economic Rhetoric*, pp. 21–30.
—— (1989) 'Short people got no reason to live: reading irony' in *Doing What Comes Naturally: Change, Rhetoric, and the Practice of Theory in Literary and Legal Studies*, Oxford: Clarendon Press, pp. 180–96.

REFERENCES

Fontana, Biancamaria (1985) *Rethinking the Politics of Commercial Society: The Edinburgh Review 1802–1832*, Cambridge: Cambridge University Press.

Forbes, Duncan (1954) ' "Scientific" Whiggism: Adam Smith and John Millar', *The Cambridge Journal* 7, pp. 643–70.

—— (1975) 'Sceptical Whiggism, commerce, and liberty', in Skinner and Wilson (eds) *Essays on Adam Smith*, pp. 179–201.

—— (1982) 'Natural Law and the Scottish Enlightenment' in *The Origins and Nature of the Scottish Enlightenment*, edited by R.H. Campbell and A.S. Skinner, Edinburgh: John Donald, pp. 186–204.

Foucault, Michel (1986) 'What is an author?' in *The Foucault Reader*, edited by P. Rabinow, Harmondsworth: Penguin, pp. 101–20.

Fox-Genovese (1976) *The Origins of Physiocracy*, Cornell: Cornell University Press.

Griswold, Charles L. (1991) 'Rhetoric and ethics: Adam Smith on theorizing about the moral sentiments', *Philosophy and Rhetoric* 24, pp. 213–37.

Groenewegen, P.D. (1969) 'Turgot and Adam Smith', *The Scottish Journal of Political Economy* 16, pp. 271–87.

—— (1987) 'Political economy' in *The New Palgrave Dictionary of Economics*, vol. 3, London: Macmillan, pp. 904–7.

Haakonssen, Knud (1981) *The Science of a Legislator: The Natural Jurisprudence of David Hume and Adam Smith*, Cambridge: Cambridge University Press.

—— (1985a) 'Hugo Grotius and the history of political thought', *Political Theory* 13, pp. 239–65.

—— (1985b) 'John Millar and the science of a legislator', *The Juridical Review* 30, pp. 41–68.

—— (ed.) (1988) *Traditions of Liberalism*, Sydney: Centre for Independent Studies.

Heilbronner, Robert L. (1982) 'The socialization of the individual in Adam Smith', *History of Political Economy* 14, pp. 421–31.

Hirschkop, Ken (1986) 'A Response to the forum on Mikhail Bakhtin', in G.S. Morson (ed.) *Bakhtin: Essays and Dialogues on his Work*, pp. 73–9.

Hogan, Michael J. (1984) 'Historiography and ethics in Adam Smith's Lectures on Rhetoric, 1762–1763', *Rhetorica* 2, pp. 75–91.

Hollander, Samuel (1973) *The Economics of Adam Smith*, London: Heinemann.

—— (1987) *Classical Economics*, Oxford: Basil Blackwell.

Hont, Istvan (1983) 'The "rich country–poor country" debate in Scottish classical political economy', in Hont and Ignatieff (eds) *Wealth and Virtue*, pp. 271–315.

Hont, Istvan and Ignatieff, Michael (eds) (1983a) *Wealth and Virtue: The Shaping of Political Economy in the Scottish Enlightenment*, Cambridge: Cambridge University Press.

Hont, Istvan and Ignatieff, Michael (1983b) 'Needs and justice in the *Wealth of Nations*: an introductory essay' in Hont and Ignatieff (eds) *Wealth and Virtue*, pp. 1–44.

Horne, Thomas A. (1981) 'Envy and commercial society: Mandeville and Smith on "Private Vices, Public Benefits" ', *Political Theory* 9, pp. 551–69.

Howell, Wilbur Samuel (1967) 'John Locke and the New Rhetoric', *The Quarterly Journal of Speech* 53, pp. 319–33.

—— (1971) *Eighteenth Century British Logic and Rhetoric*, Princeton, NJ: Princeton University Press.

—— (1975) 'Adam Smith's Lectures on Rhetoric: an Historical Assessment' in Skinner and Wilson (eds) *Essays on Adam Smith*, pp. 11–43.

Hutchison, Terence (1988) *Before Adam Smith: The Emergence of Political Economy, 1662–1776*, Oxford: Basil Blackwell.

Ignatieff, Michael (1986) 'Smith, Rousseau and the republic of needs', in T.C. Smout (ed.) *Scotland and Europe 1200–1850*, Edinburgh: John Donald Publishers.

Inwood, Brad (1985) *Ethics and Human Action in Early Stoicism*, Oxford: Clarendon.
—— (1987) 'Commentary on Striker' in Cleary (ed.) *Proceedings of the Boston Colloquium*, pp. 95–101.
Jackson, R.V. (1990) 'Government expenditure and British economic growth in the eighteenth century: some problems of measurement', *Economic History Review* XLIII, pp. 217–35.
Kauder, Emil (1953) 'Genesis of the marginal utility theory: from Aristotle to the end of the eighteenth century', *Economic Journal* 63, pp. 638–50.
Kaushil, S. (1973) 'The case of Adam Smith's value analysis', *Oxford Economic Papers* 25, pp. 60–71.
Kennedy, George A. (1980) *Classical Rhetoric and its Christian and Secular Tradition from Ancient to Modern Times*, London: Croom Helm.
Kerferd, G.B. (1972) 'The search for personal identity in Stoic thought', *Bulletin of the John Rylands Library* 55, pp. 177–96.
—— (1978) 'What does the wise man know?' in J.M. Rist (ed.) *The Stoics*, Berkeley, CA: University of California, pp. 125–36.
Kidd, I.G. (1971) 'Stoic intermediates and the end for man', in Long (ed.) *Problems in Stoicism*, pp. 150–72.
—— (1978) 'Moral actions and rules in Stoic ethics', in J.M. Rist (ed.) *The Stoics*, pp. 247–58.
Kindleberger, C.P. (1976) 'The historical background: Adam Smith and the Industrial Revolution', in Wilson and Skinner (eds) *The Market and the State*, pp. 3–25.
King, J.E. (1948) 'The origin of the term "political economy" ', *Journal of Modern History* 20, pp. 230–1.
Klamer, A., McCloskey, D.N. and Solow, R.M. (eds) (1988) *The Consequences of Economic Rhetoric*, Cambridge: Cambridge University Press.
Koebner, R. (1959) 'Adam Smith and the Industrial Revolution', *The Economic History Review* 11, pp. 381–91.
Kristeva, Julia (1986) 'Word, dialogue and novel', in *The Kristeva Reader*, edited by Toril Moi, Oxford: Basil Blackwell, pp. 34–61.
Lamb, Robert Boyden (1974) 'Adam Smith's system: sympathy not self-interest', *Journal of the History of Ideas* 35, pp. 671–82.
Langholm, Odd (1979) *Price and Value in the Aristotelian Tradition*, Bergen: Universitetsforlaget.
Lehmann, William C. (1960) *John Millar of Glasgow 1735–1801*, Cambridge: Cambridge University Press.
—— (1961) 'John Millar, Professor of Civil Law at Glasgow (1761–1801)', *The Juridical Review* 6, pp. 218–33.
—— (1970) 'Some observations on the Law lectures of Professor Millar at the University of Glasgow (1761–1801)', *The Juridical Review* 15, pp. 56–77.
Letwin, William (1963) *The Origins of Scientific Economics: English Economic Thought 1660–1776*, London: Methuen.
—— (1988) 'Was Adam Smith a Liberal?', in K. Haakonssen (ed.) *Traditions of Liberalism*, pp. 65–80.
Lieberman, David (1983) 'The legal needs of a commercial society: the jurisprudence of Lord Kames' in Hont and Ignatieff (eds) (1983a) *Wealth and Virtue*, pp. 203–34.
—— (1989) *The Province of Legislation Determined: Legal Theory in Eighteenth-Century Britain*, Cambridge: Cambridge University Press.
Lindgren, Ralph (1973) *The Social Philosophy of Adam Smith*, The Hague: Martinus Nijhoff.
Lodge, David (1987) 'After Bakhtin' in *The Linguistics of Writing*, edited by N. Fabb,

REFERENCES

D. Attridge, A. Durant and C. MacCabe, Manchester: Manchester University Press, pp. 89–102.

Long, A.A. (ed.) (1971a) *Problems in Stoicism*, London: The Athlone Press.

—— (1971b) 'Language and thought in Stoicism', in A.A. Long (ed.) *Problems in Stoicism*, pp. 75–113.

—— (1971c) 'Freedom and determinism in the Stoic theory of human action', in A.A. Long (ed.) *Problems in Stoicism*, pp. 173–99.

—— (1986) *Hellenistic Philosophy* (2nd edition), London: Duckworth.

Long, A.A. and Sedley, D.N. (1987) *The Hellenistic Philosophers*, Cambridge: Cambridge University Press.

Lothian, John M. (1963) Introduction to Adam Smith's *Lectures on Rhetoric and Belles Lettres*, Edinburgh and London: Thomas Nelson.

Low, J.M. (1952) 'An eighteenth century controversy in the theory of economic progress', *Manchester School of Economics and Social Studies* 20, pp. 311–30.

McCloskey, Donald N. (1986) *The Rhetoric of Economics*, Brighton: Wheatsheaf.

—— (1988) 'Thick and thin methodologies in the history of economic thought', in de Marchi (ed.) *The Popperian Legacy in Economics*, pp. 245–58.

—— (1990) *If You're So Smart: The Narrative of Economic Expertise*, Chicago and London: The University of Chicago Press.

MacCormick, Neil (1982) 'Law and Enlightenment' in *The Origins and Nature of the Scottish Enlightenment*, edited by R.H. Campbell and A.S. Skinner, Edinburgh: John Donald, pp. 150–66.

Macfie, A.L. (1967) *The Individual in Society*, London: Allen & Unwin.

McNally, David (1988) *Political Economy and the Rise of Capitalism: A Reinterpretation*, Berkeley: University of California Press.

Marshall, David (1984) 'Adam Smith and the theatricality of moral sentiments', *Critical Inquiry*, pp. 592–613.

—— (1986) *The Figure of Theater*, New York: Columbia University Press.

Meek, Ronald L. (ed.) (1963a) *The Economics of Physiocracy*, Cambridge, MA: Harvard University Press.

—— (1963b) 'Physiocracy and classicism in Britain', in *The Economics of Physiocracy*, Cambridge MA: Harvard University Press, pp. 345–63.

—— (1967a) 'Adam Smith and the classical theory of profit' reprinted in *Economics and Ideology and Other Essays*, London: Chapman and Hall, pp. 18–33.

—— (1967b) 'The Scottish contribution to Marxist sociology' reprinted in *Economics and Ideology and Other Essays*, London: Chapman and Hall, pp. 34–50.

—— (1973) *Turgot on Progress, Sociology and Economics*, Cambridge: Cambridge University Press.

—— (1976) *Social Science and the Ignoble Savage*, Cambridge: Cambridge University Press.

—— (1977) 'Smith, Turgot, and the "Four Stages" theory' reprinted in *Smith, Marx, and After: Ten Essays in the Development of Economic Thought*, London: Chapman and Hall, pp. 18–32.

Mitchell, Harvey (1987) ' "The Mysterious Veil of Self-Delusion" in Adam Smith's Theory of Moral Sentiments', *Eighteenth-Century Studies* 20, pp. 405–21.

Morrow, Glenn R. (1966) 'Adam Smith: moralist and philosopher' in *Adam Smith, 1776–1926*, facsimile of 1928 edition, New York: Augustus M. Kelley, pp. 156–79.

—— (1973) *The Ethical and Economic Theories of Adam Smith*, facsimile of 1923 edition, New York: Augustus M. Kelley.

Morson, Gary Saul (1986a) 'Dialogue, monologue, and the social: a reply to Ken Hirschkop' in Morson (ed.) *Bakhtin: Essays and Dialogues on His Work*, pp 81–8.

Morson, Gary Saul (ed.) (1986b) *Bakhtin: Essays and Dialogues on His Work*, Chicago: University of Chicago Press.
Myint, Hla (1948) *Theories of Welfare Economics*, LSE, Longmans.
O'Brien D.P. (1975) *The Classical Economists*, Oxford: The Clarendon Press.
Oncken, August (1897) 'The consistency of Adam Smith', *Economic Journal*, VII, pp. 443–50.
Pembroke, S.G. (1971) 'Oikeiosis' in Long (1971a) (ed.) *Problems in Stoicism*, pp. 114–49.
Persky, Joseph (1989) 'Adam Smith's invisible hands', *Journal of Economic Perspectives* 3, pp. 195–201.
Pesciarelli, Enzo (1986) 'On Adam Smith's Lectures on Jurisprudence', *Scottish Journal of Political Economy* 33, pp. 74–85.
Pocock, J.G.A. (1975) *The Machiavellian Moment: Florentine Political Thought and the Atlantic Republican Tradition*, Princeton: Princeton University Press.
—— (1981) 'The Machiavellian moment revisited: a study in history and ideology', *Journal of Modern History* 53, pp. 49–72.
—— (1983) 'Cambridge paradigms and Scotch philosophers: a study of the relations between the civic humanist and the civil jurisprudential interpretation of eighteenth-century social thought', in Hont and Ignatieff (eds) *Wealth and Virtue*, pp. 235–52.
—— (1985) *Virtue, Commerce and History: Essays on Political Thought and History, Chiefly in the Eighteenth Century*, Cambridge: Cambridge University Press.
Porter, Roy (1990) *English Society in the Eighteenth Century*, Penguin: Harmondsworth.
Raphael, D.D. (1975) 'The impartial spectator', in Skinner and Wilson (eds) *Essays on Adam Smith*, pp. 83–99.
Raphael, D.D. and Macfie, A.L. (1979) Introduction to *The Theory of Moral Sentiments*, Oxford: Oxford University Press; Liberty Classics imprint (1982).
Rashid, Salim (1980a) 'The policy of laissez-faire during scarcities', *Economic Journal* 90, pp. 493–503.
—— (1980b) 'Economists, economic historians and mercantilism', *The Scandinavian Economic History Review* 28, pp. 1–14.
—— (1986) 'Smith, Steuart, and mercantilism: comment', *Southern Economic Journal* 52, pp. 843–52.
—— (1987) 'Adam Smith's interpretation of the history of economics and its influence in the 18th and 19th centuries', *Quarterly Review of Economics and Business* 27, pp. 56–69.
Richards, I.A. (1971) *The Philosophy of Rhetoric*, reprint of 1936 edition, Oxford: Oxford University Press.
Rist, J.M. (ed.) (1978a) *The Stoics*, Berkeley, Los Angeles and London: University of California Press.
—— (1978b) 'The Stoic concept of detachment' in Rist (ed.) *The Stoics*, pp. 259–72.
Robbins, Lionel (Lord) (1935) *An Essay on the Nature and Significance of Economic Science* (2nd edition), London: Macmillan.
Robertson, H.M. and Taylor, W.L. (1957) 'Adam Smith's approach to the theory of value', *Economic Journal* 67, pp. 181–98.
Robertson, John (1990) 'The legacy of Adam Smith: government and economic development in the *Wealth of Nations*', in *Victorian Liberalism: Nineteenth-Century Political Thought and Practice*, edited by Richard Bellamy, London: Routledge, pp. 15–41.
Rorty, Richard (1984) 'The historiography of philosophy: four genres', in *Philosophy in History*, edited by R. Rorty, J.B. Schneewind and Q. Skinner, Cambridge: Cambridge University Press, pp. 49–75.

REFERENCES

Rosenberg, Nathan (1960) 'Some institutional aspects of the *Wealth of Nations*', *Journal of Political Economy* 68, pp. 557–70.
—— (1968) 'Adam Smith, consumer tastes, and economic growth', *Journal of Political Economy* 76, pp. 361–74.
—— (1975) 'Adam Smith on profits – paradox lost and regained', in Skinner and Wilson (eds) *Essays on Adam Smith*, pp. 377–89.
Rothschild, Emma (1992) 'Adam Smith and conservative economics', *Economic History Review* XLV, pp. 74–96.
Rotwein, Eugene (1970) Introduction to *David Hume: Writings on Economics*, Madison: The University of Wisconsin Press.
Samuels, Warren J. (1961) 'The physiocratic theory of property and the state', *Quarterly Journal of Economics* 75, pp. 96–111.
—— (1962) 'The physiocratic theory of economic policy', *Quarterly Journal of Economics* 76, pp. 145–62.
—— (1976) 'The political economy of Adam Smith', *Ethics* 87, pp. 189–207.
Sandbach, F.H. (1975) *The Stoics*, London: Chatto & Windus.
Schofield, Malcolm (1991) *The Stoic Idea of the City*, Cambridge: Cambridge University Press.
Schumpeter, Joseph A. (1954) *History of Economic Analysis*, New York: Oxford University Press.
Skinner, Andrew S. (1975) 'Adam Smith: an economic interpretation of history', in Skinner and Wilson (eds) *Essays on Adam Smith*, pp. 154–78.
—— (1979) *A System of Social Science: Papers Relating to Adam Smith*, Oxford: Clarendon Press.
—— (1982) 'A Scottish contribution to Marxist sociology?', in Bradley and Howard (eds) *Classical and Marxian Political Economy*, London: Macmillan, pp. 79–114.
—— (1983) 'Adam Smith: rhetoric and the communication of ideas', in *Methodological Controversy in Economics: Historical Essays in Honour of T.W. Hutchison*, edited by A.W. Coats, London and Greenwich, Conn.: JAI Press Inc., pp. 71–88.
—— (1986) 'Adam Smith: then and now', in *Ideas in Economics*, edited by R.D. Collison Black, London: Macmillan, pp. 16–42.
—— (1989) 'Sir James Steuart: economic theory and policy', in *Philosophy and Science in the Scottish Enlightenment*, edited by Peter Jones, Edinburgh: John Donald, pp. 117–44.
Skinner, Andrew S. and Wilson, Thomas (eds) (1975) *Essays on Adam Smith*, Oxford: Clarendon Press.
Skinner, Quentin (1984) 'The idea of negative liberty: philosophical and historical perspectives', in *Philosophy in History*, edited by R. Rorty, J.B. Schneewind and Q. Skinner, Cambridge: Cambridge University Press, pp. 193–221.
—— (1988) 'A reply to my critics', in *Meaning and Context: Quentin Skinner and his Critics*, edited by James Tully, Cambridge: Polity Press, pp. 231–88.
—— (1990) 'The republican ideal of political liberty', in *Machiavelli and Republicanism*, edited by G. Bock, Q. Skinner and M. Viroli, Cambridge: Cambridge University Press, pp. 293–309.
Spence, Patricia (1974) 'Sympathy and propriety in Adam Smith's rhetoric', *Quarterly Journal of Speech* 60, pp. 92–9.
Stein, Peter (1957) 'Legal thought in eighteenth-century Scotland', *The Juridical Review* 2, pp. 1–20.
—— (1970) 'Law and society in eighteenth-century Scottish thought', in *Scotland in the Age of Improvement*, edited by N.T. Phillipson and Rosalind Mitchison, Edinburgh: Edinburgh University Press, pp. 148–68.
—— (1979) 'Adam Smith's jurisprudence – between morality and economics', *Cornell Law Review* 64, pp. 621–38.

—— (1980) *Legal Evolution: The Story of an Idea*, Cambridge: Cambridge University Press.

Stewart, M.A. (1991) 'The Stoic legacy in the early Scottish Enlightenment' in *Atoms, pneuma, and Tranquillity: Epicurean and Stoic Themes in European Thought*, edited by Margaret J. Osler, Cambridge: Cambridge University Press, pp. 275–96.

Stigler, George J. (1977) 'The successes and failures of Professor Smith', in *Studies in Modern Economic Analysis*, edited by M.J. Artis and A.R. Nobay, Oxford: Blackwell, pp. 3–20.

Stimson, Shannon C. (1989) 'Republicanism and the recovery of the political in Adam Smith', in *Critical Issues in Social Thought*, edited by Murray Milgate and Cheryl B. Welch, London: Academic Press, pp. 91–112.

Striker, Gisela (1983) 'The role of *oikeiosis* in Stoic ethics', *Oxford Studies in Ancient Philosophy* I, pp. 145–67.

—— (1987) 'Origins of the concept of natural law', in J. Cleary (ed.) *Proceedings of the Boston Colloquium*, pp. 79–94.

Taylor, Charles (1979) 'What's wrong with negative liberty' in *The Idea of Freedom: Essays in Honour of Isaiah Berlin*, edited by Alan Ryan, Oxford: Oxford University Press, pp. 175–93.

—— (1989) 'Cross-purposes: the Liberal–Communitarian debate', in *Liberalism and the Moral Life*, edited by Nancy L. Rosenblum, Cambridge, MA: Harvard University Press, pp. 159–82.

Teichgraeber III, Richard F. (1981) 'Rethinking *Das Adam Smith Problem*', *The Journal of British Studies*, vol. XX, pp. 106–23.

—— (1986) *Free trade and Moral Philosophy: Rethinking the Sources of Adam Smith's 'Wealth of Nations'*, Duke University Press: Durham NC.

—— (1987) ' "Less abused than I had reason to expect": the reception of *The Wealth of Nations* in Britain, 1776–90', *Historical Journal* 30, pp. 337–66.

Thompson, E.P. (1991a) 'The moral economy of the English crowd in the eighteenth century', reprinted in *Customs in Common*, London: Merlin Press, pp. 185–258.

—— (1991b) 'The moral economy reviewed', in *Customs in Common*, London: Merlin Press, pp. 259–351.

Tiffany, Esther A. (1923) 'Shaftesbury as Stoic', *Publications of the Modern Languages Association of America*, vol. 38, pp. 642–84.

Todorov, Tzvetan (1984) *Mikhail Bakhtin: The Dialogical Principle*, vol. 13 of *Theory and History of Literature*, Manchester: Manchester University Press.

Tribe, Keith (1978) *Land, Labour and Economic Discourse*, London: Routledge & Kegan Paul.

Tuck, Richard (1979) *Natural Rights Theories: Their Origin and Development*, Cambridge: Cambridge University Press.

—— (1987) 'The "modern" theory of natural law', in *The Languages of Political Theory in Early–Modern Europe*, edited by Anthony Pagden, Cambridge: Cambridge University Press, pp. 99–119.

Tully, James (1991) Introduction to Pufendorf, *On the Duty of Man and Citizen*, Cambridge: Cambridge University Press.

Tuveson, Ernest (1953) 'The importance of Shaftesbury', *Journal of English Literary History* 20, pp. 267–99.

Vickers, Brian (1971) 'Bacon's use of theatrical imagery', *Studies in the Literary Imagination* 4, pp. 189–226.

—— (1985) 'The Royal Society and English prose style: a reassessment' in *Rhetoric and the Pursuit of Truth: Language Change in the Seventeenth and Eighteenth Centuries*,

edited by B. Vickers, University of California, LA: William Andrews Clark Memorial Library, pp. 1–76.
—— (1988) *In Defence of Rhetoric*, Oxford: Clarendon Press.
Viner, Jacob (1937) *Studies in the Theory of International Trade*, London: George Allen & Unwin; reprinted 1955.
—— (1960) 'The intellectual history of laissez faire', *The Journal of Law and Economics* 3, pp. 45–69.
—— (1965) 'Guide to Rae's Life of Adam Smith', in *Life of Adam Smith* by John Rae, New York: Augustus M. Kelley.
—— (1966) 'Adam Smith and laissez faire', in *Adam Smith, 1776–1926*, facsimile of 1928 edition, New York: Augustus M. Kelley, pp. 116–55.
Voitle, Robert (1984) *The Third Earl of Shaftesbury 1671–1713*, Baton Rouge, LA: Louisiana State University Press.
Waszek, Norbert (1984) 'Two concepts of morality: a distinction of Adam Smith's ethics and its Stoic origin', *Journal of the History of Ideas* 45, pp. 591–606.
Watson, Gerard (1971) 'The Natural Law and Stoicism' in Long (ed.) *Problems in Stoicism*, pp. 216–38.
West, E.G. (1971) 'Adam Smith and Rousseau's *Discourse on Inequality*: inspiration or provocation?', *Journal of Economic Issues* 5, pp. 56–70.
Wilson, Thomas (1976) 'Sympathy and self-interest' in *The Market and the State*, edited by T. Wilson and A.S. Skinner, Oxford: Clarendon Press, pp. 73–99.
Wilson, Thomas and Skinner, Andrew S. (1976) *The Market and the State: Essays in Honour of Adam Smith*, Oxford: Clarendon Press.
Wimsatt, W.K. and Beardsley, M.C. (1954) 'The intentional fallacy' in *The Verbal Icon: Studies in the Meaning of Poetry*, London: Methuen, pp. 3–18.
Winch, Donald (1965) *Classical Political Economy and the Colonies*, LSE: London.
—— (1978) *Adam Smith's Politics: An Essay in Historiographic Revision*, Cambridge: Cambridge University Press.
—— (1983a) 'Adam Smith's "enduring particular result": a political and cosmopolitan perspective', in Hont and Ignatieff (eds) *Wealth and Virtue*, pp. 253–69.
—— (1983b) 'Science and the legislator: Adam Smith and after', *Economic Journal* 93, pp. 501–20.
—— (1988) 'Adam Smith and the Liberal tradition', in K. Haakonssen (ed.) *Traditions of Liberalism*, pp. 83–104.
—— (1992) 'Adam Smith: Scottish moral philosopher as political economist', *Historical Journal* 35, pp. 91–113.
Young, Jeffrey T. (1986) 'The impartial spectator and natural jurisprudence: an interpretation of Adam Smith's theory of the natural price', *History of Political Economy* 18, pp. 365–82.

INDEX

admiration, of wealth and greatness 86–7
adulation, dangers of 139
agriculture: criticism of disruption of; natural order in WN 177, 178; discussion of in LJ 173n.; discussion of in WN: criticism of system 127–32, 154–5, 157–8, 179–80, 186, 193; on landowners 176–7; ranked above manufacturing 177, 178
  division of labour in 213; effect of mercantile system on 6–7, 123; employment of capital and quantity of productive labour 173–4n.; European policy on 200; as main source of wealth 200–1; natural order of investment in 203; producing wages, profit and rent 173–4; system based on statist assumptions about economy 162
allegory, condemnation of in LRBL 14
Anspach, Ralph and 'Adam Smith problem' 23n.
apathy, Stoic view of 77
Aristotle: on civic humanist virtue 209–10; on state and community 210; use of didactic style 17; *The Politics* 121, 210
Augustine, St, and dialogic discourse 55
author: conveyance of thoughts to reader as communication 10; 'death' of 13; intentionality of 3, 4, 10, 207: assumptions of 19, 20; and biography 20; external evidence for 19; role of biography in 23–4 as originating will defining meaning of text 12–13; propriety of 14–15; role in interplay of voices in TMS 37–8; use of authorial voice, in WN 44, use of authorial voice *see also* didactic voice
autobiography, and dialogism 55–7

Bakhtin, Mikhail: on canonisation process 22; on 'common language' in comic novels 39n.; on dialogism 21, 30–1, 55: in novelistic discourse 4–5; in Stoic discourses 5, 55–6
  on hybrid constructions 41–2n.; on monologic voice 45; *The Dialogic Imagination* 31n.; *Problems of Dostoevsky's Poetics* 30n.; *Rabelais and his World* 31n.; *Speech Genres and Other Late Essays* 31n.
Barbeyrac, Jean 107–11; *An Historical and Critical Account of the Science of Morality* 106–7
beneficence: distinction from justice 47; idea of 'concentric circles' enclosing moral agent 137; legislators and statesmen as examples of 137–8; as moral virtue 5, 26, 33, 34–5, 82; in TMS 208
benevolence, disinterested 64
Bentham, Jeremy, and science of legislation 120–1n.
Bevilacqua, Vincent M.: on concept of propriety 15; on rhetorical discourse 16n.; on Smith's thinking on rhetoric 9
biography, and authorial intentionality 20, 23–4
body, metaphors of 187n.

INDEX

Brissenden, R.F., on 'dark' side of TMS 37n.
Britain, degree of liberty in 187
Brougham, Henry: on individual and public wealth 200; on Lauderdale's *Inquiry* 205; *An Inquiry into the Colonial Policy of the European Powers* 199–200
Brown, Vivienne, on authorial intentionality and canonicity 8, 22
Buchanan, David, edition of WN 203
Burns, J.H., on concepts of legislator 121n.
Butler, Joseph: on conscience 73n.; *Sermons* 63

Campbell, R.H.: and 'Adam Smith problem' 23n.; on WN and capitalism 165n.
canon, construction of 7–8, 220; in economics 21–2; necessity for 21
Cantillon, Richard: on natural consequences 158; *Essay on the Nature of Trade in General* 145–6, 184
capital: accumulation of 214; analysis of employment of in WN 173–4n., 176, 202–3; classification of different employments of 183; sectoral hierarchy of in WN 180–1
Cicero: and Stoic concept of justice 103–6; use of didactic and rhetorical discourse 17; *De Finibus* 78–9; *De Legibus* 103–4, 108; *De Officiis* 78, 79, 85–6, 106n., 109, 209, 210
civic humanism: concept of virtue 101–2; and morality in TMS 209–10; and origins of liberalism 2; and role of legislator/statesman 121, 130
Clark, K. and Holquist, M., on Bakhtin 31n.
colonial monopolies *see* monopolies
commercial society: denunciation of materialism of 7; moral assessment of 1, 3–4, 7, 212, 216–17; and public decency 212
common sense, Smith's appeals to 10–11, 194, 196
communication: as conveyance of author's thoughts to reader 10; and sympathy 14–15, 18
community, and state 210
competition: discussion of in WN 160–1, 166–7; economic significance of 188
conscience 74; adversarial account of in Stoicism 61–3; in Butler's *Sermons* 63; dialogic nature of 75; and soliloquy 56–7
consumerism: attitude to in TMS 215; attitude to in WN 214
contracts: and uncertainty of language 12; verbal and written 12
Corn Laws 185
country, development of compared to that of towns 171, 178
Critical Review, critism of Lycurgus 131n.
cross-reading, and intentionality of author 4

Davenant, Charles: *Discourses on the Public Revenues* 122, 130, 185; *Essay upon the . . . Balance of Trade* 131n., 185
death, attitude to in TMS 67–9
Derrida, Jacques 3
despotism, legal 131–2
development, natural order of in WN 193
dialogism 21, 31: and intertextuality 5, 21; and monologism 5, 21; in novelistic discourse 4–5, 21, 31; in Stoic discourses 5, 61–3; in TMS 31–43, 195–6, 209, 218; tradition of 55
didactic discourse: contrasted with rhetorical discourse 16–17, 163–4; in LRBJ 10
didactic voice: representing true virtue 80; in TMS 38–43
discourse: dialogic *see* dialogism; didactic 10, 16–17, 163–4; ethical 21, 75; historical/narrative 16; monologic *see* monologism; moral 31; novelistic 21, 30–1; rhetorical 16–17, 163–4
Dostoevsky, Fyodor, *Crime and Punishment* 75n.
duty: moral status of 83–6; and natural law 109–10; negative 114; and virtue 65–6

Eatwell, John, on analysis of competitive prices in WN 166–7n.
Economistes 6, 7: advocating freedom of trade 157–8; belief that agriculture

235

is most productive activity 179, 198–9, 200; concept of wealth 171–2; criticism of mercantile system 171; and legal despotism 131–2; and sectoral hierarchy 175, 192, 197, 198–9, 204–5; Smith's criticism of in WN 129

Edinburgh Review: Horner's articles on labour 199; response to WN 203; review of Lauderdale's *Inquiry* 200, 201

elocutio *see* style

Endres, A.M.: on political arithmetic 123n.; on Smith's theory of reading 9

Epictetus 31, 56: on Stoicism and freedom 218; *Discourses* 57n., 59n.; *Encheiridion* 56n.

ethical discourse, dialogic nature of 21, 75

Evensky, Jerry: and 'Adam Smith problem' 23n.; on economics of WN 166n.; on imperfectibility 68n.; on voices of TMS 30n.

Ferguson, Adam, *Essay on the History of Civil Society* 126

Fish, Stanley, on irony 15

Foucault, Michel 3

freedom 216–20

frugality: and attempts to 'better one's condition' 214; praised in WN 214–15; and prudence 51–2, 214–15

Gee, Joshua, *The Trade and Navigation of Great Britain Considered* 185

gratitude, and moral rules 35, 84

Grotius: and natural law tradition 102–3; Preliminary Discourse to *The Rights of War and Peace* 100, 108, 109, 110–11

Haakonssen, Knud, on Smith's use of legislator figure 124n.

happiness: and utility 90n.; and virtue 90n., 95–6

Harris, Joseph, *Essay upon Money and Coins* 130

Heilbronner, Robert L. 193, on voices of TMS 30n.

history: in Smith's LRBJ 10; stadial theory of 177–8

Hogan, Michael J., on Smith's thinking on rhetoric 9

Hollander, Samuel: on economics of WN 166n.; on employment of capital and quantity of labour 174n.

Horner, Francis, articles on labour in *Edinburgh Review* 199

Howell, Wilbur Samuel: on development of plain style 11; on Smith's thinking on rhetoric 9

humanism, civic *see* civic humanism

Hume, David 45, 102: 'Of the balance of trade' 185; 'Of commerce' 146, 186; 'Of the jealousy of trade' 185; 'Of money' 146; *Political Discourses* 146

hunting, and natural rights 119–20n.

Hutcheson, Francis 102: separation of ethics from natural law 140; translation of Marcus Aurelius 103n.; *An Essay on the Nature and Conduct of the Passions and Affections* 64–5; *An Inquiry into the Original of our Ideas of Beauty and Virtue* 64–5; *A Short Introduction to Moral Philosophy* 64, 65, 78, 101, 145, 183–4

Hutchison, Terence, on mercantilist and free trade literature 183n.

Ignatieff, Michael, on 'dark' side of TMS 37n.

imagination: acting against reason 91–2; delusory nature of 42–3; illusions of 67–9; role in process of moral judgment 66–75; and role of spectator 69–75

individual: gains of and public wealth 200; relationship to society in WN 172

intentionality of author 3, 4, 10, 207: assumptions of 19, 20; and biography 20; and cross-reading 4; external evidence for 19

interdependence: material 109; social 108

intertextuality: as characteristic of discourse 21; as form of dialogism 21; generalised 5

irony, in Swift's writings 15–16

judges and arbitrators, role in process of legal adaptation 120–40

jurisprudence: justice based on principles of 48–50; natural law 100–1; and origins of liberalism 2

justice: based on human fellowship 111;

based on science of natural jurisprudence 48–50; for civil order and protection of property 112–13; commutative and distributive 113, 115, 219; and competitive prices in WN 167n.; discussion of in TMS 139–40, 141; distinction from beneficence 47; formulation in terms of precise rules 84; and moral obligation 47–8; and natural law 108–11; as 'negative virtue' 49; rectification of injustice 190–1; and role of impartial spectator 49–50; role of in LJ 212; as second-order virtue 5–6, 100, 188, 208; separation from moral judgment in LJ and TMS 112–20; Stoic concept of 103–6; subordinate role of in TMS 211–12; and system of natural liberty 189

Kames, Lord (Henry Home) 102: on common law 120–1n.; *Of the Foundation and Principles of the Law of Nature* 115–16; *Sketches on the History of Man* 184, 185
Kauder, Emil, on economic analysis of WN 142n.
Kaushil, S., on economics of WN 166n.
Kennedy, George A., on development of plain style 11
Kerferd, G.B., on living in accordance with nature 73n.
Kidd, I.G., on moral agents 77–8
Klamer, A., McCloskey, D.N. and Solow, R.M., on rhetoric and economics 9
Kristeva, Julia, on intertextuality 21

labour: cost of 149; division of 213: in agriculture 213; opulence attributed to 202
as property 170; quantity of and employment of capital 173–4n.
labourers, as property owners 170, 191
Lamb, Robert Boyden, and 'Adam Smith problem' 23n.
land, as property 170
language: arbitrary signification of 11–12; endorsement of plain style in LRBL 10–11, 18; figurative 11: in LRBL 13–14, 17, 18
uncertainty of 11–12

Lauderdale (Eighth Earl), James Maitland, *An Inquiry into the Nature and Origin of Public Wealth* 200, 205
laws, moral force of 37n.
legislator/statesman: and civic humanism 121, 130; economic responsibilities of 122–3; myth 121–2: rejection of 125–6
oppositional tone in references to 132–4; and political oeconomy 157; reliance on 123–4; role of 126–7, 210–11: in Steuart's *Inquiry* 159, 160; in TMS 134–40
role in process of legal adaptation 120–40
liberalism, debate over ideological origins of 2
liberty: degree of in Britain 187; natural: according with reason and commonsense 216–17; legal restraints on 219; rhetoric of 193–6; and sectoral hierarchy 215–16; seen as self-evident 195–6
perfect 216–17: in Stoicism 217–18
Lieberman, David, on attitudes to common law 120–1n.
Lindgren, Ralph, on justice and competitive prices in WN 167n.
Locke, John: and distinction between rhetorical and didactic dialogue 16–17; *Essay Concerning Human Understanding* 11; *Second Treatise on Government* 101
Long, A.A., on Stoicism 76n.
Long, A.A. and Sedley, D.N., on Stoicism 76n.
Lothian, John M.: on development of plain style 11; on Smith's thinking on rhetoric 9; on Smith's use of emotional appeal 18
luxury, economic effects of 145–6, 172–3n.
Lycurgus, and civic humanism 131n.

McCloskey, Donald N., on economic discourse 9, 21–2
McCulloch, J.R.: *A Discourse on . . Political Economy* 203; 'Introductory Discourse' to WN 203–5; *Principles of Political Economy* 203–5
Macfie, A.L.: and 'Adam Smith problem' 23–4; on metaphor of

invisible hand in TMS 26; on self-love 46n.; on Stoicism 57n.
Machiavelli, Niccolò: on civic humanist virtue 209–10; and legislator myth 121; use of didactic style 17; *Discourses* 124n.
Malthus, T.R.: on relationship between state and individual interests 205–6n.; and *Edinburgh Review* 201; *Essay on Population* 201n.
manufacturing: division of labour in 133; producing wages and profit 173–4
Marcus Aurelius 31: and dialogic discourse 55, 56; *Meditations* 57, 73, 103n.
market, and property rights 219
Marshall, David: on conscience and soliloquy 56n.; on TMS as 'philosophical novel' 31n.
materialism, of commercial society 7
meaning: and choice of interpretative frame 19–20; construction of by process of reading 13; defined by originating will of author 12–13; literal and ironic 15–16
mercantile system: alleged to be based on sophistry 192–3; analysis of 6–7; based on statist assumptions about economy 162; criticism of in WN 127–34, 154–7, 171, 179–80, 188–90, 192–4, 213–14; effect on agriculture 6–7
mercantilism, debate on use of term 143–4n.
mercantilist view of economy 183–4
merchants and manufacturers *see* mercantile system
metaphor, use of in LRBL 14, 24–7, 182
Mill, James, *Commerce Defended* 201–2
Millar, John 118n.: on boundaries between law and morality 113n.; *Historical View of the English Government* 120n.; 'The origin of the distinction of ranks' 125
Mirabeau, 'Rural philosophy' 160
mirror metaphor 59–60
Mitchell, Harvey, on 'dark' side of TMS 37n.
money, distinguished from wealth 192–3
monologism 21, 31: in LJ 209, 219; in scientific discourse 45–6; in WN 43–6, 162, 188, 191–2, 209
monopolies: colonial 177–8, 180–1, 198, 204; described as unwholesome bodies 187n.; discussion of in LJ 148–9
Montesquieu, Charles de Secondat 102: on Stoicism 103n.; *Spirit of the Laws* 121
Monthly Review: criticism of Lycurgus 131n.; on statesmen 124
moral agent, freedom of: in TMS 218; in WN 218–19
moral assessment of commercial society 1, 3–4
moral judgment: by spectator in TMS 25–6; dialogic nature of 33, 37; openness of 34–7
morality: privatisation of 208–9; relationship of state to 210–11
Morrow, Glenn R., and 'Adam Smith problem' 23n.
Mun, Thomas: on export of money 145n.; *England's Treasure by Forraign Trade* 185
Myint, Hla, on analysis of competitive prices in WN 167n.

national interest, as summation of individual interests 198–9
natural law: and legal despotism 131–2; and private property rights 103; traditions of 102–3
natural law jurisprudence 100–1
natural liberty *see* liberty, natural
natural sciences, influence of on development of plain style 11
nature: conflict with reason in virtuous man 70–5; living in accordance with 73–4; moral artifice of contributing to rise of industry 92; relationship to reason in Stoicism 74n., 77–8, 103–4
Navigation Acts 185
non-tuism in economic transactions 52

oaths, and uncertainty of language 12
oikeiosis doctrine of development in Stoicism 95–7, 137
Oncken, August, and 'Adam Smith problem' 23n.
opulence: attributed to operation of division of labour 202; discussion of in LJ 143–4; discussion of in WN

151; economic progress of 187–8; natural progress of 177–9, 205–6; and police 143–4, 153; relationship to foreign trade 144–5; and wealth 147
oratory, in LRBL 10

parsimony *see* frugality 214
persuasion, by rhetorical discourse 16–17
physiocratic literature 160, 175n., 199
Plato, dialogues 16
Playfair, William, edition of WN 203
Pocock, J.G.A., on virtue and law 101
poetry, discussion of in LRBL 10
police: and concept of wealth in WN 169–70; definition of in TMS 45–6, 135; in LJ 134; meaning of in WN 154–6; as mercantile system discourse 6; and opulence 143–4, 153; and prices 148–9; as state regulationist discourse 6
political arithmetic 122–3
political oeconomy, in WN 6–7, 128–9
Porter, Roy, on WN and capitalism 165n.
Postlethwayt, Malachy, on effect of trade surplus 146n.
power: admiration of by mass of mankind 86–7; aspirations to from vanity 90–1; disdain for in TMS 88–9
Pownall, Thomas, opposition to conclusions of WN 197–8
prices: and balance of trade 157; discussion of competitve prices in WN 150; effect of utility and scarcity on 149–50; of free competition 151; natural and market 148–9, 186; and police 148–9; revenues of rent, wages and profits 168–9
prodigality and frugality, in WN 172–3
profit, level of and benefits to society 202–3
progress, autonomy of in WN 160
property: concept of wealth and interests of property owners 170; criticism of system of landownership in WN 176–7; justice necessary for protection of 112–13; labour as 170, 191; land as 170; rights as natural or acquired rights 116–20, 217; rights of and natural law tradition 103; and role of impartial spectator 49–50
prudence: concept of in TMS 97–9; and economic sphere 98–9; and frugality 51–2, 214–15; legislators and statesmen as examples of 136–7; nature of in TMS 50–1; and reason 50; rules for 35; as second-order virtue 5, 98, 188, 208, 214–15; and self-command 50–1; 'superior' 46–7n.
Pufendorf, Samuel: and natural law tradition 102–3; *Of the Law of Nature and Nations* 100, 106, 109; *On the Duty of Man and Citizen* 113; *The Whole Duty of Man According to the Law of Nature* 100, 109–10, 111
punishment, and moral rules 84

Quesnay, François 128–9: and legal despotism 131–2; on opulence 153; 'Corn' 153; 'Men' 153, 157–8, 171; 'Remarks on the tableau oeconomique' 153–4n.

rank, distinction of in TMS 93–4
Raphael, D.D., on metaphor of spectator in TMS 24
Raphael, D.D. and Macfie, A.L., and 'Adam Smith problem' 23n.
reader, construction of in TMS 32
reading: and choice of interpretative frame 19–20; and historical reconstruction 19–20; and issues of textuality 2–3; process of constructing meaning 13; and rational reconstruction 19–20; theory of in LRBL 9–22
reason: conflict with nature in virtuous man 70–5; equivalence with nature in Stoicism 77–8, 103–4; natural law known through 111; and prudence 50; and unity of moral being 72–3
religion, and sense of duty 83
retailing, producing profits only 173–4
revenue, standard of annual revenue of society in WN 179–80
revenue components theory of value 172–3, 175–6
rhetoric: categorisation of in LRBL 16–17; delivery 11; disposition 11; invention 11; memory 11; as 'persuasion' 16–17; rejection of over-dependence on 10–11; significance for economics texts 9; style 11; of WN 191–7
rhetorical discourse, in LRBL 10

Richards, I.A., on figurative language 11

rights: acquired 113–14; natural 113–14; objective 111; perfect and imperfect 113; subjective 110n.

Rist, J.M., on Stoicism 76n.

Robbins, Lionel (Lord), on discussion of competition in WN 166n.

Rorty, Richard 3: on need for canons 21

Rosenberg, Nathan, on WN and capitalism 165n., 166n.

Rousseau, Jean-Jacques: on public virtue 121–2; *Discourse on the Origin of Inequality* 92–3n.; 'Political Economy' 158n.; *The Social Contract* 121–2

Royal Society, influence of on development of plain style 11

rules: applicability of 83–4; in Cicero's *De Officiis* 79; inferior to mechanism of impartial spectator 85; for justice 84; relieving results of self-deception 83–4; and sense of duty 83–4

Sandbach, F.H., on Stoicism 76n.

Say, Jean-Baptiste: and Say's Law 202; *Treatise on Political Economy* 158n., 202–3

scarcity, concept of 151–3

Schofield, Malcolm, on Stoicism 210n., 218

Schumpeter, Joseph A., on economic analysis of WN 142n.

scientific discourse, and monologism 5, 45–6

Scotland: legislative system, stress on judge-made law 120; 'poor country' relationship to England 146

self-command: endorsement of postponement of economic pleasure 51–2; and model of impartial spectator 70; as moral virtue 5, 26, 33–4, 36n., 82; and prudence 50–1, 98; in TMS 208

self-deception: preventing moral judgment 82; remedies for 82–3

self-improvement, and frugality 214

self-interest: and moral rules 84; and non-tuism 52

self-love: distinguished from self-interest 94; as foundation for love of others 96; Stoic concept of 94–7

Seneca 78n.

sensibility, and moral judgment 80

Shaftesbury, Third Earl of (Anthony Ashley Cooper): on unity of moral being 72; *Inquiry concerning Virtue* 63; *Philosophical Regimen* 56n., 57–8, 73; 'Soliloquy or Advice to an Author' 56n., 57, 58–9, 61

Skinner, A.S.: on employment of capital and quantity of labour 174n.; on Smith's thinking on rhetoric 9

Skinner, Quentin, on illocutionary forces and acts 19n.

Smith, Adam: 'Adam Smith problem' 53–4; consistency of *oeuvre* ? 20–1; criticism of statesmen and projectors 127–8n.; 'Letter to the Editors of the *Edinburgh Review*' 93n.; LJ: concern with lower-order virtues 209; continuity of economic analysis with WN 142–3; on contracts and uncertainty of language 12; discovery and publication of 1–2; discussion of justice 141; ED 149, 150; on justice 211, 212; monologic style 5–6, 45, 100, 219; on natural rights 116–17; on opulence 143–4, 153; on police 134, 153; on prices in rich and poor countries 147; on products of agriculture 173n.; on property rights 117–18, 217; and 'science of a legislator' 126–7; separation of justice from moral judgment 112–20; significance for overall project 54n., 101–2; on taxes and monopolies 148–9; theoretical shift between early and later versions 119; on trade 153;

LRBL: categorisation of rhetoric 16–17; didactic and rhetorical discourse in 17–18, 163–4; discovery and publication of 1–2; on Swift 15–16; theory of reading in 4, 9–22; use of figurative language 13–14, 17, 18; use of metaphor 14

on plain style 24; on public virtue 122; on science of the legislator 134–5; secondary literature on: attempts to integrate whole output 1–2, 207; concern with single texts 2–3, 207;

INDEX

shift in economic arguments 6–7;
system of natural liberty: homology between opulence and ranking system 177–8; and optimal order of development 177
TMS 1–2: attitude to consumerism 215; on beneficence 137–9; and civic humanism 209–10; contempt for standards of powerful 87–9; 'dark' side of 37–8; debate between spectator and moral agent 74–5; depiction of virtuous man 81–2; dialogism in 5, 31–43, 195–6, 209, 218; didactic voice in 39–43; and 'distinction of ranks' 93–4; doubt on viability of impartial spectator 71–2; freedom of moral agent 218; on 'great mob of mankind' 83, 86–8, 208; hierarchically-ordered system of virtues in 208–9; impartial spectator in 24–6, 38–9n., 55, 82; invisible hand metaphor 26, 89–90; on justice 139–40, 141, 211–12; on legislators and statesmen 124–31, 134–40; meaning of sympathy in 32n., 39; on moral agent 80–1; on moral rules 83–6; nature and reason seen in conflict 74–5; on prudence 50–1, 97–9, 136–7; range of 'voices' within 27–30; role of author in interplay of voices 37–8; role of reader as spectator 32–3; on self-love 96–7; sense of duty 65–6; separation of justice from moral judgment 112–20; Stoicism 208; on sympathy 14; and unity of moral being 72–3
unitary conception of works 23–4;
WN: and allocation analysis 188; as amoral discourse 46, 52–3, 162, 209, 215, 218–19; autonomy of conception of progress 160; on best investment of capital 174–5; on colonial monopoly 177–8, 180–1, 198, 204; on competition 160–1, 166–7; concept of scarcity 151–3; concept of wealth 168, 171–2; concern with lower-order virtues 209; on consumerism 214; continuity of economic analysis with LJ 142–3; criticism of agricultural system 177, 178, 179–80, 186, 193; criticism of mercantile system 171, 179–80, 188–90, 192–4, 213–14; criticism of system of landownership 176–7; description of commercial system 179; and development of capitalism 165–81; on distribution of revenue 191–2n.; on division of labour 133, 213; *Early Draft* (ED) 142–3; on economic effects of luxury 172–3n.; on economic regulation 150; and Economistes 179; editions of 203; on employment of capital and quantity of labour 173–4n.; on foreign trade 177, 185, 186, 212; freedom of moral agent 218–19; 'Introduction and Plan of the Work' 127–8, 154; invisible hand metaphor 166, 167n., 182–3; on justice 211; lack of generic name 156; meaning of police in 154–6; monologic style 5, 43–6, 162, 188, 191–2; on natural order of development 193; on natural prices 153–4; on perfect liberty 216–17; placing in broad political and philosophical matrix 165–6; on political body 187; as 'political oeconomy' 127–9, 156–60; on prices 150, 151; on prodigality and frugality 172, 214–15; relationship of individual and society 172; on relative development of towns and country 171; as response to Economistes 175; revenue components theory of value 172–3, 175–6; as rhetorical discourse 163–4; role of legislator/statesman in 127–9; on sectoral hierarchy of capitals 180–1, 197–9, 204–6; seen as text identifying state with individual interests 205–6; as statement of laissez-faire economics 1; structure of 197; symmetry of exchange relation 53; on system of natural liberty 158–9, 164–5, 188–9, 193–4, 211; on value in use and value in exchange 149; on wage levels 168n.
society: and concept of justice 105–6; relationship of individual to in WN

172; stadial conception of development of 183
soliloquy: and conscience 56–7; and dialogism 55–7; and solitariness 59n.
spectator, impartial: as analogue of Stoic divine Being 74–5; and contracts 114; and demands of justice 49–50, 115; doubtful viabilty of in TMS 71–2; and imagination 69–75; and jurisprudential basis of laws 116; mechanism superior to moral rules 85; as metaphor for self-knowledge and moral judgment 59–60; and moral agent in TMS 55, 74–5; moral judgment by 82; and possession of property 49–50; and property rights 49–50, 114; and public virtue 122; and punishment 114; relationship to society 208–9
Spence, P.: on Smith's thinking on rhetoric of 9
Spence, William: response to critics 202; *Britain Independent of Commerce* 200–1, 202
state: and community 210; identity between state and individual interests 205–6; and legal despotism 131–2; relationship to morality 210–11; role of 155
Steuart, Sir James, *Inquiry into the Principles of Political Oeconomy* 123–4, 131n., 134, 146, 156–7, 158n., 159, 184
Stewart, Dugald: lectures on political economy 199; on Smith's lectures 18
Stigler, George J., on discussion of competition in WN 166n.
Stoicism 3–4, 5, 31: on apathy 77; attitude to social position 88–9; belief in natural fellowship 104–5; on 'concentric circles' enclosing moral agent 137; concept of justice 103–6; concept of looking glass 61–2; concept of self-love 94–7; and consumerism 215; dialogism in 5, 21; and discussion of legislators in TMS 135–7; and individual freedom 217–18; on 'intermediates' between good and evil 76–9; on internal speech 56n.; model of inner debate 55; moral hierarchy in 5, 79–80; and natural law tradition 103–11; *officia* as proper functions of individual agents 79, 217; *oikeiosis* doctrine 95–7, 137; on proprieties 78–9n.; and religion 60–1, 106–7; in Smith's discourse 3–4, 209, 220; on social interdependence 108; on unity of moral being 72–3; unity of nature and reason in 74n., 77–8, 82, 103–4; on virtue and reason 6, 62
style: differences in between WN and TMS 3–4; as part of rhetoric 11; Smith's endorsement of plain style 10–11, 24; of WN 162–4
Swift, Jonathan, endorsement of in LRBL 15–16
sympathy 46, 69–70n.: absence of in WN 52–3; acting against reason 91–2; and communication 14–15, 18, 69–70; and differences of feeling 29; effectiveness of 43; and making of moral judgments 14n.; meaning of in TMS 32n., 39

taxation, discussion of in LJ 148–9
Teichgraeber III, Richard F.: and 'Adam Smith problem' 23n.; on 'invisible hand' metaphor in WN 167n.
textuality, and reading of Smith's texts 2–3
Thompson, E.P., on private property 191n.
Todorov, Tzvetan, on intertextuality 21
towns, development of compared to that of country 171, 178
trade: attitude to in LJ 153; balance of 146–7: achieving equilibrium in 184–5; international specie-flow mechanism 184–5; and price levels 157

criticism of large traders 200; foreign 212: circuitous and round-about 198; ranking of 177; as source of national wealth 185–6

free, opposition to 185; idea of inherent instability of 145–6; relationship of opulence to 144–5; relationship to agriculture and manufacturing 201; Say's Law 202
Tribe, Keith, on economics of WN 167n.
Turgot, A.M.J.: analysis of capital 172n.; on revenue 175n.

INDEX

Tuvesen, Ernest, on Shaftesbury 58

utility: concept of effective utility 150n., 186–7n.; definition of 45; and happiness 90n.

value, in use and exchange 149
Vanderlint, Jacob, *Money Answers All Things* 184–5
vanity, and aspirations to power and wealth 90–1
Vickers, Brian: on development of plain style 11; on propriety of expression 15
Viner, Jacob: and 'Adam Smith problem' 23n.; on economic message of TMS 90n.; on role of state 155; on semantic patterning of discourse 134
virtue: civic humanist concept of 101–2; and class 93–4; depoliticisation of in Stoicism 6, 210; and duty 65–6; and happiness 90n., 95–6; hierarchy of 5, 33–4, 76, 79–80; justice as 'negative virtue' 49; moral 76; and propriety 39, 49; represented by didactic voice 80; resonances of in eighteenth-century discourse 54
voices within text: as feature of novelistic discourse 30–1; in TMS 27–30
voices within text *see also* dialogism; monologism

wage levels, in WN 168n.
Wakefield, Edward Gibbon, edition of WN 203n.
Wallace, Robert: on effect of trade surplus 146n.; *Characteristics of the Present Political State of Great Britain* 186
Walras, Leon on 'effective utility' 186–7n.; *Elements of Pure Economics* 150n.
Waszek, Norbert, Stoic analysis of TMS 86n.
wealth: admiration of by mass of mankind 86–7; aspirations to from vanity 90–1; concept of and police 169–70; defined as low-price opulence 147; definition of in WN 168–9; disdain for in TMS 88–9; distinguished from money 192–3; Economistes' concept of *produit net* 171–2; and interests of property owners 170; mercantilist view of 183–4; public, and pursuit of individual gain 200
wholesaling: producing wages and profit 173–4; ranking of 174
Wilson, Thomas, on non-tuism in economic transactions 52n.
Winch, Donald: and 'Adam Smith problem' 23n.; on economic analysis of WN 165n., 166n.; on Smith's use of legislator figure 124n.; on theory of morality in TMS 46n.

Young, Arthur, *Political Arithmetic* 123, 185
Young, Jeffrey T.: and 'Adam Smith problem' 23n.; on justice and competitive prices in WN 167n.; on metaphor of impartial spectator 26n.

Zeno: on concept of self-love 95; obscurity of 135